COLLECTIONS AND OBJECTIONS

MCGILL-QUEEN'S NATIVE AND NORTHERN SERIES
(In memory of Bruce G. Trigger)
Sarah Carter and Arthur J. Ray, Editors

# COLLECTIONS
# AND OBJECTIONS

Aboriginal Material Culture
in Southern Ontario, 1791–1914

Michelle A. Hamilton

McGill-Queen's University Press
Montreal & Kingston • London • Ithaca

© McGill-Queen's University Press 2010

ISBN 978-0-7735-3754-5 (cloth)
ISBN 978-0-7735-3755-2 (paper)

Legal deposit third quarter 2010
Bibliothèque nationale du Québec

Printed in Canada on acid-free paper that is 100% ancient forest free (100% post-consumer recycled), processed chlorine free

This book has been published with the help of a grant from the Canadian Federation for the Humanities and Social Sciences, through the Aid to Scholarly Publications Program, using funds provided by the Social Sciences and Humanities Research Council of Canada. Funding has also been received from the J.B. Smallman Publication Fund, Faculty of Social Science, The University of Western Ontario.

McGill-Queen's University Press acknowledges the support of the Canada Council for the Arts for our publishing program. We also acknowledge the financial support of the Government of Canada through the Canada Book Fund for our publishing activities.

LIBRARY AND ARCHIVES CANADA CATALOGUING IN PUBLICATION

Hamilton, Michelle A., 1972–
        Collections and objections : aboriginal material culture in Southern Ontario, 1791-1914 / Michelle A. Hamilton.

(McGill-Queen's native and northern series ; 63)
Includes bibliographical references and index.
ISBN 978-0-7735-3754-5 (bound). — ISBN 978-0-7735-3755-2 (pbk.)

        1. Iroquoian Indians — Antiquities--Collection and preservation — Ontario.
2. Ojibwa Indians — Antiquities — Collection and preservation — Ontario.
3. Iroquoian Indians--Material culture — Ontario--Study and teaching. 4. Ojibwa Indians — Material culture — Ontario — Study and teaching. I. Title. II. Series: McGill-Queen's native and northern series ; 63

E99.I69H35 2010          971.3004'97554          C2010-902720-5

This book was typeset by Em Dash Design in Stempel Garamond 10.2/13

# CONTENTS

# ILLUSTRATIONS

# ACKNOWLEDGMENTS

Numerous individuals assisted me in completing this book and the doctoral dissertation from which it stems. As supervisor, Roger Hall provided his expertise on Ontario and public history, pragmatism, and good humour; indeed, without his encouragement, this research would have never even begun. During my research, I discovered others who shared my interest in the history of anthropology and early museums, including Regna Darnell, Julia Harrison, Lynne Teather, Trudy Nicks, Kate Muller, and Rick Fehr. I also appreciate the ongoing enthusiasm and archaeological knowledge of Mima Kapches, former senior curator in World Cultures of the Royal Ontario Museum. The ethnology and collections staff of the Glenbow Museum, the Niitsitapi community of Alberta and Montana, the participants of the Glenbow project *First Nations Women and Peace*, the urban Aboriginal youth of Calgary, and Tom Hill and Keith Jamieson, formerly of the Woodland Cultural Centre, helped me to shape many of the thoughts expressed here. In conducting community research, I was invited into many homes, and I thank these individuals for their hospitality. I was also aided by some truly interested archivists, librarians, and curators at the Royal Ontario Museum, the McCord Museum, the National Anthropological Archives, the Peabody Museum of Archaeology and Ethnology, the Smithsonian Institution, the Archives of Ontario, Library and Archives Canada, the University of Western Ontario, the University of Toronto, the McGill University Archives and Special Collections, the Hamilton Public Library and Special Collections, and numerous local museums and archives. Donald B. Smith provided me with invaluable information about the Peter Jones collection, now held by various museums across North America. Members of the Hamilton Association and of the Elgin, Oxford, Perth, Lambton, Wentworth, Brant, and Lennox and Addington historical societies were very helpful. Sheryl Smith (Parks Canada), Paul O'Neal (Mayer Heritage Consultants), Ron Williamson (Archaeological Services Inc.), Paul Williams (Haudenosaunee Standing Committee on Burial Rules and Regulations), Gerry Conaty (Glenbow), and Charles Garrad (Petun Research Institute) provided contemporary perspectives from the field.

Jan Trimble, Lynn Kennedy, Paul Williams, Mima Kapches, Keith Jamieson, Ian Dyck, Neal Ferris, and Doug McCalla kindly consented to read drafts in various forms. Many thanks also to John Zucchi, Sarah Carter, Arthur Ray, Kyla Madden, Claude Lalumière, the late Bruce Trigger, and to my two reviewers at McGill-Queen's University Press, all of whom shepherded me through the publication process. Small parts of chapters 1, 3, 4, and 5 appeared first in *Historicizing Canadian Anthropology*, edited by Julia Harrison and Regna Darnell and in *Lines Drawn upon the Water*, edited by Karl S. Hele, and I appreciate the permission of the University of British Columbia Press and Wilfrid Laurier Press, respectively, to duplicate the information. Don Lafreniere expertly made the two maps.

I also gratefully acknowledge financial support from the Association of Canadian Studies; the American Philosophical Society; the Lloyd Hodgins estate in London, Ontario; the Department of History of The University of Western Ontario; the Smallman Publication Fund, Faculty of Social Science (also at Western); and the ASPP program through SSHRC. A Postdoctoral Fellowship in Rural History at the University of Guelph and the generosity and guidance of Doug McCalla, Kris Inwood, and Terry Crowley allowed me to transform my dissertation into a monograph. Finally, I appreciate the encouragement of those who heartened me during the process, especially Jamie Mather, Melanie and John Docherty, Wade Baillie, Allan Fraser, Karen Gilles, and my former graduate student colleagues.

# A NOTE ON TERMINOLOGY

According to scholarly convention, the terms "First Nations" and "Native" include all groups original to Canada, with the exception of the Inuit and the Métis. "Aboriginal" includes the latter two while "indigenous" indicates the original groups of all continents. "Native American" pertains to solely those groups whose territories now exist within the boundaries of the United States. My use of the term "Indian" refers alone to the images of early collectors and museum professionals who often viewed Aboriginal peoples as one indistinguishable culture. If identified in the historical sources, I have used specific band or tribal names. Many Aboriginal peoples have multiple historic and contemporary versions of their band and tribal names, and I have tried to use whichever is most commonly used by themselves today. Where possible, I have included both Euro-Canadian and Aboriginal names and the chiefly titles of specific individuals.

I have chosen to use the terms "pre-contact" and "post-contact" rather than "pre-historic" and "historic" because the latter two suggest that history begins with European contact and places prominence on written conventions of recording the past.

It is difficult to find words to adequately describe the varied understandings of what scholars call "material culture." Words such as "object," "artifact," and "specimen" routinely used by museologists do not acknowledge that Aboriginal peoples see many items as alive, sentient, and powerful. Instead these terms reinforce the Euro-Canadian view of their inanimate-ness, and I recognize these limitations. For these reasons of spirituality, I have also chosen not to include photographs of sacred material culture, human remains, or objects buried in graves.

# ABBREVIATIONS

AARO    Annual Report of the Canadian Institute/Ontario Provincial Museum; (Annual) Archaeological Report of Ontario

AFHP    Andrew F. Hunter Papers

AMNH    Division of Anthropology Archives, American Museum of Natural History, New York, NY

AO    Archives of Ontario, Toronto, ON

BAAS    British Association for the Advancement of Science

CAA    Canadian Archaeological Association

CJ    *Canadian Journal*

DBC    David Boyle Correspondence, Royal Ontario Museum, Toronto, ON

DBP    David Boyle Papers, Royal Ontario Museum, Toronto, ON

DIA    Department of Indian Affairs

EHSI/EHS    Elgin Historical and Scientific Institute/Elgin Historical Society

GELS    George E. Laidlaw Scrapbooks, Royal Ontario Museum, Toronto, ON

HA    Hamilton Association for the Advancement of Literature, Science and Art/Hamilton Scientific Association

HAP    Hamilton Association Papers, Special Collections, Hamilton Public Library, Hamilton, ON

HI    Huron Institute

JHHP    J. Hugh Hammond Papers, Royal Ontario Museum, Toronto, ON

| | |
|---|---|
| JPHA | *Journals and Proceedings of the Hamilton Association* |
| LAC | Library and Archives Canada, Ottawa, ON |
| LLHS | Lundy's Lane Historical Society |
| LMHS | London and Middlesex Historical Society |
| NAA | National Anthropological Archives, Smithsonian Institution, Suitland, MD |
| NAGPRA | Native American Graves Protection and Repatriation Act |
| NHS | Niagara Historical Society |
| NHSC | Niagara Historical Society Correspondence, Niagara Historical Museum, Niagara-on-the-Lake, ON |
| NHSP | Niagara Historical Society Papers, Archives of Ontario, Toronto, ON |
| NMAI | National Museum of the American Indian |
| OFNC | Ottawa Field-Naturalists' Club |
| OHS | Ontario Historical Society |
| OHSP | Ontario Historical Society Papers, Archives of Ontario, Toronto, ON |
| OLSS | Ottawa Literary and Scientific Society |
| OxHS | Oxford Historical Society, Woodstock, ON |
| PCI/TCI | *Proceedings/Transactions of the Canadian Institute* |
| RCIP | Royal Canadian Institute Papers |
| ROM | Royal Ontario Museum Archives, Toronto, ON |
| SAA | Society for American Archaeology |
| TFRBL | Thomas Fisher Rare Book Library, University of Toronto, Toronto, ON |
| T/PRWHS | *Transactions/Papers and Records of the Wentworth Historical Society* |
| UEL | United Empire Loyalist |
| UWO | University of Western Ontario, London, ON |
| WCHST | Women's Canadian Historical Society of Toronto |
| WCHSTP | Women's Canadian Historical Society of Toronto Papers, Archives of Ontario, Toronto, ON |
| WHS | Wentworth Historical Society |
| WHSP | Wentworth Historical Society Papers, Special Collections, Hamilton Public Library, Hamilton, ON |

"Bone Pit in Medonte," by Father Martin, 1855
Jones, *"8endake Ehen" or Old Huronia*

Part of Chief A.G. Smith's archaeological collection
purchased by David Boyle in the 1880–90s
Royal Ontario Museum, NS 73, NS 76, NS 2013-14, NS 2021, NS 2028, NS 2039,
NS 5937, NS 6009; Photo number ROM2010_11423_1

Archaeological items collected by David Boyle from Dr Peter E. Jones c.1890
NS 8456, NS 8470–71, NS 8475, NS 8480, NS 8581–3;
Photo number ROM2010_11423_2

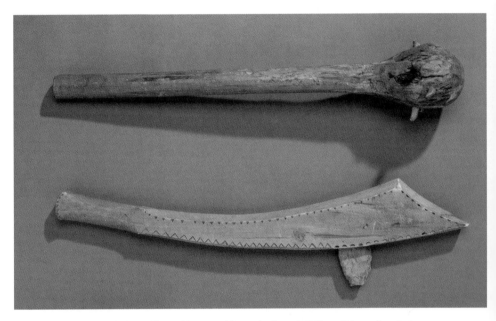

War clubs collected by David Boyle from William Henry in 1898
Royal Ontario Museum, NS 17054, NS 17056; Photo number 2010_11424_3

Knee bands and headdress collected by David Boyle from Red Cloud
(William Bill) c. 1901
Royal Ontario Museum, NS 22263-4, NS 22267;
Photo number ROM2010_11242_4

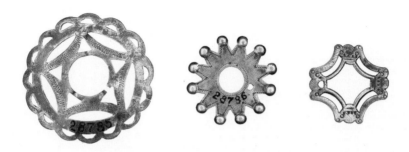

Brooches collected by David Boyle from Jacob Hess in c. 1908
Royal Ontario Museum, NS 28785-7; Photo number ROM2010_11424_5

Conch shell used to call people to Longhouse ceremonies,
collected by David Boyle in 1899
Royal Ontario Museum, NS 21464; Photo number ROM2010_11423_3

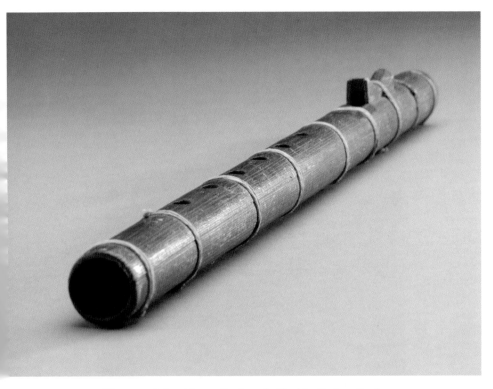

Flute, made by Abram Buck and gifted by Joshua Buck,
collected by David Boyle in 1898
Royal Ontario Museum, NS 17101; Photo number ROM2005_5896_2

Pauline Johnson posing with wampum belt
E. Pauline Johnson fonds, William Ready Division of Archives and Research
Collections, McMaster University Library, Hamilton

Quilled box depicting historical Kanienkehaka and Ojibwa conflict,
made by Jonathan Yorke for J. Hugh Hammond c. 1904
Royal Ontario Museum, NS 26988; Photo number ROM2004_948_12

Tomahawk pipe given by General Isaac Brock to Tecumseh, when he and his
warriors agreed to ally with the British in the War of 1812.
Oshawana, Tecumseh's chief warrior, preserved it after
Tecumseh's death and it was later donated to the Oronhyatekha collection.
Royal Ontario Museum, HD 6319 or 911.3 181A-B;
Photo number ROM2010_11424_2

Silver gorget given to Haudenosaunee leader Joseph Brant by King George III
and later donated to the Oronhyatekha collection
Royal Ontario Museum, HD 6317 or 911.3.209;
Photo number ROM2004_948_14

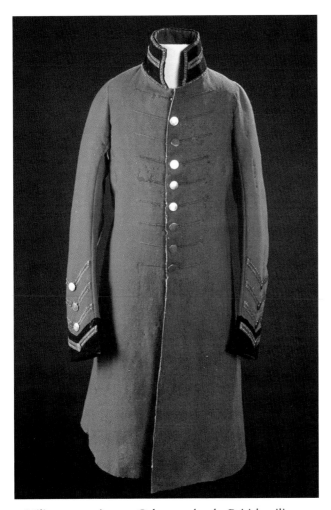

Military coat given to Oshawana by the British military;
part of the Oronhyatekha collection
Royal Ontario Museum, HD 6294 or 911.3.119;
Photo number ROM2005_1448_1

Headdresses worn by John Tecumseh Henry and wife to meet the Prince of Wales during his royal visit of 1860; later donated to the Oronhyatekha collection. Royal Ontario Museum, HD 6278-79 or 911.3.80-1; Photo number ROM2010_11424_1

MAPS

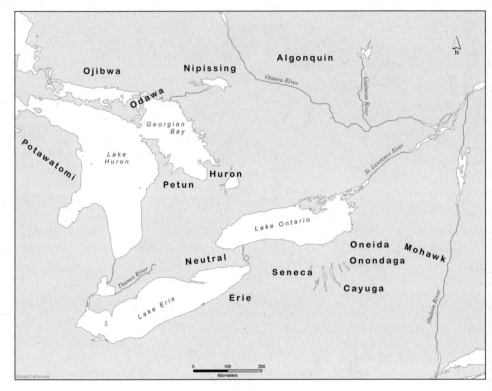

Aboriginal groups in the Great Lakes region c. 1640

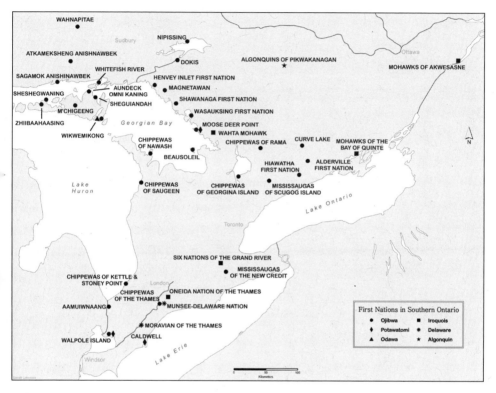

Contemporary First Nations reserves in South-Central Ontario

*Ontario First Nations Map*, www.ainc-inac.gc.ca/ai/scr/on/rp/mcaṛte/mcarteeng. asp, Indian and Northern Affairs Canada, 2008. Adapted with the permission of the Minister of Public Works and Government Services Canada, 2010

COLLECTIONS AND OBJECTIONS

# INTRODUCTION

## Museums, Collectors, and Aboriginal Peoples

Many years ago, I was intrigued by a line in Bruce Trigger's *Natives and Newcomers* (1985), which noted that farmers discovered and excavated many Wendat (Huron) burial sites in early Ontario. What, I wondered, did these farmers do with the human remains and artifacts they uncovered, how did they interpret them, and what did local Aboriginal peoples think of such activities? Who else had collected Aboriginal artifacts in the province, and where were these objects now? As I entered the museum field I became aware of the contemporary issues surrounding the collection, ownership, exhibition, and repatriation of Aboriginal material culture. In particular, my experiences at the Woodland Cultural Centre in Brantford, one of the preeminent Aboriginal-run institutions in Canada, and at the Glenbow Museum in Calgary exposed me to the very real differences between Aboriginal and Euro-Canadian views about the purpose, treatment, and interpretation of material culture. I later realized not only that these differences are the result of disparate Aboriginal/non-Aboriginal cultural values but that each society possesses many viewpoints. I also came to believe that the narrative of the past must be connected with the present concerns of scholars, museums, government officials, the public, and Aboriginal communities.

This, then, is my attempt to explore the complexities of the excavation, collection, exhibition, and interpretation of material culture of Iroquoian- and Algonkian-speaking peoples in Upper Canada and early Southern Ontario. This material culture was archaeological, items found in the soil, including human remains, and ethnographic, objects that related to and were gathered from contemporaneous Aboriginal communities. The public, historical and scientific societies, the provincial and Dominion governments, professional archaeologists and anthropologists, and Aboriginal communities held numerous, and sometimes contradictory, understandings of the significance of this material culture. Rather than privileging one understanding over another, I wish instead to emphasize the diversity of these views and the reasons that underpin them and suggest how their legacies affect current relationships between those interested in Aboriginal heritage.

Despite a call to do so in the mid-1970s by the members of the Canadian Ethnology Society at their annual meeting, one repeated by the editors of the more recent publication *Historicizing Canadian Anthropology* (2006), only a small number of scholars has examined the history of Canadian anthropology. In contrast, considerable attention has been given to the history of Americanist anthropology and to contemporary issues in archaeology, anthropology, and museology. The Canadian literature focuses upon specific individuals or the institutions for which they worked, particularly after 1910 and the establishment of the Anthropological Branch of the Geological Survey of Canada, which has been deemed the beginning of the professionalization of the discipline. Here, I examine earlier collectors and set them within a network of colleagues and other interested parties involved in the collection of Aboriginal material culture in Ontario.

In 1797, Peter Russell, the administrator of the British colony of Upper Canada, issued a proclamation criminalizing any depredation of Mississauga fisheries and burial grounds. Officially responsible for Indian Affairs in the colony as of that year, Russell had been prompted by the "many heavy and grievous complaints" from the Mississaugas and by recent rumours of Native discontent in the west, which made the loyalty of Upper Canadian bands expedient. Living along the shores of Lake Ontario, the Mississaugas were one of the first groups in the province to share their territory with early colonists, and increasing settlement had resulted in the discovery and plundering of their graves. Russell characterized these burial disturbances as violations of "decency and good order" that breached the "friendship subsisting between his Majesty and the Mississague Indians." Any future gravediggers, the proclamation concluded, would be "proceded [*sic*] against with the utmost severity."[1]

Seventy-five years later, the Anglican Minister Henry Scadding reflected upon the inefficacy of Russell's proclamation by recounting the wanton destruction of another Mississauga burial, popularly known as the "Sandhill" in York, to the members of the Canadian Institute. A founder of the institute in 1849, and of the York Pioneer and Historical Society in 1869, Scadding was greatly interested in the early days of the capital of York (renamed Toronto in 1834) and had gathered recollections from the descendants of the pioneers of the area.[2] Scadding compiled these tidbits of local history for publication in the Canadian Institute's periodical *The Canadian Journal of Science, Literature and History* in 1872 and for his popular book *Toronto of Old* one year later.

Within their broad mandate of studying and spreading historical and scientific knowledge, members of the Canadian Institute and the York Pioneers collected Aboriginal artifacts, including human remains. They undoubtedly would have been interested in the Sandhill burial and Russell's proclamation, which apparently restrained their collecting activities. Scadding suggested, however, that the proclamation had possessed only a "temporary effect." The public had carted away numerous loads of sand mixed with human bones; crushed, the bones became part of the mortar used to construct nearby buildings. Scadding dismissed the desecration of 1797 that had led to Russell's proclamation by speculating that the Mississauga had transferred their ancestral remains to another resting spot and thus had abandoned the burial. Although its closing sentiment surely belied the mandate of the societies to preserve Aboriginal culture, Scadding cited a poem whose poetic Victorian noble savage imagery implied that there were no contemporary Aboriginal peoples that needed consideration when it came to excavating their graves.

A noble race! but they are gone,
With their old forests wide and deep,
And we have built our homes upon
Fields where their generations sleep.
Their fountains slake our thirst at noon,
Upon their fields our harvest waves,
Our lovers woo beneath their moon –
Then let us spare at least their graves!

But in a contradiction that was common to nineteenth-century beliefs about indigenous cultures, Scadding also recognized that contemporaneous Aboriginal peoples had reused the ancient Sandhill burial. An Aboriginal man who had been shot out of a nearby tree during the War of 1812 had been buried in this spot "with respect" (although supposedly his scalp was taken to Washington) and a railing at some point had been erected around the site.[3]

Although these two burial disturbances concerned sites specific to the Mississaugas, Russell's and Scadding's responses illustrate some of the themes of nineteenth-century discussions about Aboriginal history and material culture in and beyond Ontario. Ideas about material culture varied widely because of the cultural differences between Euro-Canadians and Aboriginal peoples but also because they were debated within each society. Beyond an exploration of the formative years of Canadian anthropology, the struggles over Aboriginal objects and human remains in the nineteenth century inform contemporary issues of stewardship, including the control, access, study, interpretation, and repatriation of material culture.

In the nineteenth century, members of the public, particularly farmers, discovered the remains of Aboriginal villages, middens, and cemeteries during their daily work.[4] Like the York Sandhill, the location of many of these sites became common knowledge, recorded in popular memory and by newspaper reporters, historians, novelists, and travel writers. Even as the public honoured some of the Aboriginal leaders of the War of 1812 and their graves, many earlier sites were looted and destroyed out of curiosity and for entertainment. People created private curio collections to display in their homes or adapted artifacts for personal use. They planted flowers in human skulls, boiled cattle feed in copper trade kettles, or, as in the case of the York grave, turned the sand covering burials and even the human remains themselves into construction materials.[5] Professional archaeologists struggled to limit such destructive digging and careless treatment of artifacts yet also sought to harness amateur efforts in order to locate archaeological sites and to build public museum collections.

Like Scadding, most members of early historical and scientific societies were educated men and women who followed the Victorian dictates of well-rounded self-improvement through leisure learning. At each meeting, they presented and discussed papers on a variety of topics, including the natural sciences, literature, classics, and history. Members favoured object-driven lessons and spent a great deal of their time amassing and classifying artifacts in society museums that they believed contributed to scientific knowledge and spread patriotism through the preservation of Canada's past.[6] While societies distinguished themselves from the public, whose activities they often lamented as harmful, a lack of money and inconsistent community support meant that many of their own efforts never quite met the standards of the professionals whom they emulated.

Whatever their motives, Euro-Canadian collectors usually justified excavations of archaeological sites by distancing the objects found from Aboriginal communities. Scadding did so by proclaiming that European civilization had replaced Aboriginal societies and that the Indian "race" was extinct, although surely he was aware of the Aboriginal communities living in Ontario. His speculation that the burial associated with Russell's proclamation had been "abandoned" reinforced this hypothetical distance between Aboriginal peoples and their material culture. In fact, some Euro-Canadians believed that the artifacts buried in the earth could not be relevant to Aboriginal communities, either because the objects were so ancient that no links could be determined or because the people who left behind these objects were not ancestral to current communities. Although the public often used Aboriginal oral traditions to explain archaeological sites, professional collectors saw little point in consulting Aboriginal peoples because they assumed them to be almost extinct, or at least assimilated. Instead, professionals felt that material culture and the historical record contained the most significant clues to reconstruct the pre-contact Aboriginal cultures that interested them.

All collectors used progressionist or evolutionary theories to explain Aboriginal civilization but each group emphasized different aspects. To the public, archaeological remains evoked a nostalgic or ghoulish fascination for a long-dead culture that had succumbed to European superiority. Professionals disdained the public's representation of artifacts as romantic pieces from an extinct exotic culture, but they arranged material culture in evolutionary typologies of form and function that presupposed Aboriginal peoples to be less civilized. Society members sought to match the scientific standards as set out by professionals, particularly by David Boyle (1841–1911). As the secretary of the Ontario Historical Society, provincial archaeologist, and curator first of the Canadian Institute and then of the Ontario Provincial Museum in Toronto, Boyle advocated use of the classificatory-descriptive and later the classificatory-historical methodologies of anthropological practice. The museum exhibits created by historical society members, however, often celebrated the seemingly inevitable conquest of the Canadian wilderness and establishment of villages and towns by their local ancestors, and thus the displacement of Aboriginal communities.[7]

In seeking ethnographic artifacts, historical society members, and professional anthropologists preferred to collect items they considered to be traditional and authentic, that is those of pre-contact origin or those that did not show the influence of European society. The communities they visited to purchase material culture were "modern" to varying degrees, incorporating Christianity and European-style houses, clothing, and agricultural methods, but collectors did not often document these aspects. Typical of the salvage anthropology paradigm of the nineteenth century, these collectors believed themselves to be recovering the remnants of a true or pure Indian culture.[8]

Peter Russell's mention of the friendship between the Mississauga and King George III in his proclamation implied a nation-to-nation alliance, and thus Aboriginal sovereignty, concepts recognized by government officials in the late eighteenth century but increasingly disregarded as the nineteenth century progressed and threats of colonial war diminished. This made it easier to ignore Aboriginal protests over the excavation and sale of their material culture. In fact, no-one was ever charged with violating Russell's proclamation, and only a few individuals were punished under subsequent legislation despite widespread excavation of burials across Canada. In one case, the Department of Indian Affairs (DIA) sided with excavators because they were believed to be pursuing valid scientific enquiries. Yet the DIA turned down requests by local historical societies and by professional archaeologists such as David Boyle for financial support of their research and preservation activities. This, too, was based upon evolutionary ideas; unlike collectors, who preferred what they deemed traditional Aboriginal culture, DIA officials wanted Aboriginal peoples to assimilate and forget their historic customs and the material culture associated with them. The provincial Department of Education, which did give grants to historical societies, preferred to fund David Boyle at the Canadian Institute and the Ontario Provincial Museum, because it viewed local groups as unprofessional and dependent upon the fickle whims of community enthusiasm. The minister of Education feared that money given to local societies would be wasted and the material collected would be lost if a society became inactive.[9]

The territory that became Upper Canada in 1791 experienced several waves of Aboriginal occupation and settlement after European contact. In the mid-sixteenth century, the Iroquoian-speaking peoples of the Neutral, Wendat, and Tionontati (Petun) inhabited the southwestern area, with Algonkian-speaking groups of the Ojibwa, Odawa (Ottawa), Potawatomi, Nipissing, and Algonquin to the north and west. Disease, depopulation, and existing rivalries exacerbated by the fur trade and European conflict led to the dislocation of these peoples. By 1600, various Neutral communities across the southwest had coalesced in the Niagara peninsula and at the western end of Lake Ontario, in response, it is thought, to attacks from the west by the Fire Nation, an Algonkian-speaking group. From their earlier homeland along the northern shores of Lake Ontario and in the Trent River Valley, the Wendat and Tionontati retreated closer to Georgian Bay because of attacks by the Haudenosaunee (League of Five Nations or Iroquois), for trading purposes and later to congregate at Jesuit missions.[10]

In 1649, the Haudenosaunee launched major offensives on Wendat and Tionontati villages, taking prisoners and causing many others to flee to Quebec or north and west to join bands of Algonkian-speaking peoples, who had also retreated further into the interior. By 1651, the Haudenosaunee had expelled the Neutral from their territory. The Neutral fled west and south or were adopted by the Haudenosaunee. The Haudenosaunee began to use the area as hunting grounds and, by the 1680s, had established villages along the north shore of Lake Ontario and in the interior. As some Wendat, Nipissing, Ojibwa, and Odawa returned, clashes with the Haudenosaunee increased, and by the late 1690s the Five Nations had largely withdrawn to their land in the colony of New York. In 1701, the Haudenosaunee concluded a formal peace with their Aboriginal enemies and allied French. Thus when European settlers and the United Empire Loyalists came to Upper Canada in the late eighteenth and early nineteenth centuries they encountered Algonkian-speaking peoples as the Aboriginal residents of Upper Canada, although they often stumbled across Iroquoian archaeological sites.

To accommodate settlement, the British government pressured the Aboriginal peoples to surrender increasing amounts of land in Upper Canada and accept small reserves. The Odawa and Ojibwa settled mostly along the shores of Lake Huron and Georgian Bay. The Mississauga, a related group given this separate name by British settlers, lived along Lake Ontario and in the Trent River Valley. The US policy of removal to the west, especially during the 1830s and 1840s, forced increasing numbers of Odawa and Potawatomi from their homelands in the United States. Many chose to settle on already established reserves in Ontario. These groups are now known collectively as the Anishinabeg.[11] The Anishinabeg were joined by Delaware or Munceys from the United States, who established Moraviantown in the 1790s and Munceytown in the 1830s.

There were also several Iroquoian communities in the province. Akwesasne, which now borders on Ontario, Quebec, and New York State, had been an established community since the mid-1750s. After their participation as British allies in the American Revolution, the Haudenosaunee and descendants of their adopted Wendat, Tionontati, and Neutral refugees and other groups from their wars in colonial America, returned to the province, to lands granted along the Grand River and at Tyendinaga on the Bay of Quinte. In the 1840s, a group of Onyot.ka (Oneida) purchased land and established the Thames reserve near London. A mixed group of Tionontati and Wendat, or Wyandot, resided on the Anderdon reserve near Amherstburg. Many later migrated to the United States, and in 1876 the remaining families applied for enfranchisement, resulting in their land being divided into severalty and their apparent disappearance into pioneer Ontario. In the 1880s, a group of Kanienkehaka (Mohawk) from Quebec established the Gibson reserve in the Muskoka region.[12]

Although these Aboriginal peoples sustained and interpreted their history and material culture within these communities, that is not the focus of this book. Rather, it considers their engagement within a cross-cultural debate, as people from these communities responded to and participated in Euro-Canadian attempts to collect and exhibit their material culture. Historical records featuring Aboriginal viewpoints are limited but do permit the exploration of their perspectives. Aboriginal individuals aided archaeologists in excavations, including those of burials, welcomed collectors into their communities, and sold or donated artifacts to them. Others protested grave disturbances, demanded the return of items, restricted the activities of collectors, or used them for their own political purposes. A few established and exhibited their own private collections or studied their history independently.

Because of their conflict over the territory that became Southern Ontario, Anishinabeg and Iroquoian peoples shared some burial sites and objects such as wampum belts, used to formalize peace treaties. They did not, however, always agree on the interpretation of these sites or artifacts. But, whatever the context, Aboriginal peoples in many cases interpreted archaeological sites and material culture as still vital to the well-being of their society. For example, as in Scadding's anecdote, it was customary to continue interment in earlier burial grounds. Thus, despite Scadding's assertion that the York Sandhill cemetery had been abandoned, the site was still relevant at least until the early nineteenth century. Likewise, the nineteenth-century sale of an ethnographic object by an Aboriginal person did not necessarily mean, as collectors presumed, that it was considered to be irrelevant to contemporary life. Instead, its sale could mean its preservation in a time made uncertain by missionary coercion to convert to Christianity, by the presence of Indian agents, and by fears that an assimilated youth would no longer be able or willing to participate in their culture. Certainly, colonial policy and the changes it wrought, from financial pressures to altered religious and political beliefs, form the context of the alienation of material culture from its community stewards. Even when Aboriginal peoples spoke of their material culture as part of their past, they often emphasized it as a symbol of their "civilization" rather than as remnants of a dying or primitive society.

While grounded in historical evidence, this book also draws upon inter-disciplinary writings about material culture and upon the links between anthropology, museums, and colonialism. Material culture theory suggests that the purpose and significance of objects are shaped by the class, status, education, and cultural background of the owner and the viewer of an artifact or by the values of the popular culture in which these individuals invest. Thus people can impart varied meanings to one artifact, a tenet key to this book.[13]

Museums, and by extension, the collection and exhibition of material culture, have been characterized as contact zones of colonial encounter in which coercion, inequality, and conflict occurred.[14] Scholars further suggest the elements of museum exhibitions – the choice of objects, their labels, and the order in which they are organized – are socially constructed texts.[15] The authors of these texts, usually anthropologists who claimed to be experts, portrayed Aboriginal societies as primitive, inferior, and on the verge of extinction or assimilation due to contact with European civilization. Anthropologists aimed to salvage the Aboriginal past by collecting material culture, particularly items that represented pre-contact life, which was considered to be more authentic or traditional.[16]

Museums have also been characterized as "political arenas in which definitions of identity and culture are asserted and contested," and as forums for discussion.[17] The nineteenth-century collection and exhibition of Aboriginal artifacts did generate a conversation about the history and culture of Aboriginal peoples; it may have been rather one-sided and sometimes marked by coercion, inequality, and conflict, but Aboriginal peoples did enter into the debate. And arguably their refusal to do so in other cases can be construed as the rejection of the interpretations of their culture by Euro-Canadian collectors. Anthropology has always been a "'plural' or 'multi'-discourse," in which Aboriginal "auto-anthropologists" and "anti-anthropologists" participated.[18] Similarly, studies of "cultural brokers" show that many individuals, often of multicultural descent, have skilfully mediated between Aboriginal and non-Aboriginal worlds and ancestral and anthropological knowledge.[19]

Anthropology is currently divided into the four branches of archaeology, linguistics, physical anthropology, which studies human remains, and ethnography, which documents living cultures. The history of these fields in Canada has been dominated by an emphasis on individual anthropologists and their careers and on the institutions at which they worked.[20] As a result, we have studies of missionaries and gentlemen elite[21] and of the now legendary figures of late nineteenth- and early twentieth-century Canadian anthropology such as George Mercer Dawson, Horatio Hale, Edward Sapir, Diamond Jenness, and Marius Barbeau, who were employed by the first national anthropological bodies.[22] In 1884, the British Association for the Advancement of Science met with Canadian scholars in Montreal and established the Committee on the North-Western Tribes of Canada, which included Hale and Dawson, who was then an assistant director of the Geological Survey of Canada. In 1910, the Geological Survey established an anthropological division and hired Edward Sapir as its director, Barbeau, Jenness, and Frederick W. Waugh as ethnologists, and Harlan I. Smith and William J. Wintemberg as archaeologists shortly thereafter.[23] The creation of this new agency stimulated the beginning of federal funding for research, the collection of Aboriginal artifacts for the Victoria Memorial Museum, which opened in 1912 in Ottawa, and according to scholars the professionalization of anthropology. Not surprisingly, then, most works focus on these formative individuals and institutions, or on the influence of notable anthropologists like Franz Boas, who came to Canada to collect for US museums.[24]

This book assesses instead the role of the public, historical societies, and Aboriginal peoples, largely in the pre-1910 period, and places these groups in a network that included professionals Daniel Wilson (1816–92), a professor of history and ethnology at University College in Toronto, and the more active David Boyle. Only a few brief or site-specific studies examine the activities of the public.[25] The role of the prominent Canadian Institute in early archaeology has been explored, but the Ontario Historical Society and the plethora of local bodies either lack scholarly attention or have been examined only in regards to their overall function.[26] To fully understand the development of early anthropological collecting in Ontario, the roles of the public, avocational society members, professionals, and Aboriginal peoples also need to be connected together as a cohort, rather than examined individually.

Like the broader writing of historical Canadian anthropology, Aboriginal involvement in collecting has focused on key individuals such as George Hunt, who worked with Franz Boas, or William Beynon, one of Barbeau's informants.[27] Additionally, most writings explore those who acted as informants or "pickers" in the gathering of material culture, rather than individuals who objected to collecting. The latter has been only briefly noted, and many of these examples are drawn from US anthropology.[28] Aboriginal scholars who interpreted their material culture and created their own museums have often been "anthropologized" as informants or mediators, rather than acknowledged as collectors or anthropologists themselves.[29] For those individuals who engaged in anthropology, their motives and scholarship were shaped by religious and political beliefs, education, family, clan and friendship ties, financial concerns, the influence of colleagues or mentors, pressures to assimilate, and the hope to preserve material culture and beliefs at a time when the younger generation expressed disinterest in learning about their traditional culture.[30]

A historical look at anthropology in Southern Ontario also informs current relationships among professional anthropologists, archaeologists, museologists, government agencies, the public, historical societies, and Aboriginal communities. There is a voluminous literature that addresses the purpose of museums, stewardship of heritage, the right to interpret other cultures, the validity of oral knowledge, the study of human remains, repatriation and the development of cultural legislation, and successful attempts to overcome conflicting ideologies through collaborative projects between indigenous and non-indigenous groups. But few scholars connect the present with the past although these debates possess a long history and to deal with them now requires an understanding of their roots, particularly because many of the issues have remained the same. The stories of how and why objects were collected also contextualizes those still in the custody of museums, the underlying messages of power inherent in exhibits, and the efforts of indigenous peoples to control their heritage.

Many collectors in Southern Ontario consulted others throughout North America and the United Kingdom, but this cohort mainly revolved around David Boyle and his work in Toronto at the Canadian Institute, the Ontario Historical Society, and the Ontario Provincial Museum. Equivalent nineteenth-century networks of collectors and museums operated across North America. In Northern Ontario, for example, collecting centred around the efforts of the staff of the Geological Survey of Canada, even before the creation of its Anthropological Division in 1910. Outside Ontario, the northwest coast attracted many international collectors in the late nineteenth century who believed the Aboriginal peoples there to have maintained much more of their traditional lifestyle and to possess more visually spectacular material culture than others. In isolated or northern parts of Canada, a transitory non-Aboriginal population resulted in the belated development of museums and historical societies. As in South-Central Ontario, collecting in parts of Quebec and Eastern Canada occurred in the context of a settled non-Aboriginal population within which reserve communities appeared to be on the path to assimilation. But these areas also had their own circle of colleagues. In Southern Quebec, for example, the English-speaking network included John William Dawson, David Ross McCord, the founder of the McCord Museum, lawyer and novelist William Douw Lighthall, and groups such as the Natural History Society of Montreal.[31]

Similar cohorts existed in the United States, although they developed differently than they did in Canada. While Franz Boas's theories influenced the methodology of George Mercer Dawson and Edward Sapir, in the United States his training of a new generation of anthropologists who then molded their own students in Boasian methodology had wider-spread significance.[32] Further, the earlier establishment and greater funding of institutions such as the Smithsonian and the Bureau of (American) Ethnology, publications like its *Bulletin*, national organizations such as the American Association for the Advancement of Science, and university training characterized the development of US anthropology. Protective archaeological legislation also occurred earlier.

There have been several attempts to periodize Canadian anthropology, but most agree that the creation of the Anthropological Division in 1910 symbolizes the break between the pre-professional and professional stages. Regna Darnell has suggested the transition between the two was marked by the "establishment of firm disciplinary boundaries, standardized training programs, positions enabling scholars to make their living as anthropologists, growth of publication outlets, consensual evaluation of quality of work, and a recognized community of scholars."[33] In nineteenth-century Ontario, these conditions largely did not exist.

Nevertheless, the perception of 1910 as the only pivotal point in the professionalization of Canadian anthropology is too simplistic. A small literature recognizes some early anthropologists – once deemed "dilettantes" – as professionals despite the fact that they worked in the pre-1910 period.[34] These men include David Boyle, Sir Daniel Wilson, Henry Montgomery (1849–1919), the curator of the scientific collections of the

University of Toronto, and Sir John William Dawson (1820–99), geologist, professor of natural history at McGill University, and a founder of the Redpath Museum in Montreal.[35] I posit here a more complex chronology of professionalization for Southern Ontario: 1791–1851, a time of little professional oversight; 1851–84, a period marked by the incorporation of the Canadian Institute and the attempts by its early members, including Daniel Wilson, to improve archaeological standards; and 1884–1911, the career span of David Boyle as Ontario's most preeminent nineteenth-century anthropologist, and his work at the Canadian Institute, the Ontario Provincial Museum, and with the growing number of local historical societies through his leadership of the Ontario Historical Society. Amateur activity continued apace in all these periods however. Thus my use of the terms "amateur" and "professional" stem more from the standards used to excavate, collect, and exhibit material culture than the time period in which these activities occurred.

Proceeding in an approximate chronology, this book covers pioneer settlement, early tourism, the birth of historical societies, the emergence of David Boyle as an influential professional leader, the appearance of early Canadian literature and history about Aboriginal peoples, the passage of archaeological legislation, and the struggle of Ontario Aboriginal communities to deal with colonial policies. Boyle died in 1911, and after 1914 historical societies largely turned their attention to supporting the war effort. By then, the disciplines of history and anthropology had begun to change because of the advent of the Anthropological Division of the Geological Survey.

The sources available to explore the history of anthropology are diverse. Matching the donor names from museum accession lists with census records confirm Bruce Trigger's assertion that many collectors were farmers and their families. Newspapers of the time contain hundreds of scattered bits of information regarding local archaeological finds; together, these provide a pattern of how the public collected, used, and interpreted objects found in the soil. The more dedicated collectors wrote to David Boyle, asking for information or inviting him to visit the locations of their local finds. Boyle's more professional colleagues, particularly Andrew Frederick Hunter (1863–1940), a lawyer and historian who surveyed the archaeological sites of historic Huronia, also frequently commented on the activities of the public.

The membership lists of the local historical societies of Ontario tell us that doctors, ministers, teachers, and businessmen and their wives joined such groups. Only a few women rose to prominence in these societies or played a role in the building of museums. Most notable are the influential Janet Carnochan of the Niagara Historical Society, Sarah Curzon, who established the Women's Canadian Historical Society of Toronto, and Clementina Fessenden of the Ontario Historical Society. Others included Mary Rose Holden of the Wentworth Historical Society, Sarah E. Carry, who helped organize the museum at Dundurn Castle in Hamilton, and Helen Merrill of the short-lived Prince Edward County Historical Society, who collected and wrote about archaeological artifacts.[36] Society reports, minutes, correspondence, and artifact listings provide a window into society activities and their struggles in establishing themselves as permanent institutions. Their descendants are some of today's community museums; while these institutions possess few records from their early years of collecting, sometimes the artifacts that remain have information recorded on them or were stored with the labels that once accompanied them.

David Boyle left an enormous body of documents including his annual reports for the Canadian Institute and the Ontario Provincial Museum, unpublished papers, and his correspondence with Ontario citizens, other North American professionals, historical society members, and government officials. These records make his leadership and expertise clear. Three of the colleagues he trained - Andrew Hunter; George E. Laidlaw (1860–1927), a soldier and farmer of Victoria County; and J. Hugh Hammond (1858–1923), a solicitor in Orillia - also kept records that show how they became Boyle's voice in their local areas.[37] Unfortunately, another of his protegés, Dr Thomas W. Beeman (1858–1920) of Perth, did not keep such records; William J. Wintemberg (1876–1941), a smith in Toronto, and Frederick Waugh (1872–1924), both of whom were later hired by the Geological Survey of Canada, kept few records before this employment. Those of Boyle's predecessors, Daniel Wilson and Horatio Hale, have been largely destroyed. Wilson's will asked that his papers be destroyed after his death, although some escaped this fate. Fire consumed Wilson's ethnological museum, university lectures, and correspondence housed at University College in Toronto, as it did Hale's study in Clinton, Ontario.[38]

The paucity of nineteenth-century documents that describe Aboriginal viewpoints toward collecting activities means that their reactions are underrepresented. Few Aboriginal people publicly complained since not many visited museums and even fewer felt safe to criticize openly the activities of non-Aboriginal individuals. Some communities were unaware of archaeological excavations within their territories or feared that bringing attention to digs might bring "greater inhumanity" to the situation.[39] As an added complication, most Aboriginal reactions are recorded by Euro-Canadians and thus are clearly distorted either by cultural misunderstanding or guile by those who wished to represent their own actions as noncontroversial. The catalogue and the artifacts collected by and for Dr Oronhyatekha (Peter Martin), a Haudenosaunee, still exist, but he never recorded his purpose for the museum or his interpretation of the artifacts. Statements about material culture and heritage made by Aboriginal individuals such as E. Pauline Johnson, John Ojijatekha Brant-Sero, Peter Jones (Kahkewaquonaby), or his son, Dr P.E. Jones, are typically couched in romantic Victorian language intended for presentation or publication for North American or European audiences. Consequently, I have tried to "read beyond words," using known historical and contemporary Aboriginal beliefs regarding material culture and the historical narrative of how Aboriginal communities reacted to the intrusions of colonial agents.[40] For the chapter on ethnographic collecting, oral interviews and the archival records of the traditional Six Nations Council, written by the Council members themselves, would have been useful. At the time of research and writing, however, the traditional council, which authored these records, and the elected council, which now houses these records, were negotiating their access and use by outside researchers and the protocol to be established to conduct oral interviews. Understandably, their efforts have now been shelved by the need to resolve the ongoing Caledonia land-claims settlement. In the meantime, I hope that my research provides useful information for the Haudenosaunee to further explore the history of the collecting of material culture from their community.[41] Despite these drawbacks, the historical evidence clearly presents a diversity of motives to collect, exhibit, and interpret archaeological and ethnographic objects in Southern Ontario from 1791 to 1914.

While the 1791–1914 period is a long one, there were only a few changes over this time. Despite Russell's 1797 proclamation, excavations were left mostly unchallenged until the incorporation and growth of the Canadian Institute in 1851. At this point, its members, particularly Daniel Wilson, attempted to curb archaeological destruction and harness the efforts of the public. Upon the appointment of David Boyle as curator of the Canadian Institute in 1884, such efforts increased. Although Wilson and Boyle used and preached an increasing level of professionalization, amateur activity continued, and attempts to legislate against archaeological destruction, either through enforcing laws or enacting new ones, proved mostly ineffective. Even after the establishment of the Geological Survey's Anthropological Division in 1910, amateur collectors continued undeterred, although their contributions were increasingly devalued.

The nature of the evidence may obscure other changes. There are few collectors' notebooks. The sources on amateur activities written by professionals do not specify the dates of excavations. Newspapers do, but because most only survive from the mid to late 1800s, they cannot be an effective source for tracing change over the entire century. Any correspondence between Wilson and Boyle has not survived. As they were Canadian Institute members of overlapping generations, such a source could have illustrated the transition between the middle periods of professionalization. It is also impossible to fully trace the development of the Canadian Institute collection between Wilson's and Boyle's purviews since there are few records relating to the early days of the museum, before Boyle became curator.

The late nineteenth century saw a spurt of historical and ethnographic work because of the reconstitution of the Pioneer and Historical Association of Ontario into the Ontario Historical Society, the subsequent appointment of Boyle as its secretary, Boyle's fieldwork at Six Nations of the Grand River, and the increased activity of the Six Nations in historical matters as a way to preserve their sovereignty. But, again, the remaining records do not allow us to assess whether, for example, earlier established societies operated with less scientific standards than those established in the late 1800s. In fact, it is difficult to judge society activity as a whole because members acted individually, despite the societies' overall mission statements. At the same time, local societies often could not meet rising professional standards because they did not have the monetary support, professional training, or steadfast community enthusiasm to do so.

As a result, this book is not organized purely chronologically. Instead, each chapter examines the relationships and diversity of goals between two or more groups. As chapter 1 demonstrates, when settlers came to Upper Canada, they discovered ample evidence of Aboriginal occupation of the land. The high level of contact and local knowledge of archaeological sites held by the public meant that amateurs had a substantial influence over the collection of artifacts, excavation standards, and the development of museums. As a result, the public and more professional collectors, such as Daniel Wilson and David Boyle, had an uneasy relationship as the latter two tried to both curb destructive digging and harness amateur efforts. This chapter also discusses how levels of professionalization increased over the nineteenth century, particularly after Boyle became the curator of the Canadian Institute in

1884. Chapter 2 turns to the members of the historical and scientific societies that arose in Canada West beginning in the mid-nineteenth century and their struggles to mediate between professional museum standards and local community needs and realities. Aboriginal responses to and engagement in archaeology, particularly burial excavations, follow in chapter 3. While the previous chapters focus on the relationships between various Euro-Canadian groups, chapter 3 centres around the archaeological beliefs and activities among all these groups and Aboriginal peoples. This structural division implies that Aboriginal communities often reacted similarly to archaeologists regardless of the level of professionalism, because Aboriginal spiritual beliefs mandated serious consequences to burial disturbances. While true, reactions to burial disturbances cannot be entirely explained through Aboriginal/ non-Aboriginal cultural differences. Some Christians also protested burial disturbances, but whether one applauded or protested excavations, particularly of burials, also depended on one's beliefs in human rights and on whether the uncovered archaeological objects could be used for political or financial ends. Aboriginal protests against, participation in, and manipulation of ethnographic collecting, particularly at Six Nations of the Grand River, is the subject of chapter 4. How all groups interpreted and disagreed over the meanings of archaeological sites and material culture is the subject of chapter 5. In the conclusion, I turn to the larger issues that underlay the collecting of material culture and the relationships among the groups involved and their links to contemporary discussions. These groups debated issues of scientific objectivity versus religious subjectivity, the purpose and morality of the excavation of human remains, the development of cultural legislation, the validity and accuracy of oral knowledge, and the mandate of museums, all which related to the stewardship of material culture. These historical issues are relevant to current relationships between the many groups involved in the collection and exhibition of Aboriginal material culture; despite the enormous changes in the practice of studying Aboriginal peoples since the nineteenth century, these issues remain contentious.

# 1

## "BRIC-A-BRACKERS AND POT-HUNTERS"
*Professionals and the Public*

In spring 1902, the *Toronto Daily Star* reported that residents of the town of Bradford "Dug Up Hundreds of Human Bones" from a Wendat (Huron) ossuary.[1] This mass grave had been exposed when John Stibbs, a Bradford baker, had the foundation of his house excavated. According to David Boyle, who witnessed the spectacle, news of the discovery spread quickly and the "next day, Sunday, there were nearly two hundred people, jostling one another with spades and shovels."[2] A bank clerk informed Boyle that he planned to cut off the top of a looted skull and use it as an inkstand.[3] Appalled, Boyle noted that in town a "ghoulish craze seemed to have taken possession of many people ... so that in passing along its principal street, skulls were seen on window-sills, while in not a few sitting rooms they occupied prominent places on centre-tables!"[4] Boyle, by then the archaeology curator and super-intendent of the Ontario Provincial Museum in Toronto, was disturbed by such use of human remains and the resulting loss of valuable sci-entific information. Probably prompted by Boyle, Stibbs appealed for the return of the plundered skulls in the local *Bradford Witness and the South Simcoe News*, so that the Provincial Museum could make a proper scientific study.[5] No-one responded. In explanation, Boyle remarked that the donation of these artifacts would deprive collectors of a "grue-some specimen–that which he might show to his or her more rural visitors, especially ladies, and over which utterances might be bandied in solemn tones with deep-drawn sighs."[6]

Although the striking of an ossuary was the most sensational of dis-coveries, the Bradford scramble was by no means unusual in Ontario.

This and many similar incidents reveal the important role of the public in archaeology and the tensions between amateur collectors and professional archaeologists. Amateur collectors generally gathered specimens as a byproduct of their daily work, particularly farming, or as a leisure activity and thus spent less time in archaeological pursuits than members of historical and scientific societies. But they had extensive hands-on contact with archaeological specimens and common knowledge of site locations. Their amateur local knowledge – "embodied in life experiences," "reproduced in everyday behaviour," founded on community events and intergenerational oral transmission, and rooted in an understanding of the landscape – significantly affected the development of archaeology.[7] Ontario residents often led professionals to new discoveries, and as frequent excavators themselves they affected excavation standards, the preservation or destruction of artifacts, and the study and treatment of specimens. Their centrality to early Ontario archaeology resulted in an uneasy relationship with their professional colleagues, who increasingly attempted to raise the standards in their discipline as the nineteenth century progressed. But in the absence of protective archaeological legislation, and underfunded and with no supporting staff, professionals were usually forced to rely upon the tenuous good will of the public.

In Southern Ontario, the concern to professionalize archaeology was driven by the Canadian Institute in Toronto and its members, including Sandford Fleming and Daniel Wilson, but particularly David Boyle. Before 1851 and the incorporation of the Canadian Institute, there were few institutions or individuals to advocate more scientific or professional standards in archaeological excavation and study.[8] Originally conceived as an organization for engineers, surveyors, and architects, the Canadian Institute soon broadened to many areas of study, and became one of the preeminent scholarly societies in nineteenth-century Canada. In 1852, Sandford Fleming, an engineer, issued a circular that sought public assistance in locating and preserving archaeological sites and asked for the donation of artifacts to build a museum.[9] This circular generated only modest results. Daniel Wilson wrote two articles attempting to educate amateurs in proper excavation techniques, but his diverse interests and growing responsibilities as a professor and administrator at University College in Toronto precluded any comprehensive study of Ontario archaeology or instruction of amateurs. Wilson also belonged to the generation of armchair anthropologists who did not necessarily think it essential to conduct extensive fieldwork. The

Canadian Institute's museum may have also suffered from Wilson's focus on his own personal teaching museum at University College.

But by 1884 archaeology had become the main focus of the Canadian Institute museum, having acquired David Boyle's personal collection and his talents as curator. Boyle, at first a teacher in Elora, then a book-seller in Toronto, had become fascinated with archaeology and eventually was recognized by his North American colleagues as a self-taught professional.[10] Boyle redistributed the Canadian Institute circular in 1885. Following the leads produced by the public's response, Boyle began to investigate Ontario archaeology in earnest, with an emphasis on fieldwork and scientific methods. When the institute collection was transferred to the Ontario Provincial Museum in 1896, Boyle became its curator and ultimately the superintendent, until his death in 1911. As the institute's first paid full-time curator, Boyle far surpassed Wilson's efforts to professionalize the discipline. Boyle wrote extensive annual reports that always discussed proper techniques, promoted professional standards in newspapers, sought out the advice of international museum specialists, and more frequently lobbied the government to enact protective legislation. Boyle also received government funding for fieldwork and the maintenance of the museums under his care, resulting in the donation or procurement of tens of thousands of artifacts. He also trained several individuals as his local representatives.

Wilson, Boyle, and the avocational archaeologists he coached – Andrew F. Hunter, George E. Laidlaw, William J. Wintemberg, J. Hugh Hammond, and Dr Thomas W. Beeman – possessed an awkward relationship with the public. Even as they scorned amateurs as "bric-a-brackers and pot-hunters," and tried to deter what they saw as archaeological plunder, these men attempted to harness amateur efforts and local knowledge for their own ends.[11]

## THE ARCHAEOLOGICAL RECORD

With little known about pre-contact Aboriginal societies, nineteenth-century amateur collectors, let alone professionals, often could not distinguish the culture associated with the archaeological sites they found or the time period in which its residents had lived. Many reports do not associate any particular peoples with archaeological sites or material culture. Current archaeological theory and terminology characterize the sites the public stumbled across as belonging to the Paleo-Indian (12,000–9,500 years ago), the Archaic (10,000–2,800 years ago), and the Early, Middle, and Late Woodland (2,900–450 years ago)

David Boyle at the Ontario Provincial Museum, c. 1900

The Ontario Provincial Museum, also known as the Normal School Museum, 1912

periods. During the Paleo-Indian period, typical archaeological objects included stone items such as dart heads, knives, and scrapers used to prepare hides and to make wood and bone tools. These were mobile peoples who followed large game, as reflected in their tools and small campsites.

Peoples of the Archaic Period manufactured various chipped-stone and ground-slate tools, polished-stone axes and adzes used for wood-working, stone tubes, winged bannerstones, and bird-shaped stones. The stone used in toolmaking was usually obtained locally as compared to Paleo-Indian tools. Sites may also contain bone items such as fishing hooks and harpoons, needles and awls, and decorative pieces such as beads and combs. Archaic peoples obtained copper from the shores of Lake Superior through trade and made this highly prized material into arrowheads, needles, and jewellery. Along with shells from the East Coast and the Gulf of Mexico, such copper items are often found in the more elaborate Archaic graves. Little is known, however, about village and housing patterns, and many sites are now under water.

The break between the Archaic and Early Woodland periods has been marked only by the appearance of pottery at archaeological sites. Archaeologists divide the material culture found into the Meadowood and Middlesex complexes. Much of what has been learned from these two cultures comes from gravesites, which often include cremated bodies and rich grave goods such as large quantities of flint blades, bird-shaped stones, tubular pipes, slate ornaments, bar amulets, gorgets, and natural materials used to paint the dead.

The four main Middle Woodland complexes are the Couture in Southwestern Ontario, the Saugeen located just east, the Point Peninsula around the Grand River, and the Laurel in Northern Ontario. Only a few minor differences are evident between their material culture and that of the Early Woodland. Pottery became increasingly decorated, and burials more elaborate. At the end of this period, archaeologists theorize the presence of two cultures: the Princess Point on the shores of Lakes Ontario and Erie, and to the west the Sandbank complex. These cultures manufactured and decorated their pottery differently and likely began to grown corn and tobacco.

The Late Woodland Period is characterized by larger villages; the appearance of cannibalism; the smoking of tobacco; increased reliance on the cultivation of corn, beans, and squash; and the use of pictographs. Warfare was common, as reflected by the palisades erected around villages and by cut and burnt human bones, which also suggest cannibalism. Archaeologists identify several cultural areas during this period, including the Algonkian Western Basin people in the southern-most part of Ontario, the Ontario Iroquois in the central part, the St Lawrence Iroquoians along the eastern end of Lake Ontario and the St Lawrence River, the Odawa in the Bruce peninsula, and the Nipissing and Algonquin further north.

Before European contact, the central Iroquoian peoples of the Wendat, Tionontati (Petun), and Neutral lived in semi-permanent villages, moving every twelve to twenty years to seek out fresh agricultural lands, game, and woodlots. Archaeologists commonly find garbage middens, hearths, storage pits, fields of small hills mounded up to grow corn, beans, and squash, and remains left from the posts of their longhouses and palisades. Agriculture was the main subsistence strategy, although it was supplemented by hunting, fishing, and gathering. These early Iroquoians buried their dead singly, with the Neutrals using scaffold burials. Periodically, they held Feasts of the Dead, during which their ancestors were exhumed, decorated, feasted, and reburied in bundles in mass graves along with gifts, food, and status items. These ossuaries could hold up to one thousand people. After European contact, grave gifts became increasingly elaborate and included trade items such as copper kettles, beads, and iron axes.

During the Late Woodland Period in Northern Ontario, Algonkian-speaking peoples were more mobile, following seasonal subsistence patterns of hunting, fishing, and gathering. In Southwestern Ontario, however, the Western Basin peoples seemed to have traversed smaller distances due to the abundance of local resources and perhaps had permanent summer villages.[12] In some warmer areas, Algonkians grew small patches of corn but more likely traded with Iroquoians to obtain winter stores of grain. As a result, they most often lived in more temporary camps in smaller groups of people, which is reflected in their archaeological sites. An exception was the Odawa, who sometimes established year-round villages for their women, children, and elderly. Generally, Algonkian houses appear to have been shorter versions of Iroquoian longhouses. In Northern Ontario, Algonkians buried their dead in several ways. They were most often buried singly, with the graves of prominent people covered by a triangular wooden roof and a pole that marked the identity of the deceased. The Odawa also used scaffold burials and cremation. On the edges of historic Huronia, Algonkian peoples sometimes were buried with their Iroquoian neighbours in Feast of the Dead ossuaries or conducted their own version of this funerary ritual. All buried grave gifts, including European trade materials, with their deceased.[13]

## AMATEUR COLLECTORS AND DISCOVERIES

The public found many of the pre- and post-contact villages, middens, agricultural fields, and burials left by these peoples. Because new discoveries generally followed in the wake of surveying, settlement, land-clearing, and the construction of a transportation network in Upper Canada, they occurred at different times throughout the province. After the American Revolution, the United Empire Loyalists settled along the Niagara and St Lawrence rivers, and their allies the Six Nations were awarded territory along the Grand River and at Tyendinaga north of Belleville. By 1800, settlement lined the easternmost edge of the Niagara peninsula, the Thames and St Clair rivers, and the northern shores of Lake Ontario and the St Lawrence from Burlington Bay to the Ottawa River. In the 1830s, settlers began to penetrate the territory owned by the Canada Company and the forests south of Lake Huron and the Georgian Bay, which is today's Simcoe, Grey, and Bruce Counties, and by mid-century the southern periphery of the Canadian shield.

Amateur excavators and collectors are often anonymous in the historical record, but many were farmers, as suggested by Bruce Trigger.[14] His assertion is confirmed by early sources. For example, in 1888, it was noted in *Four Years on the Georgian Bay* that ploughing the land "continually" turned up relics in that area.[15] Andrew F. Hunter, a lawyer, historian, and associate of Boyle, wrote that between 1819 and 1909, farmers had exposed over 150 ossuaries in his local county of Simcoe alone.[16] Hunter also sometimes identified amateurs by name and occupation in his copiously detailed series of *Notes*, which documented site locations and artifacts found on those sites. Other individuals are recorded in the museum accession lists contained in the annual reports of the Canadian Institute and the *Archaeological Reports of Ontario* written by Boyle. Matching these names with the 1901 Canadian census corroborates that many were farmers. Innumerable tidbits in rural and city newspapers in Ontario also attest that farmers unearthed artifacts while ploughing, gardening, digging for fence posts, clearing forests, or draining ponds or during periods of low water levels.[17]

Boys, particularly those on farms, also sought out archaeological specimens. In the 1860s and 1870s, it was said that, around Mary Street, "the boys of Orillia used to make quite a business of digging up pots and tomahawks and skulls for the curious."[18] Eric Harvie, the founder of the Glenbow Museum in Calgary, collected Aboriginal items as a boy in Orillia. He had been inspired by stories about an amateur archaeologist who excavated local sites, including one on his family's farm, several decades earlier in the 1870s.[19] Similarly, in 1879, an Elora boy discovered a cache of wampum in nearby caves, and, according to local history, the find so resonated in the collective memory of the community that many children began to search for archaeological objects.[20] Fred Storry of Smithdale and brothers Aubrey and Wellington McPhee of Orillia donated artifacts to the Ontario Provincial Museum in the early 1900s. Both collections originated from their family farms.[21] Howard Kelcey of Vine, another donor of artifacts to the Provincial Museum, began his cabinet at the age of ten.[22] Children from the school of Southwold Township gathered some of the earliest accessions of their local society, the Elgin Historical and Scientific Institute of St Thomas.[23] George Laidlaw, William Wintemberg, and J. Hugh Hammond, the men Boyle would later gather around him, all began collecting as youths. Writing to Hunter, Hammond, a solicitor from Orillia, explained that

> In the early seventies, as a schoolboy, I spent the greater part of some Saturdays and holidays with my play-mates in excavating Indian graves ... Our school-master (Samuel McIlvaine) urged us to make all available collections of any objects such as beads, wampum and the like. He was making a collection, and utilized our muscles in furthering that object ... These excursions lasted over three years and were pursued by us every convenient Saturday during the summer seasons.[24]

Hunter's *Notes* and Boyle's records also include the locations where artifacts had been found. From this information, it appears that most of these farmers, their sons, and other amateurs collected only from their own land or on nearby property, rather than searching throughout their county or even farther afield, as the members of historical societies did. But beyond farm work, a variety of other activities accidentally revealed objects. As many provincial newspapers reported, road and canal workers, loggers, ditch, drain- and gravediggers, brickyard and quarry men, gas-pipe layers, and construction excavators all discovered archaeological sites during their daily work. Occasionally sawmill workers struck arrowheads buried in logs.[25]

Land surveyors also came across signs of past Aboriginal occupation. Patrick McNiff, a deputy surveyor for Upper Canada, found several sites. His 1790 map of the Thames River noted the ruins of a Neutral village on the south bank of the river near Jeanette's Creek and a knoll of human remains on the other side. McNiff also stumbled across

Exposed graves on the Dutton farm in Simcoe County, c. 1919

the remains of "huts" on the north side of Rondeau Bay during his work.[26] While surveying London Township in 1826, Mahlon Burwell found a field of cornhills.[27] James Dickson of Fenelon Falls donated an "excellent collection" from Victoria County to the Ontario Provincial Museum in the early 1890s, objects presumably gathered during his survey work.[28]

During the railway era, which began around mid-century, construction also uncovered archaeological sites. In 1840, for example, the Kingston local paper noted that employees of the Marine Railway Company struck burials on Mississauga Point. Near Windsor in the early 1850s, Great Western Railway workmen cut through a large grave containing copper kettles, pipes, silver pins, brooches, and other ornaments. Grand Trunk labourers dug into a cemetery near Hamilton.[29] Local Oxford County history told of two burial pots with skeletons inside found near the Wolverton station during railway construction.[30] Workers for the Lindsay, Beaverton and Port Hope, and the Canadian Pacific railways also found skeletons during their daily work in 1904–05.[31] The Canadian Institute perceived railroad cuttings to be so potentially productive of artifacts that it urged all such workers to observe and record any discoveries found during their daily labour.[32] Colonel Charles Coote Grant, the curator of the Hamilton Association for the

Advancement of Literature, Science and Art, also recognized this fact. Although railway employees feared an accident, for Grant was absent-minded and had poor vision, he frequently walked along railway tracks seeking geological and archaeological specimens turned up by the laying of the lines.[33]

Other discoveries were more singular. In 1793, for example, Major Edward Baker Littlehales, accompanying Upper Canada's Lieutenant-Governor John Graves Simcoe to Detroit, found a stretch of scattered bones on the banks of the Thames River, the same as noted by McNiff three years earlier.[34] In 1889, a US camping club unearthed a grave when digging a hole for their flagpole near Port Colborne, a find that drew many amateurs from both sides of the border and also David Boyle, who spent three days collecting at the site.[35] The vagaries of nature also played a part in revealing archaeological sites. Wave erosion on larger bodies of water uncovered archaeological sites, as did lower water levels.[36] At Lake Massanoga (also called Mississagan) in Central Ontario, it was said that human bones washed up after storms.[37] Storms also pulled up trees and the craters left by displaced roots often contained human remains and other objects.[38] Even the rooting and burrowing of animals such as pigs and woodchucks threw up objects.[39]

Whether through farming or other means, once an archaeological site had been accidentally discovered, a variety of amateur collectors frequently turned out to excavate. Author Stephen Leacock satirically immortalized a relic-hunting physician in his 1912 *Sunshine Sketches of a Little Town*. Knowledgeable about Canadian history, the character Dr Gallagher possessed a collection of arrowheads dug from his garden, a tomahawk, and a skull obtained from a railway embankment.[40] While Leacock based his *Sketches* upon his personal experiences in Orillia, Gallagher can also be considered an archetypal character, since numerous doctors in Ontario collected Aboriginal objects. David Boyle certainly recognized the many who collected.[41] In 1856, Dr Thomas Reynolds of Brockville explored a grave found during the excavation of the St Lawrence Canal at the Les Galops Rapids, and although the bones crumbled on contact with the air he kept the copper tools buried with the skeletons.[42] While quartered at the military barracks in Penetanguishene, Dr Edward W. Bawtree excavated several Wendat ossuaries in the 1840s and sent objects to the Fort Pitt Museum and the Museum of the Army Medical Department in England.[43] Among others, J.O. McGregor of Waterdown, Clarence Campbell of London, Thomas G. Johnston of Sarnia, William L.T. Addison of Byng Inlet, Charles and James Tweedale of St Thomas, a Dr Noble of Maple, James

N. Harvie of Orillia, F.B. McCormick of Pelee Island, James E. Brown of Arkona, and George A. MacCallum of Dunnville all took part in excavations or possessed Aboriginal artifact collections.[44] Medical students, who often procured bodies for anatomical dissection, dug up two mass graves in Oro Township in the late nineteenth century, and, in the 1870s, Toronto students found skeletons they obtained from an ossuary in Kent County to be "exceedingly useful" in their studies.[45] This may have been a Neutral "battleground" near Rondeau also recorded as the source of bones for anatomical study by Edwin Jones, a member of the Chatham-Kent Historical Society. Jones had been told by Chatham doctor George McKeough that in his school days he had studied a skull found nearby.[46] McKeough himself recorded that a Dr McCully of Cedar Springs took many skeletons from a Rondeau site for himself and his fellow students in the mid-nineteenth century.[47] Dr Rowland Orr was perhaps the best-known physician and collector in Ontario; after David Boyle's death in 1911, Orr succeeded him as the archaeology curator at the Ontario Provincial Museum and donated his large collection of objects to this institution.

Tourists considered excavating an archaeological site a way to obtain memories and mementoes. The most famous visitor to an Ontario site must have been François d'Orléans, the third son of King Louis Philippe of France, who travelled to the famed Kinghorn grave in Simcoe County in 1862, accompanied by the Lord Edward Cholmley Dering of Kent and his new wife, who were on their honeymoon tour.[48] But more ordinary vacationers also expressed fascination with archaeological sites. As early as 1817, John Savery Brock, the brother of the War of 1812 hero Sir Isaac Brock, inspected the Southwold earthworks, now a national historic site, during his stay with the land agent Colonel Thomas Talbot.[49] Excursion steamers regularly stopped at the serpent mound near Peterborough.[50] The times when locals dug – Sundays and holidays such as the Queen's birthday and Christmas Day – also reflected the relationship of these activities to leisure.

## LOCAL KNOWLEDGE AND HISTORY

Andrew Hunter considered archaeological sites, especially burials, to be "almost always well-known, and the topics of general conversation" among local citizens.[51] Indeed, beyond accidental discoveries, the general public had opportunities to excavate sites because many locations were preserved in community memory. The Kinghorn grave, for example, was touted as "one of the seven wonders at the time" to which people "flocked."[52] Another site called "'Pottery Hill'" was "well-known to every person in the locality."[53] As the location of historic Huronia, the last home of the Wendat and Tionontati before their dispersal by the Haudenosaunee (Iroquois), Simcoe County abounded with archaeological sites. In fact, in 1894, the Toronto *Empire* remarked that "relic hunting has become quite a popular fad in recent years up in that picturesque and historic country around lake Huron and the Georgian bay."[54]

Another place, the Rock Glen near Arkona, was reputed for several decades as a sure spot to find fossils and Aboriginal artifacts.[55] Boyle reported that the Shaw-Wood (now Lawson) site near London had also "long been known to relic-hunters."[56] Locals also knew that many artifacts from an old Neutral village and burial site could be found on the banks of Lake Medad and more generally throughout Wentworth and Halton Counties, which were "prolific of Indian relics."[57] In the Niagara region, "every bank examined" along the Welland River, it was said, gave "proof of occupation" by Aboriginal peoples, and graves could be found all around the Bay of Quinte.[58] An 1885 local history of Toronto and the County of York stated that evidence of a large Aboriginal population was "frequently discovered," and in particular a two-acre village site in Whitchurch Township had been known to residents since the time of the early pioneers.[59]

In addition to community memory, various types of publications spread word of site locations. The establishment of newspapers followed settlement patterns, and so, by the early 1800s, towns in the Niagara peninsula had newspapers that advertised artifact finds. After the establishment of the Canadian Institute at mid-century, the Toronto *Globe* and other newspapers began to cover its activities and archaeological discoveries across the province. Beginning in 1886, David Boyle began to produce more extensive annual reports for the Canadian Institute and later for the Ontario Provincial Museum, and newspapers reprinted excerpts that featured site locations.

The development of a homegrown history over the nineteenth century also led to wider-spread knowledge of the Aboriginal past. Late nineteenth-century local histories and illustrated atlases of the Counties of York, Simcoe, Victoria, Peterborough, Elgin, Kent, Middlesex, Brant, Dundas, and Wentworth, among other areas, recorded the presence, location, and looting of archaeological sites and often described the artifacts found.[60] George Copway, or Kah-ge-ga-gah-bowh, the Ojibwa missionary and lecturer, noted in 1850 the remains of a fort built by the Haudenosaunee in their battles against the Anishinabeg near Pigeon

Earthworks in Whitchurch Township, c. 1918

Lake, a Wendat grave, and various places where lost weapons of warfare could be commonly found.[61] His half-brother Peter Jones, also a missionary, recorded the graves from these conflicts in his 1861 *History of the Ojebway Indians*, describing their location at Skull Island on Lake Huron, near the former Government House at the south end of Burlington Bay and at the north end near the home of Joseph Brant, a leader of the Six Nations. Jones also included illustrations of archaeological material.[62] One of the latter graves was also noted by the biographer of the Methodist minister William Case in 1867.[63]

First appearing that same year and reprinted several times, Francis Parkman's popular *The Jesuits in North America in the Seventeenth Century* generally noted that settlers could find Neutral and Wendat ossuaries throughout Ontario.[64] More specific references could be found in the seventy-three volumes of the *Jesuit Relations and Allied Documents*, which were published between 1896 and 1901. These feature frequent annotations and maps of Wendat, Tionontati, and Neutral archaeological sites and the remains of Jesuit missions (sometimes with specific lot and concession information), the names of those who investigated these sites, numbers of artifacts gathered and donated to the Provincial Museum, and references to related publications. Much of this commentary was written by Andrew Hunter or excerpted from his *Notes*.[65]

Memoirs by Upper Canadian residents Samuel Thompson, Thomas Conant, John Carruthers, and Thomas Need all recorded archaeological discoveries, indicating these events as significant or at least interesting to their readers.[66] In his *Twenty Seven Years in Canada West* (1853), Samuel Strickland, the brother of the author Susanna Moodie, recorded finding a grave during a logging bee at his sister's house. Only a broken stone pipe and two arrowheads accompanied the skeleton, though Strickland stated that he had heard others discussing similar burials that contained tomahawks, metal ornaments, and copper "sugar-kettles."[67] William Brown, a "Leeds Clothier" who temporarily lived in Toronto in the 1840s, also described a burial site near a sawmill he had rented on the Red River. During his stay, he made "many curious discoveries," which he supposed were "quite familiar to older settlers." One day, several of his employees found a spot where pigs had rooted up the ground, uncovering broken pottery, guns and pipes. Brown himself went to investigate the site and estimated that forty acres of a steep river bank were covered with burials only two feet below the surface.[68]

Travellers began to tour parts of Upper Canada as early as the 1790s, and shortly afterward travel guides began to promote archaeological sites as interesting places to visit. *The Northern Traveller*, an 1826 guidebook for eastern North America, included a stop at an ancient tumuli about four miles from Queenston Heights and near Stamford Park, the summer house of Sir Peregrine Maitland, the lieutenant-governor of Upper Canada. This burial had been discovered when a tree had blown down, and underneath had been found skeletons, beads, pipes, brass or copper utensils, and conch shells from the "Tropics." The guide further suggested that visitors would see that the ground had been "defended with a palisade."[69] George Munro Grant's *Picturesque Canada* (1882) included an old village and burial ground outside of Streetsville and a mound at the edge of Hamilton.[70] A promotional booklet for the Fenelon Falls area suggested, under points of interest, a stop on Ghost or Ball Island on Balsam Lake where it was rumoured that missionaries had buried treasure.[71] Describing the Hotel Brant near Burlington, the *Canadian Summer Resort Guide* of 1900 observed that the remains of Indian mounds and burials could be seen on the hotel property, likely the same described by Peter Jones in his autobiographical writings.[72]

34

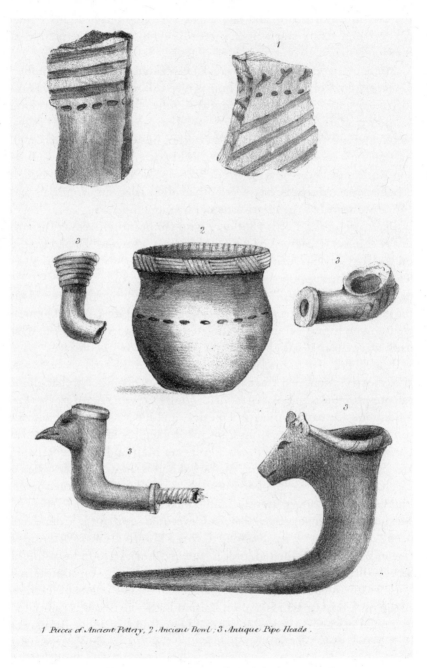

*1 Pieces of Ancient Pottery, 2 Ancient Bowl, 3 Antique Pipe Heads.*

Sketch of "Domestic Implements," artifacts from the Peter Jones collection, c. 1861

Personal travelogues mentioned visits to sites, particularly burials. British traveller Henry Cook Todd noted that "ancient entrenchments" and bones of "enormous" size had been found in Vaughan Township in the 1830s.[73] In 1838, Anna Jameson published the first edition of her *Winter Studies and Summer Rambles*, a book reprinted numerous times. Throughout the three volumes that documented her travels across the province, she recorded and sometimes visited the location of several gravesites of the Wendat, the Haudenosaunee, and the Anishinabeg.[74] In his *Wanderings of an Artist* (1859), Paul Kane also described burial mounds and a number of bones protruding through the earth near an Ojibwa village. Even the promotional material of the 1901 railway tour for the Duke and Duchess of Cornwall and York mentioned an old Onodowahgah (Seneca) village just outside Toronto.[75]

In the late nineteenth century, Canadians began to turn to the forests and lakes north and west of Toronto for vacationing. Relaxation, camping, and other outdoor activities in the clean and invigorating air of these areas were thought to counteract the increasingly hectic and stressful life of cities.[76] Magazines or guides produced for fishermen and hunters included archaeological sites. For example, the *Rod and Gun* noted burial grounds and pictographs passed by when hunting or fishing. Another guide, written by a staff member of the *Field* in 1912, explained that Wendat graves from the Feast of the Dead ceremony could still be found in historic Huronia. The 1888 *Four Years on the Georgian Bay* called this area a "Mecca" for ardent sportsmen and amateur archaeologists. It recommended visiting several sites of the Wendat.[77]

An examination of Beverly Township suggests how the existence and location of archaeological sites could be continuously documented over time and thus easily found by the public. Shortly after the discovery of one ossuary, John McIntosh noted this "golgotha" of supposedly one thousand skeletons buried with guns and cooking vessels in his 1836 *Discovery of America by Christopher Columbus and the Origins of the North American Indians*.[78] This may have been the Call Farm site, also visited by the Reverend C. Dade, who wrote about his 1836 excavation seventeen years later in the *Canadian Journal*.[79] In the 1840s, American Indian agent and ethnologist Henry Schoolcraft visited what would be later called the Dwyer site with a local minister. He described its location and the artifacts he found in several of his publications. According to Schoolcraft, its discovery also received much attention by the local press. Daniel Wilson also discussed this site in two articles published by the *Canadian Journal* in the 1850s.[80] Quebec Justice of the Peace Stanley Clark Bagg noted a Beverly site in his 1864 article about archaeology.

Bagg's article, probably read to the Numismatic and Antiquarian Society of Montreal, was also published by the *Montreal Daily Transcript*. Egerton Ryerson, the superintendent of Education in Canada West, appears to have reprinted Bagg's article in his own *Journal of Education for Upper Canada*, a periodical distributed to all the teachers in the province.[81] In 1885, David Boyle investigated the adjacent Dwyer and Rae farms, and his exploits were publicized by the Toronto newspapers.[82] The Reverend Dean Harris mentioned one otherwise unidentified Beverly Township site in his 1895 publication about the history of the Catholic Church in Niagara, and numerous ossuaries and village sites, including their exact lot and concession numbers, were recorded by Joseph Smith in his 1897 *Historical Sketch of the County of Wentworth*.[83]

Beyond excavating artifacts and making private collections themselves, the Ontario public had other opportunities to be exposed to archaeological objects. Children, and potentially their parents, learned about archaeology through school museums. Hunter and Boyle recorded the visits of numerous teachers to archaeological sites, and others requested that Boyle send them his archaeological reports, although it is unclear whether these individuals kept collections at their schools. But there were several known school museums in Ontario. J. Hugh Hammond noted the inspiration of his childhood teacher Samuel McIlvaine, who made just such a collection, and David Boyle's interest in archaeology had begun when he created a museum for his own students at an Elora school. Dr James B. Tweedale donated part of his collection to the Alma Ladies College near St Thomas to encourage the study of ethnology.[84] The Toronto *Mail* recorded a Mr Shaw near Midland who also had a school museum.[85] At the Picton high school, an E. Ackerman collected Aboriginal items and fossils and tried to interest his students in these.[86] The Iroquois high school also possessed a museum and in 1900 Principal J.A. Jackson asked Boyle to speak to the students to inspire them to collect and thus expand the museum.[87]

The public encountered displays of archaeological specimens within an eclectic variety of other places, including doctors' and newspaper offices, agricultural fairs, and community buildings. Andrew Hunter noted that a Dr Murphy of Phelpston and a Dr Pass exhibited skulls in their surgeries.[88] During his stay with a Dr Lefferty of Lundy's Lane, William Lyon Mackenzie noted his personal cabinet, in which Lefferty displayed a mix of pottery, Aboriginal and non-Aboriginal human remains, taxidermic specimens, a mammoth tooth, pharmaceuticals, and guns, powder horns, and other military items.[89] Dr Solon Woolverton of London exhibited his collection in his dentistry office.[90] The Collingwood YMCA established a curio cabinet when their building excavators uncovered skeletons.[91] Two collectors in Burford exhibited several cases of objects at a gathering to raise money for the Trinity Rectory in the early 1900s.[92] Newspaper staff often displayed items found locally in conjunction with printing reports of discoveries. Louis Kribbs of the Toronto *Empire*, for example, hung a human skull over his doorway. Robinson's Drug Store in Orillia displayed and sold artifacts, as did Thomas Wilson's general store in Kingston, and Amos and Wilfrid Jury exhibited their collection in the window of Clark's Cigar Store in London.[93] R.C. Burt and Edwin Jones, two collectors from Kent County, often displayed their finds in the window of Burt's drugstore. For one exhibit, Burt placed a skull with a hole in one side as the centrepiece and surrounded it with a stone club, a stone tomahawk, and rows of points. Arranged in a horseshoe shape, these artifacts were flanked by "handsome apothecary jars, bottles of Eau de Cologne, Yardley's Lavender, Essence of White Violets, Ayer's Cherry Pectoral, Beef, Iron and Wine, Lydia Pinkham's Female Tonic." When Jones asked "if such grim relics among the aids to health and beauty were not incongruous," Burt replied that "he thought them appropriate."[94] Thus the public had many opportunities to come into close contact with archaeological specimens, whether through excavations or other methods, and to learn the locations of archaeological sites through experience, local knowledge, and a variety of accessible publications.

## DOCUMENTATION OF SITE LOCATIONS

Amateur local knowledge meant that they were often crucial to the documentation of site locations. They guided members of scientific and historical societies to places found on their own property and to others known to them by local gossip and memory. At a time when the Dominion and provincial governments only reluctantly funded any type of research, the documentation of amateurs equalled a moderate substitute for county archaeological surveys, a major objective of David Boyle and other professionals. A dedicated individual such as Andrew Hunter could combine local knowledge, artifactual evidence, historical works, and his own investigative research into a fairly reliable survey. Together with Hunter's field books, his series of *Notes* and other writings published between 1889 and 1911, plotted and mapped more than six hundred sites in several counties.[95] George Laidlaw recorded another fifty-six sites in Victoria County through his own investigations and oral evidence from others.[96]

While most historical and scientific societies were interested in the location of archaeological sites, Ontario residents most frequently aided the Canadian Institute and later the Ontario Provincial Museum. As early as 1852, the institute called upon the public to assist in documenting site locations and establishing a museum. Inspired by the discovery of graves on the Great Western Railway line near Windsor and by the Smithsonian Institution publication of Ephraim George Squier's 1849 *Aboriginal Monuments of the State of New York*, which catalogued, surveyed, and described sites partly based on public assistance, Sandford Fleming composed a circular for mass distribution and publication in the Canadian Institute's periodical the *Canadian Journal* in September 1852. Targeting engineers and surveyors, the circular solicited specific information about the location of archaeological sites, including any "Intrenchment or Mound." It also asked for general descriptions or notification about areas in which the discovery of objects such as axes, arrowheads, pottery, or weapons suggested Aboriginal occupation.[97]

Without a dedicated curator, the Canadian Institute was initially unable to follow up on much of the information that resulted from the distribution of its circular. Daniel Wilson, the main institute member interested in archaeology, only made a few visits to archaeological sites.[98] This would change with Boyle's appointment as curator in 1884. The next year, Boyle sent one thousand copies of the circular to men "of all classes" and republished it in the institute's annual report for 1886.[99] His *Notes on Primitive Man*, targeted to teachers, also invited readers to inform him of any discoveries.[100] The requests Boyle received to visit sites, and the number of these discussed in his annual reports attest to the level of public assistance he received throughout his years as curator of the collections at the Canadian Institute and the Provincial Museum.

As recorded by the report of his first fieldwork season of 1886-87, Boyle visited numerous sites upon personal invitation and was assisted by individuals who shared local knowledge.[101] In April, he visited sites in York Township to collect artifacts, including one owned by a teacher. In early May 1886 he visited Tidd's Island in the St Lawrence River to explore a series of mounds.[102] The private landowners granted permission for Boyle to dig, provided him with accounts of their own previous discoveries, and donated artifacts for the Canadian Institute museum. Later that month, he visited a palisaded fort in Beverly in response to an invitation from Wallace McDonald, the township clerk. McDonald remembered a series of decayed posts found on a nearby farm when the land had been cleared. In preparation for Boyle's visit, McDonald planted flags to show the boundaries of the fort, and, upon digging, Boyle found remains of pine stakes. Two weeks later, Boyle visited the Township of Humberstone in the Niagara peninsula after being informed by a local teacher of a recently discovered ossuary in the area. Cyrenius Bearsse, whom Boyle described as an "enthusiastic amateur," showed him the spot and donated some articles he had found himself.[103] Next, Boyle explored parts of the Baby Estate near Lambton Mills, assisted by Raymond Baby, who indicated where remains had been found during ploughing. The Baby family hence promised to notify the Canadian Institute of any other objects found in the future, a promise they apparently kept in 1896 and 1899, years in which they sold or donated artifacts to the Provincial Museum.[104] Touring the Township of Nottawasaga in late June, Boyle recorded that many individuals donated items to the institute and provided him with information about previous finds. In October, Boyle returned to Beverly Township (probably to the Dwyer and Rae farms), and while wet weather prevented excavation he received more donations from locals. He ended his fieldwork season with trips to the London area to visit several large private collections, during which he was assisted by Public School Inspector Joseph Carson. Summarizing his fieldwork, Boyle concluded that, while he had accomplished less than he planned, "still a good beginning has been made and a great deal of valuable information has been gleaned for future use."[105] In fact, through his explorations, donations and purchases, almost eight hundred objects had been added to the institute's museum. His subsequent seasons of fieldwork continued to be as profitable partly due to amateur efforts and their invitations to visit local sites.

## EXCAVATION STANDARDS

While the public was invaluable in the documentation of site locations, only a few amateurs appear to have protected such sites from common destruction. With little archaeological legislation, only private property owners could control what happened to sites located on their own land. A few did attempt to prevent excavation. In Collingwood, for example, townspeople tried to stop excavations since they were "so wanton," while several individual landowners across the province refused to allow amateurs to excavate, although the reasons are unknown.[106] Early surveyor Mahlon Burwell specified in his deed of the Southwold earthworks in Elgin County that the site was to remain undisturbed. Its late nineteenth-century owner Chester Henderson did not plough or plant crops on this part of his property in order to protect the site.[107]

More frequently, the public destroyed much of the information
to be gathered from archaeological sites. When lumbermen damned
Massonaga Lake, for example, the rising water covered the pictographs
drawn on the rocky banks.[108] Bones in graves were broken by shovels
or crumbled to dust when exposed to the air.[109] Farmers filled ossuaries
with stones, logs, or other refuse, limiting future professional investigations.[110] One farmer told Boyle he wished to have a mound levelled,
perhaps because it was too difficult to plough.[111]

Many digs had little documentation. As T.W. Edwin Sowter, a member of the Ottawa Field-Naturalists' Club, wrote, if an archaeologist
hoped to excavate properly, the discovery of a new site should be kept
secret from relic hunters.[112] Hunter portrayed the unearthing of an
ossuary in 1882 near Phelpston as frantic. Several boys, who had been
employed to cut logs, had decided to dig into an "unnatural depres-
sion" rumoured to be the work of Aboriginal peoples. Their excavation
turned up human bones. The news of this discovery "spread like wild-
fire within a few days," and the next Sunday "the place swarmed with
men and boys … One or two men … dug furiously until they became
tired, when they were relieved by fresh diggers. They kept this up for
the greater part of the day." Throughout that summer, visitors to the
area continued to excavate this grave. Reflecting upon its archaeological importance, Hunter lamented that many skulls had been taken as
curiosities, others decorated tree stumps in the hopes of frightening visitors, and many bones were simply left strewn upon the ground, some
of which were later crushed by passing vehicles. When Hunter visited
the spot in 1886, this "sad havoc" had left little, he said.[113] Boyle called
another excavation of an ossuary in 1901 by seventy people at once a
"wild resurrection mania." The result was "deplorable" according to
Boyle; an opportunity to study an undisturbed ossuary in a part of the
province where such burials were rare was lost, and most items had
been taken away.[114] Clearly, these scrambles meant that little detail about
the sites themselves was recorded.

Some archaeological discoveries stimulated rumours of treasure, further creating a mania for digging and destruction. William Wintemberg
told of the discovery of two burial pots uncovered during railway construction. The Italian labourers, cast here as uneducated, "immediately
began breaking the pots to pieces crying, 'Gold! Gold!' much to the
chagrin of the foreman in charge."[115] The caves of the Elora Gorge were
thought to hide treasure.[116] The Rice Lake and Williamsburg mounds
supposedly contained riches, causing fortune-seekers to surreptitiously
excavate the latter at night in search of wealth.[117] Andrew Hunter

repeated several local stories about buried treasure. In recording one site location, he noted that two men actually drowned one stormy spring looking for treasure in a small boat. In Sturgeon Bay, the postmistress told him that she had heard of buried treasure in the area.[118] All the Jesuit towns were associated with legends of buried treasure as well. Hunter speculated that a story told by the artist George Catlin was the basis of these hopes of finding treasure. He recounted that an Aboriginal individual named Onogongway had dug up a "'kettle of gold'" – a mistaken allusion to the brass of which the container was made rather than its contents.[119] A late nineteenth-century tourist handbook bolstered dreams of riches by repeating an Aboriginal story about gold; the Great Manitou had forbidden Aboriginal peoples to seek it past a certain point on Lake Huron, or else they would be punished.[120] Occasional finds, such as the body of a trader buried with nineteenth-century coins at Cameron's Point, may have also stirred up such stories.[121] According to Hunter, such treasure rumours caused some residents to be tight-lipped when asked for information about archaeological sites.[122]

Professional archaeologists often expressed their frustration with the lack of excavation documentation and information they received upon the donation of artifacts. Andrew Hunter believed in the need for documentation as it was "only in this way that relic-hunting [was] of any value as an aid to history."[123] He hoped his 1899 article on Tiny Township, which precisely documented the archaeological sites and artifacts of this area and published by the Department of Education as part of Boyle's annual report, would stimulate the public to closely observe archaeological remains.[124] In a following report about Tay Township, however, Hunter lamented that his descriptions of many archaeological sites possessed "[m]uch sameness" because farmers and others had only observed "only the most general features" rather than "noted facts with more minuteness."[125]

Others attempted to remedy the situation more directly. In 1855, Daniel Wilson provided advice in his *Canadian Journal* article, "Hints for the Formation of a Canadian Collection of Ancient Crania." He noted that many graves would continue to be exposed by farmers and rail workers and expressed little hope that the "rude railway navy, or the first agricultural explorers" would be interested in scientific objects. And, he assumed, most discoveries would occur by chance, and therefore the prevention of the destruction of objects would be more accidental than purposeful. Accordingly, he suggested that, throughout the province, members of the Canadian Institute should assist its efforts, although he did not indicate whether he meant direct collecting or the supervision of communal excavations. Thus, Wilson continued, it would be expedient to give a few tips for the excavation, documentation, and preservation of skeletal material. As soon as a skull or skeleton had been revealed, Wilson advised, the excavator should turn from using a shovel or pick axe to a smaller tool such as a garden trowel. While removing the soil around the human remains, the excavator should carefully watch for other buried objects. Bones should only be removed after all the earth had been cleared away, particularly if they were fragile. Any bones made soft by moisture should be laid in the sun to dry, then wrapped in newspaper and placed in a box with hay for protection during their transport.[126]

The Canadian Institute's 1852 circular also appealed to amateur archaeologists to increase scientific standards and offered guidance in excavations. Several points instructed amateurs on how to properly document a site. The area of the archaeological find should be measured and ideally presented as a plan with sections. The ground was to be inspected for evidence of the remains of posts or palisades. It suggested that dendrochronology was the proper way to date a site; the annual rings in tree stumps should be counted and the age of standing trees estimated to do the calculations. Finally, the circular asked for any local Aboriginal traditions attached to the site that might explain its significance.[127]

These publications also tried to encourage the complete collection and documentation of objects found during excavations. For example, the circular asked for sketches of any objects or pictographs found. As Daniel Wilson wrote, the goal was not "the mere gratification of an aimless curiosity, or the accumulation of rarities … but the preservation of objects calculated to furnish valuable scientific or historical truths."[128] He asked that all pieces of broken skulls or bones be saved because they could be pieced back together. Further, all parts of bones or objects from separate individuals or separate graves should be stored independently to prevent confusion. He also addressed the public's fascination for collecting only the skulls of the dead, and suggested that the lower jaw, with its teeth intact, also be collected. Even loose teeth could give information about diet and race. The nose bones, he indicated, were extremely fragile but also a good indicator of race, as were hand bones. In fact, according to archaeological practice, Wilson said, the whole skeleton contained evidence of race and life history, although it was rare that whole skeletons could be kept. Wilson added that the sex, and the position and cardinal direction of the body, and the placement of objects should be recorded, each specimen labelled and the boxes marked with their locality. Afterward, such information should be recorded on the object itself. Finally, no detail could be trusted to one's memory, and Wilson advocated that notes should be made at the time of excavation.[129]

Such detailed instructions reveal that the activities of most amateurs were unreliable. In 1889, three years after he republished the circular, Boyle reported that, although there was increased archaeological activity, amateur collecting was "good so far as it goes, but does not accomplish what is required from the Institute's standpoint." He stated that "at least moderately accurate surveys of all aboriginal locations, with drawings of fortified works, and exact data relating to materials, patterns, depths, soils, ash-heaps, position of bodies, with particulars relating to skulls, modes of burial, presence or absence of European influences, and many other details requiring experience, time and labor" were badly needed.[130]

## MUSEUM PRESERVATION

To promote the preservation and study of specimens, the Canadian Institute's 1852 circular also called upon the public to donate specimens of tools and crania for its museum, and in his articles Wilson invited railwaymen and farmers to donate skeletal remains to the institute. The *Canadian Journal* noted that the circular had resulted in artifact donations, but the subsequent annual reports feature few of these.[131] Boyle later wrote that, despite the circular, "there is no reason to suppose that the results were very encouraging. The nucleus of an archaeological collection was formed, but as no case-room was provided (the specimens being simply placed on open shelves) the relics in possession of the Institute in 1886 were neither numerous nor valuable."[132] Many objects, in fact, were lost over time.[133] The bulk of donations began to arrive after Boyle became the curator of the Canadian Institute and subsequently of the Ontario Provincial Museum. In fact, less than one year after Boyle reissued the circular, he reported more than one thousand donations of archaeological artifacts.[134] He also aimed his annual report and exhibits at the 1886 and 1887 Toronto Exhibition to rouse farmers and others to turn over their specimens for preservation.[135] The "safe keeping" of artifacts at the provincial museum, Boyle believed, would preserve "many such scientifically valuable objects as have, too often, hitherto been lightly esteemed, or neglected and lost."[136] The Toronto newspapers summarized the circular and echoed his sentiments, calling upon all farmers, commercial travellers, and teachers to support the goals of the institute.[137]

To further cultivate donors, the Canadian Institute adopted a bylaw in June 1886 to announce donations at every meeting and to record the names of the donors. Boyle listed all new accessions and donors in every annual report after this date.[138] This appears to have been a successful tactic. In 1904, J. Hugh Hammond remarked that those who had channelled artifacts through him were "all dead anxious to get their names in the paper thus showing their notoriety, and the fact of owning a farm is thus passed down to posterity in the Report." A year later he requested copies of the annual report for several donors, commenting that farmers enjoyed seeing their names in print.[139]

George Laidlaw, another of Boyle's protegés, promoted the donation of artifacts from Victoria County, his local area. In 1896, Laidlaw placed an ad in various Ontario newspapers, which explained that he collected for the Canadian Institute. Shipping charges would be paid and donors would be acknowledged in museum exhibit labels and in Boyle's annual reports as well.[140] Articles about Laidlaw's research, accumulated artifacts, and personal donations, sometimes excerpted from Boyle's annual reports, were featured in the Orillia *Packet*; the Lindsay *Watchman*, *Post*, and *Warder*; the Beaverton *Express*; the Woodville *Advocate*; the Toronto *World*, *Mail and Empire*, and *Evening Telegram*; and other newspapers.[141] Laidlaw hoped these articles would stimulate other individuals to explore the area for relics, and indeed over the years he passed on numerous artifacts to Boyle for preservation.

Beyond distributing the Canadian Institute circular and curating exhibits for the Toronto Exhibition, Boyle targeted people working in specific occupations to promote the donation of archaeological specimens, and thus their preservation. He invited provincial land surveyors to tour the museum during the institute's 1887–88 session, hoping to encourage them to donate artifacts found in the line of their work. Boyle especially acknowledged James Dickson of Fenelon Falls, who bestowed objects to the museum. After the meeting, other surveyors "expressed their intention to aid the collection as soon as opportunity offered."[142]

Boyle also believed that teachers could promote his interests. It seems likely that Boyle sent some of the one thousand copies of the reissued circular to teachers and education officials across the province. In his first fieldwork report in 1886, Boyle thanked three teachers, the headmaster of the Ganonoque high school, and the public school inspectors for West Middlesex and Wentworth County for donations and assistance.[143] A year later he wrote that he was "still convinced that from the five thousand teachers of rural schools in this Province, there is much valuable information to be gleaned. The question is how to reach them. Shall it be by a circular, or by a card in the educational journals?" As a result, in 1895 he produced his *Notes on Primitive Man in Ontario*, which discussed common archaeological sites and artifacts for this audience. In its preface, Boyle explained that teachers and other individuals, although interested in the Aboriginal peoples of Canada, did not have the "time or opportunity" to study the latest research. Thus Boyle's publication summarized the information in "a handy and condensed form," as these individuals wished.[144] Over the years, numerous individuals from the school system led him to archaeological sites and donated the artifacts. Perhaps cued by Boyle's efforts, Andrew Hunter also looked to teachers for aid in establishing an archaeological collection in Barrie.[145] Similarly, James Coyne, president of the Elgin Historical and Scientific Institute, called upon the educators of Elgin County to help the society collect and preserve Aboriginal relics for the "benefit of future generations."[146]

Interested individuals aided Boyle's collecting in other ways. Dr Thomas W. Beeman introduced Boyle to Mrs Peter McLaren of Perth, wife of a successful lumberman and senator. Beginning in 1891, she lent her steam "yacht" *Geraldine* and its crew to Boyle and Beeman to explore sites on Lake Rideau. McLaren, Beeman observed, took "an active interest in the work," and the boat enabled archaeological explorations.[147] When he conducted fieldwork on the Dwyer farm in Beverly Township, Boyle discovered a large stone that bore marks from rock polishing and sharpening. James Dwyer took the stone to the nearest train station, in order for it to be shipped to the museum in Toronto; in Boyle's annual report, Boyle praised Dwyer's philanthropic spirit, hoping that others would emulate him.[148] To Boyle, it was the public duty of all to aid in such collecting enterprises.[149]

Indeed, many citizens agreed that to educate the public about the province's past, it was the duty of museums to collect, preserve, and exhibit material culture. While most nineteenth-century historical and scientific societies received archaeological material, the public donated the bulk of Southern Ontario artifacts to the Canadian Institute of Toronto. From Boyle's appointment as curator of the institute to his death in 1911, his efforts, and those of Hunter, Laidlaw, Hammond, and Beeman, resulted in the accession of almost thirty thousand artifacts.

But others believed archaeological sites and the artifacts found within them to be private property, not material for public education, and refused to allow excavations or to donate artifacts. The Midland Parks Association in 1889, for example, threatened prosecution of trespassers seeking out graves on their land, although it later displayed human remains in its agricultural building; clearly, the Midland Parks Association did not protest on the grounds of disturbing graves.[150] James Koch, owner of the Humboldt Summer Resort Club, refused to allow David Boyle to investigate a mound, as he wished to excavate it himself.[151] Two legal cases are also illustrative. In 1901, the Hamilton law firm of Carscallen and Cahiel contacted Boyle on behalf of a client, demanding the return of all relics removed from his property. According to the lawyers, these specimens unequivocally belonged to their client and were valuable as they could "command a good price." They also stipulated compensation for "wrongful trespass upon and injury" to his land.[152]

The outcome of this case is unknown, but the following year Boyle became embroiled in another lawsuit, which he won. Alerted to its existence by two teachers, in 1902 Boyle visited the Yellow Point mound near St Catharines. The landowner, a Mr Bradt, accused Boyle of trespassing on private property and of damaging his land. Further, Bradt calculated that the mound – unexplored, that is – increased the sale value of his property by $2,000. Boyle claimed he thought he had received Bradt's permission to excavate, but it was the second argument made by the archaeologist that is most significant. Boyle, and ultimately Judge John A. Boyd, argued that human remains and artifacts buried in the soil had no intrinsic monetary worth. Instead, such objects possessed educational importance. It was not until objects were collected, classified, and arranged within a museum that they acquired value. Only then the public would be able to study the customs of the Aboriginal peoples, compare them to that of the ancient Celts, and understand the origin of the human race, Boyle argued. Further, Boyle contended that museums were the proper place for artifacts; for every one person who would look at the mound, one thousand would visit the museum containing the objects from that mound. After a mere five minutes of deliberation, the judge decided in favour of Boyle's case.[153]

Interestingly, Boyle distinguished between those who had only a few specimens and willingly donated them for public education and amateur collectors who were "very loath to part with their 'treasures.'"[154] Boyle must have hoped that many Ontario residents would echo the sentiments of collectors such as Wodehouse farmer Frederick Birch, who donated his collection to the Provincial Museum because his family dismissed it as "so much trash" and thus he feared it would be discarded after his death. Birch also believed himself to be personally saving parts of the archaeological record by purchasing objects from others' "careless hands."[155] Clearly, some collectors were attached to their specimens. One individual referred to his artifacts as "old friends."[156] Laidlaw wrote sarcastically to Hunter about an old "codger who would not let his relics out of his sight, unless he had a string tied on them."[157] The Elgin Historical and Scientific Institute may have had this type of reluctance in mind when they advertised for donations in 1895. For those not willing to give up ownership of their collections, the Elgin Institute suggested it would take objects on temporary loan, the length of time to be determined by the donor.[158]

Others only bequeathed their objects to museums after death, or sold them when in need of extra money, frequently at an inflated cost. In the 1890s, for example, Charles Coote Grant, curator of the Hamilton Association, declared that the farm boys who sold artifacts to him had raised their prices, and he needed a government grant in order to purchase them.[159] J. Hugh Hammond once exaggeratedly remarked that many people demanded prices "that would ruin Astor to pay."[160] William J. Wintemberg also commented that many

> actuated by mercenary motives, preserve such relics, and there are some collectors who offer fabulous prices for everything that is curious, and the finders, knowing full well that some collector, with more money than brains, will pay it, usually demand an exorbitant price for their specimens, and this frequently results in a scientifically valuable relic finding its way into some obscure collection, where students will never see it, or else it is sold to some dealer in a foreign country.[161]

Collectors and tourists indeed dispersed artifacts to other countries, including those sent to friends, family, and international museums in Russia, Scotland, England, and the United States.[162]

## OBJECT LESSONS

Some eager collectors used Boyle's annual reports to learn more about their cabinets and often wrote to him when they had not received their yearly copy of his annual report or to ask for recommendations of additional reading. Such avid individuals often created rudimentary cataloguing systems, numbering artifacts chronologically, and kept notebooks of the location, description, measurements, and sketches of specimens with varying amounts of detail. The degree of knowledge amassed by such collectors provided valuable documentation when they donated their cabinets to museums. For example, donations by Dr William Addison and the Reverends Peter and Arthur Addison to the Canadian Institute included their catalogues, which featured artifact measurements, materials, finishes, use, descriptions, and very specific locations of their discovery.[163]

But those who refused to donate artifacts to museums most often did not keep them for their educational value. While Boyle believed that all pieces were valuable to show working methods and the evolution of artifact form, many collectors only preserved the best or most unusual or attractive specimens, leaving fragmented or unfinished pieces behind. Boyle and his colleagues also advocated the labelling of objects for educational purposes and to communicate artifact research. Some amateur collectors, like Perry Leighton of Essex County, organized their artifacts typologically, similar to the arrangement of museums, but most arranged their private displays aesthetically rather than for educational purposes.[164] The nature of Victorian household decoration dictated a cluttered array of natural history items, exotica, and bric-a-brac in public rooms. Some, like the citizens of Bradford, placed objects in their homes for shock or curiosity value. Most typically, archaeological specimens were vertically mounted on a board in artistic patterns.

If those who kept artifacts did not value their educational potential, they did see them as useful in other, more fanciful and ghoulish ways. As the most desirable and fascinating objects, skulls were often used as drinking vessels, while one farmer used them as flower planters suspended from his verandah.[165] Andrew Hunter recorded that a boy attended a "masked skating carnival" draped with a sheet and a skull placed on his head, and later archaeologist Wilfrid Jury noted that poor pioneer families searched graves seeking "highly ornamented playthings for their children."[166] The Steele family of Coldwater used a conch shell, once a high status grave gift, as a dinner horn that could be heard by the neighbours two miles away. They irreverently remembered that the sound of "'Steele's horn'" always stirred their hunger.[167] Another collector, George Allison of Waterdown, melted down brass and copper kettles into a small cannon. Allison also displayed a large stone originally used as a corn mortar on his front lawn.[168] While these examples may be singular and eccentric, they show the regularity with which archaeological objects were used, and that, compared to protective collections care even in early museums, nineteenth-century amateurs used artifacts in quite cavalier and often destructive ways.

Other uses were more pedestrian. An owner of a slaughterhouse in the Georgian Bay area used skinning stones rather than knives in his daily work.[169] One man carried a human tooth in his pocket, perhaps as a charm, and another smoked an old pipe.[170] Farmers boiled sugar, soap, and cattle feed in copper kettles found in graves or sold them with iron axe-heads and tomahawks to scrap-metal or junk dealers.[171] One farmer decoratively mounted more than seventy iron trade axes on the pickets of his garden fence.[172] Compared to a nineteenth-century museum's reverence for artifacts, amateurs sometimes altered objects. One smoothed out a rough stone implement and then darkened it with coal oil, to make it more aesthetically pleasing.[173] One used one specimen as a "razor-hone" and cut it in half and gave part of it to a neighbour.[174] Such treatment continued despite the best efforts of Wilson and Boyle to promote the preservation of objects.

Some created artifacts where none existed. One prankster in Simcoe County carved the date 1441 onto a pipe, smeared it with mud, and then enjoyed the confusion it caused. Locals pondered how Aboriginal peoples could have known the European system of dating before contact. The pipe was traded, presumably for its unusualness, for a necktie.[175] At the Bradford ossuary, as a joke, a local observer threw in "metal rubbish for the entertainment of the diggers." Those who discovered it puzzled over the possibility that Aboriginal people had the ability to forge metal, a skill supposedly found only in "civilized" societies.[176]

Perhaps the most publicized potentially forged object was the so-called *adjedatigwum* or "death stick," a gravemarker found on the Baby farm in the 1880s. This item was procured by avocational collector Charles Hirschfelder of Toronto. During the resulting debate in the city newspapers, Hirschfelder wrote that he believed the artifact to be likely authentic since it had genuine pictorial writing and he had found others like it before.[177] Others attacked his reputation saying that his collection housed several fakes.[178] One writer, alias Pickwick, informed the public that he knew the two youths who had recently produced this artifact. Three local boys frequently dug on the Baby farm and two had decided to pull a prank on the third.[179]

A minority of the public was not overly interested in archaeological discoveries, yet this also lead to artifact destruction, dispersal, or incomplete documentation. Many large private collections were lost or desultorily dispersed after the death of the collector. A farmer in Malahide Township, whose fields yielded many artifacts, simply piled them "up out of the way," while another left the only skull found on his property atop a fence post until it rotted away.[180] Others simply gave items to those more interested, ruining the picture of a village or burial site that could have been obtained by gathering all artifacts.[181]

Such stories suggest why amateur collectors have been dismissed as unworthy. As local knowledge is replaced by a universal set of concepts, in this case the paradigm of scientific professionalism, it is dismissed as amateurish and as "'belief'" or "'superstition.'"[182] Nineteenth-century avocational and professional archaeologists were often contemptuous of their amateur colleagues, particularly after the establishment of the Canadian Institute in 1851, and even more so after David Boyle became its curator in 1884 and of the Ontario Provincial Museum in 1896.

After Boyle's death, the next generation of Ontario archaeologists continued to comment upon the difficulties of dealing with amateurs. These men, such as Wilfrid Jury and William Wintemberg, had been influenced by the increasing desire for scientific professionalism in the discipline of archaeology as wrought by the establishment of the Anthropological Division of the Geological Survey of Canada in 1910. Visiting the Train Farm site, Jury, himself once a farmboy collector, conservatively remarked that it "would be hard to estimate the numbers of relics carried away."[183] Wintemberg, now a professional archaeologist employed by the Geological Survey, investigated the Southwold earthworks in 1935. He lamented that relic hunters had destroyed most of the evidence of postholes and that two dozen typical kinds of Neutral artifacts were missing, perhaps taken by amateurs. Similarly, he said that the Roebuck site in Grenville County, known to collectors since the 1840s, had suffered losses of artifacts. During the first professional survey of the Lawson site in London for the Geological Survey, Wintemberg stated that it, "like many others in Ontario, suffered considerably from the depredations of collectors, who in the eagerness to get 'curios' for their collections destroyed many valuable evidences, and many of the specimens secured by them have been lost."[184] Despite these disparaging remarks, the nineteenth-century public also substantially aided the discipline of archaeology, particularly by documenting site locations, donating a significant number of objects to Ontario museums for preservation, or retaining them in private colletions that could be accessed for study by professionals.

# 2

# "FOR THE GENERAL GOOD OF SCIENCE"
## Historical and Scientific Society Museums

In early 1906, Andrew Hunter wrote to George Laidlaw about an ossuary that had been discovered the previous year during the digging of a cellar. Hunter explained that he had managed to save the bones "for the general good of science."[1] As members of the Canadian Institute, both were dedicated to the preservation and study of material culture. This focus on the scientific practice of archaeology was a common one in the writings of professionals and some members of historical societies, a contrast to the public who pursued archaeology for ghoulish excitement, novelty, curiosity, or exotic mementoes. According to David Boyle, the simple digging up and collecting of artifacts could not even be called archaeology – that was only what farmers and amateurs did. Instead, the recording, sketching, measuring, and mapping of sites and the long-term preservation, exhibition, classification, and study of specimens equalled archaeology.[2] Many of these goals, which Boyle attempted to fulfill as curator of the Canadian Institute and the Ontario Provincial Museum, and as secretary of the Ontario Historical Society, were adopted by other historical and scientific societies of the province, but with varying degrees of success.

The incorporation of the Canadian Institute in 1851 marked the birth of longstanding historical and scientific societies in the province. The establishment of the Hamilton Association for the Advancement of Literature, Art and Science followed in 1857, the York Pioneers and the Ottawa Literary and Scientific Society in 1870, the Ottawa Field-Naturalists' Club in 1879, and the Lundy's Lane and Wentworth historical societies in 1887 and 1888. But it was the reconstitution of the

Pioneer and Historical Association, originally founded in 1888, into the provincial Ontario Historical Society (OHS) ten years later that inspired the creation of a spate of enthusiastic local bodies which subsequently affiliated themselves with the OHS.[3]

Like the Canadian Institute, these societies followed the Victorian principle of well-rounded education and accordingly encompassed a wide variety of subjects, including the natural sciences, literature, classics, linguistics, and engineering as well as history and archaeology. They viewed collecting as a sign of learning and industrious leisure, and a curio cabinet as a status symbol. The professional and avocational historians and archaeologists of these groups formed a self-contained community that corresponded internally, compared notes and artifacts at meetings, developed society collections, and spent a lifetime investigating Aboriginal cultures.

While Daniel Wilson was highly regarded within the Canadian Institute (and in the Royal Society of Canada), he did not become involved in other societies, and he died before the transformation of the Pioneer and Historical Association into the OHS. David Boyle, well known to local communities through his Canadian Institute fieldwork, was more influential. His leadership role grew after his appointment by Minister of Education George Ross as curator of the Provincial Museum in 1896 and the OHS secretary in 1898. In addition to administrative duties, the OHS constitution charged Boyle with acting as superintendent of its planned library and museum, the editing and supervision of its publications, and the accession and exhibition of artifacts.[4] Boyle's widespread influence continued until his health declined in 1908.

The OHS set out lofty goals in 1898. Its members wished to

> engage in the collection, preservation, exhibition and publication of materials for the study of history, especially the history of Ontario and Canada; to this end studying the archaeology of the Province, acquiring documents and manuscripts, obtaining narratives and records of pioneers, conducting a library of historical reference, maintaining a gallery of historical portraiture and an ethnological and historical museum, publishing and otherwise diffusing information relative to the history of the Province and of the Dominion, and, in general, encouraging and developing within this Province the study of history.[5]

After 1898, many of the local societies simply adopted a modified version of the OHS constitution, emphasizing the collection and research of historical and archaeological records and artifacts and the preservation of objects and historic sites, all in order to educate the public. The two groups seen as most worthy of study were their own pioneer ancestors and Aboriginal peoples. Moreover, societies wished to encourage the study of the history of Ontario or of Canada as a whole to inspire feelings of patriotism. To do so, many societies planned to establish libraries and museums and publish their research and documents written by members' ancestors.[6]

As Donald Wright has argued, in their own time the men and women of local societies were considered to be important historians, some of whom exhibited aspects of modern scholarship, not the amateurs they have been cast as after the professionalization of history in the early twentieth century.[7] Certainly, many members could claim successful achievements: they educated the public about their local past, organized community celebrations, lobbied for the preservation of historic sites, and collected a great deal of the material that remains in today's museums across Ontario. However, unlike David Boyle, society members were volunteers, not paid employees, and so had less time to focus on developing scholarship, limited access to professional historical, anthropological, and museological literature, and fewer contacts with professionals outside the province. Many societies experienced fluctuations in local enthusiasm and did not possess adequate public exhibition space. All groups, including the Canadian Institute, received little monetary support from the Dominion or provincial governments, which sometimes expressed disinterest or disagreement with their goals. As well, local societies had to mediate the interests of enthusiastic community members who looked for local recognition of their own contributions or of their ancestors' achievements. Consequently, local societies often failed to match their own high standards.

## UNCOVERING THE PAST

Societies advocated a cautious and scientific approach to collecting artifacts. As discussed earlier, the Canadian Institute outlined the most detailed instructions, through two articles written by Daniel Wilson and the circular written by Sandford Fleming in 1852 and duplicated by David Boyle in the mid-1880s. These instructions appear to have influenced some collectors. At one Canadian Institute meeting, for example, Thomas Campbell Wallbridge, later an MPP for Belleville, described his 1859 investigation of a series of mounds in the Quinte region, which had been known to the community for over fifty years. Wallbridge's report, also submitted to the *Canadian Journal*, revealed his excavation standards. In a fairly scientific manner, he opened, measured, and cross-sectioned five tumuli and dated the site through dendrochronology. On a subsequent visit, he had sketches of the mounds and artifacts made. Wallbridge noted details such as the position of skeletons, looked for tool markings on rocks, and surmised that bones found near the surface likely represented intrusive graves, all sophisticated observations for the time. He also referred to the work of Henry Schoolcraft and Ephraim George Squier, both important scholars in anthropology at the time, indicating his level of knowledge.[8]

Andrew Hunter, also a founder of the Simcoe Pioneer and Historical Society, believed that "a relic has but little value unless it is accompanied by detailed particulars of its discovery."[9] For more than twenty years, he combed many townships of Ontario seeking artifacts and how they were discovered, clocking a total of 3,600 miles on foot and by boat, bicycle, "horse-vehicle," and rail.[10] In interviewing farmers and collecting objects, Hunter relied on his own rigorous scrutiny to gather information, because he judged others as "untrained to observe."[11] He believed he only reported what could be verified[12] and compensated for any shortage of information by obsessively pursuing details. If he was told about even a single artifact collected from a site, he attempted to contact the owner for information concerning its excavation and description, even if the person had moved from the area. Although he stated that his "promiscuous or disconnected methods of enquiry from the present occupants have doubtless prevented me from learning … more," he still posited that his published surveys contained the most important sites.[13] To him, a good fieldworker was better than a dozen "book students."[14] Indeed, his notebooks reflect his extensive research.

David Boyle considered George E. Laidlaw, a Canadian Institute and OHS member, to be no longer an amateur but an individual who had studied archaeology, contributed to the literature, and was "scrupulously careful in the preservation" of locally found objects.[15] From his publications, we know that Laidlaw followed several aspects of scientific practice in archaeology. His late nineteenth-century articles in the *American Antiquarian* and in the annual *Archaeological Report* minutely described typical Ontario archaeological sites and specimens, showing his extensive research.[16] In excavations, Laidlaw sieved the loose earth he removed to capture corn kernels, beans, acorns, and other small or vegetal matter that might otherwise escape notice.[17] In 1912, he

Andrew Frederick Hunter, 1863–1940          George E. Laidlaw, 1860–1927

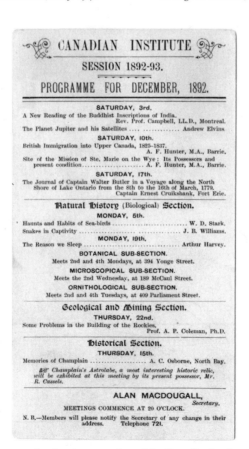

Program for the 1892–9 session of the Canadian Institute

wrote about how he used dendrochronology to date archaeological sites. Laidlaw determined that pine saplings grew over a deserted site within twenty to twenty-five years. He averaged the number of tree rings per inch in pine stumps, multiplied this amount by half of the diameter, and added the time since the tree had been cut down plus the initial twenty-five years.[18]

Few members of other historical societies pursued archaeological excavation so continuously or so thoroughly as those of the Canadian Institute. One individual who did was William J. Wintemberg of the Oxford County Historical Society. Modelling himself after Hunter, Wintemberg utilized similar canvassing methods in Waterloo and Oxford Counties, although he lacked Hunter's compulsiveness. In 1902, Wintemberg stated that, although he was reporting on only one season of fieldwork in Blenheim Township, he was certain that "few, if any, new village-sites can be added to my list, unless in some locality which is at present uncultivated. A canvass was made of nearly every farm in the township, and by this method not one village-site, unless the farmer himself is ignorant of its existence, would be left unrecorded."[19] Boyle also personally mentored Wintemberg, training him to lay out five-foot grid squares for excavation, remove the earth layer by layer, trace remains of wooden posts, and carefully document each object as it was removed from the soil. In later years, Wintemberg assisted Boyle in organizing the exhibits at the Provincial Museum and the province's archaeological display at the 1901 Pan-American exposition in Buffalo.[20]

T.W. Edwin Sowter, the head of the archaeological section of the Ottawa Field-Naturalists' Club (OFNC) was another who recommended intensive investigations. He instructed excavators to examine the site surface on their hands and knees, sift through ashbeds with a sieve, note the material used in pottery to determine whether it had been locally obtained, and collect discarded pieces like flint detritus to understand tool-manufacturing processes.[21] Under Sowter's guidance, the OFNC made expeditions to a quarry outside of Ottawa in 1883 and 1884, and in 1899 the club visited an Aboriginal camping ground in Aylmer, Quebec, and collected human remains.[22] The club returned to the quarry during its 1904–05 session, although this time members were led by Henry Ami, a professional paleontologist employed by the Geological Survey of Canada.[23]

Other local societies made similar excursions. Every Sunday, the Hamilton Association walked around the Burlington Bay area seeking specimens.[24] The London and Middlesex society often visited the Shaw-Wood (now Lawson) site, which offered middens and earthworks for

Helen Merrill of the Prince Edward County Historical Society and Dr R.W. Ells, former President of the OFNC, collecting pottery sherds during a geological excursion to the sand banks, Prince Edward County

exploration. The Elgin Historical and Scientific Institute frequently organized trips to the Southwold earthworks and other nearby spots such as Jaffa for outdoor jaunts that included excavations and picnics. In 1891, for example, members visited the farm of Albert White, who showed them several Aboriginal campsites where they excavated artifacts for their museum before a picnic lunch.[25] The Huron Institute of Collingwood also made numerous explorations in the early twentieth century. On a 1907 trip to the Currie property, members of the Huron Institute dug over a potato patch before seeking the location of Ekarenniondi, the legendary standing stone past which the Wendat dead filed toward the afterlife. The members' evening ended after a rustic dinner cooked over a fire.[26] In 1908, the Huron Institute officially formed an exploration commission to investigate Tionontati (Petun) archaeological sites. That year, it visited numerous farms to excavate and photograph sites and view family collections.[27] In all, the commission located ten large villages, and a number of smaller ones, burials,

An Elgin Historical Society outing at the Southwold earthworks, 1891

and trails and gathered artifacts for the Huron Institute museum before dissolving.[28] Unfortunately we know little about the excavation standards during these excursions, but their purpose certainly possessed social as well as scientific functions.

We know more about J. Hugh Hammond, a member of the Huron Institute and another of Boyle's local voices, who embodied a curious mix of the scientific and the amateurish. Like others, Hammond volunteered his time and archaeological services as he believed it benefited the public.[29] In a manuscript describing his fieldwork methodology, Hammond said one should go "slowly and thoroughly," "exhausting every point available." He advocated the use of a compass, the documentation of strata depths, sketching topography, the mapping of villages, middens, ashheaps, graves, water sources, and artifacts, and careful verification of all information extracted from amateurs. He also suggested the use of an aneroid barometer to determine the height of villages above sea level.[30] Like Hunter, he verified all information obtained from the public, and took "nothing for granted unless proven by ocular demonstration."[31] Hammond presumably wished to remain up-to-date on anthropological literature since he contacted the prestigious Bureau of American Ethnology for suggestions of scholarly reading material.[32]

Yet aspects of Hammond's collecting seem more reminiscent of those of the Ontario public. He described his work as romantic rather than educational. Despite the need to be well read, Hammond believed an archaeologist should be an adventurer and have "the love of the wild places in his bones."[33] He portrayed the pleasure of finding artifacts, rather than keeping them, as a craving and fancifully suggested that if he continued to collect he would "become an Indian."[34] Again, both images carry overtones more romantic than educational. Minister J.P. Secord depicted Hammond rather unscientifically as well, although his statement was also coloured by his displeasure over secular activities on a Sunday. Hammond, Secord wrote in 1904, had "been seen by respectable people on their way to Church last Sunday, with a Spade shoved down the leg of his Pantaloons ... a Bag containing a Compass, a Trowl, two chunks of Balognie Sausage and 3 Soda Biscuits and the Scull and some bones of a departed ancient all jumbled together."[35] This could not have met Boyle's standards of artifact treatment.

## PRESERVING THE PAST

In addition to finding objects during their excursions, societies asked the public to donate artifacts to build their museums. Like the Canadian Institute, groups such as the Essex Historical Society of Windsor, the Lennox and Addington Historical Society of Napanee, the Wentworth Historical Society of Hamilton, the Town and County Historical Society of Peterborough, and the Elgin Historical and Scientific Institute all employed circulars or advertisements to solicit donations.[36] Ideally, historical societies believed that the donation of items resulted in artifact preservation and widespread public education of the community through museum exhibitions. In reality, some societies found it difficult to even obtain a permanent museum space in their community.

For example, before the construction of its Memorial Hall museum, the Niagara Historical Society met in the public library and the court house and held its first exhibit in 1896 in a Mr Rowley's store in Niagara-on-the-Lake.[37] The Elgin Historical and Scientific Institute, founded in 1891, first displayed its small collection in the town hall.[38] The Lundy's Lane Historical Society first organized its collection in an observatory tower over the Lundy's Lane battlefield. Opened in 1893, the approximately 100-foot-high tower was funded by a joint stock company. The reception rooms featured a mix of relics from the battlefield below, weapons from the War of 1812 era, a wooden plough used by the first United Empire Loyalist settlers of the area, and a large collection of arrowheads, pipes, and wampum on loan from Alexander Stephenson, a local collector.[39] By late 1896, the company was in liquidation, forced to sell off the tower, land, and machinery by public auction.[40] Soon after, the society fell dormant; by the time of its reorganization in 1909 and allocation of space for a museum at the Niagara Falls public library, the society had lost much of its artifact collection.[41]

The 1882 Free Libraries Act allowed for museums to be housed in these institutions, a law of which some societies took advantage.[42] Still, many groups could not sustain their museums. In addition, many society members did not wish to donate their collections, or wished to sell them for profit, and numerous groups could not maintain community enthusiasm for their work after the first few years. All these factors affected the preservation of artifacts.

Hugh Nichol of the Perth County Historical Society of Stratford donated some specimens to the Canadian Institute, but the bulk of his collection remained in his private possession, partially exhibited in his superintendent's office at the Stratford jail, until after his death. Nichol may have been possessive of his cabinet, as many collectors were, but he must have also been concerned about its fate if he donated it to his own society. Founded in 1899 during the period of abundant historical enthusiasm following the establishment of the OHS, the Stratford society experienced problems in sustaining community interest. The county council originally allowed the society to meet in its chambers, but by 1903 its eccentric artifact collection – mostly consisting of a cobbler shop diorama, a model ship, and taxidermied squirrels – was located in the new Carnegie Public Library.[43] After an initial report to the Ontario Historical Society in 1900, no further meetings were recorded. Apparently community interest lapsed, because in 1922 a new society was organized.[44] At this point, Nichol's daughters donated his archaeological collection to the society. Four years later, the contents of the historical room in the library basement were transferred to the historic Fryfogel Inn, and the space converted into a public washroom.[45]

The County of Oxford Historical Society in Woodstock experienced similar problems. In May 1897, the same year of its founding, the Oxford society decided to establish a community museum. By 1899 there was already a lull in activity. The allocation of space by the county council in the courthouse and the potential donation of more than six hundred Aboriginal specimens by William Wintemberg partially spurred its rebirth.[46] The Oxford society even considered the cost of suitable museum cases.[47] But in 1906 it again reported it was in a "diseased condition," having not met in "some time" due to a lack of meeting rooms.[48] In the meantime, the society waited upon the construction of a public library, in which it had been promised a room for a museum. Meetings

Part of the Hugh Nichol collection, c. 1920, now at the Stratford-Perth Museum

were suspended again during 1907–08. In 1909 the Carnegie Library opened in Woodstock, but Wintemberg had donated his collection to the Ontario Provincial Museum in Toronto approximately seven years before because no permanent space could be found in Woodstock and he likely feared the loss of his artifacts, a fear that would prove justified.[49] A 1908 basement plan of the library shows a museum located between a workroom and a smoking room, and in 1910 the local newspaper reported that the beginnings of the long-awaited museum included a piece of the first macadam road in Canada, fossils, South Sea shells, a Chinese "idol," and part of the first local fire engine.[50] But the society fell defunct after 1912. Its next meeting did not convene until March 1930, and in 1933 the museum reopened in the courthouse.[51]

The London and Middlesex Historical Society (LMHS) also encountered troubles establishing its museum. It designated Dr Solon

Woolverton, a dentist and private collector who exhibited Aboriginal and natural history specimens in his Dundas Street dental office and on the upper floor of his Grand Avenue home, to be its curator. He attempted numerous times to secure a place for the society and offered his cabinet as a substantial contribution toward its creation. In 1900, he proposed to lend his cabinet to the London Public Library; his offer was referred to the finance committee, but no action was taken.[52] Upon organization in 1901, the LMHS obtained room in the library for meeting space, and although the society placed artifacts on display it continued to discuss the idea of an official museum. Woolverton's 1904 offer to sell his collection to the Geological Survey of Canada indicates the lack of results.[53] Because the group despaired of ever receiving money from the city, it next debated whether to amalgamate its collections with the Teachers Association, which planned to form museums in schools.[54] The idea of an exhibit on the third floor of the city hall was also raised. Again, Woolverton agreed to the donation of his cabinet.[55] Ultimately, Woolverton placed eight to ten cases of his artifacts at the library, but the collection had grown too large for the space, and so eventually the collection was given to the archaeological museum at the University of Western Ontario, before he died in 1943.[56]

While Nichol, Wintemberg, and Woolverton may have been concerned about the preservation of their collections, Aylmer collector David H. Price appears to have been more interested in making a profit, although he vaguely advertised the price of his artifacts as "little more than the bare cost of collecting." He had previously donated artifacts to the Canadian Institute and was also a member of the OHS, and thus was familiar with David Boyle's curatorship of the archaeological collection at the Provincial Museum. But instead of donating his collection of seven thousand Neutral specimens to Boyle, Price printed up a flyer and solicited buyers. He did, however, include the names of David Boyle and George Mercer Dawson, the director of the Geological Survey of Canada, as references to bolster the professional nature of his collection. Price invited prospective buyers to drop by his Toronto address to inspect his collection. Such a sale of material culture would have been too expensive for local societies, and indeed the Geological Survey purchased his collection, grown to nine thousand items, in 1904 for almost $6,000. Even Boyle, whose yearly budget totalled only a few thousand, could not have purchased Price's museum.[57]

## A PROVINCIAL MUSEUM

In its aim to preserve material culture, the Canadian Institute also desired the establishment of a provincial archaeological museum in Toronto, one which would have sufficient funding to conduct archaeological research and purchase important collections. Two years before Boyle became the Canadian Institute's curator, President J.M. Buchan and Charles Hirschfelder, himself a prodigious collector, appealed to the Dominion Bureau of Statistics for the financial support to create a formidable museum of Canadian archaeology. They also reminded the provincial government of the rampant destruction and loss of artifacts to persuade them that aid was urgently required.[58] George Laidlaw further publicized the cause in Toronto newspapers in 1885.[59] That same year, Boyle suggested the formation of a committee to petition the attorney general for an archaeological research grant.[60] Consequently, in 1886, a committee that included Daniel Wilson approached the Ontario government for a $5,000 subsidy to establish a provincial archaeological museum in which students could study and conduct original research, purchase private collections, and conduct a "systematic, thorough, and scientific examination of all monuments, sites, and localities" related to Aboriginal cultures. In response, Premier Oliver Mowat asked the group to research US museum structures and funding.[61] The Canadian Institute was more successful that year in its negotiations with the Minister of Education George Ross. He agreed to increase its annual grant from $750 to $1,000 for "general purposes," although the institute had requested an additional $1,500 for research alone.[62]

With the exception of a brief revocation in 1894, the Department of Education provided this grant yearly. Though large by the standards of the time–most societies received a few hundred dollars, if anything at all–this amount only covered Boyle's paltry salary, minimal accession purchases, and museum maintenance, limiting research to basic investigations. It certainly could not have covered the expansion of the Canadian Institute collection into a provincial museum. In fact, Boyle had previously estimated that a proper investigation of Ontario archaeology alone required a minimum of $5,000–6,000 annually for four to five years.[63] Discouraged, in 1891 he wrote to George Brown Goode of the Smithsonian Institution seeking employment, or at the very least Goode's written support to the minister of Education for an increased grant for the Canadian Institute museum.[64] By 1892, Boyle reported he had received so many invitations to visit sites that it would take two or more seasons to do so by himself, and he feared that farming would eventually destroy significant sites before he could document them.[65]

Several of Boyle's colleagues supported his bid for increased funding and an expanded facility. Thomas Beeman complained to George Ross after a disappointing visit to the Canadian Institute museum in 1894. He found most artifacts stored in the basement rather than placed on exhibit. Certainly by the early 1890s Boyle reported that the museum, located in the upper story of the institute building, was overcrowded. Further, Beeman wrote, specimens continued to filter out of the country to the United States to those willing to pay higher prices.[66] The Pioneer and Historical Association of Ontario (later to be the OHS) supported the establishment of a provincial museum. Henry Scadding, its first president, had always desired a provincial museum that would focus on the early days of Canada. At its 1891 annual meeting, this organization resolved to appeal to the provincial government for funds for a museum, in support of the petitions of the historical section of the Canadian Institute. It passed a similar resolution to fund the collection of artifacts at an 1893 meeting.[67]

Throughout the 1890s, the Canadian Institute pressed various federal and provincial agencies to establish a provincial archaeological museum. A subcommittee continued to investigate not only US, but also Canadian, British, Australian, and New Zealand museums in order to present a well-informed petition to the government.[68] To further lobby the government, the institute also formed a committee consisting of two individuals each from its own membership, the University of Toronto, and the Ontario Bureau of Mines.[69]

The Canadian Institute also appealed to the Department of Indian Affairs (DIA) for funds for research and for maintenance of its existing museum. In his reply, Deputy-Superintendent Lawrence Vankoughnet recognized the importance of the institute's work but feared a contribution would set an expensive precedent for other groups engaged in similar studies. Really, he said, the provincial government should fund it, while federal government money should support the Geological Survey. In response, the institute compiled a report of the provincial government funding it had received but argued that no group, including the Geological Survey, did as extensive work as itself did. Vankoughnet did not, however, change his mind.[70] His correspondence with Superintendent-General of Indian Affairs Edgar Dewdney is revealing. After perusing the institute's 1889 annual report, Vankoughnet concluded that, although he could see the value of its work in archaeology, its goals would not help Aboriginal peoples.[71] The DIA was more interested in

assimilating Aboriginal peoples than helping them to remember and preserve past traditions and material culture. In fact, the Indian Act made the
following of many Aboriginal traditions illegal. Thus, a later memorial to
Dewdney in 1891, and another in 1892 yielded little results.[72]

The Canadian Institute's appeals were partly answered in November
1896, when George Ross appointed Boyle curator of a new archaeological department at the Ontario Provincial Museum, which was housed at
the Toronto Normal School. This museum had been earlier established as
the Museum of Natural History and Fine Arts by Egerton Ryerson, the
chief superintendent of Education in Upper Canada, but the collections
had languished. To expand facilities for the Canadian Institute museum,
Ross transferred its collections to the Ontario Provincial Museum.
But Boyle continued to receive only the annual amount of $1,000 for
research and curatorial work and thus was still hampered in fulfilling his
goal of building a professional scientific museum. Ross, as most politicians did, saw museum work as simply organizing a finite exhibit, not an
ongoing process of research and changing exhibits to represent new findings.[73] Promoted to superintendent of the Provincial Museum in 1901,
Boyle continued to assert that the institution was underfunded. After
attending the International Congress of Americanists in New York the
next year, Boyle told Richard Harcourt, the new Education minister, that
museums south of the border were much better funded. Boyle proceeded
to request an annual grant of $5,000 for new acquisitions and for assis-
tants to maintain and renew exhibits. Instead, Harcourt provided $1,950.
By 1904, Boyle was disparagingly comparing the Provincial Museum to
a vaudeville performance, a far cry from his goals of scientific education.[74] As before, Boyle's complaints were supported by several of his
colleagues.[75] In 1905, however, after a change in government, R.A. Pyne,
the new minister of Education, provided additional money for increased
staff and raised Boyle's salary.

In 1898, when the Pioneer and Historical Association reorganized as
the OHS, its constitution advocated the collection and preservation of
documents and relics and the establishment of an ethnological and historical museum. With David Boyle at the Ontario Provincial Museum
for the previous two years, it seemed logical to expand the existing historical collection through the work of the OHS. As secretary of the OHS,
Boyle was responsible for the collection and exhibition of artifacts, but
the group only received a grant of $500, much less than it had requested.[76]

Nevertheless, the OHS appointed a committee to assist Boyle in
the collection of artifacts and issued a circular canvassing its affiliated societies to determine what historical relics they held. After an

overwhelming response, in February 1899 the OHS proposed an exhibition to showcase these collections, an idea that had been under discussion for several years. This exhibition, the OHS hoped, would catch the attention of politicians and underscore the need for an expanded provincial museum. The Women's Canadian Historical Society of Toronto (WCHST) took on the task and pressed local societies to lend their own artifacts and persuade private collectors to lend their cabinets.[77]

The provincial government had already responded favourably to the idea of a provincial historical exhibition, cast earlier as a celebration of John Cabot's 1497 landing in North America and the progress Canada had made since then. In 1896 the provincial government had passed the Canadian Historical Exhibition Act, which established a board of commissioners under the honorary presidency of the Earl of Aberdeen, the governor general of Canada. The commissioners consisted of twelve people: two each appointed by the governor general, the lieutenant governor of Ontario, and the city of Toronto, and the remaining six by the exhibition committee. The scope of the project was originally very ambitious, encompassing "musical and other entertainments, ceremonies, pageants, ethnological camps, zoological and botanical gardens, military and naval reviews, regattas, sports," and a "congress of representatives of governments, universities, law societies ... for the purpose of considering the history and nature of the principles of government as applied to the constitution and government of the British Empire."[78] In addition, supporters agreed that it was "in the public interest that a permanent public museum of Canadian history, art, science and natural history should be established in this Province" and that the profits of the exhibition could be used for that purpose, or for the erection of statues and monuments, or the creation of zoological and botanical gardens.[79]

A much smaller and later event than the provisions of the act suggested, the Canadian Historical Exhibition took place over two weeks in June 1899 at Victoria College in Toronto. Its exhibits featured Canadian art and furniture, military memorabilia, silver and china, fancy dress, and Aboriginal archaeological and ethnographic objects. Afterward the Women's Canadian Historical Society retained custody of numerous artifacts held in trust until the future opening of the proposed OHS museum. The exhibition also generated a profit of $330.24 for the museum fund.[80] Despite this small sum, the society's final report concluded that it had saved many objects from loss, demonstrated that a large number of artifacts existed, which might form the basis of a museum, and raised public interest in Canadian history.

Indeed, the WCHST asserted that "work such as this may be regarded as of greater value and importance for the future than the mere acquisition of dollars."[81]

Despite the government's original support and that of Education Minister George Ross, who had provided a room at the Provincial Museum to store the collected artifacts, little progress was made. In fact, in 1904, the women's society was even asked to vacate the room, as it was needed for other purposes. For years afterward, its artifacts were kept first at the Women's Welcome Hostel and later at the home of the curator Mrs Seymour Corley.[82] In 1906, the Women's Canadian Historical Society of Toronto was still seeking significant monetary aid for an expanded provincial museum. At the yearly meeting of historical societies on the Canadian National Exhibition grounds, it called upon wealthy men for help.[83] In the end, however, the movement for an expanded provincial institution faltered for several reasons. Boyle was reluctant to acquire historical objects for the archaeologically focused Ontario Provincial Museum, because his resources and time were already stretched thin. The OHS was beginning to turn its attention to the commemoration of historical sites. Finally, the development of the Royal Ontario Museum (ROM), driven by Charles Trick Currelly and his colleagues, who emphasized European and Asian civilizations rather than Canadian history and archaeology, eclipsed the project. Eventually the ROM acquired the collections of the Ontario Provincial Museum in the 1930s.

## PROTECTIVE LEGISLATION

Historical societies also wished to preserve archaeological sites and the artifacts that could be unearthed from them, agreeing that government action was badly needed. They especially championed federal legislation, commonly referring to Britain, which had implemented the Ancient Monuments Protection Act in 1882. Government disinterest and lack of funding, however, hampered the fulfilment of these ideals. Not long after his appointment as curator of the Canadian Institute, the *Toronto Daily Mail* wrote about Boyle's call for funding to make an immediate examination of all Aboriginal sites in Ontario before their destruction.[84] Shortly after, Arthur Harvey, a journalist and member of several historical societies, advocated the same.[85] The next year, Boyle and others formed a committee that drafted a petition for an ancient monuments bill to be passed.[86] The Canadian Institute's annual report politely described the lack of action as a result of the "heavy work falling upon the Minister this session," which "made it impossible for him to bring in an Ancient Monuments bill." Boyle hoped it would come to pass the following session, yet it seemed such a bill never appeared before the legislature.[87] Accordingly, in discussing an earthwork in Moore Township in his 1901 report, Boyle could only hope that the private owner of the site would continue to protect the landmark from destruction and maybe in the future official legislation would be enacted.[88] In 1910, the Ontario Historical Society took a different approach and requested that the federal Department of Indian Affairs should protect archaeological sites and remains on reserve lands.[89] Not until 1953, however, did the federal government pass the Archaeological Sites Protection Act.

In particular, societies expressed concern about two unique sites in the province – the Southwold earthworks in Elgin County and the serpent and egg mounds near Peterborough. When Boyle first investigated the earthworks in 1890, the property was then owned by farmer Chester Henderson. Boyle wondered in his annual report at the indifference of the municipality and wealthy individuals toward the potential destruction of the only double earthworks in Canada, particularly because the cost to purchase the area would be small. In fact, he compared this site to the fantastic serpent mound in Ohio and lamented its possible erasure through cultivation.[90] A few years later, he emphasized that only a few hundred dollars from the Elgin County government could purchase this land and save it from being destroyed.[91]

Likely prompted by Boyle, in 1891 the Ontario Historical Society requested that the local society, the Elgin Historical and Scientific Institute (EHSI) of St Thomas, survey the site in order to document its characteristics before it was ruined. City engineer A.W. Campbell completed the survey and Boyle had a model made of the site for the Canadian Institute, presumably so its features could always be studied even if the site was later destroyed. The EHSI also hoped to obtain legislative protection for the site. At the annual 1903 OHS meeting in St Thomas, the OHS Council resolved to represent Elgin County and take steps for the site's security. Three years later, the group appealed to the Royal Society of Canada for cooperation in this endeavour.[92] James Coyne, a long-time EHSI president, and E.A. Cruikshank of the Lundy's Lane society, continued to push for protection of the earthworks while they were members of the Historical Landmarks Association (later the Historic Sites and Monuments Board). At one point, Coyne and Cruikshank even considered purchasing the property themselves, but this never occurred.[93] Finally, in 1929, almost forty years after Boyle's first visit, the earthworks were purchased for $2,500.[94]

Like the Southwold earthworks, the serpent and egg mounds were privately owned. David Boyle first visited this site in 1896, and in his annual report he strongly suggested that the government should purchase the plot and create a small park for the benefit of the public. He estimated the cost to do so to be only a few hundred dollars even if the whole surrounding sixty acres were purchased.[95] The formation of the Town and County Historical Society of Peterborough that same year was partly motivated by this issue, and, concerned about vandalism, the group resolved to be advocates for the site's protection. Society member Henry Strickland, who owned part of the property consulted with the other owner, G.W. Hatton, and both agreed to sell. According to Boyle, however, they asked too high a price.[96] In 1897, the Peterborough society approached both the minister of Education and the Otonabee County Council for aid. The council did not see it as a local matter and instead adopted a memorial to the Ontario legislature.[97] Advised by Boyle, the Peterborough society also asked the council to invite the British Association for the Advancement of Science (BAAS) to inspect the mounds.[98] The BAAS agreed to take steps toward preservation at its 1897 meeting in Toronto, but Boyle expressed his disappointment with the lack of interest shown by the council by disparagingly asking: "what is there in an earth-heap to stimulate a town councillor, unless it has to be removed from his door-step?"[99] The Peterborough society was still calling for government intervention in 1907, although this lack of attention likely partially resulted from the floundering nature of the society itself.[100] Finally, in 1955, the mounds were turned into a provincial park and marked by the Historic Sites and Monuments Board.

## STUDYING THE PAST

Despite the failure to significantly expand the funding and facilities of the Ontario Provincial Museum and to enact legislation to protect sites and the artifacts found at them, many societies possessed a significant number of objects. The selection and arrangement of objects were paramount; one could not properly study the artifacts if they were haphazard choices, or classified or labelled improperly. To David Boyle, museums should be dedicated to research and the education of the public. They should not be "merely a raree show, or a junk-shop, or an idle place of resort," "a mass of bric-a-brac, or a heap of curiosities." Rather, each specimen should "illustrate a point, enforce some statement, or elucidate something otherwise obscure" and should have a "clear and copious label."[101] In fact, labels were equally if not more important than the objects since they communicated information.[102] Through the "close and patient study" of artifacts and their attached information, one could understand "modes of thought, manners of life, and conditions of early society."[103] As a follower of Pestalozzian educational philosophy, Boyle also believed that hands-on experience with and observation of objects, rather than memorization of facts by rote, was a more effective pedagogical approach.[104]

In the late nineteenth century, professional archaeologists used the classificatory-descriptive system, an arrangement that combined some speculative theory with abundant description and the beginnings of categorization based upon artifact typologies. These typologies were often organized along an evolutionary scale that linked technological development with increasingly sophisticated levels of civilization. The dating of specimens and sites could only be roughly achieved through dendrochronology, or by the absence of trade goods, which could indicate that the site was pre-contact. As a result, archaeologists had little understanding of culture change over time. As well, primitive groups were considered unprogressive; archaeologists explained marked differences in artifacts at long-occupied sites by the in-migration of another group rather than internal advancement of one culture.[105] It was under this rubric that David Boyle first organized the collection of the Canadian Institute.

Particularly concerned with the function or use of objects and the method and material of their manufacture, Boyle classified the Canadian Institute's specimens and his own, which he donated upon his appointment, into four categories: those of known use and production; those of known production but not use; those of known use but not production; and those which had neither no known use nor production.[106] The function of specimens, that is essentially the object type, was the most important piece of knowledge, the method and material of manufacture the second. Boyle described artifacts lacking information about their origin and use as "valueless for scientific purposes."[107] The 1889 catalogue describing the museum's organization reflected Boyle's thinking. Exhibit cases with titles such as Bone and Horn, Copper and Hematite, Partly or Wholly of European Manufacture, Broken and Unfinished Articles Showing Methods of Working, Flaked Tools and Weapons, Stone Pipes, and Clay Pipes suggested his emphasis on the type/use and production method and material of objects.[108]

True to the classificatory-descriptive system, Boyle subsumed the cultural association, geographic origin, and date of artifacts under type and function. The 1889 catalogue shows, for example, that cases C, D, and E featured flints in the categories of rough, typical, and miscellaneous, but mixed together examples from England, Ireland, the United States, and Canada. Boyle arranged case D to specifically show the differing size, materials and the modes of hafting stone points to shafts. Only the items in case W, Clearville Specimens, were configured by locality. Boyle deemed two miscellaneous cases only temporary until a reorganization of the permanent cases allowed for space to include objects in their typologies.[109] While dating artifacts was speculative at best, Boyle also rejected the chronological categories of paleolithic and neolithic, then revolutionary in Europe. They did not suit Ontario archaeology, he believed, because objects that seemed to be from these different stages of cultural progress were actually contemporaneous.[110]

In 1893, Boyle mounted an exhibition for the World's Columbian Exposition in Chicago through the auspices of the Department of Education. He chose six hundred artifacts from the Canadian Institute collection to fill twelve table cases. Although he reported that he was busy with the mineralogical exhibit half a mile away and that another individual was responsible for the arranging and labelling of the archaeological items, it seems more than likely that he had given instructions for its organization.[111] Indeed, the Chicago display evinced similar organizational principles to the Canadian Institute museum. Overall, the objects depicted an evolutionary development from "the ruder to the more elaborate designs."[112] One area featured stone tools and other objects that demonstrated methods of working, such as pecking or the boring of holes to cut stone, and most of the other objects were displayed by type or object use. Some items were grouped by material, such as miscellaneous objects made out of slate, bone, horn, shell, or copper. While the geographical areas in which the objects were found were listed, this was not the primary level of organization. There was also no attempt to identify or distinguish between the cultures or time periods associated with these objects, with the exception of one post-European case.[113]

This typological organization also characterized the discussion of artifacts in Boyle's publications. His regular section Notes on Specimens within his annual reports accented the method and material of construction and function of the items he highlighted. Boyle's 1895 *Notes on Primitive Man In Ontario*, which he wrote as a teacher's guide, also separated archaeological objects first by object type or function, and then

Provincial Museum main archaeological room showing typological
arrangement of artifacts, c. 1911

Provincial Museum archaeological display, including the Laidlaw collection, c. 1928

by descriptions of their material, production, and purpose. Typologies were so important that they overwhelmed the uniqueness of certain pieces; for example, Boyle deemed a bone fish hook from Victoria County of European influence because such an object was so rare.[114]

Early on, Boyle advocated that the larger and more varied the collection the better, so that scholars could compare artifacts, true to the nature of establishing typologies.[115] Later, Boyle no longer emphasized the comprehensive collection of specimens. Instead, he stated that there were so many artifacts in the Provincial Museum that it was really only necessary to add new types of objects, those that documented an unresearched locality or that facilitated innovative comparisons.[116] This suggests that Boyle believed the utility of the classificatory-descriptive system had reached its limit, or was perhaps cynical about ever receiving more funding to expand the museum.

Whatever the reason, by 1890 Boyle had begun to express interest in examining artifacts by their location in order to make comparisons between geographical areas and, hence, different cultures. This organization scheme has been called classificatory-historical methodology.[117] Noting the generous donation of the Laidlaw collection, which focused on life in the Balsam Lake area, Boyle remarked, "what is of even more importance is the increase of our knowledge relative to the areas occupied by different tribes," including the sources of tool materials, burial rites, methods of fortification, the character of towns and housing styles, and the methods of making tools. While "savage life is or was, much 'the same with a difference,'" across the world, Boyle suggested that it was this difference that illustrated the "history of our race." For example, he elaborated, all people historically used stone for tools at one point, but chose different types of stone and worked them in different ways. Even a comparison of the William Long and George Laidlaw collections at the museum, which were collected at close localities, showed noticeable differences, especially in pottery, he said. Boyle hoped that in the future the acquisition of specimens from other areas in Ontario would result in even wider comparisons.[118]

In 1895, Boyle corresponded with staff of the United States National Museum to ask how they had organized its collections. For ethnographic artifacts, George Brown Goode advised him to first divide material culture by geographical location, then by culture and technology. For pre-contact archaeology, Goode recommended emphasizing locality and technological aspects, to show the evolution of each artifact type if possible. Boyle apparently had already proposed this classification scheme, for Goode expressed his approval of his plan.[119]

In 1900, Boyle reported that he had rearranged the Laidlaw collection. These 1,500 objects were now organized by the location of thirty-one Balsam Lake village sites, illustrating daily life of that area. Similarly, Boyle preserved James Heath's donation in its original order, as representative of Neutral culture in Brant County. Boyle, however, did not plan to reorganize the rest of the museum in this manner, because he believed that each system had its own virtues. At the time of his death in 1911, photographs of the Ontario Provincial Museum show numerous floor and wall cases still arranged by artifact typology, although all artifacts are not visible. Later photos reveal rough divisions in locality; Haudenosaunee masks and Plains items mingled in one cabinet, and items from the Arctic were grouped together, although several geographical areas were represented.[120]

Some society members associated with Boyle copied his organizational schemes. George Laidlaw and J. Hugh Hammond discussed artifacts in their collections also by use or typology and then described their method of construction, finish, size, form, and materials.[121] Laidlaw also emphasized the descriptive aspect of the classificatory-descriptive system. In one article, Laidlaw stated that his purpose was not "to theorize or speculate on various recurrent forms" but rather to provide "minute descriptions" of his artifacts and to compare them with others.[122] Andrew Hunter organized his catalogue on a descriptive basis of measurements, finish, use, location, and materials or, as Laidlaw did, grouped artifacts by village sites.[123]

Although Boyle was considered to be the guiding influence of the OHS and its affiliated societies, local groups often chose other organizing principles than the classificatory-descriptive and classificatory-historical methodologies. The Niagara Historical Society (NHS) appears to be most influenced by Boyle. One of its scrapbooks features a newspaper clipping describing Boyle's museum methodology that all artifacts on display should be educational; the society also published his lecture "History Taught by Museums," in which he explained this philosophy.[124] In 1902, Boyle agreed to assist in the reorganization of the NHS collection. After two days, however, Boyle concluded that the museum was still "semi-chaotic"; little classification and reorganization could be done because of the small space and crowded collection.[125]

When the NHS finally established its new museum Memorial Hall in 1907, it did not follow the model laid out by the Provincial Museum exhibits and instead focused on recognizing the donors of the artifacts. Like its earlier accession catalogue, the NHS museum separated Indian relics from other artifacts but otherwise grouped objects by donor and

Niagara Historical Society museum, 1927

not by type, function, method of manufacture, or attribution to various
Aboriginal groups.[126] Not surprisingly, this focus upon donors emphasized appreciation for local supporters, without whom smaller societies would collapse. The 1911 catalogue reveals a continuation of this
type of classification. A collection by E. Shepard combined military
and archaeological items in one case, although the remaining space was
taken up with non-Ontario ethnographic pieces from other donors.
Two other cases in the gallery almost exclusively displayed Aboriginal
artifacts, but because they were again organized by collector, several
non-Aboriginal artifacts were incorporated. A grouping of 196 archaeological objects may have been an exception to the organization by
donor, as no name was given; this may have been the result of numerous
donations, possibly suggesting arrangement by racial origin rather than
donor.[127] Cultural origin was defined rather loosely. Nineteenth-century
definitions of race – Indian versus White – rather than the comparison
of different Aboriginal groups as Boyle was beginning to explore, was
of primary interest. But characteristic of the classificatory-descriptive
phase, in those cases designated Indian, the NHS combined items of the

Indian Room at the 1899 Canadian Historical Exhibition,
including part of the Brant-Sero collection

Indian Room at the 1899 Canadian Historical Exhibition

Wendat, Neutral, Sioux, Inuit, Anishinabeg, and Metis. As well, there
was little indication of the date of Aboriginal artifacts.

The 1899 provincial exhibition at Victoria College used a similar
mix of museological philosophy and organizational schemes. In solic-
iting artifacts from other groups and private collectors, the Women's
Canadian Historical Society stated that it did not desire objects of simple curiosity or those without educational value, a statement similar to
Boyle's beliefs.[128] James Coyne, then president of the OHS, reinforced
this message in his 1899 address to the society.[129] Concepts of race dictated that Indian relics be separated into a discrete display, although
numerous objects could have been instead subsumed under major categories such as Portraits, Silver, or Fancy Work. Internally, the Indian
Exhibit, as it was called, was arranged by lender, combined archaeological, ethnographic, historical, and photographic relics, and mixed objects
from the Wendat, Neutral, Haudenosaunee, Cree, Sioux, Anishinabeg,

Haida, Dene, Metis, and others.[130] There were a few exceptions, however. For example, the WCHST incorporated depictions of Cartier at Hochelaga into both the Indian and the Portrait division. Aboriginal tools used in curing hides were also included in the Military section. The integrity of some collections took precedence as well; the exhibit of the Niagara Historical Society and a collection of relics from the arctic search for Franklin contained Aboriginal items but were presented as discrete exhibits.[131] This mix of organizational styles was also partly based on the short time frame for exhibit development, the division of the exhibition team into thematic subcommittees, the availability of collections, and the ease of using their pre-existing organization and interpretation.[132]

Other societies, such as the Hamilton Association, possessed enthusiastic individuals who organized museums around their own personal efforts and family legacies. In 1896, Sarah E. Carry donated her father's collection of Aboriginal, Oriental, conchological, and ichthyological items to the Hamilton Association.[133] Although Carry believed that her family's heirlooms should be on display for the "pleasure and instruction" of visitors, she was possessive of the objects and retained control, reserving the right to open the cases of her cabinet.[134] When the city of Hamilton purchased Dundurn Castle, the former residence of Sir Allan MacNab, the Hamilton Association and the Wentworth Historical Society transferred its collections to this building, which officially opened on 24 May 1900. Sarah Carry spent eight weeks in the Dundurn drawing room, organizing her seven cases of artifacts. It appears as if the items were divided by broad subjects such as natural history and Aboriginal and Asian cultures.[135] A later description of Dundurn revealed that these objects were still exhibited in this room. The walls displayed framed newspapers from 1827, portraits of MacNab, Senator McInnes, another owner of Dundurn, and Sarah Carry herself, while bronze busts of 1812 heroes Tecumseh and Brock rested on the mantlepiece.[136] Some of the portraits were likely later additions, but the rest of the living room had possibly remained intact since 1901.

Beyond Carry's efforts, Dundurn Castle combined the exhibit strategy of donor appreciation with still another type of organization common to Victorian historical societies. Clementina Fessenden, the first curator, preserved the integrity of private collections, but her exhibits also reflected a typical nineteenth-century house as a living history site. She contextually arranged items in logical rooms, although the contents had not belonged to MacNab or other owners. Still, some artifacts were whimsically located, such as the busts of Mexican presidents featured in the breakfast room, and a 1924 *Hamilton Spectator* delighted in the relative disorder of the exhibits since the "very charm of such a vagarious peregrination is the aimless flitting about" – a description that Boyle would have found disturbing had he been alive.[137]

Over thirty years later, Royal Ontario Museum archaeologist Walter Kenyon reorganized the Aboriginal objects at Dundurn Castle. They were too "helter skelter," he said, and needed to be organized properly before they could be used to teach, one of the main goals historical societies had hoped to fulfill when they began their museums.[138] As Donald Wright has shown, members of nineteenth-century societies were increasingly thought of as amateurish as it became possible to specialize and professionally train in history and archaeology in the early twentieth century.[139] Many societies, however, did create and sustain successful museums that educated the public and preserved objects for future generations. But even before this process of professionalization began, local historical and scientific societies often did not match the scientific standards in archaeology as laid out by David Boyle and his colleagues, because their focus was often more community-centred than scholarly. And they often could not fulfill their own high standards because of difficulties in securing museum and meeting space, lack of funding, and sporadic community interest.

# 3

# ABORIGINAL RESPONSES TO ARCHAEOLOGY

In the 1780s, when Captain John Deseronto established the Kanienkehaka (Mohawk) territory known as Tyendinaga, he chose a location that happened to be near pre-contact burial mounds. In 1800, when Joseph Brant, another Kanienkehaka leader, established Brant's Landing on Burlington Beach, he built his estate near a mass grave. This interment, commonly known to early settlers in Upper Canada, was thought to be the result of a battle between the Haudenosaunee (Iroquois) and the Anishinabeg. Tourists often visited tumuli on the Walpole Island reserve, and the Mississauga of the Trent River Valley resettled on reserves near the Rice Lake serpent mound. On Christian Island, the remains of the Jesuit mission Ste Marie and its associated Wendat (Huron) village could still be seen by Anishinabeg who lived nearby. The Six Nations of the Grand River reserve contained several large Neutral villages and burials often excavated by prolific collectors in the nineteenth century. Aboriginal collectors such as Chief Alexander G. Smith (Dehkanenraneh) and Peter E. Jones also collected here and on the nearby Mississauga New Credit reserve. In fact, the 1883 *History of the County of Brant* suggested that many objects were "frequently found" along the Grand River and on the Six Nations reserve.[1]

Clearly, the Aboriginal peoples of Upper Canada were familiar with these and other archaeological and historic sites, some of which their ancestors had created. Unfortunately, there are relatively few documented Aboriginal opinions about the accidental discoveries and deliberate excavations of such sites. Most Aboriginal protests stemmed from religious concerns about the disturbance of their dead, evidencing an utter dismissal of the level of professionalism, the factor that so often concerned non-Aboriginal excavators. But Aboriginal individuals also aided anthropologists in their excavations and collected artifacts for themselves. Thus disagreements about archaeological excavations and the exhibition of objects and human remains cannot only be seen as the result of Aboriginal and Euro-Canadian individuals choosing to follow their different cultural values. Each could privilege or protest curio-hunting and public spectacle, scientific dispassion, or religious understandings of the dead, intellectually distance the dead from the living through the attribution of an ancient sense of time or through denial of cultural affiliation, and devalue Aboriginal human rights or elevate certain Aboriginal individuals to heroic status as part of the broader nationalistic fervour of United Empire Loyalism or in defense of Aboriginal sovereignty.

## LEGISLATION AND REGULATION

Not surprisingly, most controversy centred around the excavation of burials. In the nineteenth century, there was little to protect Aboriginal burials or any archaeological site, either on or off reserve.[2] What little legislation did exist stemmed mostly from Aboriginal protest, as it did in 1797. But, when Peter Russell issued his prohibition against grave-digging that year, it was neither precedent setting nor a legal or moral deterrent, despite its apparent seriousness. As Henry Scadding of the York Pioneers and the Canadian Institute noted, it was considered "prosaic" and of "temporary effect."[3] Indeed, although there were sporadic instances of protection for Aboriginal sites, they were largely left undefended.

Subsequent protection for interments in Upper Canada fell under local jurisdictions. In 1859, An Act Respecting the Municipal Institutions allowed municipalities to pass bylaws to deter destruction of "cemeteries, graves, tombs, tombstones or vaults," although this was not specific to Aboriginal burials.[4] Seemingly no municipality in the province used this act to protect Aboriginal gravesites. British Columbia, however, enacted the Indian Grave Ordinance of 1865 in response to Aboriginal protests against graverobbing. "[E]xpedient for the preservation of the public peace," the penalties for grave depredations included a possibility of six months imprisonment, a £100 fine for the first violation, and a maximum of twelve months hard labour for a second infraction. Although it applauded the protection of Aboriginal graves, the *British Columbian* newspaper complained that these penalties were too severe a punishment and encouraged magistrates to exercise what it deemed common sense in their rulings. In 1867, the fine was converted to $100 and the prison terms reduced to half the original provisions. Tellingly, these were considered crimes against the Crown, as it claimed to own all antiquities, not an offense against Aboriginal peoples, the descendants of those interred.[5]

The 1886 federal Larceny Act subsumed these British Columbia laws, although its provisions were still only applicable to this Western province. This act punished anyone who "cuts, breaks, destroys, damages or removes any image, bones, article or thing deposited in or near any Indian grave" or induced another to do so. Knowingly purchasing stolen grave material was also prohibited. A first offense resulted in a maximum $100 fine or up to three months in prison, with subsequent violations extending the potential term to six months with hard labour. The statute included a proviso, however, that allowed substantial flexibility. Because human remains and associated grave goods were still considered to be the property of the Crown, it, and not Aboriginal communities, had the control of their protection or disposal. Thus, the Larceny Act provided for the legal excavation of burials with the approval of the lieutenant governor.[6]

In 1892, the national Criminal Code ruled that it was unlawful to interfere with any dead body or remains. In 1906, the code encompassed the earlier Larceny Act (omitting the inducement, purchase of stolen items, and Crown ownership clauses), finally making the disturbance of Aboriginal graves a national crime.[7] But these laws had little effect on the excavations of graves in Ontario. Commenting on the Criminal Code in 1907, J. Hugh Hammond confessed that he knew of its provisions but seemed to think the biggest danger was the potential bribery farmers might demand in order not to notify the authorities. Writing to William Holmes of the Bureau of American Ethnology, Hammond promised that "As soon as the Spring comes I will send you some [skulls] if I can keep clear of the Criminal Code which my friend the farmer if he thought he had a ghost of a show would put into force to squeeze a few shekels out of yours truly." Even this possibility he did not consider to be overly distressing, for he concluded that "I am not easily terrified I have gone on these quests before and got off safely likely will do so again."[8] Indeed, there were few tests of the legislation, but the following cases demonstrate the lack of seriousness with which various levels of government enforced these laws, and the ways in which Euro-Canadians qualified the disturbances of Aboriginal burials.

In his 1853 memoirs, Samuel Strickland, an Upper Canadian magistrate, described the disturbance of a child's grave. Isaac Iron and his family had buried one of their children at Deer Bay and, upon returning a few years later, discovered the grave violated and the child's skull mounted on a stick nearby. Although Strickland expressed his personal horror, as a justice of the peace he could not act without proof of the offender's identity. Unfortunately, Iron suspected but could not ultimately swear that he knew the perpetrator. But Strickland also suggested that there was a difference between the disturbance of ancient and recent burials, commenting that, "If the person who disturbed the remains of Isaac's child had, out of mere curiosity, opened the grave, not knowing but that it was an ancient tomb, some excuse might be offered."[9]

Several decades later, another case brought much wider spread attention, but the outcome was similar. In 1897, George Dorsey, a curator of the Field Columbian Museum of Chicago, flagrantly ravaged burials on the northwest coast. Dorsey was arrested, but, when he promised restitution, the charges were dismissed.[10] Aboriginal protests led the Reverend John Keen, a missionary at Masset on the Queen Charlotte Islands, to write to Victoria's *Daily Colonist* newspaper to condemn Dorsey's actions. "The Indians told me," Keen wrote, "they found that almost every grave had been rifled, and the boxes which contained the bodies left strewn about. In one case some hair, recognized as having belonged to an Indian doctor, and a box which had contained a body, were found floating in the sea."[11] Keen's letter brought the matter to the attention of the anthropological community of North America, and the response is significant. Franz Boas of the American Museum of Natural History and one of the most influential anthropologists at the time, noted that he himself had robbed graves but had never raised such conflict. This was a fine distinction, since two of Boas's agents had been arrested for graverobbing in British Columbia, but again the charges had been dropped. Boas was seemingly more upset at the attention than at Dorsey's act. Graverobbing was "most unpleasant work," he wrote in his diary, but "someone has to do it."[12] In Ontario, while George Dawson of the Geological Survey was outraged over Dorsey's actions, David Boyle attempted to defend his colleague. Even the fact that Dorsey had plundered graves only thirty years old did not seem to faze him.[13]

The Indian Act did not prohibit the destruction of graves or other archaeological sites. When protests arose, the Department of Indian Affairs (DIA) evaluated each case based on the intent of the collector. In 1892, when James Coyne of the Elgin Historical and Scientific

Institute and a few colleagues excavated burial mounds on the Walpole Island reserve, the DIA tolerated the community protests it caused because Coyne argued the dig had been a scientific endeavour. Of individuals looking for curios the DIA was less tolerant. In 1898, one A.J. McCordie was arrested for removing a skull from a grave near Alberni on Vancouver Island. It must have been a fairly recent burial for there was still flesh attached to the skull. McCordie had decided to procure the skull to send as a present to a friend but later changed his mind and disposed of it in a canal, where an Aboriginal individual discovered it. McCordie was charged under Section 352 of the Criminal Code. Prosecutors Langley and Martin condemned McCordie's theft stating that "We disapprove of the indiscriminate gathering of the remains of the dead, even those of Indians" and recommended to all Indian agents that the law should be "strictly enforced." Indian Affairs Superintendent A.W. Vowell agreed, noting that Aboriginal people were very sensitive about the disturbance of their dead relatives. He further recognized that many curio-hunters and scientists dug up graves but lamented that evidence was difficult to find. This fact, plus McCordie's retention of a good lawyer, resulted in a fine of ten dollars rather than a recommendation of a jail sentence.[14] Still, McCordie's punishment was lenient. Ten dollars was a relatively small amount; the mean yearly income of adult males in British Columbia in 1901 equalled $781 dollars, and the Criminal Code allowed a maximum fine of $100.[15]

If there was little legislation to protect Aboriginal graves, historical and scientific societies did not possess official or ethical policies regarding gravedigging either. In 1872, when discussing Russell's 1797 proclamation, Henry Scadding included a poetic stanza that asked for the graves of the "noble race" to be spared, but this seemed to be more a rhetorical than heartfelt request.[16] Certainly the Canadian Institute deplored the random destruction of burials by the public. In 1852, its council "distinctly disown[ed] any wish or desire to disturb native burial places of comparatively recent date, and strongly recommended they be treated with respect," although the exact meaning of "recent" was left undefined. In the institute's 1886–87 *Proceedings*, David Boyle lamented the desecration of graves "for the purpose of satisfying a craving for curiosities."[17] Both of these statements suggest a condemnation of non-scientific research rather than any empathy with Aboriginal peoples and their feelings toward the excavation of their ancestors' resting places. Throughout his employment as curator of the Canadian Institute and the Provincial Museum, Boyle accepted donations of skeletal specimens from collectors across North America, and himself excavated burials all over Ontario, though these seem to have been more of an ancient origin than those plundered by Dorsey.

Arthur Harvey, another member of the Canadian Institute, believed that Aboriginal graves should be as respected as Euro-Canadian burials and protected by the government. But like Boyle and the DIA, he qualified this statement by distinguishing between amateur and scientific excavation. Not surprisingly, Harvey argued that control of graves should favour the interests of science and that government funding to professional groups would ensure no disrespect would be shown to Aboriginal remains.[18] Protection, in this sense then, meant stopping excavation by amateur curio-hunters, not from scientific professionals. The presumption was that museums or the members of historical societies - not amateurs, or even Aboriginal communities - were the proper stewards of Aboriginal graves. G.W. Bruce, an officer of the Huron Institute in Collingwood agreed. Part of the Huron Institute's mandate was to preserve Aboriginal interments from "indiscriminate rooting" by placing the research under "intelligent supervision," presumably that of its own members.[19] Certainly, the commonplace exhibition of human remains and grave goods as a matter of science at the Canadian Institute and the Ontario Provincial Museum would have suggested to members of other societies that gravedigging was a justifiable scientific and educational activity.

## PERCEPTIONS OF DEATH AND THE DEAD

For some, particularly scientists and physicians, the excavation and study of human remains could be separated from religious beliefs or emotions that might cause others to be offended. Anatomical dissection, an increasing part of Canadian medical education at the turn of the twentieth century, taught students to dehumanize and view bodies with a sense of detachment. Medical students also learned from anatomical and pathological teaching museums, which included skeletal material and tissue preserved as wet specimens in jars.[20] Many Euro-Canadians believed in the Cartesian dichotomy of body and soul, which meant that, once dead, the body was simply the discarded shell of the more important soul, which had moved on to exist purely in a spiritual realm.[21] Consequently, scientists and doctors could choose to see Aboriginal skeletons not as human remains from desecrated graves but as specimens or educational material to be looked at with dispassion.

The language used by the prosecuting lawyers and the DIA in the McCordie legal case is also revealing. The lawyers disapproved of the indiscriminate collecting and treatment of human remains, "even those" that were Aboriginal. Vowell condemned McCordie's treatment of the skull as showing "little consideration as though it had been the head of a dog or of a cat and not that of a human being albeit an Indian!" Such comments suggest that grave disturbances of non-Aboriginal remains would have been considered much more seriously. Whether one believed in Darwinism or earlier Enlightenment thought, the common nineteenth-century view that Aboriginal peoples were of a lesser race, or of a lesser evolved stage of human evolution, could be used to justify this differential treatment of the dead.[22] As the scholars of graverobbing and dissection have shown, the bodies of minorities and the marginalized were buried as people and extracted as resources.[23]

It was also more commonplace in the nineteenth century to have physical reminders of the dead in everyday life. In the Victorian period, families valued mementoes to honour or remember the dead, which consoled them in their grief. These could be photographs taken after the death of loved ones, which would assure the family that the departed were now at peace, as portrayed by the atmosphere in the picture; or jewellery and decorative items made of physical remains such as the deceased's intricately woven hair.[24] Perhaps the skulls that the public placed in their living areas, as in the Bradford case, can be contextualized in this way as well.

Naturally, ministers, missionaries, and strong followers of Christianity were more likely to protest the disturbance of Aboriginal burials as Reverend John Keen did. These men and women often emphasized the equal human rights of Aboriginal peoples, even as they believed that First Nations needed to be assimilated into mainstream culture. Christianity did not suggest that the human soul stayed with its physical body after death, as many Aboriginal peoples believed, but that it was resurrected and lived in an afterlife. But some Christians, those, for example, who disagreed with cremation in the nineteenth century, believed that the body needed to be preserved in order to be resurrected. For these individuals, the collection and distribution of human remains would prevent an afterlife in heaven.[25]

The traditional spirituality of Iroquoian- and Algonkian-speaking peoples provides alternative beliefs about death and the dead. Our earliest understanding of the Iroquoian perception of bodies and burials, particularly the ritual of the Feast of the Dead, emanates from the *Jesuit Relations*. According to the Wendat, after death, bones (*atisken* or "souls") retain a sentient presence. Humans possess two souls: one leaves the body after the Feast of the Dead, but the other remains with the physical body forever, unless it is reborn as a child. These souls require care even after death, and the disturbance of their buried remains is dangerous because it angers the dead. Father Gabriel Sagard wrote that the disruption or removal of items from graves was offensive and courted a "cruel and painful death."[26]

One of the most noted ways to care for souls was through the Feast of the Dead or *yandatsa*, which was described by Father Jean de Brébeuf. The Wendat and Tionontati (Petun) conducted this ritual every eight to twelve years in respect of those who had passed. The Neutral also held Feasts of the Dead, though less frequently. During the ten-day ceremony, Iroquoian peoples unearthed single interments, washed the bones, decorated them with jewellery, feasted in their honour, and reburied them in a large pit lined with fur and bark. On the last morning of the ceremony, the families arranged and mixed the bones of their dead with great care. Gifts, food to be eaten on the way to the afterlife, tools for hunting, and prestige items marking individual status were added to the ossuary. After contact, as trade with the French increased, these presents included items such as iron axes and other metal tools, copper pots, and glass beads. After 1580, as wealth increased through European trade, Wendat burials became more elaborate in gifts and the largest in number of people, sometimes reaching one thousand individuals in one ossuary. Although the Haudenosaunee partly dispersed the Wendat and Tionontati in the mid-1600s, they continued the Feast of the Dead in their new homes.

While the *Jesuit Relations* mainly describe the Feast of the Dead among Iroquoian-speaking peoples, the Nipissing and the Odawa conducted their own version of this ceremony.[27] As well, the Haudenosaunee maintained similar spiritual beliefs as recorded by twentieth-century anthropologists. Working for the Geological Survey, Frederick W. Waugh attended a ceremony similar to the Feast of the Dead at the Oneida on the Thames reserve in 1912. In the 1930s, Frank Speck observed the ritual conducted by the Gayogoho:no (Cayuga) of the Six Nations of the Grand River. In the 1940s, Simeon Gibson of Six Nations told William Fenton that when a group of Gayogoho:no had previously moved to another spot on the Grand River reserve, a Feast of the Dead had been held to let their ancestors interred in a cemetery know that they were leaving. Many Onondage'ga' (Onondaga) who moved from Middleport to a more southern spot on the reserve did the same. Fenton and Gertrude Kurath recorded similar ceremonies in the mid-twentieth century.[28] In the 1950s, Annemarie Shimony confirmed that the Grand River community still held dead feasts. She noted that even families who subscribed to Christianity conducted the ritual because they felt guilty if only a Christian funeral had been performed.[29] Fenton and Kurath also noted the commonly held belief that one soul remains in the community of the living and needs "propitiation" through tobacco, food, song, dance, and other gifts.[30]

These ongoing beliefs suggest why the Iroquoian-speaking peoples in Ontario would be angry at burial excavations. In his 1881 book Tuscarora Chief Elias Johnson expressed his anger over such incidents. Euro-Canadians expected Aboriginal peoples to "look merely on while the graves of their fathers were robbed of their treasures, and the bones of their fathers were left to bleach upon the fields," he wrote. But instead, they were "fierce with indignation and rage, on seeing themselves treated as without human feeling, and the sacred relics of the dead ploughed up and scattered as indifferently as the stones, or the bones of the moose and the deer of the forest."[31]

Algonkian-speaking peoples held similar spiritual beliefs around the death, burial, and disturbance of their ancestors. Basil Johnston, a contemporary Anishinabeg writer, provides one account of the origin of their burial rites. His version begins with an Ojibwa man named Beedut or Coming Storm, who had been injured during a skirmish with their traditional enemies, the Dakota. While Beedut lay wounded, his spirit met another, who gave him the proper protocol to bury the dead. Beedut was eventually found still alive, and upon recovery told his people of these rituals, which they promised to perform after every death. All warriors should be buried in a sitting position, facing west, and wearing battle clothes and with weapons nearby, in order to fight the enemy if necessary. For four days, mourners were to sit near the grave with a fire burning to keep the soul and the spirit of the person warm as the individual travelled to the land of the souls. The spirit that Beedut met said that if people were not buried in such a way, their spirits would wander.

In this and other stories about "Pagidaendijigewin" or the "Ritual of the Dead," the Ojibwa were also told to bury the dead with food for their travels to the afterlife, cover the grave with a lodge of birch bark anchored with stones in which the soul and spirit could find shelter, and erect a post over the grave carved with their totem upside-down. A widow should visit her husband's grave every night for a year to mourn.[32] Some versions of these rituals included the celebration of an annual Feast of the Dead, during which the dead were resurrected and reburied in a common grave.[33]

In the mid-nineteenth century, the Mississauga Methodist missionary Peter Jones recorded similar burial rituals of his people. The dead were to be buried wearing their best clothes, wrapped in skins or blankets, and laid alongside their hunting, war, and personal items such as a bow and arrow, gun, pipe and tobacco, knife, kettle, and medicine bag. The grave would be covered with earth, and then by a small house made of bark or mats laid over poles. Mourners then sat in a circle at the head of the gravesite, offering meat, soup, and alcohol to the soul by burning these items in a fire. For one year, the spouse or relatives of the dead would daily offer food to their loved one. Jones also described a funeral at Munceytown during which the coffin was bored with several holes for the soul to move in and out at will.[34]

Informants shared similar beliefs and rituals with Frances Densmore in her early twentieth-century Bureau of American Ethnology study of American Ojibwa (Chippewa) communities. They told Densmore that the dead should have personal items buried with them to use during their four-day trip to the afterworld and have food left nearby the grave. A fire burned for these four days next to the grave for warmth and to allow for cooking of the food. The grave was to be covered with a small birchbark house, or, in later times, one made from lumber. A gravemarker with the person's totem documented the ancestry of the individual and the fact that it was carved upside-down indicated death.[35]

Diamond Jenness, another anthropologist of the Geological Survey, recorded much the same information in his 1935 ethnography of the social and religious life of the Ojibwa of Parry Island. In his fieldwork, he discovered that tobacco was placed in the hand of the dead so the soul could pay for its passage across the river of death on the way to the afterlife. The souls of any other object placed in the grave would also be used by the dead in the afterlife. If a person died in the winter, Jenness documented, the body would be placed above ground over which a miniature wigwam or, in more recent times, a grave house would be built. Later, relatives would return to bury the individual in the ground. Jenness also added that this local community believed that even after the soul left the body of the dead, his shadow (seemingly the spirit as discussed by Johnston) continued to hover near its grave. Thus, the Parry Island Ojibwa feared the despoilation or the taking of items from graves in case the shadow took offence and caused the disturber harm. Those who travelled by graves often left offerings of food and tobacco for the shadow.[36]

Peter Jones also described the methods with which the Mississauga kept away the spirits of the dead and encouraged them to move on to the afterlife. If a husband had died, a woman could leap over the grave and run in a zigzag pattern through surrounding trees to lose her spouse's spirit. Men could fire guns at night and women could knock and rattle the family's wigwam to scare away the dead. Inside the wigwam, hanging folded shapes of thin birchbark that moved in the air served the same purpose. To protect children, Jones said one could singe the hair from a deer's tail and rub it on their faces, and the smell would keep away the dead.[37] All these stories suggest that Anishinabeg peoples believed that the dead or their spirits needed to be treated with care and that disturbance of burials could result in community or personal harm.

## REACTIONS TO ARCHAEOLOGICAL EXCAVATIONS

Accordingly, many Aboriginal peoples in Ontario were upset with the disturbance of their ancestral graves by Ontario collectors, whether or not they were engaged in a scientific endeavour or a quest for curios. But some Aboriginal individuals participated in burial excavations, or gathered burial goods including human remains for their own collections. There are only a few documented cases, but they illustrate the variety of perspectives held by Aboriginal and Euro-Canadian individuals.

After the Mississauga protests that led to Russell's 1797 proclamation, the next recorded instance of burial disturbance occurred near Lake Simcoe in the 1830s. Although the cultural affiliation of the graves is unknown, an Anishinabeg band protested the removal of a skull and "trinkets" from a burial by a surgeon and his companion. The next morning, an Aboriginal individual confronted one of the men, and the "whole tribe were in commotion," resulting in Indian Superintendent Captain Thomas G. Anderson reporting the matter to the "Governor." The opinions of DIA officials are unknown, but the Reverend George Hallen, who recorded the conflict in 1835, thought the excavation "impudent" and "unfeeling." This particular incident was such a "serious business," Hallen said, that these burials had not been touched since.[38]

In 1870, the Haudenosaunee requested that Thomas Barnett, the owner of the Niagara Falls Museum, rebury an exhibited Anishinabeg skeleton, presumably because they found its display offensive. They also felt reburial would be a sign of reconciliation with their traditional enemies. In June, one thousand people attended the ceremony, which included the display of a closed coffin on a dais, funeral addresses by Seneca Johnson of Grand River and a Chief Cusick of the New York Tuscarora, songs, a "war dance," and a ritual joining of two wampum strings, which signified peace between the Haudenosaunee and the Anishinabeg. The skeleton was finally placed in a ten-foot pyramidal vault within the garden of the museum. Needing a relative to transfer the spirit to the Creator as custom dictated, the Haudenosaunee representatives elected and named Barnett "The Good Word." Dressed in feathers and war paint, carrying war clubs and bows and arrows, twenty chiefs in all attended the funeral, including John Buck, Isaac and Alexander Hill and Henry Williams of Six Nations of the Grand River, and Samson Chew and Simon Cusic of the Tuscarora nation in New York. Unfortunately we do not know how the Aboriginal participants viewed this mix of tradition and elaborate spectacle, but their original request likely came from their religious views about death. In contrast, Barnett used the opportunity to organize an exotic public event and published a description of the reburial ceremony in a tourist pamphlet, "Visitors to Niagara," to promote his museum.[39]

In 1886, Andrew Hunter recorded in one of his field notebooks a story of Aboriginal reactions to excavations. Peter Yorke, one of his Ojibwa informants, told him that Aboriginal people were "superstitious" and therefore disapproved of strangers digging up relics, but he also admitted that sometimes they did pair with excavators. Yorke himself had dug in the company of Aboriginal individuals at the old Jesuit fort on Christian Island, the last haven of the Wendat before dispersal. In one instance, he sold metal items found there to a collector. During another excursion, Yorke had been chased around the island, seeking refuge with the lighthouse keeper, in order to prevent from being shot at by other Aboriginals. Yorke, however, was not a popular member of the community since he had been accused of taking a large amount of a government grant to his band, and it is unclear whether the fracas was caused by the excavation or by personal dislike.[40]

During his 1890–91 fieldwork season, David Boyle received assistance from several Aboriginal individuals, including some who had dug up burials themselves. That summer, Boyle and two colleagues, A.F. Chamberlain and Dr T.A. Beeman (a relative of T.W. Beeman), visited a small village on an island in Lake Baptiste, an area known to possess archaeological sites. Here, the three collectors met François Antoine, or Ag-wah-setch, originally from the Oka reserve, and engaged his son Jean Baptiste to take them by canoe to a spot called Grassy Point at which objects had been previously found by others. After only superficially examining this area, Antoine suggested visiting a cave his grandfather had told him was used by their ancestors to conceal weapons. Whether or not any artifacts were found here went unrecorded, but the senior Antoine did give to Boyle several stone pieces he had found previously and an example of porcupine quillwork that had belonged to his father.[41]

That same year, Boyle also visited the Powles Baptiste farm on the Grand River reserve near Brantford. He had been alerted to the spot by Dr Peter Edmund Jones of the neighbouring Mississauga of the New Credit community. Jones, the son of the Methodist missionary Peter Jones, was a collector himself and thought a pottery-making site had once been located on the Baptiste property. Boyle hired Baptiste and three other Aboriginal individuals to help him dig for two days. Questioned by Boyle, Baptiste revealed that he had uncovered an ossuary when he dug his cellar. He was able to describe the complex placement of the seventeen skeletons, suggesting that he did not stop digging as soon as he detected the human remains. But it is curious that Boyle did not describe how Baptiste proceeded after discovering the bones. Surely Boyle would have commented on their donation to a museum or lamented as usual about the destructiveness of amateur archaeology, so perhaps Baptiste reburied the skeletons. Boyle did remark upon the reaction of Baptiste and the labourers to the discovery of other human remains. He stated that they "exhibited no superstitious fears," but their silence could have equalled discomfort as well.[42]

An instance of gravedigging on the Walpole Island reserve in 1892 further illustrates the different viewpoints within Aboriginal peoples and among Aboriginal communities, archaeologists, and the DIA toward archaeology. Methodist Minister Jeremiah W. Annis of Chatham had arranged with Chief Joseph White and Reverend William Elias, the Aboriginal minister for Walpole Island, to excavate burial mounds on the reserve. Annis invited James Coyne, founder and president of the Elgin Historical and Scientific Institute of St Thomas, to accompany them. One mound, located at the north end of Walpole Island, was well known, likely because of its size: approximately sixty to seventy feet in diameter and a height of six feet. Annis also likely knew of its existence through his familiarity with the community. Elias, White, and a neighbour—all Aboriginal individuals—did the actual digging under Annis's supervision, who had obtained printed excavation instructions from the Smithsonian Institution. Excavating it from the outside to the centre, they found there a large animal skull. The next discovery was a human skull, depicted by Coyne as "evidently belonging to the warrior or chief who had been deemed worthy of so notable a tomb." The men were in the midst of examining this skull when they were confronted by a community member. This was John Yahnodt, a Potawatomi, who by Coyne's description, "snatched" the skull, "threw it back" into the mound and began to refill the excavation "in a fury of rage, whilst abusing us all in the most violent manner for disturbing the remains of his 'ancestor.'"[43]

Subsequently, Yahnodt and Chief Ashkebee officially complained to their Indian Agent Alexander McKelvey, who referred the matter to the Department of Indian Affairs and to the Anglican Bishop Maurice Baldwin in London. Yahnodt and Ashkebee also wrote a petition to the DIA requesting an end to gravedigging for "all time."[44] The DIA instructed McKelvey to write a letter to Annis asking for an explanation of the incident; in turn, he asked Coyne to respond to the department. The agent was also directed to question Reverend Elias. McKelvey accidentally met Elias in the local post office and, upon showing him this Indian Affairs correspondence, feelings turned from acrimonious to violent. Elias later accused McKelvey of striking him in the face and attempting to push him through a window in order to snatch back the letter from his hands.[45]

The response of the collectors illustrates common nineteenth-century thinking about archaeology from a scientific perspective. Annis addressed the issue by asserting their credibility as conscientious citizens and accomplished scientists. Annis explained that the excavation had been conducted under the supervision of Coyne, who was not only Elgin County registrar but president of the Elgin Historical and Scientific Institute. Both gentlemen had intensively studied the Aboriginal groups of Ontario, therefore they perceived their investigations to be conducted in the "interests of science."[46] Coyne echoed these sentiments and even called their visit "harmless."[47] Five years later, Coyne wrote to Ontario Minister of Education George Ross and argued that the skulls that had been reburied by Yahnodt were of "considerable value, archaeologically," and needed to be preserved at the Provincial Museum.[48]

Using an argument common to anthropological collectors, Coyne also stated that the skeletons found at Walpole Island were not biologically related to the current residents. Instead, he believed the tumuli to be remnants of the Moundbuilder culture that had preceded the Walpole community by centuries; it was "in no way connected with the present races," Coyne wrote. Despite this allegedly ancient origin, Coyne acknowledged that Yahnodt "appeared to have a vague idea that it was of … sentimental value to the tribe" or that he calculated the burials to have a monetary worth.[49] But as Yahnodt had said at the time of the confrontation, the complainants called the skeletons "our dead," suggesting that he, Ashkebee, and perhaps others believed them to be their ancestors. In contrast, Elias reported that oral tradition designated them as their enemies not their forefathers.[50] This designation was also later reported by Coyne, who said that once Yahnodt had calmed down at the excavation site, he acknowledged those buried there were Onodowahgah (Seneca), not his ancestors but rather their traditional enemies. Coyne used this to further reinforce his opinion that the people buried in the mound were not related to the current residents of Walpole Island, especially since he said that Yahnodt knew nothing of the history of the grave.[51] Finally, Annis and Elias used another common argument to vindicate their actions: they suggested the mounds were not graves in a literal sense, since they were not situated in an official cemetery. Similarly, they deemed other nearby burials as "unenclosed" and "entirely neglected."[52]

Annis and Coyne also justified their excavations based on factors of respect, assent, and ownership. Coyne stated that graves dug up near the Council House were very respectfully treated.[53] Both men declared that one site had been excavated many times before, as if this implied implicit consent by the Walpole Island community, and, as it was located near an excursion spot, Annis assumed the mound would be visited by future tourists also looking to dig. As well, they said that Agent McKelvey had permitted the excavations, and, though the landowner was absent, his brother who resided next door had agreed to the digging and even conducted most of the labour himself. Lastly, the presence of Chief Joseph White was considered to be a form of approval.[54]

Both Annis and Coyne dismissed the complaint as a genuine concern for the disturbance of the interred human remains, ancestral or otherwise. They felt their visit had been greatly exaggerated and posited a few other theories to explain the protests by John Yahnodt and Chief Ashkebee. Coyne suggested someone was trying to anger the chief, while Annis proposed that the petition was part of a prevailing quarrel of Chief Ashkebee and John Yahnodt with William Elias.[55]

Annis wrote that he was sure that, had the DIA understood the facts, it would have found the Aboriginal complaint "unwarranted and untrue."[56] Indeed Indian Affairs did eventually take the side of the excavators. At first, McKelvey had admitted that the archaeologists had not asked either the department or the Walpole residents for permission to dig and called it "repugnant to the feelings of the Indians," an opinion that Indian Affairs believed to be justified.[57] Both the archaeologists and the DIA presumed the burial sites and their contents to be the property of the department, rather than important cultural sites or ancestors stewarded by the Walpole community, the opinion expressed by the complainants. In the exchange of letters between the archaeologists and Indian Affairs, Annis and Coyne apologized to the officials of the DIA for not seeking their permission before their visit.[58] Later, in Coyne's correspondence to Education Minister George Ross, he suggested the understanding of the Walpole community would be needed for future explorations, but no apologies were ever extended to the Walpole Island residents.[59] In the end, McKelvey agreed that Coyne and Annis had not intended to desecrate the graves and had "innocent" motives. In the future, however, he recommended formal permission be sought, adding that the department would "always be glad to aid competent scientists."[60]

In some cases, the Euro-Canadian public was also horrified at the disturbance of Aboriginal graves. In their dealings with Aboriginal peoples, the extended Strickland-Moodie-Traill family seemed to possess genuine empathy and human compassion for Aboriginal peoples. In addition to the attempts of Samuel Strickland to aid Isaac Iron in prosecuting the individual who violated the grave of Iron's daughter, the Aboriginal bones discovered during the logging bee at the house of Strickland's sister Susanna Moodie were reinterred "where there was little chance of their being disturbed," although only after it was ascertained that few relics were buried with it.[61] Strickland's other sister, Catharine Parr Traill, also expressed concern about more recent Aboriginal burials. In 1893, hearing of the sale of an island in Stony Lake where Polly Cow, a "poor Indian girl," was buried, she wrote to the DIA to see if she could purchase it in order to protect the grave from desecration. It should be "held sacred," she wrote in her short piece "The Indian Maiden's Grave." It had, however, been earlier desecrated and the skull taken by a collector. Traill's request was granted on behalf of her contributions to Canadian literature and the publication of information of benefit to immigrants, but not because of the need to protect Aboriginal burials.[62]

In other cases, public anger about the disturbance of Aboriginal burials seemed only to rise over those famous individuals, such as Joseph Brant and Tecumseh, who were considered to be heroes in the broader scope of British and Upper Canadian history. Nineteenth-century historical societies and communities spent much time and money honouring and decorating the graves of United Empire Loyalists and the non-Aboriginal soldiers of the War of 1812. As an important Aboriginal leader and ally of the British during the American Revolution who later settled in Upper Canada, Ontario residents often included Joseph Brant as one of their military heroes. Brant's original grave was located on the property of St Paul's, Her Majesty's Chapel of the Mohawks on the Six Nations reserve near Brantford. When citizens heard that it "seemed forbidden to remain undisturbed; and in its unprotected condition was exposed ... to the depredations of the animals who grazed upon the common," these conditions were judged "a disgrace to Canada" since Brant was a "celebrated Indian Chief – one of the most valiant and distinguished military leaders." A widespread appeal for redress resulted in the erection of a tomb at the Mohawk chapel and the reinterment of Brant's bones in November 1850 at the partial expense of the public. Great festivities, including speeches, a gun salute over the tomb, and a procession of schoolchildren, Freemasons, the Brantford band, Odd Fellows, Orangemen, the mayor, and Sir Allan MacNab accompanied this occasion.[63] Brant's new grave still suffered depredations from relic hunters, including the destruction by one tourist who "hacked the tomb until there was a large hole in it." Finally in 1879, the Council of the Six Nations of the Grand River reserve erected a six-foot iron fence for its protection. How successful this measure was in deterring collectors is uncertain, for in 1899 the grave was still described as having a "chipped appearance."[64]

Numerous attempts to locate and excavate the bones of Tecumseh also infuriated Ontario residents, many of whom wished to erect a monument in honour of this warrior of 1812.[65] This story also demonstrates the divisions within and between Aboriginal and non-Aboriginal communities over the excavation of graves. The idea to find Tecumseh's burial originated with US supporters of William Henry Harrison during his presidential campaign of 1840, who wished to honour him by collecting artifacts from his military triumphs over Aboriginal groups. The resulting excavation in Ontario was met with outrage, and a condemnation by the Montreal Gazette, although it seemed unlikely that the bones found were, in fact, Tecumseh's. A year later, inspired by a burst of patriotism caused by the supposed US-led destruction of Sir Isaac Brock's monument at Queenston Heights, a Canadian committee was established to erect a monument for Tecumseh. Subsequently, various communities and historical societies took up the cause to erect a monument near Tecumseh's grave or at a place deemed honourable for his reinterment.

One of these groups was the United Canadian Association, whose general mandate was to boost Canadian nationalism. Members of this association conferred with Chief George H.M. Johnson of the Six Nations of the Grand River reserve in 1876. Johnson apparently owned a map that indicated the location of Tecumseh's burial based on the oral tradition given to him by Ockawandah, a Shawnee man who lived at Six Nations. This location was confirmed by Timothy Snake of Moraviantown, who claimed he had been present at Tecumseh's burial. These directions indeed led to *a* grave, its alleged authenticity further confirmed by two men from the reserve at Moraviantown shortly after the United Canadians began excavation. The Canadians stopped their dig when it grew dark and did not return until several months later, when they procured a skeleton and a few items buried with it.

This excavation led to local opposition, not against gravedigging itself, but against the removal of Tecumseh's bones and the erection of a monument at another spot. Others claimed this was not the remains of Tecumseh at all. In contrast, those at Moraviantown and the Grand General Indian Council, a body of various representatives of First Nations in Ontario, approved of the excavation of Tecumseh's remains. Later, however, the United Canadians heard that Timothy Snake had said that Tecumseh was buried elsewhere, on the farm of Chief Jacobs. Jacobs led the United Canadians to a spot on his property, allowed them to dig and when it appeared unlikely that the remains found were Tecumseh, he still presented the bones to the party. The United Canadians were then shortly accused of ransacking a Christian missionary's grave, for Chief Jacobs's property included the cemetery of the Fairfield Moravian mission. Despite the outrage, the United Canadians said Jacobs had the right to dispose of the bones as he wished because he owned the property. In the meantime, the bones obtained from the original site had been examined by Daniel Wilson, who proclaimed them to be an assortment of animal and human bones. Wilson suggested that the gap of time between the first and second excavation had allowed the swapping of remains by individuals at Moraviantown.

Another excavation occurred at Walpole Island in 1910. A party of men from the Wallaceburg Board of Trade and individuals from the reserve together uncovered a grave, once again assumed to be that of Tecumseh. Fearful of graverobbers once the news of the discovery had spread, the men from Wallaceburg asked for possession of the bones. The Aboriginal individuals reluctantly turned over the skeleton to Dr George Mitchell of Wallaceburg, a member of the excavation party, with the stipulation that it be returned upon request. Shortly afterward, Chief Joseph White, presumably the same individual who accompanied J.W. Annis, William Elias, and James Coyne on their excavations at Walpole, visited Mitchell and asked for the bones to be returned. In 1931, these bones supposedly resurfaced, found in a burlap bag in White's attic after his death. Upon investigation, White's stepson informed the interested parties that these bones were not really part of Tecumseh's skeleton, but rather items White had used to deceive excavators; really, it was said that White had moved Tecumseh's actual bones several times on his property to prevent their discovery.

In the meantime, the 1910 search for Tecumseh caused another uproar. A Moraviantown resident wrote an open letter to a London newspaper objecting to the disturbance of this grave, and argued that it was not the burial of Tecumseh in any case. Further, the Macaulay Historical Society of Chatham believed that the bones should be "reverently replaced" not ghoulishly examined. The Wentworth Historical Society, alerted to this incident, passed a resolution similarly condemning this "act of Vandalism."[66] The Macaulay club, however, may have possessed the underlying motive of wishing to have a monument to Tecumseh in Chatham rather than in Wallaceburg.[67] It seems unlikely, however, that the Wentworth group, based in Hamilton, protested on the basis of wishing to have the monument in a city so removed from the area of Tecumseh's death.

The search for Tecumseh's grave, and the battling historical, mythical, and Aboriginal oral traditions that suggested its location continued until a cairn was erected at Walpole Island in 1941 with a reinterment of one supposed set of Tecumseh's bones, and another monument and plaque erected by the Historic Sites and Monuments Board in the 1960s in a park near the site of the Battle of the Thames. The divisions over the excavation and reinterment of Tecumseh's skeleton and the memorialization of his military efforts were always coloured by political motives, but it is also clear that there was little consensus over the disturbance of graves. While many historical societies and Ontario communities expressed eagerness to locate and excavate Tecumseh's grave as a way to honour him, the Wentworth Historical Society, and perhaps the Macaulay group, disapproved of the idea as an act of vandalism. Regarding the Aboriginal position, whether or not Chief George Johnson or Chief Jacobs believed the burials they pointed to were actually that of Tecumseh, neither appeared disturbed by the possibility that someone's resting place would be despoiled. Parts of the Moraviantown community and the Grand General Indian Council approved of the search for Tecumseh. Yet Chief Joseph White, and the two men who validated the first location of the grave dug up by the United Canadians, appeared to have participated in a complicated deception in order to stop the search. Members of the Moraviantown reserve also accused Chief George Johnson not only of leading the United Canadians to Tecumseh's secret burial but also of trying to profit financially from the information.[68]

## ABORIGINAL COLLECTORS

Aboriginal peoples also collected and displayed archaeological items, including human remains, for their own purposes. Throughout his career David Boyle received artifact donations from various Aboriginal individuals. While there is little context about these donations or Boyle's relationship with the donors, the accession lists for the Provincial Museum show these objects to include wampum, and a bird-shaped amulet found on the Oneida reserve by Johnson Paudash of the Hiawatha band; a Mississauga cradle and a slate gouge presented by Pashigeezhik (Richard Black), a student at Victoria College in Toronto; a stone pipe from the north shore of Lake Superior from Chief John Montague of Christian Island; and numerous archaeological items from John Bay (Wahsatch), a Haudenosaunee from the Akwesasne reserve, and from Jacob Hess of the Grand River reserve.[69]

There are also glimpses into Aboriginal collecting activity exemplified by the Indians of Ontario exhibit at London's Western Fair. Between 1888 and 1901, the Western Fair Association invited Aboriginal reserve communities to enter agricultural, household and handicraft items in this special exhibit approved by the DIA. Although there were no categories set aside for such items, Aboriginal individuals also brought archaeological items for display. These objects, such as stone axes and other tools, clay pipes, arrowheads, bone needles, corn grinders, and pottery pieces, likely had been discovered by Aboriginal farmers in their fields just as Euro-Canadian settlers had done.[70] No human remains were exhibited however. Unfortunately, reporters make no mention of the interpretation of these artifacts by the Aboriginal communities themselves, although it is curious that such items were included when the Department of Indian Affairs only wanted to showcase agricultural products as symbols of assimilation.

The Six Nations' own agricultural fair featured similar archaeological collections and may help contextualize the exhibits at the Western Fair. The Six Nations 1911 prize list included a category for Best Collection Numismatics, Indian, and Other Articles, Not Less than 25 Articles in the Miscellaneous Section. The 1922 and 1941 lists offered prizes for the Best Collection Indian Relics.[71] Though the Six Nations displayed such artifacts they presented a non-evolutionary interpretation. Speaking in general about handmade items past and present, a Six Nations Agricultural Society publication argued these objects demonstrated that "industry, patience, economy, endurance, originality and skill" were part of the Aboriginal character.[72] This statement contrasted with the Victorian idea that such items were simply rude remnants of an extinct or primitive culture.

Some Aboriginal individuals were serious collectors. These include Kanienkehakas Peter J. Maracle, the family of Chief George H.M. Johnson, Chief Alexander G. Smith (Dekanenraneh), Dr Oronhyatekha (Peter Martin), and the Anishinabeg doctor Peter Edmund Jones. Peter Maracle contacted Boyle in 1903 after learning that he was purchasing items for the Ontario Provincial Museum. He offered a few hundred arrow points, a skinning stone, and stone pipes, as well as ethnographic items.[73] Clearly he had built his own personal collection. The children of George H.M. Johnson also collected, although most of their items were ethnographic rather than archaeological in nature. As an adult, his daughter Evelyn reminisced that she, her sister, E. Pauline, and their brothers played with human skulls in their garret at their home of Chiefswood. The skulls had been washed into the Grand River from a burial ground. When the family moved into Brantford after the death of the George Johnson, they left them behind, but apparently they had no spiritual objections to handling human remains.[74]

Chief A.G. Smith had become involved in anthropology even before he met Boyle. In the 1880s, he had helped noted anthropologist Horatio Hale understand a traditional condolence ceremony at the Six Nations of the Grand River. At that time, he had asked Hale to recommend sources about Aboriginal peoples as he wished to build a personal library.[75] He was also elected as a corresponding secretary and honorary member of the Wentworth Historical Society in 1897.[76] Smith appears to have adopted the Victorian practice of establishing a personal collection and exhibiting it at provincial and agricultural exhibitions.[77] During the late nineteenth century, Boyle purchased from Smith over 150 archaeological pieces including stone, metal and bone tools, pipe parts, wampum, gorgets, pendants, beads, and pottery sherds for $105. Many of these items had been found on the Six Nations reserve.[78] This sale of items to Boyle saved these pieces: a house fire later that year consumed the remainder of the collection.[79]

Dr Oronhyatekha, or Peter Martin, is perhaps the best-known Aboriginal collector in Ontario. He was a Kanienkehaka from the Grand River reserve and was one of the first Aboriginal individuals in Canada to obtain a medical degree. After studying at several universities in the United States, at Oxford, and at the University of Toronto, he practiced medicine near the Tyendinaga reserve and in London. In 1881 he became the chief ranger of the Independent Order of Foresters. During his leadership, he built an eclectic museum collection that was

Chief Alexander General Smith, 1898

displayed in the Forester's temple in Toronto. In 1911, after his death, the order donated his artifacts to the future Royal Ontario Museum.

Dr Oronhyatekha's museum included typical Ontario archaeological artifacts from all over the province, including human remains and grave gifts. His catalogue lists three skulls from the Erie nation, two skulls from Canada, two skull gorgets, and an Egyptian mummy.[80] The grave goods included several arrowheads, a scalping knife and a stone axe from Walpole Island, a hunting knife found near Hamilton, an adze from Niagara Falls, a beaver jaw from Manitoulin Island, a pistol from Orillia, and a pipe head and a stone tomahawk from a mound near London. This last object had been originally discovered by Dr Solon Woolverton of the London and Middlesex Historical Society.[81] In fact, it is unlikely that Dr Oronhyatekha excavated most, if any, items; rather, many objects had been collected by George Mills McClurg. McClurg's success appears to have rested on the trust that other Aboriginal individuals placed in Oronhyatekha[82] but also on the relationships he himself built with many Anishinabeg people. McClurg acted as the general secretary and treasurer for the United Bands of the Chippewa and Mississauga but, perhaps more importantly, as their lawyer in obtaining compensation from the federal government for the violation of the 1850 Robinson treaties in Ontario. The United Bands clearly knew about Oronhyatekha's museum at the Forester's temple, because they met there in 1904.[83] Unfortunately, McClurg's papers only

contain one brief reference to additional objects.[84] Mary E. Rose Holden
of the Wentworth Historical Society may have also collected or organized Oronhyatekha's collection; in 1900, she told Boyle that she was at
the beck and call of the Foresters under Oronhyatekha.[85]

A newspaper review of the opening of the museum in 1902 stated
that, though McClurg collected and organized the museum, the thought
behind it was Dr Oronhyatekha's.[86] Unfortunately, he himself never
recorded his motives for collecting or, more specifically, his feelings
about the burial material in his museum. He may have been inspired
by the museums he had visited, which included the British Museum,
the Ashmolean in Oxford, and the Ontario Provincial Museum, as
well as by his association with Daniel Wilson of the Canadian Institute
in the 1860s.[87] Anthropologist Trudy Nicks asserts that the collection promoted a good corporate image for the Foresters and that
Oronhyatekha, as a man of two worlds, aimed to fulfill both Victorian
and Kanienkehaka cultural traditions. Keith Jamieson, who curated an
exhibit of Oronhyatekha's artifacts in 2002 agreed, as suggested by its
title: *Mohawk Ideals, Victorian Values*. His museum certainly reflected
the Victorian ideal of combining natural history, archaeology, and indigenous material from around the world for educational and scientific
purposes. F. Barlow Cumberland, who prepared the original catalogue
for the Foresters, further suggested that Dr Oronhyatekha would be
pleased that his collection aroused "an increased interest in history,
nature, and art, and beyond all, thought and reading in the Home,
the centre of every Forester's heart."[88] This comment implied that he
subscribed to the Victorian ideal of learning through collecting. But
Jamieson sees another, more traditional message behind Oronhyatekha's
collecting, particularly of the archaeological objects. Jamieson argues
that these specimens supported Aboriginal claims of their ancient presence in North America.[89]

Peter Jones, the Methodist missionary, also began a museum that
included archaeological and ethnographic material. Illustrations of pottery sherds, clay pipes, and various weapons from his collection appear
in his *History of the Ojebway Indians*, but little else is known about it.[90]
After inheriting his father's collection Dr Peter Edmund Jones expanded
it. A local resident of Hagersville remembered that Jones, also a taxi-
dermist, exhibited his animal specimens in his home so that "It was the
delight of many visitors to stroll past his window, or enter his abode, to
view the fascinating array of wild creatures."[91] Jones himself described
the collection of stuffed animals, coins, fossils, insects, old books, and

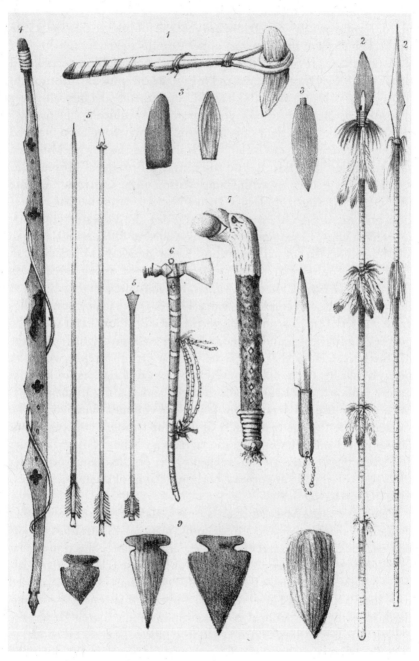

"Weapons of War," artifacts from the Peter Jones collection, c. 1861

Indian relics as making his home "a pleasant-one for friends to visit who have a taste for such things."[92]

P.E. Jones also knew David Boyle. Remember that he invited Boyle to the Powles Baptiste farm on the Grand River reserve to investigate what he thought to be a pottery-making site. Under Jones's guidance, Boyle investigated Baptiste's property and the surrounding area in 1890.[93] The museum catalogue shows that Jones donated numerous artifacts, seemingly found during his collaboration with Boyle in 1890.[94] Like A.G. Smith, he also displayed his collection at the 1893 World's Fair in Chicago.[95] In 1898, Jones also sold several items – stone tools, pottery sherds, and a clay pipe – to the Bureau of American Ethnology, now in the Smithsonian, some of which were found on his own New Credit reserve.[96]

Typical of Victorian collectors, Jones was possessive of his cabinet. He valued the twenty-nine books, paintings, and Anishinabeg ethnographic objects he lent to the 1899 Canadian Historical Exhibition in Toronto as "Inestimable. Minimum $500.00."[97] When Janet Carnochan, president of the Niagara Historical Society, asked Jones for artifact donations in 1898, he replied that "I cannot break my own collection." A few duplicates he owned only consisted of points and spearheads, so common that he supposed that Carnochan had such artifacts already represented. In the end, however, he did send a few items, some wampum, beads, and a gorget, with short descriptions.[98]

Fortunately, we know more about the purpose of Jones's collecting than of Dr Oronhyatekha's. He was a corresponding member of the Hamilton Association, read papers at its meetings, and may have been influenced by their mandate to collect archaeological objects.[99] In 1885, Jones established a bimonthly publication called *The Indian* to present Aboriginal biography, history, and archaeology along with agricultural and religious news.[100] In general, the paper proposed to "educate" and "elevate" Aboriginal people to the "social, agricultural, and commercial" level of Euro-Canadian society. The paper also advocated a society and museum in which to preserve artifacts. A modified version of the Canadian Institute's circular appeared in the very first issue of the serial, arguing that a museum was necessary to stop the flow of artifacts across the border into the United States. The newspaper therefore requested information about sites and collectors and donations of specimens, especially from farmers and teachers.[101] In the third volume, a report of the 1886 memorial to the Dominion government for funding presented by Boyle, Daniel Wilson and others reinforced this message.[102] *The Indian* proceeded to print papers by collectors such as Charles Hirschfelder and Andrew Hunter. While Jones did not personally author any articles on archaeological collecting, clearly his position was supportive of these endeavours of scientific education.

Explaining these Western-style motives as a result of his upbringing is ambiguous. Only one-quarter Mississauga by blood, Jones was raised by a Methodist minister father who was part Mississauga himself, and later by a governess. His formal education included the Brantford Grammar School, the University of Toronto, and Queen's College in Kingston. In 1873, he married Charlotte Dixon, a non-Aboriginal woman. On the other hand, for eleven years he served as head chief of the Mississaugas at the New Credit reserve and lived nearby the community in Hagersville. According to Donald Smith, Jones identified himself as Aboriginal, although perhaps more traditional members of New Credit did not.[103]

Like Dr Oronhyatekha, Peter E. Jones, the Johnson sisters, and A.G. Smith can all be considered to be individuals living in two worlds, Western and traditional, who encompassed traits of both. As such, their collecting and exhibiting activities have been recorded by their non-Aboriginal colleagues. Less is understood about the reaction to or participation in archaeology of the more anonymous Aboriginal peoples of Ontario due to the inadequacy of primary documents. There are no local newspapers or personal diaries for most communities. Indian Agent records rarely discuss any kind of archaeological activity. There are also numerous ambiguous or incompletely recorded incidents. For example, chiefs of the Tutelos, a group who lived at Six Nations of the Grand River, confronted corduroy roadworkers about to continue their work through a Neutral village site between Woodstock and Brantford in the nineteenth century.[104] We do not know what happened or how the Tutelos heard of the situation. The 1861 memoir by Upper Canadian resident John Carruthers recorded that Aboriginal individuals requested that a local farmer near Bradford stop his ploughing because a grave was known to be underneath.[105] In 1884, the Grand General Indian Council invited a Mr J. Grensell, a reporter from the Detroit *Free Press*, to address the gathering at the Cape Croker reserve. Grensell professed his belief in the civilized nature of Aboriginal peoples and his interest in them by recounting his archaeological exploits. Lately, he said, he had been present at the opening of a mound near Detroit that revealed various objects, including a copper tool. Since then he had been told about the pre-contact copper mines found by mining agents around Lake Superior, which surely suggested that ancient Aboriginals had been quite civilized.[106] What response this mix of praise for indigenous intelligence and disclosure of Grensell's assistance to mound excavation elicited from the council is unknown.

We also often do not know why Aboriginal individuals assisted collectors. In summer 1888, A.F Chamberlain, a Canadian Institute member, visited a Mississauga village on Scugog Island to conduct fieldwork. Seeking to record their history and folklore, he collected archaeological artifacts with the help of an informant, Nawigishkoke, or Mrs Susan Bolin, considered to be "the wisest of the Indians in the matter of the history of her people and their beliefs in the past."[107] She told him about several spots where relics had been found locally, including an ancient encampment at Oak Orchard, Sturgeon Point, and a place where an "earthen kettle" had been discovered when the soil had washed away. These, she interpreted as Kanienkehaka, the latter in particular, because the pottery took a different form than Mississauga styles. Bolin also informed Chamberlain about Albert C. Stevens, a local farmer and amateur collector. Stevens, who lived nearby on Nonquon Island, showed Chamberlain the spots in his fields where he had found archaeological remains. Eventually, and with some monetary persuasion, Stevens transferred his collection to the Canadian Institute.[108] Bolin aided Chamberlain in his studies and collection of artifacts, but her feelings about burial excavations are enigmatic. While she told him about the opening of a grave near her home twenty years earlier, and that she had seen a knife and other items obtained from the burial and judged them "no doubt" from a grave of her ancestors, Chamberlain provided no indication of the feelings Bolin might have experienced upon viewing items interred with the remains of her people.[109]

Overall, however, there are discernable patterns in the history of archaeological excavation in Ontario. Aboriginal and Euro-Canadian individuals reacted to archaeological excavations and the exhibition of objects from the soil, including human remains, based upon factors such as scientific and spiritual beliefs, varying interpretations of the cultural and familial links between the dead and the living, racism, monetary gain, political goals, and patriotism. Ministers and others who followed a form of spirituality, whether Christian or Aboriginal, most often protested against grave disturbances. For example, like Hallen and Keen before him, the Reverend J.P. Secord was presumably concerned about the fate of all human remains as an advocate of the Christian faith, when he wrote to Andrew Hunter, protesting the activities of J. Hugh Hammond. Secord, who shared office space with Hammond, called his excavations "profaning" and "desecrating" graves.[110] A few individuals did rebury uncovered graves or attempted to protect them from further excavation. A Mr Tobin in Kent County surrounded a mound on McGregor Creek with a fence in order to protect it from desecration out of "respect to the dead."[111] In the 1850s, a Mr Harmon buried the human remains at the site noted by surveyor Patrick McNiff and by Major Littlehales.[112] In his memoirs, "Leeds Clothier" William Brown stated that he persuaded his employees to curb their burial excavations and let the dead rest in peace.[113] An owner of an ossuary in Nottawasaga Township protected it from excavation.[114] Other instances were cast as examples of superstition, but they may have really been motivated by religious reasons. According to William Wintemberg, one farmer in Blenheim Township uncovered a grave and, "overcome with superstitious dread," reburied the human remains and never ploughed that part of the field again.[115] Hammond wrote to William Henry Holmes of the Bureau of American Ethnology that farmers' superstitions sometimes hampered his work.[116]

Like Coyne and Annis, professionals and historical society members tended to emphasize archaeological items and human remains as educational resources and consequently de-emphasized or denied the links between sites and living communities. Such individuals also saw themselves as the stewards of archaeological remains and advocated for protection of sites, but only against amateur diggers. The press had little sympathy for Aboriginal burial disturbances, with a few exceptions. For instance, the author of one 1889 article in a Penetanguishene newspaper wondered upon viewing several skeletons on display how these individuals would have reacted if they knew they were the subject of jokes, thoughtless remarks, and pranks such as making their bones rattle and their teeth chatter.[117] Others, both Euro-Canadian and Aboriginal, saw excavation and sometimes reburial of human remains as a means to a financial, political, or patriotic end. There was little consensus about the purpose and intent of excavating archaeological sites, particularly burials, in Ontario.

# 4

## COLONIALISM, ETHNOGRAPHIC COLLECTING, AND ABORIGINAL ENGAGEMENT

While the public and members of historical and scientific societies engaged in archaeology for curiosity, leisure, or study, fewer individuals interacted with Aboriginal communities in order to collect ethnographic pieces not made for the souvenir trade. Ethnographic work in Southern Ontario centred around David Boyle and the Six Nations of the Grand River reserve near Brantford in the late nineteenth century. As the only Canadian reserve with members of all Six Nations, including a reinstituted Haudenosaunee Confederacy Council following the post-Revolution migration to Upper Canada, it was perhaps seen to offer more potential for ethnographic collecting. Boyle also presumably targeted this reserve because of its proximity to Toronto and his increasing contacts within the community. As typical in the nineteenth century, Boyle was more fascinated by the pre-contact, supposedly more traditional Indian, those "most noble" rather than the contemporaneous, partly Christian Aboriginal communities that seemed assimilated, at least outwardly, to collectors.[1] Like others, Boyle believed it was necessary to collect older, more traditional material culture before assimilation destroyed its use and meanings.

Aboriginal individuals protested against, collaborated with, and sought to use ethnographic collectors for their own reasons. Like archaeological collecting, the varying motives of those involved in ethnography cannot be explained simply as differences between Euro-Canadian and Aboriginal cultures. Across North America, indigenous individuals acted as community conduits for collectors because they agreed with some of the goals of nineteenth-century ethnography.

Others formed genuine bonds of collegiality or friendship with them. For David Boyle, these individuals were primarily John Ojijatekha Brant-Sero, Chief Alexander G. Smith (Dehkanenraneh), William Williams, Dahkahedondyeh, and the Davis family at the Six Nations of the Grand River.[2]

The separation of material culture from Aboriginal communities, including Six Nations, and how the community reacted to collectors, must also be contextualized within the mounting pressures of colonialism. As restrictions of the Indian Act tightened around Aboriginal communities, traditional leaders sought ways to be recognized as sovereign peoples and sometimes used influential scholars as allies in their political struggles. Collecting and fieldwork, then, became part of a reciprocal relationship. Over the nineteenth century, the Six Nations traditional hereditary council became increasingly dismayed by its community's enforced transition from autonomous loyal allies in the British colonial wars to wards under the Canadian government. The Six Nations viewed their wampum belts as official records of their status as sovereign nations. The matter was further complicated by the fact that not all nations and not all chiefs agreed on a way to resolve this most unwelcome discrepancy. Missionary activity among the Six Nations had resulted in the decrease of the traditional spiritual beliefs of the Longhouse religion and the adoption of Christianity by some, making it easier for collectors, including Aboriginal ones, to obtain sacred objects. Attitudes toward communal ownership and stewardship of objects such as wampum belts also changed, and those who felt such items should be treated as private property or family heirlooms sometimes chose to sell despite community resistance. In contrast, in the face of assimilationist pressure, some individuals felt that museums were the best places to preserve material culture, because they feared its dispersal if it remained in the community.

## BOYLE'S ETHNOGRAPHIC FIELDWORK

David Boyle's initial contact with the Six Nations of the Grand River occurred in 1886. After corresponding with their Indian agent, Jasper Tough Gilkison, Boyle visited the farm of Chief John Buck (Skanawati), the traditional Onondage'ga' (Onondaga) wampum-keeper, along with Chief A.G. Smith, the government interpreter, two Kanienkehakas (Mohawk), and Thomas Whitehead, a teacher from England. Buck spread a cloth upon the grass and laid out twelve Haudenosaunee Confederacy wampum belts, which he interpreted for Boyle.[3] By 1889,

John Ojijatekha Brant-Sero, c. 1910

Boyle had met John Ojijatekha Brant-Sero, a Kanienkehaka individual who was greatly interested in the history of his community. Brant-Sero had delivered a paper entitled Pagan Beliefs on Religion at the Canadian Institute in April of that year and more than likely made contact with Boyle at that time, if not before.[4] In 1892, on the Queen's birthday, a day of celebration at Six Nations, the community adopted Boyle and named him Ahewanoneh, "one who is sent on tribal business" or more simply, "an ambassador." Asked to choose his tribe and totem, Boyle selected the Turtle clan of the Kanienkehaka nation.[5] One month later, Boyle recommended the purchase of A.G. Smith's collection for the Canadian Institute. Valued at $105, it included mostly archaeological pieces but also several northwest pipes, four silver bracelets, and fifty-six Iroquoian silver brooches that Smith had collected from several other people.[6] Two years later, Boyle purchased two wampum belts from Joshua Buck, the son of the man who had interpreted the twelve belts for him in 1886.[7]

By 1896, Boyle had met E. Pauline Johnson, the famed poetess and "Mohawk princess," who sold or donated to the Ontario Provincial Museum a dance mask originally owned by Onondage'ga' Chief Crow.[8] In 1897, she also sold to Boyle a "Medicine" mask, a turtle shell rattle, one wampum belt, and a belt of dentalium shells.[9] That same year, numerous Haudenosaunee chiefs attended the annual meeting of the Pioneer and Historical Society (shortly to become the Ontario Historical Society) in Niagara-on-the-Lake. It seems likely that either Boyle or Brant-Sero, who was also a member, had suggested the invitation. At the meeting, the Six Nations treated the general membership to a traditional council meeting and an otherwise unidentified Longhouse ceremony. The Six Nations officially affiliated themselves with the provincial society, and consequently they were allowed to form their own local society and appoint one delegate with voting powers for each nation. The chiefs invited the Ontario Historical Society (OHS) to hold its next annual meeting at Ohsweken on the reserve.

The bulk of Boyle's ethnographic fieldwork at Six Nations began in 1898. During ten days in January and February, Boyle attended the Mid-Winter or New Year's Festival at the Onodowahgah (Seneca) Longhouse.[10] In May, he returned for the Gayogoho:no (Cayuga) After Seeding or Spring Sun Dance. In June, eighty OHS members and several hundred Haudenosaunee gathered at the Six Nations Council House for the society's annual meeting.[11] Chiefs A.G. Smith, John Gibson, Alexander Hill, Nicodemus Porter, Benjamin Carpenter, and Richard Hill acted as representatives to the OHS, one for each of the nations, in addition to Nelles Monture of the Delaware. In autumn Boyle witnessed the Green Corn Dance and, at harvest, the Big Corn Feast. During several of his ethnographic field trips he lodged with William Williams (Kanishandon) and Dahkahedondyeh, who lived together, because Williams was one of the ceremonial leaders who aided Boyle in understanding the rituals performed. John Ojijatekha Brant-Sero also served as his interpreter and authenticated the details later recorded in Boyle's 1898 *Archaeological Report*. With the approval of the Onodowahgah Longhouse, William Williams also came to Toronto in order to record ceremonial songs on wax cylinders for Boyle and the Department of Education. Boyle's report for 1898 described the range of his fieldwork. He had investigated their housing, food, clan structure, origin and other stories, naming traditions, and various spiritual, marital, political, and funerary customs and related material culture. According to Brant-Sero, this report inspired many other Haudenosaunee to share their own knowledge with Boyle.[12] Certainly, some had provided him with ethnographic objects. The 1898 report described Boyle's accessions of three rattles, two masks, two war clubs, two silver crosses, one pair of moccasins, and one whistle or flute.[13]

William Williams, or Ka-nis-han-don, 1898

The next year Boyle returned for the Gayogoho:no Sun Dance. His 1899 report showed further acquisitions of two game sets, two pairs of moccasins, three rattles, three masks, two paddles for stirring ashes in Longhouse rituals, one drum, and a conch used for calling people to the Longhouse.[14] That year William Williams and Dahkahedondyeh recorded more songs on wax cylinders. In 1900 Boyle again attended the Mid-Winter Festival. His ongoing relationship with the community spurred further collecting in the next few years, including one cradle model, one rattle, one pair moccasins, over thirty Iroquoian silver brooches, and ceremonial regalia owned by Captain William Bill (Red Cloud).[15] Two years later, William Bill visited Toronto to record songs for Boyle. In 1904, the Gayogoho:no invited Boyle to view the installation of one of their chiefs. That year Boyle appears to have established a relationship with a man named Jacob Hess, who served as a community middleman collector and facilitated the transfer of a number of ethnographic objects to the Ontario Provincial Museum.[16] In 1905, one of the last few years of Boyle's ethnographic fieldwork, he obtained numerous ethnographic pieces from Chief Austin Bill (Sawgawwis).[17] In 1908, Hess procured a flute, four silver brooches, and a pair of silver earrings for Boyle. The next year, Boyle wrote to Hess that he wished to attend the upcoming New Year's Festival, but it seems unlikely he did so.[18] He had suffered a stroke in 1908, and, although he recovered after a few months, he was hit with a second attack in April 1909 that paralyzed him.[19]

## PRESERVING THE TRADITIONAL AND AUTHENTIC

In addition to preserving material culture and related ethnographic information, Boyle hoped to increase the public's understanding of the Haudenosaunee. As he explained in the preface to his 1898 report, he hoped it would "not only assist white people in arriving at some intelligent conclusions respecting our Iroquois, but that it would prove beneficial to the Indians themselves, as every word [had] been written in a spirit of sympathy with the past, present, and possible future of the Red Man."[20] Like most nineteenth-century ethnographers, however, Boyle's approach was also clearly influenced by the evolutionary theories of the day. In particular, Boyle used E.B. Tylor's theory of survivals, which proposed that remnants of cultural characteristics from past evolutionary stages could be used to reconstruct a pre-contact lifestyle. Accordingly, Boyle focused upon what he considered to be the traditional aspects of Haudenosaunee culture.[21] Ethnographers also believed that pre-contact life supposedly possessed an Indian character much more authentic than the nineteenth-century Aboriginal societies that had been tainted with assimilation. Pre-contact culture was also imbued with more romantic appeal, especially its spiritual aspects, which, at Six Nations, supposedly could be found in the longhouses on the reserve rather than in its houses, farms, and churches, which were similar to those of their off-reserve neighbours.

Unsurprisingly, then, Boyle observed Longhouse religious rites rather than Christian ones and perceived his attendance at these rituals as a glimpse into life in the past rather than insight into an ongoing and vital part of the contemporary community. "In the music, songs, dances, speeches and peculiar rites," Boyle wrote, "one may picture to himself what an event of the same kind must have been when celebrated by savages in the old-time long-house, lighted only by the glare of two huge fires."[22] Consequently, he tried to figure out the ancient origins of ceremonies, such as that of the burning of the white dog. During one

Red Cloud, or William Bill, c. 1901

group conversation in 1898, Boyle asked for individual names, but only to see if the traditional reluctance in giving one's name still existed.[23] Boyle also pointed out what he thought to be discrepancies between old and new practices. For example, at the Spring Sun Dance, Boyle's notes distinguished between traditional and modern dancing and clothing.[24]

Also typical of nineteenth-century ethnography, Boyle sought out material culture that represented older or conservative customs at the Grand River. The definition of old to Boyle was clearly pre-contact: he judged one mask once kept by E. Pauline Johnson as not old enough because steel tools obtained through European contact had been used in its carving.[25] Boyle also preferred items that he felt did not show European influence. For example, though he purchased this object, he scorned the idea that a flute made by Abram Buck was of Aboriginal origin, rather than of European influence.[26] Judging from his accession lists, Boyle also preferred ceremonial or spiritual items such as rattles, False Face and corn husk masks, and other regalia worn during Longhouse religious ceremonies. Fewer objects of daily life were gathered, and even these – war clubs and archaeological tools – stemmed from past daily life rather than modern times. Objects made for the tourist industry received little attention from Boyle during his curatorship. Most ethnographers perceived such objects as hybrid forms of craft, too influenced by European culture. Only one object that Boyle purchased – a model cradle – may have been a tourist piece, or perhaps it was a toy or charm.

## COMMUNITY RESPONSES

Boyle apparently communicated his greater valuation of what he considered to be traditional and authentic objects to his informants and donors. Jacob Hess, one of Boyle's middleman collectors at Six Nations, wrote in 1904 that he knew Boyle prized old and authentic False Faces and, although he had been unable to procure one yet, asserted that all the masks he had obtained had been used in ceremonies. He stated he would not bother carving a new one for this reason.[27] Writing to Boyle in 1896, Pauline Johnson validated that all her wampum belts were old, suggesting that Boyle had stated his preferences in previous communications. One belt was one of the oldest of all belts, she said, and suggested it might be the Hiawatha treaty belt that documented the formation of the Confederacy of the Five Nations. She wished to obtain Boyle's opinion on the matter. In reality, this wampum was not the Hiawatha belt, but Johnson may have been attempting to emphasize the age and traditionality of this item, or perhaps she designated all wampum belts as Hiawatha in reference to their relationship with the Confederacy. Describing one of her masks as so old it was crumbling, she recognized that Boyle would therefore place a high value upon it.[28] Johnson also asked anthropologist and family friend Horatio Hale to authenticate a False Face to be sold to the Canadian Institute as a "genuine ceremonial mask," an act witnessed by Chief A.G. Smith, and to formulate a certificate of authenticity to accompany the sale of her masks in general.[29] Later Johnson played upon Boyle's partiality for traditional artifacts when she described several items as once belonging to "our most blue-blooded Onondagas," one of the Six Nations thought to have remained more traditional than others.[30]

Johnson also sold parts of her collection to others, and in a 1905 communication with naturalist and writer Ernest Thompson Seton, she emphasized the exceptional nature of one of her belts. A "treasure," this belt was one of the "greatest," because it was an original "Hiawatha League" wampum from the formation of the Confederacy. Johnson also described it as one of the largest and the most famous, since her grandfather John Smoke Johnson was pictured holding it in his hands in the photograph of the Haudenosaunee chiefs taken by anthropologist Horatio Hale in the late nineteenth century for his *Book of Rites*.

She also stressed the romantic nature of the wampum, for traditional Six Nations kept the belts and their history confidential; according to Johnson, only Hale had learned their secrets, from "a *reliable old* Indian."[31]

In contrast, Evelyn Johnson, Pauline's sister, objected to Boyle's focus on the traditional. In an angry letter to Minister of Education Richard Harcourt, she accused Boyle of presenting a distorted impression of the Haudenosaunee in his 1898 annual report because he had mostly interviewed Longhouse people, attended their ceremonies, and collected their material culture. He "seldom was seen among the more educated Indians," she wrote, nor were there any photographs of brick homes, churches, or "accomplished" people, those who showed "advancement and civilization." In particular, Johnson was outraged over the depiction of the poor state of health at Six Nations, including the statement that it was common for children to pick worms out of their noses and throats. The previous summer she had addressed Boyle personally about this matter; "annoyed," he suggested that she write a correction to his report, although she never did. Corresponding with Harcourt, Boyle pled innocence, stating that he did not research Christian Indians and that he included nothing untrue or unkind in his report.[32] In truth, Boyle had not written the specific section that had initially angered Johnson (though he included it for publication), but the charge of skewed interpretations of Haudenosaunee culture was nevertheless accurate.[33]

## COLLEGIAL TIES

Others from Six Nations of the Grand River both questioned and assisted David Boyle's ethnographic fieldwork and even collected for themselves. As was the case for many other nineteenth-century collectors, Boyle's relationship with the Six Nations was facilitated by members of the community. Boyle's entrée into the Grand River reserve occurred through his previously established relationships with Chief A.G. Smith and especially John Ojijatekha Brant-Sero. After Boyle's death, Brant-Sero fondly remembered him as having a genuine "personal and emotional" interest in Aboriginal research. He also suggested that a memorial should be created in Boyle's honour, perhaps a fund to sponsor similar studies by Ontario students.[34] Although he worked as a machine-hand in Toronto in the late 1880s, Brant-Sero clearly aspired to be a professional anthropologist and may have been inspired by Boyle's own self-made career. Brant-Sero was a fellow of the

Anthropological Institute of Great Britain and Ireland, and a member of the Canadian Institute, the York Pioneers, the Hamilton Association, and the Wentworth Historical Society, serving as second vice-president for the latter body in 1899. He belonged to the group that reconstituted the Pioneer and Historical Association of Ontario into the Ontario Historical Society in 1897 and assumed the second vice-presidency for the 1898-1900 sessions. He and his wife Frances Baynes Kirby were also collectors and owned items from the Grand River and the Siksika and Kainai reserves on the prairies, some of which were displayed in the Indian Exhibit of the 1899 Canadian Historical Exhibition.[35] For the latter, Brant-Sero also served on the exhibition committee.

By 1899, like Pauline Johnson, he travelled a lecture tour circuit in Canada, the United States, Britain, and Europe. His lectures were a curious mix of Victorian entertainment and anthropology. An advertisement for Squire's Hall in Stoney Creek featured songs and recitations by the Brant-Sero family, who were costumed in "old English Lace and Indian Bead Work," all for a cost of twenty-five cents for adults and fifteen cents for children.[36] At other performances his wife played the piano, a woman named Lizzie declaimed poetry in costume, and Brant-Sero explained the history of the Haudenosaunee Confederacy, delivered a Shakespearean address of Othello in both the Kanienkehaka and English languages, and performed "Mohawk yells."[37] Much of Brant-Sero's performances included information from Boyle's fieldwork at the Grand River. At one point, he also wished to incorporate the ceremonial songs recorded by Boyle, but the minister of Education forbade the loan of these precious wax cylinders.[38]

Brant-Sero also researched and published on the history of his people. In 1899, he attempted to have documents concerning the Haudenosaunee Confederacy published, enlisting the support of David Boyle and James Coyne of the Elgin Historical Society. He also suggested that the Six Nations Council might agree to underwrite a portion of the publication costs. By autumn, however, he had dismissed the idea, reporting that there was considerable "friction" in the community over the issue, though the council had approved his possession of these documents.[39] During 1899 and 1900, Brant-Sero researched "Pagan Rites" and Kanienkehaka genealogies. Unsponsored, he asked Boyle to solicit money from the minister of Education, who agreed to give Brant-Sero twenty-four dollars to conduct his research.[40]

Disappointed in his attempts to be an employed anthropologist, in 1900, Brant-Sero moved to the United States, where he hoped to find a better-funded market for his talents.[41] He wrote for the Chicago

*Evening Post* and continued his lecture tour, but he still wished to be fully employed as an anthropologist. He had previously corresponded in 1889 with Major J.W. Powell of the Bureau of American Ethnology, offering legends and traditions for sale.[42] In 1900 he appealed to Powell for employment at the bureau. Although he acknowledged that the Ska-ru-ren (Tuscarora) anthropologist J.N.B. Hewitt was by now conducting fieldwork at the Grand River reserve, he believed that there was much more work to be done and that he had the "friendship" of the community.[43] He also targeted the American Museum of Natural History in New York and asked James Mooney of the bureau and Reuben G. Thwaites of the State Historical Society of Wisconsin to contact anthropologist Franz Boas there with references. Boas was unable to offer him a position at the museum but suggested that it might be possible at a later date.[44] By July 1900, however, Brant-Sero had left for South Africa to unsuccessfully join the Boer War effort, and then in autumn travelled to England to continue his lecture tour. Yet he still held out hope to work for Boas, suggesting that he could attend the Mid-Winter ceremonials the next year at the Grand River or at the Cattaraugus reserve in New York State.[45]

In his pleas for employment, Brant-Sero sounded similar to the avocational anthropologists of Ontario. Studying the Haudenosaunee was his "Life work," and he desired opportunities to "ripen" his "scholarship." Like Boyle, he felt this task to be fairly urgent because of the large amount of work among the Haudenosaunee to be completed. Using the salvage anthropology paradigm, he stated "No time should be lost in collecting every available material before the old people die. Changes will rapidly take place over these people."[46] Like Boyle, Brant-Sero also emphasized the traditional side of Haudenosaunee culture. In 1899, he agreed to procure for Janet Carnochan, president of the Niagara Historical Society, a False Face mask and a turtle rattle for one dollar each and a complete set of corn-processing tools, including a pounder and winnowing baskets. He noted that he could obtain a new pounder easily, but he assumed that Carnochan "would value an old pounder much more than a new one."[47] In another suggested research prospectus entitled An Iroquoian Proposal, he advised that he should study the Onodowahgah and the Onondage'ga', the nations who had preserved their old ways the most. This research should include, he wrote, the uses and beliefs of herbs, roots, minerals, food preparation and taboos, and a collection of food preparation tools, clothing, and silver ornaments.[48]

According to Boyle in 1898, the "men in this group consented to dance outside, that a photograph might be taken, but at the last moment one suggested that it would not be pleasing to Rawen Niyoh."

Thus in many ways Brant-Sero and Boyle were kindred spirits. They both attempted to carve out a career in anthropology for themselves at a time in Canada when such an occupation barely existed. They joined numerous historical societies and believed in their goals of preservation and education. They both feared that assimilation was erasing the traditional ways of the Haudenosaunee and wished to conduct ethnographic fieldwork and collect objects in order to salvage the remaining knowledge about older customs. They believed material culture should be preserved in museums. Clearly, then, Boyle would have found Brant-Sero useful as a conduit into the Six Nations community. But how did the Grand River residents respond in turn?

## FRIENDSHIP AND FICTIVE KINSHIP

Not everyone was pleased with Boyle's presence. John Styres, a leader of the Onodowahgah Longhouse, questioned the propriety of Boyle taking notes during ceremonies.[49] Boyle also met resistance after asking to photograph dancers outside of the Longhouse. At first the men consented, but then one suggested that the Creator would be displeased. The resulting photographs show the dancers posed as a group, rather than in the action of dancing.[50]

Lizzie Davis, wearing pieces collected by the Brant-Seros, c. 1898

But some, in fact, welcomed Boyle and accepted him into the bonds of friendship and fictive kinship that were often extended by Aboriginal communities to ethnographic fieldworkers. Besides Brant-Sero, the Davis family at the Grand River seemed to have taken Boyle under their sponsorship. According to the 1901 census of Canada, Chief Isaac Davis (Shorenhowane) was a seventy-seven-year-old Kanienkehaka farmer who belonged to the Anglican Church. His wife Susannah was English. Three adult children lived at home: Sarah, Lizzie, both teachers, and Perry, a farmer.[51] John Roberts Davis, presumably of the same family, and his wife also assisted Boyle. He is listed in the census as being forty-nine years of age, retired, and of the Anglican faith. His wife, also named Susannah, is recorded as a Longhouse Onondage'ga' who spoke Gayogoho:no, although Boyle's report referred to her as a Tutelo.[52]

It is not known how Boyle met the Davis family, but their correspondence began before his 1898 winter visit to see the New Year's Festival. It is possible that Lizzie Davis was the Lizzie of the Brant-Sero lectures, as she appeared in a northwest Aboriginal costume in a photograph in the 1898 *Archaeological Report*. The photograph had been provided by Frances Brant-Sero, and the clothing she wore had been collected by the Brant-Seros.[53] Perhaps the Brant-Seros had introduced them. The

Captain John Roberts Davis and his wife Susannah demonstrate
how to pound corn to Boyle, 1898

sister of John Buck, whom Boyle had visited in 1886, was also the aunt
of John Roberts Davis's wife, which may also explain the connection.[54]

In any case, Lizzie Davis had received a letter in mid-January from
Boyle asking to attend the Mid-Winter ceremonies and had taken this
appeal to her father at a council meeting. The chiefs agreed to host
Boyle on the 31 January 1898 and agreed he could bring a photographer.
Lizzie Davis invited Boyle to stay with her family and promised to help
him understand the rituals. Isaac Davis also personally responded to
Boyle's letter, inviting him to the ceremony of the burning of the white
dog, an important part of Mid-Winter.[55] John Roberts Davis issued
other invitations in March 1898 and November 1899.[56] During the New
Year's Festival in 1898, his wife taught Boyle how to pound corn in a
wooden mortar and pestle and to make it into corn cake.[57] In January
1900, in a letter signed "Uncil [sic] Bill and Bob" and addressed to our
"Dear Nephew," Davis asked Boyle to attend that year's False Face
dances and white dog ceremony, sending an invitation stick with wampum in the traditional manner.[58] The Davises also channelled messages
to Boyle; a Mrs Davis wrote in September 1899, informing him that
Susan Buck wanted him to know the date of the Green Corn dance.[59]

According to Gerald Killan, his biographer, Boyle's "friends along the Grand River appreciated his attempts to reconstruct Iroquoian prehistory and his efforts to preserve their cultural heritage." Killan further cited Boyle's adoption and naming as "ambassador" by the Kanienkehaka in 1892 as proof of their gratitude.[60] Brant-Sero believed that Boyle's adoption was in honour of his research as well as his role as the "voice between races."[61] Indeed, Boyle stated that he received "unqualified Indian courtesy, perhaps to some extent on account of being an adopted Mohawk" during his fieldwork.[62] At the Gayogoho:no After-Seeding ceremonies in 1898, although he appeared to have been unaccompanied by interpreters or acquaintances, he once again stated that he was "treated with perfect courtesy."[63]

Although Boyle was warmly received by the Davises at Six Nations, the significance of his self-identified acceptance, and particularly his adoption, may be overemphasized. Certainly some perceived it as a genuine bond, and accordingly expected a reciprocal relationship. For example, in 1900, elders asked Boyle to bring tobacco to Mid-Winter.[64] Another year, Boyle offered to bring beef for a feast or to give a cash donation for the construction of a new longhouse.[65] The community also anticipated an exchange of information; Boyle received numerous requests for his archaeological reports and other research information.[66] But his adoption in 1892 occurred before the bulk of his ethnographic work and the building of community relationships in 1898. And, interestingly, Boyle was not the only individual to receive this specific name upon adoption. In an 1896 ceremony performed by Chief William Wage, the Six Nations conferred the name "Ra-vi-wa-non-neh" ("Ambassador") upon William Wilson, the county master of the Orange Order, and declared him an honourary member of their people.[67] In this light, Boyle's adoption seems simply part of a wider system of seeking outside allies.

As well, current scholarship on naming and adoption has suggested that these supposed acceptances may have alternative meanings. Adoption may indeed have been motivated by feelings of affection, or a fear that younger generations were not interested in traditional knowledge, and thus elders looked for others on which to bestow their learning. Adoption may also be a way to socialize strangers, to have respected professionals educate the public against stereotypes, to exert control over an outsider so that he or she will not embarrass the community or reveal sensitive information as a family member, or to create political allies. Significantly, although anthropologists feel that adoption is a validation of their research, most indigenous societies see it as an acceptance of the person rather than their studies.[68]

## SEEKING SOVEREIGNTY

In his 1898 presidential address, James Coyne suggested that the affiliation of the Six Nations with the OHS would bolster Boyle's work, as they would "no doubt feel the responsibility resting upon them as affiliated with this Society to give him full and accurate information."[69] Killan argued this was the stimulus behind the original OHS affiliation offer to the Haudenosaunee, in conjunction with the generation of good publicity that would help in their appeals for government grants.[70] The Haudenosaunee appear to have had other priorities in mind, looking to Boyle, among others, as an ally in their endeavours to regain recognition of their political independence.

Boyle's fieldwork at the Grand River reserve occurred at a time of political uncertainty in which the Canadian government attempted to impose increasing restrictions through the Indian Act and refused to recognize the Six Nations' sovereign status, which they had earlier accepted. The Six Nations also protested the transfer of the Indian Affairs administration from the British to the Canadian government after Confederation in 1867. As military allies, they had possessed political bargaining power, but within Canada they were considered to be only subjects. Further, the loss of direct communication with the Crown symbolically and literally represented a loss of leverage.

The Haudenosaunee attempted to resolve the discrepancy of their status numerous times throughout the nineteenth century. In 1876, many Six Nations chiefs sent a petition to Indian Affairs stating that they were not subjects but allies to the British and they would "follow our Ancient Laws and Rules and ... not depart from it."[71] In 1888, residents at Tyendinaga petitioned to have their government-imposed elected council abolished and their traditional council structure reinstated. The petitioners explained that they had no confidence in the elected representatives because liquor and bribes had played a role in the election. Further, they wanted to be exempted from the Indian Act. In response, Superintendent General of Indian Affairs Edgar Dewdney simply suggested that the petition was only from individuals who had been unsuccessful during this election and thus recommended that the council remain as chosen. A second memorial, written by Joseph J. Brant two years later, again requested for the hereditary government to be restored at Tyendinaga.[72]

That same year, numerous chiefs, warriors, and headmen of the Grand River reserve petitioned Governor General Frederick Stanley. They argued that they had never made any treaty with the British Crown that forced the Haudenosaunee to live under any but their own traditional laws and customs. As proof, they referred to two important wampum belts in their keeping. The first, a dark blue and white belt, showed the formation of the Five Nations Confederacy and thus symbolized the establishment of their own laws and political system. The second belt, often referred to as the two-row wampum belt, depicted two white parallel lines within a sea of darker wampum. The two rows represented the British in their vessel and the Five Nations in their bark canoe existing together but never touching - that is, never interfering with the other autonomous nation. This latter belt, the petition stated, promised that the British would never force their laws upon the Five Nations, nor would they make them British subjects.[73]

The matter was referred to Dewdney, who proclaimed there to be no grounds for such claims made by the Six Nations. Deputy Superintendent General Lawrence Vankoughnet agreed. He said he recognized and appreciated the loyalty of the Six Nations, but that it did not equal a special status in legal matters – they were still Crown subjects. Both Dewdney and Vankoughnet referred to an earlier claim made in 1839, which had concluded similarly. At that time, provincial Judge James Buchanan Macaulay had decided that the Six Nations were naturalized subjects and, as they resided within the "organized portion" of Ontario, fell under its and the national jurisdiction. Thus, for the Department of Indian Affairs (DIA), the matter had already been decided. Notably, Dewdney dismissed the wampum belts as valid evidence of any "(so called) treaties." Instead, he recommended that the governor general pass an order-in-council dismissing the petition of the Six Nations.[74]

The matter was not settled in the minds of the Six Nations chiefs, however. In early 1892, Chief Isaac Hill complained about the seizure of wood under Canadian law. He again asserted that the Six Nations were allies, not subjects, and thus not bound to any law but their own. Not surprisingly, Dewdney stated that this matter had been already addressed by the order-in-council in 1890 and the result had been communicated to the chiefs. Afterward, Hill and his supporters again petitioned the government to request that the chiefs retain control of their own matters. In response, the DIA suggested to Governor General Stanley that the chiefs could be allowed to decide on certain issues unless it was not in the interest of the Six Nations community. There was, of course, no agreement that the Six Nations were autonomous allies not subjects of the Crown. In a later communication about a Six Nations appeal to Prince Arthur, the duke of Connaught, Dewdney bluntly stated that the British North America Act gave Canada the full power to legislate for the Six Nations whether they liked it or not and that the Six Nations must conform to the Indian Act. In closing, he derided the appeal as being the same old tired claim of the Six Nations that had been resolved in 1890.[75]

These problems may have been further complicated by divisions within the Six Nations community itself. Anthropologist Sally Weaver has suggested that, as early as the 1860s, the Haudenosaunee Council possessed numerous factions, both Christian and Longhouse, and those who promoted political reform versus those who supported traditional procedures. According to Weaver, the mostly Longhouse Onodowahgah, Onondage'ga', and Gayogoho:no preferred the traditional council, while the more acculturated, largely English-speaking, Christianized Kanienkehaka, Onyot.ka (Oneida), and Ska-ru-ren nations desired some measure of governmental reform, including the possibility of an elected council. All, however, demanded the preservation of Haudenosaunee sovereignty. The latter nations believed that they could protect the sovereignty of their government by a pragmatic transformation of the council into a local government. In contrast, the traditional element protested any relinquishment of power. The community was also divided between those who regarded the council as part of their founding spiritual doctrines and those who believed it to be a secular political body. These disagreements were particularly dangerous in the wake of the Indian Act of 1869 and the Indian Advancement Act of 1884, which promoted the imposition of elected councils.

According to Weaver, in the 1890s, the pro-reform group maintained the majority of council and acted as the administrators and interpreters. Another group known as the Progressive Warriors unsuccessfully petitioned the Canadian government to institute an elected council at Six Nations, while the conservative faction sought federal recognition of Haudenosaunee sovereignty. In 1906, the Progressive Warriors reorganized as the Indians Rights Association and appealed again to the Canadian government for an elected council in 1907 and 1910. They were supported by a small number of the Kanienkehaka, Upper Gayogoho:no, Ska-ru-ren, Onodowahgah, and Delaware nations.[76]

Weaver's description of factionalism at Six Nations of the Grand River has been questioned recently by Haudenosaunee scholars. Sue Hill has suggested that as an anthropologist looking for acculturation,

Weaver overemphasized the numbers and control of the so-called pro-gressive faction within the Six Nations Council and community and under-represented the influence of the Longhouse or conservative group. Further, the idea that the reserve could be broken down into only two sides – the progressive versus the traditional – is too simplis-tic, Hill argues. Andrea Capatano agrees, noting that families have alternately supported the elected council and the hereditary council depending on the issue, that divisions exist within each council anyway, and that even the traditional council members were often considered progressive. Paul Williams argues that despite their differences, council members agreed to leave their religious disagreements outside of the Council House.[77]

Aside from the debated severity and consequences of the "factional-ism" on the reserve, it does seem clear that under pressure from the federal government and the DIA, the Six Nations of the Grand River fought to maintain autonomy of their own political affairs. Thus the Six Nations considered the 1898 OHS meeting and a relationship with David Boyle to be a political opportunity to gain support for their claim to sovereignty rather than solely a method to preserve their history. One of their strategies to regain recognition of their political indepen-dence centred around the use of the United Empire Loyalist myth, an interpretation of the history of Upper Canada and its founders cher-ished by most historical society members. This myth proposed that the United Empire Loyalists had been steadfast in their alliance with the British during the American Revolution and had thus had given up their wealth and lives in colonial America to eke out a harsh living in the untamed wilderness of Canada.[78] This interpretation happened to coin-cide with the beliefs of the Haudenosaunee. As important military and political allies of the British who had moved to Upper Canada after the American Revolution, they indeed saw themselves as having sacrificed their homes and territory in colonial America. Receiving territory at the Grand River and near Belleville for their loyalty, they also saw them-selves as founders of Upper Canada. And if they were considered to be allies, not subjects, their sovereign status seemed to follow logically. If they were considered founders of the province, their level of civilization seemed equal to other UELs, and thus they should not be treated as legal wards of the government.

Most historical societies widely recognized the Six Nations as Loyalists, and the Six Nations had stressed this during their partici-pation in the 1860 royal visit of the Prince of Wales and the Loyalist centennial celebrations in 1884. The organizing committee of the centennial celebrations had recognized that the Six Nations were loyal and had made progress in the civilization of their society.[79] At the 1897 Pioneer and Historical Association annual meeting, Janet Carnochan welcomed the Six Nations representatives and affirmed that their people had "fought bravely for our country," after which their Indian agent, E.D. Cameron, proclaimed that there were "none so loyal as the Six Nations," who had even fought in the Northwest Rebellion.[80]

In the month just before the OHS 1898 annual gathering at Ohsweken, the United Empire Loyalist Association held a ceremony to award a medal and an honourary vice-presidency to War of 1812 veteran John Smoke Johnson of the Grand River and Chief Samson Green of Tyendinaga. At this event the association stated that, without the Six Nations, Canada would have fallen to the United States.[81] That summer the UEL Association visited the Tyendinaga reserve. Here, Samson Green welcomed them and in his address asserted his people had been British allies for over two hundred years. Their loyalty, he continued, was still as strong as ever. Unlike those who would speak at the OHS 1898 annual meeting, however, Green used the term British "subjects" to describe those at Tyendinaga. Responding to Green's speech, Edward Chadwick, who had written a history of the Haudenosaunee, also acknowledged their loyalty, a talk printed in the society's annual transactions for 1900.[82] Thus it must have seemed possible that the political support of the OHS could be gained by appealing to the pride and Loyalist ancestry commonly cherished by most historical societies.

In his 1898 address to the OHS, Chief Nelles Monture emphasized the loyalty of the Six Nations to the British Crown. In his speech, Chief A.G. Smith used language strikingly similar to the United Empire Loyalist myth. He welcomed the OHS members "as brothers whose forefathers fought side by side with ours ... in defence of our country–as brothers whose fathers were devoted and loyal through many dangers and difficulties, privations and sorrows to this land and country, and to the throne of Great Britain ... brothers who are with us still in loyalty and love to the same flag under which our fathers fought and fell." Both Monture and Smith stressed the civilized and advanced nature of the Haudenosaunee. The chiefs hoped that the OHS would improve the public's understanding of Aboriginal peoples in the province, and Monture added that perhaps this could lead to an acknowledgment that the Haudenosaunee were ready to govern their own affairs rather than being regulated by government officials.[83]

The idea that the Six Nations looked to Boyle and the OHS for political support rather than for pure historical goals seems reinforced by

other factors. Few Haudenosaunee visited the museum of any historical society, perhaps a comment on their perceived utility to Aboriginal
communities. Besides Dr Peter E. Jones and John O. Brant-Sero, who
were members of several societies, existing museum registers for Ontario
institutions exhibit few signatures of Aboriginal individuals. Using visitor books as potential commentary on the purpose of museums suggests
that those individuals who signed these books had specific reasons for
their visits.[84] During the annual meeting of the Pioneer and Historical
Association in 1897, for example, four members of the Six Nations visited the Niagara Historical Museum in Niagara-on-the-Lake. In 1898,
approximately seventy members visited the Niagara museum in June as
part of a military camp at Niagara-on-the Lake.[85] A few other scattered
visits by individuals occurred in 1900, 1902, and 1909.[86]

Further, the Six Nations of the Grand River never formed their own
society, as they were permitted to do under the OHS affiliation, and
instead sent Confederacy Council representatives to OHS meetings.
Even the brief spurt of interest following their affiliation with the OHS
was short-lived. Elected a vice-president in 1898, Brant-Sero continued
in this position until 1900, and he and his wife were regular members
during the 1898–1900 sessions. Nelles Monture sat on the two commit-
tees for Monuments and Tablets and Addresses and Publications until
1901. But no other Haudenosaunee filled officiate roles or joined the
membership. Even the election of Brant-Sero as a vice-president was
considered suspect by some chiefs, as they did not feel that he represented the entire Haudenosaunee; indeed, he had been appointed internally by OHS membership rather than by the Confederacy Council.[87]

Several years later in 1907, Elizabeth Thompson, the new OHS secretary, wrote to Indian Agent E.D. Cameron asking whether there was
any hope in reorganizing historical work at the Grand River reserve.
He replied that there was some potential as the chiefs had decided to
celebrate the 100th anniversary of the death of Joseph Brant.[88] But it was
not until 1909 that the Haudenosaunee made an overture to the OHS.
That year, the council invited the OHS to speak at the Six Nations' celebration of King Edward's birthday on Victoria Day. Again the council emphasized the Six Nations' loyalty and service as military allies.
Council Secretary Josiah Hill suggested to the OHS that their address
should discuss the participation of the Haudenosaunee during the
French and British wars in colonial North America. Hill's letter arrived
too late, however, for the OHS to attend.[89]

In their continued political struggles for confirmation of their status
as allies, not subjects, and to shed the restrictions of the Indian Act,

in 1911 the Six Nations again sought recognition from the Ontario Historical Society as joint founders of Upper Canada. During the annual meeting held in Brantford, the OHS met at the Council House in Ohsweken. Chief John W.M. Elliott addressed the gathering, emphasizing the longevity of their traditional government and the significant role of the Haudenosaunee as British allies in the French colonial wars and in the American Revolution. With this in mind, he pointed out the incongruity of their new rank as minors under the Canadian government and, as all descendants of the United Empire Loyalists, requested the help of the OHS to influence the federal government to reinstate their rights and privileges as sovereign peoples. Elliott also distinguished between the Haudenosaunee and other Aboriginal groups, suggesting it was unfair to classify them all the same under the Indian Act. At the same meeting, in a move reminiscent of David Boyle's adoption in 1892, the Six Nations awarded David Williams, then the president of the OHS, an honourary chieftainship of the Onondage'ga' nation and named him Shagoeiwatha (One Who Keeps Awake).[90] Williams agreed that the OHS would investigate the status of the Six Nations' claims, and, if they proved true, the OHS would advocate for fairer treatment. Thus Williams referred their appeal to the OHS Council for consideration, but it ultimately decided against supporting their claim, based upon a clause in the society constitution that stated that it should refrain from any political involvement.[91]

Three years later, members of the Six Nations reserve participated in the 100th anniversary of the battle of Lundy's Lane. Their placement as third in the parade, behind the army and a veterans' association, reflected their important role in the War of 1812. As one of the celebration's speakers, a Chief Hill from the Grand River reserve described the unfair treatment of Aboriginal peoples. Significantly, he apologized for airing problems at a celebration but emphasized that it was the only place such complaints would receive a hearing.[92] In 1921, similar issues were raised once again at an OHS meeting at Niagara-on-the-Lake. Asa Hill, the secretary of the Six Nations Council read a paper that described the alliance between England and the Haudenosaunee and thus asked the OHS to support their petitions to resolve the "unwarranted and unjust" treatment they received from the federal government. Augusta Gilkison, the daughter of the previous Six Nations Indian Agent Jasper T. Gilkison, and Colonel A.E. Belcher, the OHS treasurer, asked for the society to pass a resolution and send it to the government. The OHS, however, simply referred the matter to its council, which once again decided the constitution prohibited them from advocating political causes.[93]

Thus, despite a brief initial interest in historical matters, the Six Nations of the Grand River seemingly turned to the OHS only for political support, rather than for preservation of their history. The Haudenosaunee Council did decide to record its own history during the late nineteenth century, but again as a way to solidify the legitimacy of the Confederacy, and it did not act in conjunction with the OHS or any other historical society. In the 1880s, Seth Newhouse compiled this history, but, because of the preeminence he placed upon the Kanienkehaka nation, council rejected the document.[94] In 1899, the council allowed US anthropologist William Beauchamp to write down Confederacy procedures. Soon after, the chiefs appointed respected and knowledgeable Onodowahgah Chief John Arthur Gibson to record the oral history of the Confederacy, which was hence considered to be the official version.

Other groups also saw the OHS as a potential political advocate. At the 1904 annual meeting of the OHS in Windsor, a member of the Peterborough historical society read a history of the Mississaugas, as recorded from Chief Robert Paudash and his son Johnson of the Hiawatha band. At the end of the piece, the Paudashs included a political appeal for land or annuities on behalf of an Aboriginal band near Moose Point on the Georgian Bay. These people, the Paudashes explained, were the descendants of Tecumseh and possessed war medals, familiar allusions to their loyalty to the British, but had not been included in a treaty and thus had no reserve or monetary support. The Paudashes believed that if the government knew about their situation they were sure to be awarded aid.[95]

## SPIRITUAL BELIEFS

If Boyle was genuinely accepted by some individuals at Six Nations of the Grand River, and seen as a political ally by others, further elements of colonialism also shaped the reactions of Haudenosaunee during his collecting fieldwork. One of these factors was religion, which played a role in both the refusal to part with material culture and the reason behind its sale to Boyle and to other collectors such as Dr Oronhyateka and Peter Jones, the Mississauga missionary. The maintenance of traditional spirituality meant that many sacred objects needed to be retained while the conversion of individuals to Christianity often resulted in the sale or donation of such objects.

The sale of False Face masks, used to cure illness in humans and animals and control crop-destroying winds, is still contentious because of their spiritual meaning. Traditionalists consider objects such as masks and rattles to be alive. Only to be viewed at certain ritual times of the year, masks are not to be reproduced through photography, drawing, or any other means. They also require rigorous care; the keeper of a False Face mask is responsible for maintaining the spirit's life through the feeding of corn mush, rubbing oil or grease on the wood, and blowing tobacco smoke into its mouth. Considered communal within the False Face society, masks could be lent to others. When not in use, a mask could be hung out of general view in one's home but was more likely to be wrapped up with the accompanying turtle rattle. After the keeper's death, a mask was usually destroyed, buried, or transferred to another individual, though it must be someone within the False Face society.

Many continue to believe that grave repercussions follow the disrespect, ill treatment, or neglect of the powerful entities that are represented by the masks. Simeon Gibson, an informant for anthropologist William Fenton in the 1940s, detailed three stories of the serious results caused by inappropriate treatment of the False Face spirits earlier in the century at Six Nations. In the first episode, a man had insulted the False Faces and called them names. His face became twisted to one side, in the manner of many masks, and could not be cured until a False Face feast was conducted. Gibson's uncle, Chief Abraham Charles, was also affected by False Faces. He sang a song that belonged to a medicine man despite warnings from his elders. Until a similar feast was promised, Charles's mouth and nose were bent crooked and he repeatedly tried to jump into a burning fire. The third afflicted individual was a Christian Kanienkehaka, who, before he was cured, mimicked the actions of a False Face by pursing his mouth as if blowing ashes and emitting sounds as if appealing for tobacco. Again, a feast was recommended.[96]

Accordingly, Boyle encountered some reluctance when he enquired about False Faces during his fieldwork at Six Nations of the Grand River. As well, Indian agents and missionaries discouraged the practice of traditional spirituality and in response, many Aboriginal communities hid their ongoing rituals. "For a long time," Boyle wrote, his enquiries about a False Face Society on the reserve were met with denials of its existence. Persistent, Boyle learned that there were two societies, one secret and one whose members were known.[97]

Although individuals did sell Boyle False Face masks, many were hesitant to do so. In 1899, with the help of Dahkahedondyeh as interpreter, Boyle recorded his purchase of a seventy-year-old mask.

Abram Buck, brother of John Buck, 1898

According to Boyle, the keeper – Abram Buck, or Hyjoongkwas (He Tears Everything) – was "too old to act in his official capacity" as "Chief Medicine Man," and therefore allowed the mask to be sold. Boyle noted Buck's hesitance, however. Buck explained to the False Face that he was leaving his company. In order to placate its spirit, he burnt tobacco to keep it "calm and well pleased" despite this transition. He tied a small bundle of tobacco to the mask so that it would "always have some when you want it" and asked Boyle to rub its face with oil every year as it was "used to such attention … and would be pleased to be remembered in this way." He assured the mask that they "shall not be very far apart, and we will often think of you, and will often burn some tobacco for you."[98] Fenton's informants in the 1940s confirmed this as proper protocol upon the transfer of a mask, a ritual to prevent harm to the new keeper.[99]

Obviously, Buck regarded the mask as an animate being rather than a static object, and one that could affect the health of the Six Nations community. Boyle described Buck as "affectionately stroking" the hair of the False Face, and Buck's request for Boyle to rub the mask with oil yearly and his own promise to burn tobacco for it – both part of the important ongoing care of False Faces – suggest that Buck wished to ensure it remained alive and cared for. Further, it is significant that Buck also suggested to the Face that it "may still do good where you are going."[100] Although he did not specify its future purpose at the Ontario Provincial Museum, Buck obviously believed that the spirit still possessed a relevant role to society at large and was not a remnant or symbol of the past, as Boyle believed.

Jacob Hess, a middleman collector for Boyle, also observed that it was difficult to purchase False Face masks because people resisted their sale. He had "worked hard" to obtain the five specimens that he sent to Boyle in autumn 1904.[101] He also indicated that older masks demanded a higher price, perhaps in order to offset opposition to their purchase or because sellers knew that traditional objects commanded an increased value.[102] Brant-Sero noted that such pieces could only be bought at the Mid-Winter Festival, perhaps because it was the time of year when families were hungry and short on money.[103]

Dr Oronhyatekha's museum also included sacred objects. In most cases we do not know how these pieces came to be in his collection or why their keepers decided to give them up. For example, one False Face mask in Oronhyatekha's collection received a lengthy label in his catalogue, but it was simply an excerpt from David Boyle's 1899 report that described the hesitant donation of the mask by Abram Buck.[104] Another case, however, shows that conversion to Christianity often resulted in the sale of objects, a pattern found within historical collecting more generally. This case concerns the donation of an Odawa "Little Indian Idol" by Chief Shanghonose of the St Clair River area. The chief explained that this wooden "god" had been given to him by his great-grandfather Aligognoyenk who went west searching for the "'Happy Hunting Ground.'" At long last, Aligognoyenk and his party reached a great salt water, placed in their way by the spirit of the idol in order to stop him from reaching the afterlife. Because the water was salt, Aligognoyenk would have nothing to drink if he continued his journey, so he turned back. Upon reuniting with his people, a great council was called to discuss his trip, and it resolved that all dead should be buried with food and water from then on, to prepare them to cross this great water. But, as a Christian, Chief Shanghonose said he himself gave up this idol to "our friend Mr McClurg," the collector of many of the objects in Oronhyatekha's museum.[105]

Peter Jones, the Mississauga and Methodist missionary, also collected sacred objects, many of which he passed down to his son Dr Peter Edmund Jones. Like the Odawa figure given to Oronhyatekha, Peter Jones appears to have acquired religious items after the conversion of Aboriginal individuals, likely those he himself helped to convert. One "idol," exhibited to the Parent Missionary Society in 1829 in New York,

Jones said, had been "delivered up to me by a noted conjurer named Peter Omik."[106] Similar items were featured in his 1861 *History of the Ojebway Indians* and were likely collected during his 1841–49 ministry at Munceytown. One idol labelled "Me-Zeengk" had been "Delivered up" by Joseph Nicholas, a Muncey, after his conversion, and another was described as "A Muncey Devil Idol" that "Formerly belong[ed] to the Logan Family Delivered up on the 26th of Jan^y 1842." He also possessed two "family gods": Pabookowaih, the "god that crushes or breaks down diseases"; and the "goddess" Nahneetis, the "'guardian of health.'" The latter was accompanied by clothing and silver brooches given to the goddess as annual offerings and was "delivered up" to Jones by Eunice Hanks of Muncey, who after her conversion "had no further use for it."[107] Other sacred objects, including another mask similar to Pabookowaih, a water drum stick, two rattles, four bone sucking tubes used in healing practices, a "god" made of snake and weasel skin, a miniature racquet used for divination, a box that had contained "love powder," and a shaman's headdress, may have been given to him for similar reasons.[108]

Unlike Abram Buck, who continued to believe in the power of his False Face after he gave it to Boyle, it is difficult to know what those who gave up other spiritual items thought about the power of these objects after their conversion to Christianity. Many Aboriginal people who became Christian continued to believe in aspects of their traditional religion and observed rituals of both belief systems, but giving up such items would have made this difficult. In his writings there is no hint of whether Jones coerced converts into giving up such items, but this certainly occurred in other cases across North America. Like False Face masks, these religious objects, often considered to be sentient beings, carried cultural protocols for their care, respect, treatment, and use, which did not match their acquisition into a Victorian-style collection. For example, Nahneetis was to be celebrated every year with feasting, dancing, and offered food and clothing. Pabookowaih and similar masks used for healing and sometimes divination were hung in little bark houses when not in use.[109] It seems unlikely that either Jones followed such protocol once these beings were in his artifact collection.

While the published writings of the senior Jones would have been scrutinized by his religious colleagues, his opinions about Christianity as the one true religion appear to be genuine. He showed objects during public speeches, like one to the Parent Missionary Society, to demonstrate "the power of the Gospel in pulling down the strong holds of Indian superstition and idolatry, and thus to bring the red man of the forest to cast away his idols to the moles and bats." At a visit to the museum of the London Missionary Society, Jones stated he was "much pleased to see the trophies of the Gospel in demolishing idolatry and superstition."[110] Further, in reference to Pabookowaih and Nahneetis, personal gods that one obtained by fasting and dreams, Jones stated he had fasted but never had had a vision. Indeed, he concluded it was a "mercy ... that neither our happiness nor success depends upon the supposed possession of these imaginary gods, but that there is *one* only true and living God, whose assistance none ever did, or ever can, seek in vain!"[111] His son, P.E. Jones, was also a Christian and sold much of his collection to the Smithsonian Institution through W.J. McGee of the Bureau of American Ethnology and to Mark R. Harrington, an agent who collected for private individuals.

The Johnson family collection also contained sacred objects. Pauline Johnson sold to Boyle a "Medicine" mask and turtle shell rattle once owned by the wampum keeper John Buck in 1897.[112] Buck had died several years earlier and his children, particularly his son Joshua Buck, began to sell his belongings. Presumably, Johnson had obtained the items in this manner. Other items in the Johnson family collection had been obtained more forcibly. Anthropologist Horatio Hale told a story about the acquisition of part of a Delaware idol by George H.M. Johnson, Pauline's father. Johnson had visited the Delaware nation in the midst of feasting and dancing around an idol carved from wood in the shape of a woman. Johnson struck off its head with an axe, splitting the statue in the process. The Delaware chief had agreed to this, apparently because he had partly converted to Christianity himself although his people had not. Johnson at first threw the head on top of a shed at the Anglican parsonage. His other daughter Evelyn remembered that children played with it and broke off its nose in the process. Her father also displayed the head in his study, and after his death it was kept underneath the parlour table.[113] Certainly such treatment would have been offensive to Delaware traditionalists.

Some contemporary community members from Grand River suggest, however, that Chief Johnson's destruction of the Delaware idol and appropriation of masks was more posturing for the missionary who accompanied Johnson in some versions of the story, the Anglican Church who employed him as an interpreter, and the Indian agent than personal belief. Horatio Hale's telling of the story characterized Johnson as a fervent Christian who went to the Delaware ceremony alone because he believed their religion to be "monstrous." A Brantford historian portrayed Chief Johnson similarly in the telling of another story about Johnson who once visited a carver of a False Face mask with an axe and a pistol and destroyed it in process of its creation.[114] But, in her interpretation of the story of the Delaware idol, Pauline Johnson said that, while her father was Christian, he distinguished between those who worshipped the Great Spirit, such as his own Kanienkehaka ancestors, and those who were idolatrous like the Delawares. The Kanienkehakas were "pagans," she said, but not "heathen."[115]

Pauline, her sister Evelyn, and their siblings inherited their father's artifact collection. Although she travelled frequently, Pauline Johnson often brought objects such as quill mats, ceremonial stones, baskets, pouches, and an Onondage'ga' rattle with her.[116] In the 1890s, Johnson took a mask to England and displayed it on her mantelpiece with her performance costume draped over a screen nearby.[117] At least one of her recitals included the display of a mask on her platform.[118] Such treatment of traditional spiritual items may have been offensive to Longhouse members who considered them to need care and dedication and not to be viewed except during ceremonial occasions.

This issue may not be so straightforward, however. In her writings she claimed to be both Christian and pagan, and it is unclear whether these identities changed over time, were a form of religious hybridization, or mere rhetoric.[119] It is possible that the public display of False Face masks became less common as missionaries pressed the Haudenosaunee to convert to Christianity and thus religious items were used or shown more secretly. In this sense, Johnson's public use of the masks may represent an earlier traditional protocol. Certainly, others had allowed anthropologists to photograph masks, including Boyle who, during his fieldwork, took a picture of John Key, a Tutelo, outside his house with a False Face hanging next to him.[120] Anthropologist William Fenton's twentieth-century informants also distinguished between types of masks. Those that visited an individual in a dream and were carved especially for the keeper as guardians were considered to be more inviolate, while extra masks could be lent to others or even sold.[121]

## CHANGING IDEAS OF STEWARDSHIP

Sales of material culture also revealed changing attitudes about the stewardship of objects of cultural patrimony. As Aboriginal individuals adopted values of the wider Euro-Canadian community, including the preference for private property, traditions concerning the care and custody of objects changed. When traditional Onondage'ga' wampum keeper Chief John Buck died in 1893, his son Joshua negotiated the

Pauline Johnson, 1861–1913, wearing a wampum belt as part of her performance costume

sale of the Confederacy Council wampum belts and strings with museums and collectors in the United States and Canada. The Six Nations Council, who wished to appoint a new wampum keeper, was understandably concerned about the custody of the wampum. Traditional ownership of wampum was communal and therefore not for individual sale. The 1890s was also the era in which the Six Nations struggled to regain recognition of their sovereignty from the federal government and, as in their 1890 petition to Governor General Frederick Stanley, they used wampum belts as evidence of their claim. Thus the retention of the belts at Six Nations was important. In contrast, Joshua Buck appears to have treated the belts as private family property.[122] Several years later, in a letter to Ska-ru-ren anthropologist J.N.B. Hewitt, Buck enigmatically remarked: "I will tell you I sold it for the chiefs twenty-one single [wampum] strings for forty dollars. That shows the chiefs they can't cliam [sic] on these things. You know what I mean."[123]

Pauline Johnson wearing a dentalium shell belt as part of her costume

In 1893 the council appointed several members to approach the Buck family and demand the strings of wampum, the pipe of peace and all other property belonging to the council. The group appointed Johnson Williams (Dehayadgwayeh) and David John, who then requested a certificate validated by council before they confronted the Bucks. Apparently unsuccessful, a week later the council charged six chiefs to visit the family and obtain these items "without any further trouble."[124] The objects remained in the Bucks' possession.

Ultimately, many of the belts were purchased by US collectors and museums.[125] As part of a larger investigation seeking the whereabouts of numerous belts sold to several individuals, the Six Nations chiefs discovered that Boyle, at the Canadian Institute, had purchased two of these in June 1894. In January 1895, Chief Smith, presumably the same individual who sold his own individual archaeological collection a few years earlier, requested that the wampum be returned to the Six Nations. Boyle agreed, on the condition that the institute be reimbursed the sixty-five dollars in advance. He also requested that, if the belts came upon the market again, he would have first right of purchase.[126] That same year, council chiefs appointed Jacob Salem Johnson to care for all remaining belts until a definitive arrangement could be made.[127] The council decided not to take action against those who sold the wampum belts and did not report the sale of these items to their Indian agent. In a retroactive gesture, the council secured the remaining four belts in a vault at Jacob Salem Johnson's general store in Ohsweken and in 1899 refused to lend them for the Canadian Historical Exhibition in Toronto.[128]

Pauline Johnson obtained at least four of these belts, presumably from the Buck family, and wore at least two of them, along with her father's hunting knife and two scalps, at her waist as part of her performance costume. Later, she sold a belt each to David Boyle and US collectors George Heye and Harriet Maxwell Converse, and gifted another to the British artist Sir Frederic Leighton, whom she had met in England during her travels.[129] Johnson must have known about the council chiefs trying to stop the Bucks from selling the wampum to collectors, later attempts to have other belts returned by their US purchasers, and council's use of the wampum belts to prove the Six Nations' status as allies not British subjects.

Biographers have deemed Pauline Johnson a profligate spender.[130] Certainly her correspondence suggests financial need, but being raised as a Christian and by a Euro-Canadian mother who instilled non-Aboriginal values likely would have made the choice of selling sacred objects, and items of significant cultural importance like wampum belts, easier. In 1897 she agreed to Boyle's purchase price of fifty dollars for several items. "I am at a standstill," she wrote, "and alas! my treasures must go for money must be had at all costs." She assumed that he would have all her artifacts eventually anyway.[131] In 1905, she requested the aid of naturalist Ernest Thompson Seton to find a buyer for her Hiawatha League wampum belt. She was "compelled" to part with it if she was to tour again in England. She calculated it to be worth $1,600 but she was willing to accept a lesser amount.[132] One year later, Johnson sold this belt to the prolific US collector George Heye. Because she found herself in a better financial position than expected, she suggested to Heye that she would sell him the belt for $500 with the opportunity of repurchasing it within the next two years at a rate of six percent interest once she was settled in England. Johnson also offered a "medicine mask" to Heye as she disliked to have these objects scattered more than necessary. Heye agreed on the amount of fifty dollars, with a similar clause for its redemption by Johnson.[133] In 1907, Johnson offered an Onondage'ga' turtle rattle, among numerous other pieces in her collection, to Montreal lawyer and collector William D. Lighthall, as security for a $100 loan.[134] In later years, Pauline Johnson appealed for the return of the wampum belt she had previously sold to Boyle, but this was only because she required it as a prop for her lectures rather than for traditional political purposes. Boyle replied that he had no authority to sell items and suggested that she contact the minister of Education.[135]

Her sister Evelyn Johnson looked to museums, rather than the community, to steward and preserve Haudenosaunee material culture, particularly wampum belts. She twice offered the Brant Historical Society the possessions of her late sister in hopes of forming a museum, and she also later willed seven False Face masks to this society.[136] She was also concerned about US collecting expeditions that targeted wampum belts, and she believed that her community would eventually regret their sale to the United States. "I cannot tell you how I love these relics of the former grandeur of our people," she wrote to Charles Currelly of the Royal Ontario Museum (ROM), "and hope they may still be saved to our own museums."[137] Another common fear by those who wished to preserve traditions and material culture was that the communities could no longer be relied upon to do so. Instead, some individuals looked to museums as a new location for preservation. Indeed, Evelyn Johnson tried to convince the Grand River Confederacy Council to entrust the four remaining belts to a museum for safekeeping. Two of the four belts were the very ones that David Boyle had purchased and then returned in the 1890s. Johnson suggested to Currelly that this should be a loan not a sale and that the chiefs could borrow and exhibit them whenever needed and then return them to the fire-proof museum in Toronto. The chiefs insisted that their Council House was the suitable place for the storage of the wampum. In the 1920s, however, Evelyn Johnson somehow obtained these four belts and six strings of wampum and placed them in Currelly's hands. She stipulated that her name was never to be connected with these items and that the objects were not to be exhibited until after her death. If the belts were still retained by the museum upon her death, then ownership was to be transferred to the ROM, which later occurred.[138] Like the Onondage'ga' in New York, who believed they transferred care but not ownership of several belts to the state museum in 1898, Evelyn Johnson seems to have feared the further loss of material culture and thus viewed the preservation of wampum belts and other items in museums to be a viable alternative in a community under pressure from assimilation and political differences.[139] It is unclear, however, if she shared the common Euro-Canadian nine-teenth-century presumption that material culture was best preserved by museums, not by Aboriginal communities, or rather if she simply suspected the motives of a few individuals at the Grand River who had sold belts before.

What else might explain the sale and donation of these wampum to collectors and museums? Anthropologist William Fenton has contro-versially argued that there was an increasing neglect of wampum belts in the late 1800s, perhaps caused by the decreasing orthodoxy in council protocols. Thus professional anthropologists pushed for their care by museums and may have influenced community members to agree.[140] Strings of chieftainship wampum, such as the one Emily Carryer sold to David Boyle, may have been considered anachronistic as many Haudenosaunee chiefly titles had become extinct or unfilled after the partial migration of the Haudenosaunee to Canada after the American Revolution.[141] In contrast, contemporary members of the Six Nations have suggested that the wampum belts began to symbolize divisive politics in the Confederacy Council and thus some believed they were better off preserved outside of the community. Anthropologists have also theorized that various levels of access to traditional knowledge exist within cultures, which in turn affect the degree of understanding among individuals, and the way in which ethnographic items are valued and utilized. As assimilation undermines the power of traditionalists, the significance of the objects that legitimize their authority declines. Teleologically, as this material culture is dispersed, the authority of traditionalists further decreases. Some individuals may even seek to decrease the power of traditionalists. This may, then, also contextualize the sale of sacred objects or those of cultural patrimony.[142]

Ambiguity surrounds the transfer of many objects to David Boyle and other collectors. For some artifacts, even the seller is unknown. For instance, Boyle recorded the accession of numerous sacred pieces – three masks, four rattles, two games, two ash stirring paddles, a drum, and a conch shell used to call people to the Longhouse – but not their previous owners, nor how he obtained them.[143] For other objects, the previous owners are known but not their reasons for giving up these items. Josiah Hill sent Boyle war clubs.[144] Peter J. Maracle, who sold archaeological items to Boyle, also offered him numerous Iroquoian silver brooches, an ink stand used by Joseph Brant to make Bible translations and the translations themselves.[145] In addition to the chieftainship wampum, Emily Carryer offered to sell Boyle brooches, earrings, bracelets, corn processing items, a knife, and a basket and tumpline, stating that these objects would add curiosity and complete Boyle's collection. Carryer also suggested she could procure additional items from others.[146] William Bill, although he was a Longhouse follower, gave numerous sacred "pagan" dance rattles to Boyle.[147] William Sandy, a Gayogoho:no "pagan" according to the 1901 census, presented Boyle with a woman's rattle, possibly a sacred item.[148] Pauline Johnson was not the only one to obtain items from the Buck family. John Roberts Davis also possessed a rattle, once belonging to Chief John Buck, which he later gave to Boyle in 1898.[149] Why Davis, an Anglican, procured this rattle before giving it to Boyle is unknown, or perhaps he procured it specifically for Boyle.

The sale of objects did not mean that the original owners did not later regret their loss. For example, two of Pauline Johnson's biographers have suggested that her compositions may have reflected ambiguity toward her involvement in anthropology.[150] In 1893, her short story "A Red Girl's Reasoning" mocked anthropologists through its depiction of the marriage of protagonist Charlie McDonald to a young Métis woman as the consummation of "his predilections for Indianology," which had begun by relic-hunting and studying archaeology and folklore. Christine Robinson teased her husband that she someday might exchange him for another, just as he did with the "duplicate relics" in his artifact collection. In the end, she leaves McDonald, for he ultimately cannot understand her Aboriginal culture and upbringing.[151] Johnson's 1911 *Hoolool of the Totem Poles* described a West Coast Aboriginal woman who adamantly refused to sell a family pole despite poverty and numerous tempting offers. One night, her son dreamt of many small totem poles. The mother interpreted this as a sign that she should carve tiny replicas for sale and yet protect the original pole. The moral of the story: the family could be prosperous and still preserve custom as the proud owners of the totem.[152] Johnson did later express regret over the disposal of the "ancient National Belts Thus destroying our Archives" after the death of the wampum keeper Chief John Buck. Her thoughts about her own role in this dispersal went unstated.[153]

Pauline Johnson died childless, as did all of her siblings, a fact that some at the Six Nations of the Grand River see as a spiritually determined consequence of their family's role in the dispersal of material culture. A similar belief surrounds the death of Joshua Buck, the seller of most of the Confederacy Council's wampum belts and several sacred objects, who died after being crushed by a steamroller during roadwork. Such regret and ambiguity surrounding the sale of ethnographic material culture is not unique to this community. In comparison, many anthropologists ethnocentrically believed that they, not Aboriginal communities, were the best caretakers of these unique items and were thus preserving traditional culture before assimilation completely wiped out past lifeways. The reactions of Aboriginal communities to collectors were also shaped by colonialism and pressures of assimilation. Changes to political structures, religious conversion, differing ideas of ownership, and the disruption of the intergenerational transmission of knowledge all affected the relationships between collectors and Aboriginal communities. By the early twentieth century, a significant portion of the Six Nations' material culture had been separated from the community and rested in the hands of US and Canadian collectors and museums.

# 5

## USABLE PASTS
### *Interpreting Aboriginal Material Culture*

Here is all that is left of a once powerful race,
The tribes that first roamed all over this place.
This is all that remains of all that they done,
All the rest is tradition from father to son,
And the next generation will look for in vain
Mementoes of man that they held in disdain.[1]

So wrote Dr Solon Woolverton, who was poetically inspired by his own
private natural history collection which he housed on the top floor of
his London home. A typical nineteenth-century scholar, Woolverton
had diverse scientific interests. He was a dentist and a geology professor at Western University. He belonged to the Entomological Society
of Ontario and the London and Middlesex Historical Society and acted
as one of the latter's first curators. David Boyle described his collection
of archaeological items as comprising "much rare and correspondingly
valuable material." In 1894, Woolverton introduced Boyle to several
archaeological sites, including the Shaw-Wood site, once a large Neutral
village, which had been known to area residents for several decades.[2]

Found in his scrapbooks, Woolverton's poem captures themes
common to the Euro-Canadian portrayal of the culture and future
of Aboriginal peoples in the nineteenth and early twentieth centuries. Aboriginal peoples were thought to be extinct or on the verge of
extinction because their culture could not survive in the face of the so-
called superior European civilization. Thus only artifacts in museums
remained, or would remain, to tell "of all that they done." In this sense,

collectors and historical societies saw themselves as the stewards who should preserve and interpret Aboriginal material culture, and the existence of contemporaneous communities and their own ongoing oral traditions could be ignored. There is no mention in Woolverton's poem of the many post-contact factors – epidemics, conflict and war, enforced assimilation, alcoholism, poverty, appropriation of land – that led to the dispersal and reduction of the Aboriginal population. Rather, it was common in early Canadian history and literature to gloss over these factors or to depict a peaceful succumbing to an inevitable evolutionary force. Some members of historical societies recognized the loyalist contributions of deceased Aboriginal leaders like Joseph Brant or Tecumseh, but these individuals were only briefly noted. So, one could be nostalgic about the decline of the Aboriginal population, but with no guilt attached.

The average Euro-Canadian also believed in evolutionary paradigms that proposed that Aboriginal culture was more primitive than their own and spoke of Aboriginal peoples through the imagery of the noble and barbaric savage, which had been popularized earlier in the eighteenth century. Even some Aboriginal individuals used this imagery. As noble savages, Aboriginal peoples supposedly lived harmoniously in a golden age of nature. They acted instinctually, were brave, dignified, loyal, hospitable, eloquent, of strong physical form, and pure and innocent, the latter two traits often symbolized by nakedness. They lacked religion and societal rules but produced artifacts of beautiful craftsmanship. Alternatively, barbaric savage imagery characterized Aboriginal peoples as cruel, dirty, indolent, deceitful, and lacking in letters, religion, and artistic abilities. Writers emphasized the scarcity of food, poverty, short lifespan, cannibalism, and torture of war captives. Seen through this trope, Aboriginal artifacts were characterized as rough, rude, and primitive. In both sets of imagery, Aboriginal peoples teetered on extinction because of their seeming inability to adjust to the advanced civilization introduced to North America by European settlers.[3]

In the late nineteenth century, the accepted scientific theory was cultural evolution. Cultural evolutionists like David Boyle believed in a hierarchy of societies, in which all societal characteristics evolved from simple to complex. Yet the doctrine of progress and perfectibility meant that all groups could advance, although perhaps not to equal levels of civilization. Popularized by US ethnographer Lewis H. Morgan, the developmental structure of savagery to barbarism to civilization was mostly based on the level of technology and economic development, and often placed Iroquoian peoples as culminating at a high degree of barbarism and ahead of Algonkian-speaking peoples. This process of evolution could be demonstrated by the comparative method, which assumed that earlier stages of humanity could still be seen in contemporary primitive societies. British armchair anthropologist E.B. Tylor's idea of survivals – existing remnants of cultural traits from past evolutionary stages – was integral to the comparative method and used to reconstruct past cultures. Darwinism mixed with cultural evolution suggested that societal development was based upon biological or racial factors.[4] While David Boyle used both cultural evolution and the earlier, more popular images of the noble and barbaric savage, he could not ignore the fact that Aboriginal peoples had not died out since he conducted fieldwork among them. Instead, Boyle emphasized Aboriginal assimilation, including his belief that oral tradition had been too corrupted by European influence to be of much use. This, too, was a way to assume that someone other than an Aboriginal individual, in this case a professional scholar, was better placed to interpret their culture.

The public was exposed to oral traditions as well, mainly those of the Anishinabeg, which told of their battles with the Haudenosaunee (Iroquois) and their struggle over what became Upper Canada. Travelogues and popular literature commonly recorded these stories. To Boyle, the historical and archaeological record contradicted them. Many Aboriginal peoples continued to believe in the accuracy and importance of their oral traditions, but the historical conflict between Iroquoian- and Algonkian-speaking peoples meant that they disagreed about the meanings of some sites and material culture preserved through that tradition. Both groups, however, agreed on their importance to the founding and defense of Upper Canada, beliefs similar to the United Empire Loyalist (UEL) myth cherished by historical societies.

Thus differences in the method and content inherent in the interpretation of material culture and historic sites were not just culturally based. Usefulness was another factor. As Norman Knowles has shown, usable pasts are (re)invented traditions that often serve a purpose beyond celebration or documenting historical content. For Euro-Canadians, the idea that Aboriginal peoples were dying out justified the expropriation of their land. An emphasis on their warlike qualities suggested that conflict with European powers was inevitable. To professional collectors, Aboriginal assimilation and corruption of oral knowledge bolstered their own authority as scholars and provided a reason why they should be the stewards of traditional material culture preserved in museums. Historical societies included the actions of Aboriginal leaders in the founding of Upper Canada in their celebration

of United Empire Loyalism but denied Aboriginal peoples a contemporary presence. Under pressure from colonialism, the Aboriginal groups
of Ontario used collectors and collecting to assert their traditional ter-
ritorial rights and fight back against land appropriation and increasing
restrictions under the Indian Act.

## IMAGERY IN POPULAR PUBLICATIONS

It is not surprising that the nineteenth-century public continued to
believe in the images of the noble and barbaric savage, while professional scholars began to discard their more extreme interpretations.
Popular English-Canadian publications, including national magazines and literature, certainly reinforced them.[5] Such publications
also emphasized the sublime and the picturesque, two concepts that
included similar imagery to describe the sites and peoples of Ontario.
Sublime experiences meant encountering natural elements previously
considered as gloomy or threatening while the picturesque encompassed
more romantic, artistic, and pastoral landscapes. Euro-Canadians fit
Aboriginal people into both categories. The untamed and savage nature
of Aboriginal peoples matched the frightening wildness of Canadian
lakes and forests, which was so important to the sublime experience.
Picturesque landscapes often featured historic elements like dilapidated
building, ruins, and graveyards to stir feelings of nostalgia. Aboriginal
peoples, allegedly almost extinct, and the remnants of their former villages dotted throughout this landscape heightened the nostalgia.[6] For
example, in a history of Dundas County, the author described Point
Iroquois, one of the "favorite resorts" of Aboriginal peoples, through
these tropes. "Here, amid the peaceful groves of pine and maple, they
built their camp-fires and held their pow-wows," the book explained.
"Here," the author concluded, "they revelled in the joys consistent with
their natural tastes, and as they viewed the mighty river so picturesque
at this spot what fancies must have thrilled them? What an ideal environment it must have presented to their minds."[7]

Most Canadians in the nineteenth century read historical romance,
a genre that celebrated heroic characters and their struggles to establish
a new country.[8] For example, in *The Master of Life: A Romance of the
Five Nations and of Prehistoric Montreal* (1908), collector William D.
Lighthall described the Haudenosaunee as a people who lived in harmony in a bountiful Eden, and their nature as mystical, "chivalrous
and reverent."[9] James Dickson, the land surveyor who collected for
David Boyle, used similar images. He wrote that Aboriginal peoples

lived "in the remote ages" and if the "veil in which the unwritten past is enshrouded be withdrawn, scenes of valour, scenes of heroism, and scenes of cruelty and blood would be beheld."[10]

This literature supported the idea that Aboriginal peoples were extinct or close to it, as Ontario farmer and poet Alexander McLachlan nostalgically memorialized in his poem *To An Indian Skull* (1874):

And art thou come to this at last
Great Sachem of the forest vast!
E'en thou who wert so tall in stature,
And modelled in the pride of Nature;
High as the deer, you bore your head,
Swift as the roebuck was thy tread;
Thine eye, bright as the orb of day–
In battle a consuming ray!
Tradition links thy name with fear,
And strong men hold their breath to hear
What mighty feats by thee were done–
The battles by thy strong arm won!
The glory of thy tribe wert thou–
But–where is all thy glory now?
Where are those orbs, and where that tongue,
On which commanding accents hung!
Canst thou do nought by grin and stare
Through hollow sockets–the worms' lair
And toothless gums, all gaping there![11]

Local publications also emphasized the extinction of Aboriginal peoples. A history of the Peterborough area stated that nothing remained of the Wendat (Huron) but Jesuit records and bonepits. A similar book on Toronto and surrounding area suggested that of its previous Aboriginal residents the "last living representations of their race has disappeared."[12] A Middlesex history likewise said that "not a vestige of the unknown or early Indian occupiers of the county exists."[13] *Four Years on the Georgian Bay* (1888) recommended visiting several sites of the Wendat, which it deemed as "vanished from history."[14] A handbook of scenery noted "far-famed" picture writing at Cariboo Point on Lake Superior, created by an Aboriginal race "now supposed to be extinct."[15] Part history and part travelogue, Methodist minister William Withrow's *Our Own Country* (1889) also depicted the inevitable near-extinction of Aboriginal peoples and evoked a sense of distance and mystery between Euro-Canadian settlers and those indigenous to Canada. "To our remote descendants," he lamented, "the story of the Indian tribes will be a dim tradition ... Already their arrow-heads and tomahawks are collected in our museums as strange relics of a bygone era. Our anti-quarians, even now, speculate with a puzzled interest on their memorial mounds and barrows."[16] Indeed, much of the Ontario public believed that the Haudenosaunee had exterminated the Wendat, the Tionontati (Petun), and the Neutral in the 1600s, although the Wendat had a reserve in Quebec, a group of Wyandot still lived near Windsor, and prisoners from all nations had been adopted by the Haudenosaunee.

Ontario children were also exposed to these common images in various ways. At summer camps, instructors often incorporated the finding and excavation of a mock Indian burial ground as part of their activities. Camp staff also encouraged admiration of Aboriginal peoples, but the information presented was highly imaginative, often pan-Indian in nature, and included the use of noble savage imagery. These camps portrayed Aboriginal peoples as ageless and unchanging, possessing a "natural religion," and having little or no technology. Boys' activities such as fishing and tracking promoted the idea of Aboriginal men as hyper-masculine, while those for girls emphasized the artistic side of Aboriginal peoples through crafts such as weaving and painting.[17]

Much of the children's stories in this period portrayed Aboriginal peoples within the two stereotypes of the noble and barbaric savage.[18] Catharine Parr Traill's *Canadian Crusoes* (1850) set out both tropes. The main characters, children lost on the Rice Lake plains, dreaded meeting Aboriginal people because of their cruelty, but when they rescued a captive Aboriginal girl, she taught them how to survive in the wilderness.[19] In *Snowflakes and Sunbeams* (1856), two rivals, Redfeather and Misconna embodied the noble and barbaric savage played out against the backdrop of the fur trade era.[20] Ernest Thompson Seton, who established the League of Woodcraft Indian camps, later absorbed by the Boys Scouts of America, played a large role in shaping how young boys thought about Aboriginal peoples. In his children's book *Two Little Savages* (1903), the novel that served to exemplify many of the beliefs and activities featured at the Woodcraft camps, Yan, the main character "goes Indian." This process included making and hunting with bows and arrows, building a wigwam and a tipi, learning to identify animal tracks and wild plants, making fire without matches, tanning hides and sewing moccasins, darkening his skin through tanning, and "grunting 'Ugh' or 'Wagh' when anything surprised him."[21] Ultimately, Yan's dream was to lead an "ideal life–the life of an Indian with all that is bad and cruel left out ... he would show men how to live without cutting down all the trees, spoiling all the streams, and killing every living thing. He would learn how to get the fullest pleasure out of the woods himself and then teach others how to do the same."[22] This romanticized notion of living in harmony with nature fit neatly into noble savage imagery.

Early school texts also show that children learned about the more popular images of Aboriginal peoples, with a dash of scientific theory. Reminiscent of Lewis Morgan's theory, history books, including those approved by the provincial authorities, described the Iroquoian-speaking peoples as more settled, agricultural, and more politically sophisticated – and thus more civilized – than Algonkian-speaking ones, but still untamed. These texts described all Aboriginal peoples in terms of the noble and barbaric savage imagery; they were instinctual, freedom-loving, hospitable, loyal to their tribe, taciturn, and superstitious. They possessed no laws, arts, or sciences, and they loved to gamble, feast, and tell stories.[23] In describing the events that led to the dispersal of the Wendat and Tionontati, or in warfare generally, textbooks condemned the Haudenosaunee as revengeful warriors and cruel torturers who conducted "incessant, murderous raids."[24] Children in nineteenth-century Ontario could be forgiven for assuming that the province's Aboriginal peoples were long dead or tattered scraps of formerly glorious societies. Textbooks often ignored or glossed over the existence of contemporaneous communities, calling the Anishinabeg and the Wendat extinct or remnants of former groups. *The History of the Dominion of Canada* (1897) quickly dismissed the Six Nations of Ontario as "descendants of the once powerful and ferocious Iroquois" who now lived "largely upon the bounty of the Canadian government."[25] Most books briefly acknowledged the important role of Tecumseh and his Aboriginal allies in the War of 1812, but overall there was little discussion of nineteenth- or twentieth-century Aboriginal peoples who still lived in the province.

## POPULAR INTERPRETATIONS OF MATERIAL CULTURE

Andrew Hunter described the public's understanding of Aboriginal peoples as "at the mercy of their fancies and exaggeration."[26] Certainly, the public's interpretation of specific sites and artifacts could be rather imaginative, romantic, nostalgic, and shaped by popular imagery. Naturally formed knolls and even beaver dams were often assumed to be tumuli. As Ingersoll factory owner and poet James McIntyre wrote, "We know a hill is smooth and round, Where Indian relics may be found."[27] Local opinion in Elgin County said that the ditch between the double earthworks at the Southwold site was the remains of a medieval-style moat.[28] One magazine touted four circular ridges near a supposed serpent mound to be dance circles, the lower parts stamped down by many feet. Apparently a stone sacrificial altar had been found nearby.[29] Of such circles, Boyle simply noted that he was unaware of any documentation for such beliefs.[30] Other natural ridges were also thought to be battle embankments or serpent mounds. Hunter noted that it was common to creatively describe these sinuous formations as "'fortifications,'" "'Indian embankments,'" and even "'Indian race-courses,'" while Boyle suggested the need for "great caution, before venturing the assertion that any bank or mound is of human origin because of its external appearance."[31]

Such romantic speculation also occurred when the public found unique or beautiful artifacts. Caves among the Elora gorge were famous for the story of a local boy finding several hundred wampum beads hidden in a crevice. The tourist guide *Picturesque Canada* asked "Did some Indian beauty, flying for protection to these natural cloisters, and taking off her now useless and dangerous jewellery, confide to this secure casket the necklaces that had set off her charms at many a moonlight or firelight dance?"[32] At Clearville, at a site known as the Fort, collector J.H. Smith discovered a skull that a local history described as being carved with hieroglyphics that might represent zodiac signs.[33] The public often interpreted such artifacts as indicators of a special status. At Rice Lake, for example, a female buried with copper items was deemed a princess by the press, and another with moss, bone artifacts, silver jewellery, and other charms was claimed to be a medicine woman.[34] A man found with a shell necklace was an important warrior, and even a skeleton buried with only a single tomahawk, a chief.[35]

Artifacts could also be interpreted through barbaric savage imagery. Most Euro-Canadians assumed that early European trade goods, such as iron axes and copper kettles, were eminently superior to indigenous-made items and that Aboriginal peoples had quickly adopted them. As the *Jubilee History* of the Thorold and Beaverdams Historical Society stated, "the superior implements of the Europeans gave an irresistible impulse. Stone axes, flint knives and bone needles yielded at once to steel ones, for which there was a keen demand."[36] Artifacts interpreted through this image were commonly described as rough, rude, or unfinished. If items were elegant, well-finished or unusual they were frequently labelled as being from a superior tribe of Indians, or even from a pre-Indian race. For example, a local history of Dundas County credited tools made from an unusual blue stone to a "tribe superior to the ordinary Indian."[37] Military officer, engineer, and artist Sir Richard Henry Bonnycastle stated in his *Canadas in 1841* that a "vase" he had been given seemed too elegant to have been crafted by any Aboriginal race living in Upper Canada; instead he thought it must have been a specimen of an Eastern Old World culture, or an advanced but extinct culture related to the Aztecs, a society thought to be one of the most superior of all those indigenous to North America.[38]

In discussing the Southwold earthworks in Elgin County, the *Canadian Illustrated News* judged them to be of the Moundbuilder culture – often argued to be a pre- or non-Indian society – based on artifactual evidence. According to the author, pottery pieces demonstrated an artistry of which Aboriginals were incapable. Although clearly an extreme interpretation, this writer further argued that Aboriginal peoples were so undeveloped that they did not have pottery or arrowheads, both types of objects found at Southwold. Finally, the author contended, the depth of the ashbeds meant that the site had had substantial houses, far more than what Aboriginal groups were capable of constructing.[39]

The Moundbuilder myth did not take as strong a hold in Canada as it did in the United States. David Boyle ridiculed the idea that any mounds in Ontario had been made by a pre-Indian race. They were not constructed by any Iroquoian or Algonkian peoples he thought, but certainly they were from an Aboriginal culture. This was the less poetic interpretation he acknowledged, however, and noted that the Moundbuilder myth appealed to "man's mythologic sense very powerfully."[40]

The public often disregarded information from historical records that were relatively accessible and instead focused on aspects of popular imagery. Newspapers published information from the *Jesuit Relations*, other historical literature and excerpts from Boyle's annual reports. These articles, as some local histories and even personal memoirs did, described the Iroquoian and Algonkian ceremony of the Feast of the Dead, which demanded the periodic reburial of skeletons in a large pit with strict cultural rules about grave gifts and the placement of the bones. But, seen as savages, Aboriginal peoples were believed to have lived under constant threat of warfare, and thus mass graves were often interpreted as results of large battles. In his description of a Phelpston ossuary excavation, for example, Andrew Hunter noted that individuals who did not take part in the digging gathered around the grave and proposed "all sorts of wild theories" to explain the origin of the bones, the favourite being a war.[41]

The public thus characterized many sites as battlegrounds. The public mistakenly identified these through the supposed suitability of the landscape for war, the presence of only a thin covering of leaves overtop graves, ordinary clothing rather than one's best on the skeletons, and the presence of abundant arrowheads and tomahawks in the ground or stuck in tree trunks. The public often called small depressions rifle, battle, warrior, or surprise pits, holes that David Boyle said were really used for storage of corn.[42] Even a small pioneer lime kiln was deemed a fort despite its small size, an idea ridiculed by the newspaper that reported about it. The kiln designation was a less romantic interpretation, the reporter noted.[43]

The idea that Aboriginal peoples had been consumed by war also led to the public's interpretation that the human skeletons found in ossuaries had been tossed in carelessly or randomly, rather than arranged in the culturally determined order prescribed by the Feast of the Dead ritual. Amateur collectors also frequently commented on the supposed violence experienced by those interred in graves. Excavators delighted in finding skulls with arrowheads embedded in them, or so-called tomahawk marks or holes in skeletons, all apparent indicators of a violent death. Skulls or skull gorgets drilled with holes were considered to have been trophies, the perforations representing a tally of enemies killed or perhaps they enabled the owner to hang it on display. Others speculated the holes were made during torture.[44] A bronze tomahawk found on the bank of the Thames River was theorized to be one of those given by the Wendat to the Neutrals to dispatch the Jesuit missionaries, while alleged human finger bones must have been worn as badges of honour to prove how many enemies the wearer had killed.[45] While some sites may indeed have been battlegrounds and some individuals died by violence, the public's propensity was to assume that, because Aboriginal peoples were warlike, burials stemmed mostly from battles.

## POPULAR INTERPRETATIONS AND ABORIGINAL ORAL TRADITION

This emphasis on the warlike aspects of Aboriginal culture, the tendency to see every site as a battleground, and interpretation of mass ossuaries as battle graves, rather than products of the Feast of the Dead, likely also stemmed from the public's exposure to Anishinabeg oral traditions. This oral knowledge explained how, with French and British

allies, the Anishinabeg and the Haudenosaunee warred over the territory that became Upper Canada, after the dispersal of the Wendat,
Tionontati, and Neutral in the 1600s, a conflict that ended in 1701 with
a treaty between the two Aboriginal groups.

Nineteenth-century writers, Aboriginal and otherwise, often
repeated these stories. For example, the author of an article for *Rod and
Gun* magazine interviewed Johnny Bey, described as a "pure Iroquoian
Indian," about a site near Massanoga Lake. Here, Bey explained, the
Anishinabeg and Haudenosaunee fought a great battle and consequently
bones often washed up on the banks of the lake after violent storms.[46]
Two people–Wendausum (Lightning) and Mesaquab (Getting into the
Land), the latter a Mississauga also known as Jonathan Yorke from the
Rama reserve–told J. Hugh Hammond stories about the Anishinabeg
sweeping the Iroquois from Southern Ontario. Yorke also crafted a
birchbark box decorated with a porcupine quill design that showed two
Anishinabeg warriors brandishing weapons over a fallen Kanienkehaka
(Mohawk). This scene, according to Yorke, had been copied from a
petroglyph on Lake Couchiching, although the original rock itself had
fallen into the water years before.[47] Yorke and another Anishinabeg
informant also told Andrew Hunter that large ossuaries were the results
of war and that the bones were of Kanienkehaka dead.[48]

Anishinabeg missionaries George Copway and Peter Jones recorded
their peoples' oral traditions about these conquests. In Copway's *Indian
Life and Indian History* (1858), he related what he considered to be
five of the most important battles. The first occurred near present-
day Orillia between the Kanienkehaka and the combined forces of the
Anishinabeg and Wendat. After three days, the Kanienkehaka surren-
dered. At the second battle at Pigeon Lake, the Haudenosaunee had
erected a fort, but the Anishinabeg finally overran it, though many
of their men died in the process. Copway described the third engagement near Mud Lake as particularly bloody, with the bodies of the
dead filling a nearby river and blood dying the water red. Combat at
a village on the Otonabee River resulted in two "heaps" of the dead,
one of Haudenosaunee and one of Anishinabeg. The fifth struggle,
Copway wrote, occurred on an island in the Trent River, in which the
Kanienkehaka were entirely defeated.[49] Peter Jones recorded similar
stories in his *History of the Ojebway Indians* (1861). He spoke of an
Anishinabeg attack on the Haudenosaunee on an island in Lake Huron
called Pequahkoondebaymenis or Skull Island, so named from the number of dead left behind. The last battle, according to Jones, occurred
on the Burlington Bay beach, where traces of fortifications and two

mounds of human bones could still be seen.[50] Skull Island was also
described by Mississauga Chief Robert Paudash, in addition to various
battle sites in the Rice Lake area.[51]

Early non-Aboriginal writers repeated these oral traditions. John
Carroll, though writing about the history of Methodism, briefly summarized the conflict between the Kanienkehaka and Anishinabeg.[52]
Upper Canada's Lieutenant Governor John Graves Simcoe wrote about
a knoll of human bones on the Thames River that he encountered on a
trip to Detroit in 1793. He recorded that this grave had resulted from
a battle between the Anishinabeg and the Onodowahgahs (Seneca),
many of whom were slaughtered. Those left alive escaped across the
Niagara River.[53] Major Edward Littlehales, who accompanied Simcoe
on this journey, also documented this account.[54] In his 1838 memoirs,
Thomas Need recorded stories told to him by three Kanienkehaka individuals about a particular battle near Rice Lake. Here, a Kanienkehaka
war party had attacked an Anishinabeg one, who retreated into the
forest. That night, the Anishinabeg found the Kanienkehaka sleeping in "wigwams" and threw firebrands onto their roofs. When the
Kanienkehaka rushed out to escape the fires, the Anishinabeg picked
them off. A grass-covered mound near the lake marked the graves of
the dead Kanienkehaka, Need concluded.[55] Anna Jameson, the English
writer who travelled throughout Upper Canada, also recorded oral
traditions in her *Winter Studies and Summer Rambles* (1838). She told
of a spot overlooking Lake Superior near Sault Ste Marie, which was
the "scene of a wild and terrific tradition." Here, after a battle with
the Anishinabeg, the Haudenosaunee held a "war feast to torture and
devour their prisoners" and later camped for the night. Watching from
the other shore and "roused to sudden fury," the Anishinabeg plotted
their attack. At dawn, they fell upon the Haudenosaunee, whom after
their "horrible excesses" lay sleeping. The Anishinabeg "massacred"
them all, women and children included, and left the bodies to "bleach
on the shore." Today, Jameson concluded, one could find bones and
skulls still at this spot. Jameson may have copied this version of the
story from the earlier work of the fur trader Alexander Henry.[56] The
artist Paul Kane noted a mound erected over the dead from a battle
between the Anishinabeg and the Kanienkehaka near Saugeen.[57] In 1888,
the tourist guide *Four Years on the Georgian Bay* pointed out battle
sites and burial grounds near Sault Ste Marie and on the islands north
of Shanawaga Bay.[58] James Hamilton's *Georgian Bay* (1893) discussed
the Wendat Feast of the Dead but also recalled a story told by Francis
Assikinack, an Odawa teacher and clerk for the DIA. Assikinack had

told of a conflict between the Kanienkehaka and the Odawa along the Nottawasaga River. The great Odawa warrior Sahgimah saw the Kanienkehaka approaching, and that night, after dark, he snuck into their camp and removed their weapons. At midnight, the Odawa swept into the Kanienkehaka camp. They mounted the heads of their slain enemies on poles and released the Kanienkehaka captives so they could tell the Haudenosaunee that Sahgimah watched over the Blue Mountains. This site, Hamilton wrote, was a little west of Collingwood, overlooking Georgian Bay.[59]

It is likely that these oral traditions, pertaining to some specific sites in Ontario, reinforced the views of the public and of amateur collectors that Aboriginal peoples were savage bloodthirsty warriors, and thus that all mass graves must come from battles and their dead. Yet because of their distrust of oral tradition and their emphasis on the archaeological and historical record, many historical society members were more likely to consider ossuaries, particularly in the area of historic Huronia, as burials from the Feast of the Dead. For example, in one of his talks to the Canadian Institute, Charles Hirschfelder, a prolific collector, explained that the battle theory of graves was incorrect. If they were battle graves, he argued, women and children would not be buried in them.[60] Andrew Hunter also placed primacy on the archaeological record, since such graves contained bodies of all ages and both sexes. He also wrote that the supposed marks of violence that the public noted on bones and skulls were really made after death as part of Wendat mortuary practices. Referring to a *Jesuit Relations* written by Father Brebeuf, Hunter noted that the Wendat believed that their dead passed by the residence of Oscotarach, or "Head-piercer," who extracted their brains.[61]

## HISTORICAL SOCIETY INTERPRETATIONS

On the other hand, local historical societies did use the evolutionary images common to the public. Speaking of the Neutral who once lived at the site of the Southwold earthworks, James Coyne of the Elgin society deemed them an "almost forgotten race."[62] The Thorold and Beaverdams Society structured its *Jubilee History* so that civilization triumphed victorious over the extinct Neutral nation. Its authors ended their chapter on early Aboriginal occupation of Ontario by concluding, "the whole face of the country is changed. Instead of the continuous forests ... we have to-day a picturesque landscape checkered with meadow and grainfield ... Instead of the intricate trail of the savage, broad highways open to us vistas of orchard, farm and dwelling. The warwhoop has given place to the whistle of the locomotive."[63] In a paper for the Ottawa Field-Naturalists' Club, Edwin Sowter similarly contemplated the fate of the Wendat who had disappeared from the Ottawa River Valley. He posited both migration and cultural adaptation, two plausible possibilities, yet ended with a ghoulish suggestion reminiscent of the tropes of savagery and of the sublime: "Or, were they absorbed by the red cloud of massacre, to disappear forever in the darksome shadow of the illimitable wilderness?"[64] Such a rapid disappearance of the Aboriginal peoples and the ever-encroaching development of Ontario meant, to local societies, that they had better hurry and preserve what was left of Aboriginal culture.[65]

Fewer societies emphasized Aboriginal cultures as barbaric. In its *Jubilee History*, the Thorold and Beaverdams Historical Society described the Neutral nation as a "cruel" "warlike" group who tortured their prisoners in ways "too shocking to relate."[66] Members of the London and Middlesex Historical Society (LMHS) argued for the cannibal nature of the peoples who lived at the Shaw-Wood site.[67] In his 1895 *Country of the Neutrals*, James Coyne speculated that from the Southwold village site, Neutral "warriors set out to wage their relentless warfare ... returning satiated with blood, they celebrated their savage triumph, adorned with the scalps of their enemies."[68]

Like the public, society members interpreted specific archaeological sites using noble savage imagery. John Sonley of the LMHS argued that the Neutral Shaw-Wood site was "romantically situated on a high plateau overlooking the Medway" River.[69] E.B. Jones of the Chatham-Kent Historical Society described an open space once created by a semicircle of lodges as a forum for pow-wows, ball games, and the torture of captives at the stake, a theory offered up with no supporting evidence.[70] Several societies pronounced a village on Lake Medad, a small body of water in Halton County, to be a tragically doomed spot, a tale repeated by the Ontario public. One version was embodied in a talk at a meeting of the Wentworth Historical Society. According to the story, the residents of this Iroquoian village had been corrupted by European contact, driving the neighbouring towns away. One night, the residents roasted the chief's son as punishment for murdering another. The villagers then heard a rumbling noise, and the lake rose to swallow up the village as punishment for its evil deeds.[71] The lake itself was rumoured to be bottomless. Mary Holden further romanticized this site by mixing in allusions to Roman culture. She explained that a single grave of a "woman of rank" at Lake Medad was separate since she had not been virtuous and violated their so-called Vestal Virgin order.[72]

Images of extinction or assimilation were linked to the devaluation of oral tradition and the reliance on the supposedly more objective historical and archaeological record. In its 1898 *Jubilee History*, the Thorold and Beaverdams Society lamented "It is much to be regretted that the early settlers of this district have not left us written accounts of the customs of the Indians with whom they came in contact ... Most of the traditional lore is so corrupted as to be almost worthless."[73] During a paper read to the London historical society, Dr Clarence Campbell lamented that only ash-heaps remained as records of former Aboriginal life.[74] John Sonley, in his address about the Shaw-Wood village site in London, asserted that only the relics possessed by curiosity seekers documented the "departed race" of Neutrals.[75] In his local history, the Reverend William Richard Harris of the OHS agreed that, of the vanished Neutral nation, "there remains nothing to remind us that even they ever lived" besides a few arrowheads and axes.[76] Addressing the Wentworth Historical Society in 1915, Frank Wood, a collector with more than three thousand specimens in his private museum, echoed this sentiment; only tools and bones were left, and due to the "carelessness" of Aboriginals, he said, they did not even know about the time of their grandfathers, still less about earlier history.[77] Stanley Mills, the president of the UEL Association of Canada and the honorary president of the Hamilton Branch, suggested in his *Lake Medad and Waterdown* (1937) that Aboriginal stories had grown so old that even the storytellers themselves could not vouch for their truthfulness. Even the "scraps" known about the Neutrals had actually been saved by the Jesuits and other pioneers who had written them down. Really, his book suggested, "What we know now of them can be but guessed at by the relics found within their graves. They are a race almost entirely lost to history."[78]

## INTERPRETATIONS BY DAVID BOYLE AND COLLEAGUES

Although they interpreted Aboriginal cultures through cultural evolution, the accepted scientific theory, David Boyle and his colleagues still used the earlier noble and barbaric savage stereotypes. In his unpublished paper "What Is a Savage?" Boyle outlined his perceptions. Savages, he wrote, possessed a child's intellect, had no thought for the future, were credulous, superstitious, illogical, cruel, animistic, but also demonstrated traits of self-denial, bravery, filial love, and gratitude.[79] Boyle described their land as "nearly a real earthly paradise" with an

abundance of food and fertile soil.[80] Overall, he judged the daily life
of Aboriginal peoples to be better than that of European peasants,
although he felt their moral code was not very high.[81] Rather than
being inartistic and of low intelligence, as many thought, Boyle argued
that Aboriginal peoples possessed imagination, honour, and moderate
intelligence and reason, were good storytellers, and cleverly selected
appropriate raw materials for tools and understood how to adapt
them.[82] Their patience, he added, was demonstrated by their tools.[83]
Andrew Hunter also employed noble savage imagery. He wrote that
Iroquoian peoples had greater feelings of envy, revenge, and anger,
could detect warfare from far away, had heightened sensitivities to the
sublime, and possessed simpler perceptions than non-Aboriginals.[84]

Anthropologist Bruce Trigger has suggested that archaeologists had
less contact with contemporaneous Aboriginal communities than ethnologists, and as a result they were affected by the more popular views
of Aboriginal peoples' development.[85] Gerald Killan argued that Boyle,
both an archaeologist and an ethnographer of the Six Nations community, was motivated to negate the public image of Aboriginal peoples as
warlike and uncivilized, a position likely derived from Horatio Hale,
whose work influenced him. Hale looked back to eighteenth-century
Enlightenment views of "man."[86] He therefore also tended to roman-
ticize Aboriginal cultures. Only two collectors indicated that perhaps
a more subtle philosophy was required: J. Hugh Hammond suggested
that Aboriginal history should be studied from the Aboriginal viewpoint not from that of the "civilized man"; Hunter, in a contradictory
statement, posited that it was the individual rather than the race that
determined whether a person was savage or civilized.[87]

Boyle also followed the Victorian idea that evolutionary progress
was based upon technology. To him, archaeological artifacts, especially
tools, showed the mental development of Aboriginal societies and elu-
cidated the progress of civilization from the "rudest to the highest and
most refined manifestations of humanity."[88] Artifacts, if arranged properly, showed mechanical evolution in particular. From tumpline to train,
digging stick to plough, and from stone scrapers to a tannery, Boyle
drew evolutionary comparisons between archaeological objects and
nineteenth-century technology. He also suggested a seemingly logical
development of technology. For example, the hammerstone was likely
the first tool, he thought, and Aboriginal peoples learned which stones
served best through experience. As they needed more delicate tools and
ornaments, they developed a more refined process, hence the invention
of such working methods as pecking, flaking, saw cutting, bow drilling,

or the use of water to smooth stone. Further, he argued, mechanical evolution equalled ethical evolution and an increase in artistic taste, both which led to increasingly superior craftsmanship.[89] But while tools also showed Aboriginal originality and adaptability, he thought that their cultural development had stalled. Boyle pointed to the example that, although Aboriginal peoples had developed round clay discs for games, they had never thought to apply this concept to the creation of a wheel.[90]

Boyle also used evolutionary theories to explain artifacts of clay. He subscribed to one of Lewis H. Morgan's theories, which posited the presence of pottery on a site indicated semipermanent villages and early artistic efforts, therefore a higher level of civilization. In fact, Boyle felt Ontario pottery to be quite tasteful and skillfully made.[91] Hammond, too, believed the blending and tempering of pottery materials demonstrated an advanced state of civilization.[92] Hunter and another of Boyle's colleagues, Frederick Waugh, agreed that the Wendat were more developed as proved by their ability to shape clay and by their pottery designs, which possessed a "simple elegance." Waugh cautioned that, though pottery was a sign of the survival of the fittest, Iroquoian peoples had not reached the stage of drawing curvilinear patterns. They had, however, imprinted round shapes in clay using the ends of bones and other objects.[93]

Archaeologists devoted much attention to interpreting pipes as well. Boyle argued that this manipulation of clay required a higher degree of skill than the making of stone tools. The presence of pipes also indicated that a village was no longer mainly concerned with the production of food but had time for leisure, and thus had developed a more sophisticated culture than before.[94] Effigies on pipes also supposedly indicated the level of civilization. He compared pipes with children's drawings, concluding that they were very similar; both groups, he said, often omitted features on faces or created disproportionate parts of their bodies, supposedly indicating that their artistic ability was relatively undeveloped compared to European art.[95] In contrast, Andrew Hunter believed that Wendat human pipe effigies were accurate portraits that preserved their distinct racial features. In fact, Aboriginal peoples did not easily understand abstract representations he argued, but instead they could only make literal depictions. In examining animal effigies on pipes, Hunter stated that "in some cases even the draughtsmen and plastic workers of our own race could not have designed them with the features better portrayed."[96] Hunter, however, credited the increase of pictorial attempts on pipes to European influence.[97]

Although the evolutionary model was popular, it did not allow for minor internal changes. As a result Aboriginal cultures were thought to be static. Different periods of occupation were recognized within sites, but changes in material culture were often interpreted as migration by another group into the area rather than the development of one culture itself. Diffusion, the belief that cultures adopted and adapted elements from each other, was not popularized until later by professional anthropologist Franz Boas. The relative inability to determine the time depth of Aboriginal occupation of Ontario, due to limited technology, reinforced such supposed cultural inertia.

The interpretation of gravesites was clouded by this problem. Because the *Jesuit Relations* discussed the mass Feast of the Dead ossuaries utilized by the Wendat and the Neutral, many assumed that these nations had not ever buried their ancestors differently. Thus, single graves were often designated as Algonkian in origin, although some recognized that the Neutral used ossuaries less. Few noted the fact that the Algonkian peoples, influenced by their Iroquoian neighbours, sometimes buried their dead in mass ossuaries, too. Therefore, when considering burials just north of Toronto, Daniel Wilson believed single graves to be Algonkian in origin.[98] Edwin Sowter made a similar conclusion after discovering both single and mass graves on Lighthouse Island on Lake Deschênes. Two races must have lived on this island, he believed.[99] Burials that did not contain grave gifts were also presumed not to be Iroquoian, when, really, lavish grave goods, especially among the Wendat, increased in historic times. More ancient burials often only contained skeletons, but, again, the lack of time depth distorted interpretations. In one instance, Boyle suggested that those graves with no gifts must have been buried hastily after sickness or battle.[100]

## SCIENTIFIC COLLECTING AND ABORIGINAL ORAL TRADITION

As did local society members, Boyle emphasized the use of the historical and archaeological record to interpret Aboriginal material culture. Accordingly, he expressed skepticism about the accuracy and authenticity of oral traditions. After his first visit to the Six Nations of the Grand River reserve to meet the Onondage'ga'(Onondaga) wampum keeper Chief John Buck (Skanawati) and see the belts he kept, Boyle commented on the veracity of oral traditions. Despite the status of wampum keeper as tribal historian, Boyle concluded that Horatio Hale's *Iroquois Book of Rites*, based upon two earlier Haudenosaunee-written manuscripts, contained more information than he gained from his visit. Other traditions, according to Boyle, were "mainly fabulous" and revealed no information of how artifacts that he had collected had been either constructed or used.[101] Several years later, he stated that Ontario Aboriginal peoples were so assimilated that their traditions were "almost totally valueless."[102] In his publication for teachers, *Notes on Primitive Man*, Boyle confirmed that the "little we know ... is gathered from the writings of early travellers and missionaries, eked out by what we can deduce from the remains of ... embankments, mounds, ossuaries, other burial places, village sites, potteries, and various tools and weapons of bone, horn and stone." Even these early writers did not record much detail, Boyle continued, and therefore "Upon archaeological researches ... we must depend chiefly or wholly for any additional knowledge."[103]

Such cynicism is evident in Boyle's interpretation of the Rice Lake serpent and egg mounds site. Boyle reported that he had been told by local Mississaugas and settlers that the long mound had been erected as a defence against the Kanienkehakas.[104] But at the 1904 annual OHS meeting in Windsor, Colonel H.C. Rogers of the Peterborough society read a paper proposing a different explanation, one that recorded an oral tradition told by Mississauga Chief Robert Paudash and his son Johnson. The Paudashs said that the Mississaugas had erected the serpent and four turtle-shaped mounds (not eggs) as a "pictorial representation" of the Kanienkehaka totem in memory of them and the battle that took place there.[105] Robert Paudash carefully validated the authority of his story through the Aboriginal convention of referring to those from whom he had learned the oral tradition and their credentials: "No word ... has come from reading, or in any other way than from the mouth of Paudash, my father ... the last hereditary chief of the tribe of Mississagas ... and from the mouth of Cheneebeesh, my grandfather ... the last Sachem, or Head Chief, of all the Mississagas, who in turn had learned ... what Gemoaghpenassee, his father, had heard from *his* father, and so on." Some people had supposed the site "to mean more than this, but my father has so stated it," Paudash concluded.[106]

The OHS journal published the Paudashs' story, but in a footnote Boyle contradicted the chief. He credited him as "the very worthy and intelligent head" of the Hiawatha band of Mississaugas but stated that it "would be misleading not to point out to the reader that the Otonabee Serpent Mound is, most undoubtedly, the work of a people who occupied the soil long before the coming of the Mississagas."[107] After Boyle's excavation of the mounds, he argued that two different

The Serpent Mound near Peterborough, excavated by Boyle in 1896

cultures had used them. The intrusive or more recent burials belonged to people "to whom the structure possessed no significance, or, at any rate, a significance very different from what it had been to those who, at infinite pains, labored to put the embankment into shape." The original constructors were of an unknown stock but certainly lived in the area prior to the Wendat or Haudenosaunee. Perhaps, Boyle said, a "lingering fondness for such structures among some tribes of Ojibwa origin, until very recently, if regarded as an evidence of heredity, might warrant us in attributing to some old-time Algonkins the making of these mounds."[108] Boyle also believed that the serpent mound could not be a fortification since it was too incomplete and placed in an illogical spot for such purposes. Really, he explained, the mounds had a symbolic purpose. Both the serpent and the egg represented "rejuvenescence and perpetuity–hence of eternity," because snakes could shed their skins and new life was born from eggs.[109]

## ABORIGINAL INTERPRETATIONS

While many Aboriginal communities and professional collectors disagreed over the validity of oral knowledge, numerous Aboriginal individuals, particularly those in the public eye, used noble savage imagery. Pauline Johnson also challenged the noble savage stereotypes of

Aboriginal peoples, particularly of women, in pieces such as "A Strong Race Opinion." In this short essay, she scolded literary authors for creating an archetypal female Indian character, no matter the plot, author, or location.[110] But in her defence of the Haudenosaunee as a civilized society, she attributed many of the noble savage characteristics to them, and despite her accurate criticism of Euro-Canadian authors treating all Aboriginals alike, she did the same with the many nations and individuals of the Haudenosaunee. Johnson described them as brave, intelligent, physically strong, moral, bloodthirsty, indulgent of children, creators of a sophisticated government, and "undemolished and undemoralized" to this day.[111] John Ojijatekha Brant-Sero also used romantic Victorian language to describe the Haudenosaunee. He called his ancestors the "Romans of the West ... unequalled by any other barbaric power in the new world," who were famed for their once-powerful control of a massive territory.[112] Brant-Sero equally emphasized the civilized nature of the Six Nations, suggesting that they were in no way inferior to Euro-Canadians. In an interview with the London *Daily News* in England, a reporter asked Brant-Sero if the Indian race was degenerating. In response, he asserted their civilized status but couched it in terms of the mainstream trope of recent progress after contact. "Certainly they are not degenerating, nor are they dying out," he answered. "They have made wonderful progress, especially in Canada ... We are beginning to wake up to the possibilities which lie before us."[113]

Aboriginal peoples also shared some of the interpretative elements of United Empire Loyalism so dear to local historical societies. Many societies believed that the very study of history and its heroes was a way to inspire patriotism and loyalty and thus mandated this principle as one of their main goals.[114] As members of the Lundy's Lane Historical Society thought, gazing from their observatory tower across their War of 1812 battlefield with their artifact collections nearby, one could not help but learn "splendid lessons of loyalty of the past."[115] Yet, while historical societies acknowledged the role of Aboriginal peoples in the founding and protection of Upper Canada, creating a kind of "imagined community" with them, Aboriginal peoples had no real contemporary practical place in this British-Canadian nationalism, unless as assimilated peoples.[116] In their publications, societies portrayed Aboriginal peoples as a primitive precursor to civilized settlement, a dying culture who made way for the superior pioneer stock, or as communities whose survival depended on acculturation to North American lifeways.

But Aboriginal peoples played upon aspects of United Empire Loyalism themselves, and these meanings of loyalty attached to their

WAR MEDAL, 1814.

War of 1812 medal, given to Chief Naudee, "Warrior, Guide and Scout,"
and later donated to the Oronhyatekha collection

material culture became tools in political negotiation. Many items in Dr Oronhyatekha's museum are illustrative of this. As noted before, George McClurg, the primary collector of Oronhyatekha's artifacts, acted as the general secretary and treasurer of the United Indian Bands of the Chippewas and the Mississaugas from 1903 to 1911 and as their lawyer who helped them lobby the government for preservation of their rights under the Robinson treaties. Not surprisingly, then, most of the ethnographic items came from Anishinabeg reserves in the province. Many of these objects related to imperial-Aboriginal relations, especially during the War of 1812, and had been owned and donated by individuals recognized as important and powerful allies to the British in their military battles and in the protection and settlement of Upper Canada.

Oronhyatekha's collection included two military red coats with brass buttons and bullion braid given to George King and Oshawana, Tecumseh's chief warrior in 1812. Oshawana's knife and scabbard, a drum for feasts and other ceremonies, silver George III medal, and a red ensign from Fort Malden that "was preserved in the Chief's family as a valued relic of those stirring times," were all donated to the museum.[117] Three other George III medals had previously belonged to Puckeshinwa, Tecumseh's father, Chief Tomigo of the Munceys and Chief Wa-be-che-chake, an Anishinabeg from Sault Ste Marie. A War of 1812 medal had once been owned by Chief Naudee.[118] Another medal and a tomahawk peace pipe had been presented to Tecumseh by Sir

Isaac Brock, the latter item more ceremonial than utilitarian. Other tomahawk pipes in the collection had been owned by Chiefs Kiageosh and Macounce of Walpole Island, and Chief Miskokoman.[119] To early colonial leaders and Aboriginal peoples, military uniforms, tomahawk pipes, and medals given to their chiefs and warriors symbolized loyalty and the appreciation of the British Crown for their military alliance. Medals, often presented with a certificate, were given to mark important events such as treaty signings and also confirmed the authority of the individual upon which it was bestowed. Thus they were highly prized and respected within Aboriginal communities. George III medals were particularly significant to Aboriginal men in Canada, because they had been awarded before the War of 1812. Those who kept them were British allies, while men who fought for the American side during the Revolution had their medals replaced by US presidential ones.[120]

The museum also featured ceremonial clothing worn by Aboriginal individuals when they met royalty during their tours of Canada. John Tecumseh Henry, the president of the Ontario Grand Council of Chiefs, and his wife represented the Muncey and Oneida of the Thames reserves and presented an address to the prince of Wales, later King Edward VII, during his royal visit of 1860. Their clothing of a black beaded coat and leggings, beaded pouches, council belt, and beaded and quilled head-dresses was given to Oronhyatekha. Henry's pouch belonged to his father Maungwudaus and may have represented his passing of hereditary Anishinabeg leadership to his son, and thus his authority in representing his community to the future King of England.[121] Similar items included a golden eagle headdress worn by Chief Waubano or John B. Wampum of Moraviantown when he met Queen Victoria in 1886.[122] It was also customary for the Crown to present medals to Aboriginal peoples as symbols of their loyalty during such visits, and the Oronhyatekha museum contained a Victoria silver medal given to Waubano by the prince of Wales, and another medal presented by the duke and duchess of York in Calgary during their 1901 tour.[123]

To Aboriginal peoples, their attendance and addresses to royal visitors to Canada was a ritualistic and symbolic part of maintaining their alliance with the Crown, and thus such items of clothing and decoration carried these meanings. The ceremonial dress of Aboriginal peoples at occasions such as the 1860 royal visit brought attention to themselves and staked a claim to public space.[124] Much of the collection, in fact, symbolized Aboriginal sovereignty, international relationships and treaties, and the leaders who maintained these alliances.[125] Thus, while many of Oronhyatekha's objects depicted the "other," such artifacts also promoted the idea of Aboriginal peoples as equal nations who dealt with the Crown on equal terms.[126] Certainly Oronhyatekha himself believed in Haudenosaunee sovereignty and identified himself as a British ally not a subject.[127]

Historical society members and the mainstream public would have shared these meanings as they toured Oronhyatekha's museum. As fervent supporters of the United Empire Loyalist myth, they appreciated the importance of Aboriginal allies and gave lip service to the equality of individuals such as Brant and Tecumseh, although as shown earlier, few acted on the behalf of Aboriginal communities to preserve their sovereignty. Perhaps visitors also felt similarly to Methodist missionary Conrad Van Dusen, who believed that the wearing of "savage dress" for royal visits undermined the perception of Aboriginal intelligence and ability to be further civilized and use land productively. Thus, Van Dusen felt that rather than achieving political rights, such outfits only justified colonial treatment.[128]

While Aboriginal peoples may have agreed upon the importance of their respective oral traditions and in their Loyalist status as allies, they did not necessarily agree on the meanings of all objects. Perhaps the most politically important was the interpretation of wampum belts, which recorded treaties between Aboriginal groups and with Europeans about land use and embodied the sovereign status of each party. After the conquest of Ontario by the Anishinabeg, along with their French and British allies, they and the Haudenosaunee concluded a treaty of peace and friendship in 1701, which was recorded by a wampum belt. This belt was marked with a bowl that symbolized that both groups would eat out of one dish with one spoon - that is, they would be one people who shared the hunting territory and resources over which they had recently fought.

In the nineteenth century, increasing settlement in Southern Ontario and the influx of several thousand Anishinabeg and Haudenosaunee fleeing the US policy of Indian removal caused the meanings about land use embodied in this wampum belt to become even more important. Further, disagreements over the meaning and boundaries of land cessions had already begun.[129] In 1840, the Grand General Indian Council met at the Credit River, intending to renew the 1701 treaty for the fifth time, among other business. At this meeting, it was proposed that the various Anishinabeg and Haudenosaunee communities should join together to receive official title to their lands in the province. But a disagreement over the meaning of the 1701 wampum derailed any further collaboration. John Buck, the Onondage'ga' wampum keeper brought with him four belts, one of which represented the original treaty of 1701. The dish in the centre of the belt contained a few white wampum shells, which symbolized a beaver tail, the favourite dish of the Anishinabeg. This belt, Buck interpreted, meant that the Anishinabeg and the Haudenosaunee had agreed to share the game in the province in common. The second belt represented the renewal of the 1701 agreement, which had earlier taken place in Buffalo. The third came from the extension of this agreement to the Shawnees and allied tribes, and the fourth had been created only twenty-five years earlier as a confirmation of these treaties.[130] Chief William Yellowhead of the Lake Simcoe Anishinabeg presented another belt that contradicted Buck's interpretation. Really, he said, the symbol of the one dish meant that the Haudenosaunee were allowed to hunt in Anishinabeg territory only when they came to attend councils in the area. Significantly, this gave primacy of land ownership to the Anishinabeg. In disagreement, the Six Nations representatives left the Grand Council meeting, and the Anishinabeg petitioned the lieutenant governor of Upper Canada for their title deeds alone.[131]

If the Haudenosaunee and the Anishinabeg disagreed over the meanings of wampum belts held in common, ethnographic collectors such as David Boyle did not see the intrinsic value of wampum to be their record-keeping qualities of historical treaties and events at all. In fact, Boyle altogether dismissed the Six Nations' current knowledge of the meanings of the belts by suggesting that much more information could be learned from Horatio Hale's *Book of Rites*.[132] Even as museum artifacts, Boyle felt that most surviving wampum belts had little worth because they showed European influence. The belts "possess[ed] no archaeological value whatever," he wrote, because they had been constructed of "white-man's-make material, while ethnologically, they [were] little better than curiosities illustrative of an Indian-European combination of ideas, and workmanship. It is more likely that many of these belts were entirely made by Europeans with just enough 'Indian' in the make-up to make them pass muster among the natives for commercial and treaty purposes."[133] Rather than seeing these items as ones that maintained traditional forms and functions and whose manufacture incorporated European technology as a means of adaptability and creativity on the part of the maker, Boyle devalued them altogether. In fact, writing to fellow collector William Beauchamp in New York State, Boyle judged that "'One answers our purpose as well as a dozen or a score.'"[134]

The noted anthropologist Horatio Hale held similar beliefs about wampum belts. Like Boyle, he also emphasized the traditional and derided wampum beads that were not handmade, comparing them to counterfeit coins.[135] But, unlike Boyle, he considered John Buck to be extremely knowledgeable about the history and customs of the Six Nations, and he suggested that the reading of wampum belts was accurate. "Those who doubt whether events which occurred four centuries ago can be remembered as clearly and minutely," Hale wrote, "will probably have their doubts removed when they consider the necessary operation of this custom. The orator's narrative is repeated in the presence of many auditors who have often heard it before, and who would be prompt to remark and to correct any departure from the well-known history."[136] Hale was not so sure about the preservation of oral tradition in other communities however. In 1872 and 1874, he conducted fieldwork at the Wyandot community of Anderdon. Here, Hale purchased four wampum belts, commenting that, if all Wendat belts and their significance had been preserved, they would have equalled a bulk of diplomatic documents of great ethnographic value. But Hale believed the belts had no practical use or contemporary political meaning since he believed the community to have little memory of their original function and context. Interestingly, he noted that to the community the value of the wampum lay in its function as "evidence of a subsisting treaty or land-right. To any merely archaeological purpose which it may serve they are entirely indifferent."[137]

## USABLE PASTS

Images of Aboriginal extinction commonly used by the public and members of historical societies served several purposes. Unlike Australians, who often claimed their territory to be *terra nullius*, Canadians could instead point to the dramatic depopulation of its original residents. If all that remained of Aboriginal peoples in Ontario were relics buried in the earth, then there was no need for the average citizen to feel guilt over the appropriation of Aboriginal land. And Aboriginal peoples were cast as a casualty not of European actions but of a predetermined evolutionary fate. Euro-Canadians also often used the "other," in this case Aboriginal peoples, as a foil to examine their own culture and values and soothe their anxieties. In the late nineteenth and early twentieth centuries, Canadians felt ambivalent toward modernization and its related elements of increased technology, urbanization, poverty, consumerism, dirt and disease, and loss of community.

Such anti-modern impulses depicted Aboriginal peoples as primitive but free, healthy, unconcerned with material wealth and modern-day timekeeping, community-focused, and living on nature's bounty. Some Victorians also worried about increasing secularization and often looked back fondly on earlier days when an agricultural lifestyle seemingly promoted spiritual feelings. Thus, Aboriginal peoples, whose animistic beliefs found spirits in all things natural, seemed to be more ideal.[138] A collection of artifacts from a pre-contact age, then, could symbolize a more idealistic lifestyle.

Members of historical societies celebrated the establishment of their communities through the efforts of their loyalist ancestors. These individuals supposedly brought civilization to an untamed wilderness, and hence their celebration was a celebration of progress. If societies commemorated UELs, then they had to include Aboriginal peoples whose leaders such as Joseph Brant and Tecumseh had significant roles in the settling and defence of early Ontario. But to see Aboriginal peoples as equal contradicted the common evolutionary paradigm. Aboriginal peoples – under pressure from government officials to replace their traditional governments, sell more land, protect what they had not sold with title deeds, and collaborate with various Aboriginal communities who claimed the same territory – used the UEL myth to back up their claims of sovereignty and indigenous rights to land.

Professional scholars like David Boyle had their own reasons for interpreting Aboriginal material culture through evolutionary paradigms. If Aboriginal peoples had been assimilated and their traditional knowledge lost or corrupted, as Boyle claimed about the Six Nations of the Grand River, then he was justified in removing objects, even those still in use, and placing them in a museum collection. Assimilation supposedly meant that Aboriginal societies could not preserve the traditional meanings and uses of objects, and thus museum professionals must take it upon themselves to act as stewards, and ultimately as interpreters, of material culture. By placing primacy on the archaeological and historical record, and an allegedly objective scholarly reading of both, Boyle could suggest that he, not Aboriginal community leaders, was the learned expert. Further, by distancing contemporary Aboriginal communities from historic sites, as he did by with the serpent and egg mounds near Rice Lake, Boyle again set himself up as the most informed. As the Hamilton *Herald* suggested in 1901, "David Boyle knows much about natives and not just the present mix-up of reservation 'braves' but the real, sure-enough Indian of long, long ago. In fact it would please a resurrected Indian to find out what a really interesting being he was."[139]

While some emphasized popular images and others more scientific theory, most Euro-Canadians believed in some form of evolutionary development and used their preconceptions to interpret archaeological sites, the material culture found there, and objects collected from contemporaneous Aboriginal communities. The Ontario public seemed more likely to believe, or at least repeat, Aboriginal oral tradition, compared to David Boyle, who more often emphasized what could be derived from the historical and archaeological record. Some First Nations used popular imagery and evolutionary language to depict their own peoples, but all believed in the importance of the oral traditions attached to their material culture, even if they disagreed among themselves about their meanings.

# CONCLUSION

*Connecting the Present to the Past:*
*Contemporary Issues and the Historicization*
*of Anthropology*

On 15 June 1843, the *Bytown Gazette* reported the discovery of an Aboriginal grave: "About a fortnight since, whilst some workmen were engaged in digging sand from a pit immediately in the rear of Bedard's Hotel, at Hull, they accidentally came upon human bones."[1] Edward Van Cortlandt, a physician, private collector, and member of the Ottawa Literary and Scientific Society (OLSS), examined this site and reported his findings to the Canadian Institute in 1853.[2] From this site Cortlandt collected numerous human remains, which he likely later donated to the OLSS museum.[3] In 1909, Edwin Sowter of the OFNC described Cortlandt's excavation in the society's *Ottawa Naturalist*.[4] In 2002, 159 years after its original discovery, the *Ottawa Citizen* published several historical articles about this archaeological site, prompting the Kitigan Zibi nation of Maniwaki, Quebec, to request repatriation of these and all ancestral Algonquin human remains from the Canadian Museum of Civilization, which had inherited the OLSS collection. In 2005, the bones were returned and reburied. This case, and many others, demonstrates the contemporary implications of historical collecting. The relationships between amateurs, professionals, historical societies, government agencies, and various Aboriginal groups, and the issues raised by their activities between 1791 and 1914, continue to be reflected in today's archaeological, ethnographic, and museological disciplines.

After 1851, the Canadian Institute and other historical societies, and professionals like Daniel Wilson, tried to curb or improve public excavations, while simultaneously asking for the public's help in collecting and documenting artifacts. Overworked as a professor and an administrator, and operating in an era of armchair anthropology, Wilson was unable to significantly impose any scientific standards on amateur collectors. The appointment of David Boyle as the full-time curator of the Canadian Institute in 1884 and at the newly refocused Ontario Provincial Museum in 1896 intensified professional attempts to suppress the worst of the public's destruction of sites, artifacts, and associated information. Although Boyle's curatorship marked the increase of collections at both institutions, a result of his successful relationship with a part of the public, sometimes amateurs considered archaeological sites and their associated objects to be private property to be used in whimsical ways and not items to be donated to museums for educational purposes. Historical societies attempted to negotiate the challenges of serving their communities, keeping enthusiasm alive and finances feasible, and fulfilling nineteenth-century scientific principles of archaeological and ethnographic study, the latter particularly emphasized after David Boyle became the secretary and leading intellectual of the Ontario Historical Society in 1898. The scientific paradigm within which professionals and historical societies operated often meant that Aboriginal religious concerns about the treatment of human remains, and thus their protests over excavations, were dismissed in favour of science. But it was not that simple. Some Euro-Canadians abhorred the disturbance of the dead while some Aboriginal people assisted in their resurrection. Boyle's fieldwork at Six Nations of the Grand River operated within evolutionary beliefs; to him and other nineteenth-century collectors, Aboriginal peoples were rapidly dying off or assimilating, and thus their material culture must be preserved within museums. As Aboriginal communities struggled to deal with colonial policies, they both questioned and assisted collectors' activities. Whether they used popular imagery or the approved scientific theory to express it, most nineteenth-century Euro-Canadians deemed Aboriginal peoples less civilized and used evolutionary tropes to interpret the material culture they collected and exhibited. While the public often used Aboriginal stories to help interpret artifacts, David Boyle placed primacy on the "objective" scrutiny of the archaeological and historical record rather than consulting Aboriginal communities and the oral knowledge they held. In contrast, whether they assisted or protested collectors' activities, Ontario Aboriginal peoples saw themselves as simultaneously civilized, modern, and traditional and often used collectors and material culture for their own ends.

A comparison of these groups' activities and goals reveals numerous underlying issues about the study of Aboriginal material culture.

Centering around the key concept of stewardship, these issues include cultural representation, appropriation of voice, the legitimacy of a private artifact market, control of and access to museum collections, the mandate of museums, the validity and accuracy of oral knowledge, repatriation, and the use of scientific or religious paradigms. Many of these issues remain under debate today and cannot be understood only through Aboriginal/non-Aboriginal cultural differences. Scholars and heritage workers in Canada await a much-needed national and interdisciplinary synthesis of contemporary issues in Aboriginal/scholarly relations that draws together the enormous literature in archaeology, anthropology, and museology. Such a discussion is beyond the scope of this work, but I do wish to historicize these issues, that is, to connect the collecting past to the controversies of the present.[5]

## TURNING POINTS

Although issues of stewardship are still contested today, it is true that the disciplines and individuals that collect, exhibit, and study indigenous material culture have changed. Since the civil rights movement and the process of decolonization after the Second World War, enormous shifts in thinking and practice have occurred, and discussions of the progress and future directions of anthropology, archaeology, and museology are lively. Metropolitan museums are more likely to consult with indigenous peoples and allow them to present their stories from their own perspectives, including those informed by spirituality and oral knowledge. Consequently, the representation of indigenous peoples as primitive, dead, or dying cultures has lessened. And, certainly, the concept of a museum having social responsibility, accountability, and civic engagement has become more commonplace.[6]

While some Canadian institutions, notably the Museum of Anthropology at the University of British Columbia and the Royal Saskatchewan Museum of Natural History, have a longer history of collaborating with Aboriginal peoples, the turning point in Canada is largely credited to be the 1988 Lubicon Cree boycott of the exhibit *The Spirit Sings: Artistic Traditions of Canada's First Peoples*. This exhibit was prepared by Calgary's Glenbow Museum in conjunction with the 1988 Olympics. Although the protest began as a tactic to settle a Lubicon Cree land claims dispute, the focus quickly turned to an examination of standard museum practices. The resulting controversy highlighted issues of cultural representation, appropriation of voice, and the ownership, display, and repatriation of sacred materials. Dissenters accused the major corporate sponsor, Shell Oil, of hypocrisy, because it glossed over its resistance to land claims issues and the ruination of the Lubicon economy through oil drilling while contending to support Aboriginal culture. The almost all non-Aboriginal curatorial team was denounced as celebrating only a past history, thereby denying current social and political problems. Scholars also noted that the displayed objects symbolized the extreme change, loss, dispersal, and extermination that occurred after European contact, but that the exhibit did not address these painful messages.[7]

In response, Julia Harrison, Glenbow's coordinating curator, stated that *The Spirit Sings* explored the "richness, diversity and complexity of Canada's native cultures ... at contact" and "emphasize[d] the adaptability and resilience of these cultures in the face of the dominant influences of European cultures."[8] Artist performances and demonstrations were to represent contemporary culture not discussed in the exhibit. Harrison had also aimed to increase the public's understanding of Aboriginal peoples in order to combat commonly-held stereotypes and believed the display of artifacts from European institutions might be a first step in their repatriation. Some Glenbow staff also argued that museums should remain apolitical. Nevertheless, in the end, the museum conducted several Aboriginal consultations during the exhibit planning process, introduced a statement about current issues at the end of the display, and recognized epidemic disease, severe depopulation, alcohol abuse, forced assimilation, poverty, and the effects of changing technology in its two-volume exhibit catalogue.[9]

Responses were mixed between and within Aboriginal and museum communities. Several international institutions refused loan requests as a measure of support of the Lubicon band while others withheld artifacts based on fears of repatriation requests. The Canadian Ethnology Society joined the boycott, and anthropologist Bruce Trigger resigned his honourary curatorship at the McCord Museum after it agreed to lend items. Kanienkehaka (Mohawk) from the Kahnawake reserve in Quebec contested the display and ownership of a sacred False Face mask borrowed from the Royal Ontario Museum in Toronto, stimulating other groups to consider similar actions. In contrast, several Aboriginal groups in Alberta participated in the arts festival and crafts demonstrations.

Georges Erasmus, then national chief of the Assembly of First Nations, invited the Canadian Museums Association to co-host a symposium to discuss the controversy. It convened in Ottawa in November 1988. The resulting joint task force published its report *Turning the Page: Forging New Partnerships between Museums and First Peoples* in 1992. It advocated increased participation of Aboriginal peoples in museums, training and funding for Aboriginal individuals to enter the museum field, improved access to collections, the repatriation of certain types of items, and the portrayal of Aboriginals as living peoples who had a significant role in Canadian history, rather than as extinct and primitive societies. In 1996 the report of the Royal Commission of Aboriginal Peoples echoed many of these recommendations.[10]

Over the past fifteen years, then, Canadian institutions such as the Royal British Columbia Museum (Victoria), the Glenbow, the Manitoba Museum of Man (Winnipeg), the Royal Ontario Museum, the Prince of Wales Northern Heritage Centre (Yellowknife), and the Canadian Museum of Civilization (Gatineau), among others, have worked with Aboriginal groups and institutions to form advisory bodies, to curate permanent and temporary galleries, to rework collection management policies, to train and hire Aboriginal individuals, to conduct research relevant to both parties, and in some cases to repatriate ethnographic and archaeological objects.[11] In the United States, this trend to increase indigenous access to and control over museum collections has been most recently manifested in the new National Museum of the American Indian of the Smithsonian Institution which opened in Washington, DC, in 2004.

Museums benefit from these types of collaboration, but smaller community museums, often descendants of those created by local historical and scientific societies in the nineteenth century, often cannot follow suit. Like their nineteenth-century ancestors, these museums often have fewer paid staff, less training and experience in dealing with Aboriginal peoples and their concerns, less time to change outdated and perhaps offensive exhibits, and little government funding to pursue collaborative curatorial projects. Another problem is the lack of conjunction between critical scholarship and museum work.[12] A lack of money constrains research; in museums, it is the last item to receive money and often the first to be cut from the budget. As a result, most research conducted is tailored to the production of new exhibits or educational programs rather than for research itself.[13] These smaller institutions also struggle between balancing scholarly and community needs. How can museums present the latest academic research and celebrate community histories? Museum historian Mary Tivy argues that Ontario history museums were founded upon an anti-modernism that celebrates the pre-industrial and rural values of local communities and their pioneers. Aboriginal peoples thus appear only as savage predecessors to the pioneers and are represented mostly by their archaeological remains. For the most part, the overarching metanarrative is the banishing of the wilderness through the building of civilization and the celebration of those pioneers who constructed it, a trope that suggests Aboriginal peoples were inferior.[14] To maintain local support, museums generally must produce celebratory community-focused exhibits and activities, and many of these communities do not include Aboriginal peoples, despite the fact that most of these museums contain Aboriginal material culture.

In archaeology, many professionals now acknowledge Aboriginal concerns about their practices. In the absence of federal statutes, Canadian archaeologists operate under national ethical policies and varied provincial laws. In 1996, after consultation with Aboriginal peoples, the Canadian Archaeological Association (CAA) published its *Statement of Principles for Ethical Conduct* for its membership. It recognizes the "cultural and spiritual links" between Aboriginal peoples and artifacts, the importance of collaboration and communication, the need to follow Aboriginal cultural protocols when dealing with human remains, and respects the role of oral history in archaeological interpretation. The CAA noted, however, that the document only represented the first step in the future relations between Aboriginal peoples and archaeologists.[15] Parks Canada, a major holder of land containing archaeological sites, has similar policies. It operates under the principles of co-management of sites, repatriation of burial items, and generally that archaeological interests will not supercede those of Aboriginal peoples.[16] The Canadian Museums Association and Assembly of First Nations task force advised that human remains known by name should be returned to the appropriate community. It also suggested that the fate of bones of a more ancient age should be decided by archaeologists and Aboriginal communities together, although it advocated a combination of a limited study period and reburial. The 1996 Royal Commission on Aboriginal Peoples proposed similar recommendations. Even before the creation of these ethical statements, some museums repatriated human remains. In 1988, for example, the Peterborough Centennial Museum closed its exhibit on Aboriginal burial traditions and negotiated with the nearby Curve Lake First Nation to return its holdings of human remains and burial goods.[17]

Numerous professional bodies in the United States, particularly the American Anthropological Association, have issued similar ethical statements. This organization states that anthropologists have "primary ethical obligations to the people ... they study" and that these "can supersede the goal of seeking new knowledge" usually achieved through the "long-term conservation of the archaeological ... and historical records."[18] Unlike Canada, the United States has passed numerous pieces of national legislation that affect archaeological practice. After 1978, the American Indian Religious Freedom Act theoretically protects the right of Native Americans to practice traditional spirituality. Native groups thus argued that the holding of their spiritual objects by museums abrogated their rights to practice their religion, and some institutions did agree to return selected objects or to remove them from exhibit, but the legislation had little enforcement. The Archaeological Resources and Protection Act of 1979 requires Native American consent for the excavation and removal of objects from tribal land and protects burials less than one hundred years old from excavation. Perhaps the real turning point was the enactment in 1990 of the Native American Graves Protection and Repatriation Act (NAGPRA), which officially sets out a protocol to repatriate human remains and objects of cultural patrimony and spirituality. With the exception of the Smithsonian Institution, which is similarly governed by the National Museum of the American Indian Act (1989), NAGPRA compels all federally funded museums to inventory their collections, notify the appropriate groups of their holdings, and return any relevant objects. NAGPRA's protocol for repatriation is based upon the concept of cultural affinity or continuity, that is, all human remains and associated grave goods to be returned must be proven to be ancestral to a living group.[19]

Many non-indigenous archaeologists believe that their activities can offer something of value to indigenous communities, including assistance in land claims, education of their youth, management and protection of burial sites, promotion of nation building and sovereignty, and the creation of employment at cultural centres and through tourism.[20] Archaeologists have also begun to theorize different methods of practice, such as "covenantal archaeology," "decolonizing archaeology," "collaborative archaeology," and "indigenous archaeology." The first suggests that indigenous peoples should be trained in archaeology so that they may take over the direction and management of future archaeological endeavours to formulate and answer the questions they see as important.[21] Likewise, a decolonized archaeology prefaces and is informed by indigenous values and changes the traditional power structure between archaeologists and indigenous peoples.[22] "Collaborative archaeology," as defined by Jordan Kerber, involves indigenous groups and archaeologists working together, to understand and protect artifacts and human remains, although not necessarily on a voluntary basis.[23] Cara Lee Blume distinguishes between consultation and collaboration, the latter including a sharing of power. This sharing of power means

equal contributions to the decision-making process and that both partners bring valuable elements to the project and also benefit equally
from the results.[24] Joe Watkins, an archaeologist of Choctaw heritage,
has proposed a similar ideology of compromise. His suggested "indigenous archaeology" encompasses mutual education of archaeologists
and indigenous communities by the other, the recognition of diverse
decision-making processes, an awareness of indigenous concerns, collaboration that extends beyond archaeology, communication with the
communities involved, and an acknowledgment of varied interpretations of ownership and control of archaeological heritage.[25]

There is also a growing number of indigenous people involved in
archaeology. Davina TwoBears of the Navajo nation sees indigenous
anthropologists as leaders who can help determine standards in the field.
She suggests that the goals of Native American anthropologists should
include the publication of traditional information for children's educational purposes, teaching, acting as resources in establishing programs of
language preservation and to care for repatriated objects.[26] Indeed, some
indigenous communities do see the relevance of archaeology to their
own goals. For example, after the discovery of a more than 500-year-
old frozen body in the Tatshenshini-Alsek Park in British Columbia in
1999, the Champagne and Aishihik First Nations decided that this was
a unique opportunity for study and permitted the remains to be held by
the Royal British Columbia Museum in Victoria in order to be dated
and tested for cultural affinity.[27] The agreement to co-manage Kwaday
Dan Ts'inchi (or Long Ago Person Found) and the items found with
him, however, has been questioned by some as only seemingly collaborative while preserving the dominance of museums to control, study, and
display human remains as specimens and their belongings as artifacts.[28]

Some tribes have instituted their own archaeology and historic preservation programs on their reservation lands. After the 1966 National
Historic Preservation Act was established, numerous tribes took over
the role of state historic preservation officers, which allowed for greater
control.[29] In 1974, the Zuni Pueblo created the Zuni Archaeological
Enterprise (later renamed the Archaeology Program in 1978 and the
Zuni Heritage and Historic Preservation Office in 1994) for cultural
resource management, including the research and protection of cultural
objects and sacred and archaeological sites on and off their land. If projects, such as proposed development, will affect sacred sites, program
archaeologists contact Zuni religious leaders, and thus many outcomes
are determined according to traditional spirituality. Thus archaeology
can be a tool for religious preservation.[30] In 1977, the Navajo set up the

Navajo Nation Archaeology Department in order to be able to determine how their cultural resources would be managed and protected. Archaeology in this sense was a way to increase self-determination. In conjunction with Northern Arizona University and Fort Lewis College, the Navajo organized training programs for tribal members in order to have nation members who could conduct archaeological surveys and excavations, which, in turn, are used to protect historic and sacred sites from development. These training programs not only teach Western academic topics but also incorporate oral and indigenous knowledge.[31] In Canada, the Wet'suwet'en have implemented an alternative cultural resource management structure that necessitates being highly involved whenever their heritage resources are endangered by logging. This allows the Wet'suwet'en to have more input, share responsibility, help determine what is considered culturally significant to them, and train band members in heritage management.[32]

Aboriginal groups also use archaeology for very different purposes, such as gathering evidence of their ancient occupation of Canada for land claims cases. In 1984, the Musqueam of British Columbia submitted a comprehensive land claim that in part used archaeological evidence to prove their eight-thousand-year existence in and occupation of expropriated territory. This First Nation presented a similar argument in 2004 when the BC government attempted to sell off a piece of property under a land claim.[33]

Others believe that their ancestors have engineered the discovery of their human remains for learning purposes. In 1997, Paul O'Neal, chief archaeologist for Mayer Heritage Consultants in London, Ontario, collaborated with the Aamjiwnaang nation (Chippewas of Sarnia) and the Bluewater Bridge Authority to manage skeletons found during construction of a new bridge. Although these remains were designated Iroquoian according to archaeological interpretation, the Aamjiwnaang band believed them to be their ancestors. Their agreement with O'Neal barred photography and scientific testing of remains, although a physical anthropologist was allowed to visually analyze gender and other details of the bones. Age was determined by the presence or absence of nonhuman artifacts rather than by radiocarbon dating, which destroys the part of the bone tested. Members of the community helped remove the human remains, conducted daily ceremonies, and reburied the skeletons in an undisclosed location. In the end, the Aamjiwnaang nation believed that their ancestors had wanted them to learn their forgotten traditional burial practices by revealing themselves through the construction of the bridge.[34]

## STEWARDSHIP: CONTINUING CONTROVERSIES

There are many other examples of collaboration in Ontario, Canada, and the United States, but the stewardship of material culture remains contested, and, as it was historically, this debate cannot be only understood as a simple indigenous versus non-indigenous argument. Amateur and professional archaeologists still disagree whether heritage should be private or public in nature. Like they did in the nineteenth century, amateur archaeologists continue to make significant contributions to the public collection of Aboriginal material culture in Canada. The Ontario Archaeological Society and the Saskatchewan Archaeology Society consists of both professional and amateurs. In fact, archaeologists Eldon Johnson and Tim Jones argue that it is this combination that has made the latter group so successful and offer it as a model for other provincial groups.[35] These volunteers, they suggest, can assist in the recording and preservation of new site locations, act as local educators, and lobby the government for additional legislation and funding.[36]

Yet the power struggle between amateurs and professional archaeologists persists. Perhaps most problematic are excavations by serious looters who believe that material culture should be individually owned and sold for profit. In the United States, professional archaeologists report that looters still target both publically and privately owned property to obtain interesting artifacts, especially those from burials, for their own collections, or to sell their treasures for large amounts of money on the antiquities market. Archaeologists have returned to their excavations to find that pothunters have visited the site overnight. Property owners have rented out land known to possess significant burial or village sites to looters who employ bulldozers and other destructive techniques to quickly locate and loot artifacts. With the exception of some state laws prohibiting gravedigging on private land, no legislation covers private property or regulates the commercial art market. Some antiquities dealers and private collectors even lobby against the enactment of state laws to protect sites because they fear legislation will harm their businesses.[37]

A 1999 study conducted in British Columbia shows that much of the public is against excavations by non-professionals for personal and private interests.[38] But in Canada looting continues to be a problem. Staff of small community museums are often asked to disclose site locations in order for individuals to make their own personal explorations, and a number of sites have been reported as illegally excavated over the past several decades. In 1985, two men were charged under the 1974 Ontario Heritage Act, the first case to be prosecuted under this legislation.

These men and an accomplice had looted the Freelton Misner site, an untouched Neutral village and cemetery in the Hamilton area, collecting almost ten thousand artifacts and human remains. The looting was characterized as blatant and deliberate. One man had been a member of the Ontario Archaeological Society and thus knew his actions were illegal while the other was described by the court as a "'second-generation looter.'" They had even advertised the sale of some of the artifacts in a newspaper. The two men received fines of $7,000 and narrowly escaped a jail sentence. The accomplice received a sentence of eight hundred hours of community service and a $700 fine. Dr William Fox, a regional archaeologist from the Ontario Ministry of Citizenship and Culture, noted that the human remains would be repatriated to the Six Nations of the Grand River for burial and the village designated as a heritage site. A professional excavation, however, was to be conducted in the future. In the meantime, the exact location of the sites was left undisclosed for fear of further looting.[39]

Four years later, Fox commented on the continued widespread looting of Ontario sites, particularly by those crossing the border from Michigan, who target the large Wendat (Huron) and Neutral village sites of the Georgian Bay, Grand River Valley and the Niagara peninsula. These are especially attractive to Michigan collectors for most sites in this state are not so large and rich in artifacts. Archaeologists suspect, however, that Canadians assist Americans in their searches. The artifacts found are kept by private collectors, sold at meetings of collector clubs, or even farther afield when they are rare and thus can command high prices. Sometimes they are used in ways reminiscent of the nineteenth century. For example, in Northern Ontario, individuals pried away chunks of rock paintings to use in the construction of a fireplace.[40] Another case in 2003 is similar. That year, the Fisheries' Small Craft Harbour Division of British Columbia discovered nine skeletons in the process of rebuilding a harbour. These remains were taken by several individuals for an otherwise unidentified use at home and at a local firehall. The Qualicum and Cape Mudge bands demanded the return of the human remains and the protection of this site.[41] In response to such activities, archaeologists no longer talk about sites, fearing it only increases looting and destruction. "There's nothing scientific about these people," said one archaeologist, a telling comment stemming from the divide between the public and professionals that has been in place since the nineteenth century.[42]

Archaeologist Robert Mallouf suggests that professional archaeologists have used a "'milquetoast advocacy'" in dealing with hobbyists and looters, a tactic similar to that used in the nineteenth century. This approach both discourages destructive excavations and the private sale of objects but also seeks out the information these people can provide about specific sites. Some archaeologists fear that if amateur excavators are faced with severe repercussions they will simply go underground with their activities and the information they do possess will be lost. Mallouf instead argues that, although hobbyists and avocational collectors do provide information to professionals, serious pothunters do not and thus these fears are groundless. He further suggests that archaeologists have not effectively communicated to the public how their profession is different than nineteenth-century antiquarianism, a problem compounded by the publication of their research in a manner deemed incomprehensible by a non-scholarly audience.[43]

Aside from the issue of looting, questions remain. Who should steward artifacts preserved in museum collections? Whose viewpoint should have priority, or is it possible to present a balance of scholarly and indigenous perspectives? Access to and treatment of objects and interpretative control of them are closely related to the mandate of museums. Which public(s) should museums serve – indigenous groups, the local community, academia, or a combination?

As discussed above, since the publication of the *Turning the Page* report in 1992, many Canadian museums have followed its ethical proscriptions by collaborating with Aboriginal communities in order to incorporate their beliefs and priorities. But not all agree with this approach. For example, Norman Zepp, a former curator of Inuit art at the Art Gallery of Ontario, believes that allowing artists to choose works for display is a "retreat from scholarship"; it is the curator's duty to select the artifacts from an expert and scholarly standpoint.[44] In contrast, Kanienkehaka museologist and historian Deborah Doxtator criticized the *Turning the Page* report as being too conservative. She felt it supported a power imbalance by placing the onus on museums to approach Aboriginal peoples and by not advocating co-ownership rather than co-management of museum collections.[45]

A third approach can be called the indigenization of the museum, a process that could be argued as having informed Dr Oronhyatekha's nineteenth-century museum. Some indigenous peoples doubt that the museum as a collecting and exhibitionary complex can ever be reconciled with their traditional principles, but others see a middle ground with cultural centres. These institutions, which may incorporate museums, also offer language courses, artistic and performance opportunities, and the teaching of crafts. In this sense, the cultural centre promotes

the continuance and strengthening of indigenous culture, in opposition
to the museum, which is often characterized as stultifying culture or
portraying it as altogether dead and vanished.

The largest manifestation of the movement to indigenize the museum
must be the new National Museum of the American Indian (NMAI), a
part of the Smithsonian Institution in Washington, DC.[46] It officially
opened in autumn 2004 amidst a six-day First Americans Festival that
attracted approximately 600,000 visitors and indigenous people.[47] The
NMAI originated from a private New York collection owned by George
Gustav Heye, whose artifacts Congress transferred to the Smithsonian
in 1989 through the National Museum of the American Indian Act.[48]
Methodologically, the curatorial team believed it would have to "invent
a new discipline," one that would combine an anthropological and historical approach with traditional and oral knowledge.[49] Consequently,
the NMAI has dedicated itself to collaborating with indigenous peoples
of the Western Hemisphere and Hawai'i to revoke stereotypes, reaffirm traditions, recognize the diversity, adaptability and continuity
of their cultures, promote contemporary artistic and linguistic endeavours, and incorporate indigenous approaches to the care, study, and
exhibition of their material culture.[50] But the significance of the NMAI
extends beyond these achievements; to supporters, its creation signifies
the redefinition of a museum, from an institution that colonizes and
objectifies indigenous nations to a place of "cultural sovereignty," in
which indigenous voices can be reclaimed.[51] Like nineteenth-century
indigenous peoples who attempted to use their historical past to regain
recognition of their sovereignty, many indigenous people now see the
indigenization of the museum as a way to bolster their autonomy.

To many indigenous peoples, the NMAI building itself is a statement of reclamation and redefinition because its location on the Mall
in Washington, DC, the capital of the United States, re-establishes the
city as Native American land.[52] Many of the management and staff at the
museum are Native American, including Director W. Richard West, and
the curation of its shows involve collaboration with indigenous communities and elders. The NMAI currently features four exhibits that
discuss indigenous cosmology and spirituality, European contact and
its consequences, survival and adaptation, and contemporary identities
and art.[53] The museum also includes a visible storage area that houses
many artifacts and video clips by community members who interpret
objects; an ongoing demonstration of boat-building; a performance
space for dance, storytelling, plays, and music; and a restaurant that
serves indigenous foods. As the NMAI is located outside of most large

indigenous population centres in North and South America, many communities suggested that another "museum" be created, one that would be more accessible and thus more meaningful. Community outreach programs, the NMAI website, travelling exhibits, and educational and training opportunities for indigenous individuals fulfill this mandate.

The building and the collections management system both incorporate indigenous spirituality. The design of the NMAI stemmed from collaboration among numerous indigenous communities across the country, the process and results of which is contained in the document *The Way of the People*. From these consultations several common themes arose, including the belief that the museum should pay tribute to nature and be shaped by traditional spirituality. In essence, the building emphasizes the link between natural and built environments, an important theme in indigenous understandings of the world. Consequently, the door faces east toward the rising sun and toward the beach, two common elements in the construction of traditional indigenous buildings. The shape of the structure resembles a rock formation worn away by wind and water. Spiritual motifs have been incorporated into the structure and the colours used throughout derive from those found in nature. Inside, the floor plan follows a series of circles, and outside, running water, forest, meadow and wetland habitats, and gardens of plants such as corn, beans, and squash recreate an indigenous landscape. Grandfather rocks symbolize the ancient connection of indigenous peoples to the land, and other rocks from several different communities mark the four cardinal points of direction, which are also represented inside. These natural materials were blessed before their use.[54]

Because indigenous cultures believe certain objects to be living beings that need care, respect, and sustenance, the collections management system incorporates spiritual elements. As the artifacts moved from New York City into their new home in Washington, elders and spiritualists blessed them. Community leaders are allowed to leave water and food for these beings in the storage area and conduct rituals such as smudging, all considered conservation hazards in standard museum practice. Items judged to be inappropriate for display are not shown, and indeed many items have been repatriated to their descendant nations. Researcher access to culturally sensitive material is restricted or requires approval of the relevant community.[55]

Predictably, while many have applauded the final product, some visitors, scholars, and indigenous peoples question NMAI's message, mandate, and management. While the museum sees the inclusion of contemporary art and artifacts as a testament to the survival of indigenous cultures, some critics suggest that they are displayed to promote the sale of items marketed by the expensive gift shop. This is a view also shared by some indigenous peoples. In response to the goal to allow indigenous peoples to relate their own histories from their own perspective, some scholars argue that this methodology has led to a neglect of academic research, reflected in what they see as unconnected and unfocused exhibits and vague labelling. In fact, one reviewer questioned how tribal curators can be knowledgeable when there is no written pre-contact record and oral tradition has been disrupted by European influence. The cyclical interpretation of objects, judged as ahistorical and conflating of time periods, also bothers those more used to a linear scholarly approach. But there is also dubiousness from indigenous peoples; one individual complained that the "New Age Indians" who were involved did not understand their culture as fully or accurately as those raised traditionally. Others argue that the NMAI is too politically correct and does not address difficult and painful issues such as land appropriation, assimilation and religious conversion, war, disease, genocide, poverty, and substance addiction. This too has been brought forth by indigenous critics. Controversial and conflicting theories around the origin of the indigenous peoples in North, South, and Central America are not discussed. Some commentators deem its celebration of survival as romanticized, simplistic, self-validatory, and merely a vehicle to boost pride. The idea of indigenous control of artifacts is also contested. One reviewer argued that a museum should hold the collections in trust for the public and that the NMAI contravenes this mandate because access to items for research and exhibition of objects is restricted based on race and background. The idea that a federal institution promotes one religion over another is thus problematic to some. And, what will be next, many question, a museum for every different ethnicity or religious belief in North America?[56]

Debates about stewardship include the issue of repatriation. Should all objects in museums be kept? Perhaps the most sensitive issue concerns the collection and control of human remains. A spectrum of opinions exist, but as it was in the nineteenth century, one basic division revolves around whether human remains should be viewed as scientific resources or as ancestors whose disturbance through excavation violates human rights and religious beliefs. While anthropologist Thomas Biolsi and archaeologist Larry Zimmerman argue that the historical image of the vanishing Indian has mistakenly encouraged archaeologists to act as the stewards of indigenous skeletons, some proponents of the scientific argument believe that they are best suited to continue in this role.

They argue that the information obtained from bones cannot be drawn from living indigenous groups and that, in fact, skeletons are more "objective" than live informants. Professional archaeologists are therefore needed to conduct research on human remains.[57] The latter wish to keep permanent bone collections in case new scientific techniques are discovered in the future and thus more testing can be done. The scientific method also demands repeated testing, to confirm, improve, or negate previous findings. One group, the American Committee for the Protection of Archaeological Collections, refuses to participate in excavations if the remains will be reinterred, deeming it a destruction of property. As one nineteenth-century newspaper suggested, it is thought that buried remains possess a "usefulness" by being dug up and studied.[58] Some museums also believe that they respect human remains, because they define the term as careful and cautious treatment in storage. One scholar even stated that scientific examination is a very high form of deference.[59] In contrast, the group American Indians against Desecration opposes all archaeology.

While some indigenous people call for archaeologists to band with them against looters, others do not distinguish between looters and archaeologists.[60] They denounce both as being more concerned with objects than human beings and argue that, despite their rhetoric of scientific objectivity, they still perpetuate stereotypes about their cultures. To these individuals, both groups exploit human remains for money or academic advancement and are disrespectful of graves. Like those who protested against excavations in the nineteenth century, the level of professionalism during an excavation is thus irrelevant to them.[61] While not all indigenous groups take this hardline stance, many do demand the primacy of their religious rights over academic freedom. Some traditionalists argue that non-indigenous skeletons are treated differently; they are reburied because they are viewed as human beings not scientific resources and because their descendants' wishes for respectful treatment are abided with. Some deem this institutional racism and a violation of human rights.[62] Others do not reject science but the notion that science should take precedence over all other cultural beliefs.[63] In fact, in one case, Cheyenne representatives decided to leave a group of funerary and religious objects at the Smithsonian for the education of community researchers and others.[64]

Many indigenous groups see their ancestors, although dead, as members of their contemporary communities.[65] Even if a cultural link cannot be made between an ancient interment and a living group, which NAGPRA requires, many Native American groups still believe that, as present stewards of their land, they are responsible for those who are buried there. Disturbance of the dead also affects the living; angry spirits can cause earthquakes and dangerous weather, illness, and death. Consequently, as in the case of the Alaskan Larsen Bay repatriation by the Smithsonian, Native Americans are often more concerned about restoring spiritual balance than contributions to science.[66] Some traditionalists also believe that the natural world is also impacted. Burial completes a cycle of nature: bodies nourish the ground in death which enables the earth to sustain humans in life. Disinterment disrupts this rhythm. Some indigenous groups further argue that the information that archaeologists seek is present in oral knowledge; therefore to contend that reburial equals a loss of information, as anti-repatriation proponents do, suggests that indigenous cultures are extinct.[67] Some also believe that the scientific and objective stance that archaeologists have taken is really a political – not an academic – claim and should be seen as such. Others characterize science as completely subjective.[68] In contrast, some indigenous groups do not wish human remains to be returned because they fear spiritual harm from angry ancestors.

Some scholars believe that ancient skeletons belong to society as a whole because no definitive cultural link can be made with modern-day groups or because their study can benefit everyone. Alternatively, some archaeologists suggest that, the older burials are, the more they reinforce the common heritage of all humankind, rather than a sense of ethnic identity. This idea of a public trust is represented, for example, by the code of ethics of the Register of Professional Archaeologists.[69] A more medium ground has been taken by the Society for American Archaeology. The SAA recognizes the rights and spiritual beliefs of indigenous peoples and encourages communication between scholars and indigenous communities but believes that "all human remains should receive appropriate scientific study," opposes "universal or indiscriminate reburial of human remains," and advocates that repatriation be based upon demonstrated cultural affinity between the remains and modern groups, as NAGPRA requires.[70] But many members of the SAA, in fact, go beyond this code and engage in collaborative archaeology, as shown by their recent volume of case studies, *Working Together*.[71]

Other scholars champion academic freedom and the United States First Amendment, both ostensibly violated by reburial. Clement W. Meighan, an outspoken adversary of repatriation of older graves, believes that reburial sacrifices public knowledge for special-interest groups and that it is anti-intellectual to deny study on the basis of religion. Further, he sees oral tradition as mythical and since there is no written history of ancient indigenous societies, archaeology remains the only method of investigation of pre-contact cultures. He deems claims to prehistoric bones as mere mysticism, implies that the designation of items as sacred is used arbitrarily by indigenous groups, and dismisses the spiritual belief that the study of human remains can harm living peoples. Most compromises, he suggests, are unrealistic.[72] Archaeologist G.A. Clark is as adamant: "NAGPRA is an unmitigated disaster for archaeologists," he lamented, because it "puts ethnicity and religious belief on equal footing with science and thus provides a mandate for claims of affiliation by virtually any interested party ... It is simply a fact that knowledge of most pre-contact aboriginal cultures ... would have vanished without a trace if were it not for archaeology."[73]

This idea of a loss of scientific information through reburial is countered by other archaeologists who, in fact, argue the exact opposite. They suggest that NAGPRA has actually increased the number of studies on collections of human remains, since these need to be completed before NAGPRA can be fulfilled.[74] Other archaeologists see a range of benefits stemming from NAGPRA and repatriation, including increased employment of physical anthropologists, an integration of different types of knowledge, and reflexive critiques of anthropological practice, including the abrogation of the idea that archaeology is an objective and neutral science.[75]

Perhaps the most famous case that symbolizes the disagreement over the access, study, control, and purpose of human remains is Kennewick Man or Oyt.pa.ma.na.tit.tite, "The Ancient One," a more than nine-thousand-year-old skeleton that tests the limits of NAGPRA. According to some archaeologists, Kennewick Man's age negates the possibility that he is an ancestor to any present-day tribe while many Native American groups remain steadfast that oral tradition proves they have been in North America for thousands of years, and therefore Kennewick Man must be of Native American descent regardless. At first, it was decided that oral tradition proved cultural continuity between Kennewick Man and those who claimed him as an ancestor, as NAGPRA requires. He was thus slated for reburial until Dr Robson Bonnichsen, director of the Center for the Study of First Americans at Texas A&M University, and others collectively sued for the right to examine the skeleton, arguing that freedom of expression and the right to gather information under the US constitution had been violated. The plaintiffs also claimed that the denial of access to Kennewick Man based on their race (i.e., non-Native American) transgressed the Civil Rights Act of 1866. In 2002, Oregon US District Court Magistrate John

Jelderks ruled that scientists should be allowed to study Kennewick Man. He disagreed that all remains prior to 1492 were automatically Native American and dismissed the oral evidence that linked Kennewick Man to present-day groups.

A joint tribal coalition composed of the Nez Percé, the Confederated Tribes of the Umatilla Indian Reservation, the Confederated Tribes and Bands of the Yakama Nation, and the Confederated Tribes of the Colville Reservation filed with the Ninth Circuit of the US Court of Appeals, but in February 2004 the Circuit Court upheld Jelderks's ruling. Kennewick Man, unproven to be Native American, was to be governed under the Archaeological Resources Protection Act, not NAGPRA. Later that year, the Confederated Tribes of the Umatilla Indian Reservation decided not to appeal to the US Supreme Court, partly due to the fear that, if the decision was unfavourable, a legal precedent would be set. Scientists have now studied Kennewick Man at his temporary home at the Burke Museum of Natural History and Culture at the University of Washington in Seattle. Meanwhile, US Congress debates how to modify NAGPRA in order to clarify future treatment of ancient and those termed culturally unidentified skeletons, particularly changes to its wording around the need to demonstrate cultural affiliation between human remains and a living Native American group.[76]

In Canada, there are no federal statutes about the excavation or repatriation of human remains, although in the 1980s and 1990s there was an attempt to enact such legislation. The Department of Communications drafted a paper entitled *Federal Archaeological Heritage Protection and Management* for the general security of sites not under the authority of Parks Canada. The Assembly of First Nations agreed with its overall objectives at a meeting in 1989, but at a 1991 consultation, to which over one hundred Aboriginal organizations were invited, a preliminary bill was rejected. Aboriginal participants emphasized the need for respect, mutual understanding, and alternative interpretations of archaeology. They especially argued that Crown control was inappropriate since the Creator gave Aboriginal peoples the inherent right to ownership and stewardship of archaeological sites.[77] In 1999, the Assembly of First Nations passed a resolution that "condemn[s] and abhor[s]" those who "explore, exploit, disturb and remove native remains … both ancient and contemporary" and vowed it would lobby for protective national legislation, but there has been little result.[78]

Thus most Canadian archaeologists work within the boundaries of the ethical statements created by their various professional organizations. Most are collaboratively worded. The *Turning the Page* report recommends both study and reburial of human remains, to be decided by archaeologists and Aboriginal communities together. The CAA acknowledges the cultural importance of human remains to Aboriginal peoples, Aboriginal protocols governing treatment of them, and the significance of oral history and traditional knowledge in archaeology.[79] In 1996, the Royal Commission on Aboriginal Peoples advocated that Aboriginal groups should be the owners of heritage sites, rather than collaborative parties in their management. In the context of this recommendation, Margaret Hanna of the Royal Saskatchewan Museum of Natural History judged the CAA *Statement of Principles* to be too ambiguous in its definition of the relationship between Aboriginal peoples and archaeologists. Hanna states that Aboriginal peoples consider themselves related to bones by their "common experience of the land," negating the importance of genetic relationships, usually the key concept to repatriation.[80] Without the recognition of Aboriginal ownership, she argues, there is no alteration in the power relationship between archaeologists and Aboriginal communities. In contrast, the Canadian Association for Physical Anthropology advocates against repatriation and reburial. In 1979, this organization recognized Aboriginal spiritual beliefs and urged physical anthropologists to consult Aboriginal communities affected by their work, but it also stated that no one group should claim or control all of Canada's past. The association believes this heritage belongs to the public as a whole; to curtail research on the basis of religion deprives many, including First Nations, of the benefits of that research. There has been no change in this policy.[81]

Each province has its own legislation. In Ontario, the municipal Planning Act stipulates that Aboriginal communities must be notified of any development within one kilometre of their land, in case burials are discovered. The Ontario Heritage Act recognizes that First Nations have a special duty as stewards of their own culture, yet defines the government as the ultimate owner of all artifacts, a provision unacceptable to many Aboriginal groups. The Ontario Cemeteries Act requires Aboriginal consent before any removal or analysis of burials. Government mediation will follow if no agreement to manage the site can be made.

Despite the lack of specific repatriation legislation, Canadian museums have begun to return human remains from their collections amidst disagreement and controversy. In 1977, the Royal Ontario Museum received a formal request by Michel Gros-Louis of the Wendat of Jeune-Lorette in Quebec for the remains of more than five hundred ancestors excavated in 1947. Like many other Aboriginal individuals,

Gros-Louis emphasized the spiritual aspect of repatriation. He believed his ancestors had asked him to give them peace through reburial. In 1999, the bones were returned, and the ownership of the site transferred to the Lorette band, though the museum considered his request to be a political, rather than a spiritual, bid.[82] But many Wendat peoples still believe that the disturbance of the dead can lead to dangerous consequences and continue to pursue the return and reburial of their ancestral ossuaries.[83] After a Wendat cemetery was accidentally uncovered by a backhoe during construction of a hockey arena near Midland, Ontario, in 2003, David Grey Eagle Sanford of the Huron-Wendat nation told the newspaper about their beliefs about death. The Hurons "'had two spirits,'" he said, "'one to go over to the other side and another to stay with the remains, to sleep with them, to watch over them and protect them ... The spirits have been awakened and are now coming to and thinking somebody is disturbing them after all this time; people can get very sick from this. It is very powerful medicine.'" While Jamie Hunter, curator of the Huronia Museum, wished to erect a plaque to commemorate the site, the newspaper noted that the Huron-Wendat were likely to refuse in case such a plaque would only tempt looters.[84] A plaque has been erected but the text suggests the ossuary was a result of an European epidemic, rather than the traditional archaeological interpretation referring to the Feast of the Dead.[85]

In 1998, the Canadian Museum of Civilization returned Iroquoian remains dug up in the 1910s from the Roebuck site, which were reburied at the Akwesasne reserve. Museum archaeologist David Morrison prefaced the return with a reference to the public trust doctrine. "After a few thousand years," he said, "everybody is the common property of everybody." The reporter covering this story noted that now these bones had been returned, they would be unavailable for future methods of genetic testing, which could reveal the migration history of indigenous peoples in North America.[86]

The 2005 return of the Algonquin remains to the Kitigan Zibi First Nation by the Canadian Museum of Civilization was even more controversial. At first, when the Kitigan Zibi made their repatriation request, the museum was reluctant. A few individual staff members possessed concerns similar to those expressed during the Kennewick Man dispute. Some of the remains were classified as between five and six thousand years old, and thus some argued that they could not be culturally linked with current Algonquin peoples. Only those about seven hundred years old, the museum suggested, could be reliably connected to present-day communities. The museum proposed to radiocarbon test the bones to determine their age, and thus their potential for repatriation. The Kitigan Zibi First Nation at first considered the radiocarbon testing but ultimately decided against it. Gilbert Whiteduck, their spokesman, asserted that the Algonquin peoples had lived along the Ottawa River since time immemorial and thus these human remains were their ancestors, no matter their age, and needed to be laid to rest permanently. In fact, the Algonquin, once they knew the location of the site Van Cortlandt had excavated, conducted spiritual ceremonies here to honour the dead and placate any angry spirits. The museum also lamented the loss of knowledge that could come from the study of these bones. Dr Susan Pfeiffer, a physical anthropologist who originally studied some of these ancient bones, and then dean of Graduate Studies at the University of Toronto, agreed: the idea that scientists have discovered all they can from such bones, she argued, is false. In studying ancient remains, President Victor Rabinovitch said, "'it is not the purpose of the Canadian Museum of Civilization to be disrespectful, either toward any modern community nor to the individuals whose bones we hold. Rather, we keep and study these remains because of the information they hold, and our respect for the past.'"[87]

US archaeologists also spoke out against this alleged loss of scientific information. Perhaps not surprisingly, these were Smithsonian anthropologist Dennis Stanford and Douglas Wallace, a molecular biologist from the University of California, both of whom were part of the Kennewick Man lawsuit. These men lobbied the Museum of Civilization and Canadians generally to refuse to give up the more ancient remains for repatriation, arguing that research findings using new tools in genetic analysis could provide answers about the origin of indigenous peoples. In contrast, Whiteduck stated that "'There's nothing else to be learned … There's been enough research. There's been enough damage.'" After visiting the Algonquin human remains at the museum, the Algonquin elders also expressed sorrow that the officials saw them as only bones and not as related human spirits.[88] Despite all the controversy, the remains were reburied on National Aboriginal Day in 2005 on the Maniwaki reserve.[89]

One of the key issues of these repatriation conflicts revolves around the definition of cultural affinity upon which NAGPRA and many ethical statements are based and the idea that ancient remains cannot be linked to current-day indigenous groups. This is not a new idea. Remember that James Coyne and others argued that the Walpole Island community, who protested the 1892 disturbance of a gravesite, were unrelated to those buried there, an argument used to dismiss the protests. According to archaeologists Tamara Bray and Lauryn Guttenplan Grant, utilizing such an anthropological idea as the basis of a law that supposedly benefits indigenous peoples is paradoxical.[90] Tuscarora scholar Rick Hill further states that anthropologists have arbitrarily defined culture; the category of Paleo-Indians has been created by archaeologists, he says, as "if they were genetic and cultural mutants that had no relationship to modern Native Americans."[91] Others, like James Riding In, believe that the term culturally unidentified should be dismissed, since it is clear that all Native American remains in museums are related to some current-day tribe.[92] A second problem is the ambiguous NAGPRA clause that suggests objects should not be considered for return if they could be part of a major scientific study of national importance, which provides a loophole to resist repatriation.[93]

A third issue involved in the repatriation of human remains is the accuracy and validity of oral tradition. As they have been in the past, Euro-Canadian and indigenous paradigms of collecting, preserving, and transferring knowledge are treated as both incongruent and complementary. Sioux scholar and activist Vine Deloria Jr asserted the primacy of oral knowledge in his books *Red Earth, White Lies: North America and the Myth of Scientific Fact* (1995) and *Evolution, Creationism, and Other Modern Myths* (2002). In 1992, Wendat author Georges E. Sioui argued that even ethnohistory, which attempts to understand the indigenous point of view, incorporates evolutionary paradigms. He suggested that this discipline should be replaced with Amerology or autohistory, which employ indigenous values.[94] Other indigenous scholars, such as Roger Echo-Hawk, advocate a middle ground in which oral tradition and scientific evidence are combined to support each other, each having first undergone a critical examination. He believes oral and archaeological information "describe a shared past and should be viewed as natural partners in post-NAGPRA America."[95]

Like their nineteenth-century counterparts, archaeologists still disagree whether oral traditions and archaeological evidence can be used in complementarity. Ronald J. Mason argues that oral history and archaeology are distinct methodologies, while Peter M. Whiteley believes each can be used together without any loss of scientific rigour.[96] Many scholars have advocated a more wholesale acceptance of indigenous historicities. This includes alternative temporalities, a seasonality and spirituality to stories, an interconnection of the past, present, and future, ownership of intellectual property, the acceptance of elders as trained historians, the application of history to reaffirm cultural identity, and the use of material culture such as wampum belts to document the past. As a result, these scholars suggest going beyond ethnohistory, in which oral tradition is used only to confirm or support historical documents. History "'in the round,'" "multiple representations," "polyvocality" or a "dialogical" history, and plural discourse have all been proposed, in which indigenous interpretations are presented alongside those of historians with equal validity.[97] Of course, the most recent decision in the legal battle over Kennewick Man abrogated the accuracy of oral knowledge, while in Canada the 1997 Delgamuukw Supreme Court judgement regarding land claims upheld its validity.[98]

The use of scientific or religious paradigms and oral traditions in interpreting material culture, and issues of human rights and sovereignty, also partly underlie debates about the collection, exhibition, and repatriation of sacred objects. Many objects are believed to be as alive as and often more powerful than human beings, and thus some indigenous peoples feel it is offensive and even dangerous to restrict such objects in cupboards or glass cases. Many of these items carry cultural protocols about their use, handling, and viewing, and museum staff are thought to be at risk by violating these rules. These items are often used to maintain a connection with the natural and spiritual environment, and their removal from community use severs this link.[99] Thus many traditionalists wish to restitute ceremonial objects to their original use to foster traditional spirituality, to protect religious freedom of indigenous peoples, and to restore human relationships with the spiritual world.[100] Items of cultural patrimony, those that do not belong to an individual but to a community, are also targeted for return. But repatriation is also an issue of human rights and sovereignty, since, as we have seen, many objects were removed from their communities because of colonialist and assimilationist pressures. To have such items returned, then, can be seen as a way to restore sovereignty and control over spirituality and political governance, and to spur a cultural renewal.[101]

In the United States, NAGPRA partly covers restoration of sacred and ceremonial material culture and items of cultural patrimony. If an object was illegally obtained, or if it once was owned communally, it must be returned, but otherwise museums are not required to proceed with repatriation.[102] As with archaeological remains, in Canada there is no national repatriation legislation for ethnographic items.[103] Again, there is a variety of ethical policies. The *Turning the Page* report recommended several approaches, including repatriation, replication of objects for the use of the museum or community, loans of items to be used in ceremonies, and the co-management of collections. Parks Canada considers the return of sacred items based on their significance, the history of acquisition, and the interest of the Aboriginal peoples and is willing to negotiate on the meaning of sacred, a definition that changes depending on the Aboriginal group in question.[104] A movement toward virtual, digital, or information repatriation, in which photographs of artifacts and related knowledge is made accessible through the internet, has also begun. For example, the Great Lakes Research Alliance for the Study of Aboriginal Arts and Cultures led by Canada Research Chair Ruth Phillips aims to bring together information and photographs of artifacts from museums across several continents in a digital database for researchers and Aboriginal communities. Similarly, the Reciprocal Research Network through the Museum of Anthropology at the University of British Columbia facilitates research on and access to northwest coast cultural heritage. Collaboration between scholars, museums, and Aboriginal communities is key to these projects.[105]

Numerous museums in Canada have begun the process of repatriation. The Royal Saskatchewan Museum is currently developing policies with the Treaty Four Aboriginal groups to create keeping houses that will store and exhibit ethnographic material according to Aboriginal protocol. Both the Royal British Columbia Museum and the Glenbow Museum have willingly returned ceremonial items to the Nisga'a and the Niitsitapi respectively, and the latter is working toward repatriation of objects to other nations. As with other issues, not all groups completely agree with repatriation, seeing it as a loss of scientific information. For example, a current call by several Plains groups for the return of Papamihaw Asiniy, a meteorite, has met with resistance by officials of the Provincial Museum of Alberta. While these nations believe that the stone is an animate spiritual being that protects them, geology staff at the museum argue that this specimen is "'probably the best meteorite in Canada to show its scientific features'" and that there is "'other value to it besides the native, spiritual aspect.'"[106]

Traditionalist Haudenosaunee from Ontario, New York, and Quebec communities are particularly concerned with the ownership of False Face masks and wampum belts. Today, the Grand Council of Haudenosaunee states that interference with the duties of traditional societies and False Face masks is considered to be a "violation of the freedom of the Haudenosaunee and does great harm to the welfare of the Haudenosaunee communities." Traditionalist Haudenosaunee visit museums and reassure these masks, considered to be as alive as humans, that they are working toward their return, and ask them to be patient. Many traditionalists are determined to eventually reclaim all

masks, and the Haudenosaunee Standing Committee for Burial Rules
and Regulations is working toward this goal. Returned masks, with
the exception of those that have been treated with arsenic for preservation and therefore are dangerous to handle, have been restored to
their traditional use. Not surprisingly, there have been attacks on the
credibility of the Grand Council. Noted Iroquoianist William Fenton
argued that the Grand Council had been goaded into making its policy
by off-reserve activists who were seeking their Haudenosaunee roots
but whom really had no connections to traditionalists. Further, Fenton
suggested, not all Haudenosaunee traditionalists supported the Grand
Council's actions.[107]

As discussed earlier, members of the Haudenosaunee began to attempt
to have their wampum belts returned shortly after they were sold in
the late nineteenth century. The Haudenosaunee Standing Committee
states that the possession of wampum by museums and collectors violates their human and communal rights, religious freedom, and sovereignty.[108] Many of the wampum belts sold by the Buck family and others
have been repatriated. In the 1970s, members of the Six Nations of the
Grand River requested the return of four wampum belts and six strings
of wampum from the ROM. In 1999, the museum returned these pieces,
originally given by Evelyn Johnson, as it believed that it did not possess clear title to the wampum.[109] More controversial was the repatriation of wampum belts from the New York State Museum in Albany
to the Onondage'ga' (Onondaga) in the 1970s. These belts had been
transferred by them in 1898 to the museum. The Onondage'ga' claimed
that they had loaned, not sold, the belts to the state museum, and they
needed them returned in order to continue many of their traditional
rituals.[110] William Fenton objected based upon several points. First, he
stated that the Onondage'ga' cultural memory cannot be justified in
light of written documents. He also believed that wampum belonged
to all Americans, not just Native Americans. Those people who ask
for such items to be repatriated often forget or gloss over the circum-
stances of their transfer to museums, he said. To repatriate means ignor-
ing the responsibility entrusted to the museum by the Onondage'ga'
when they were originally transferred in 1898. Fenton implied that the
beliefs that the Onondage'ga' were bilked of their wampum, that the
keeping of such objects in museums denies them of their rights, and
that repatriation leads to cultural autonomy and regeneration are all
false. Wampum, because it was a post-contact invention, he said, was as
American as "apple pie, the log cabin, and the splint basket." These belts
were thus great US cultural treasures, and, if they were returned, few

people would ever see them, in contrast to the thousands who viewed them at the New York museum. Fenton set himself up as the expert who could interpret the belts for educational purposes in contrast to those he saw as merely spewing Native American propaganda. In fact, Fenton continued, many Haudenosaunee looked to academic anthropological publications for knowledge about their history and traditions. Lastly, Fenton suggested that historically many Six Nations had little interest in caring for their belts as evidenced by their sale to collectors and by the fact they no longer believed in their communal property ownership.[111] In 1988, the Museum of the American Indian (just then made part of the Smithsonian) repatriated eleven Confederacy belts, this time to the Six Nations of the Grand River. Fenton did not object this time, perhaps because the Smithsonian ultimately felt their sale had been "ethically shaky." Fenton did, however, disagree with the cultural memory of the Six Nations about how the wampum belts left their care, although he did not specify in which ways.[112]

The past collection, exhibition, and interpretation of material culture will continue to matter to ongoing initiatives, such as the potential projects to mark the 400th anniversary of the journey of the explorer Samuel de Champlain through Ontario, and particularly through historic Huronia in 1615. In 2008, the *Orillia Packet and Times* reported on a Algonquin or perhaps Wendat site, called Mount Slaven, which now lies underneath the homes and concrete of the city. This spot had been partially unearthed in the nineteenth and twentieth centuries but had been forgotten as Orillia grew in size. This story was a response to the proposal by the Huronia Museum in Midland, which seeks $1.25 million from the provincial government to locate and verify the fourteen Aboriginal villages visited by Samuel de Champlain, mark them with plaques, create historical tours, and build an interpretative centre. Part of this initiative will be to research and find the artifacts taken from these sites that are now in private or museum collections, which may include tracing the footsteps of amateur archaeologists and those more professional collectors such as David Boyle and Andrew F. Hunter. This project has begun, in collaboration with the local chapter of the Ontario Archaeological Society. A related project initiated by the French-Canadian historical group La Clé d'la Baie is the Champlain Trail proposal to erect plaques along already established historical trails to discuss the contributions of the French and Aboriginal peoples to this area. Destination Nord, a group that promotes Francophone tourism in Ontario, has proposed an even larger "Champlain Circuit" that follows this explorer's travels through the Ottawa Valley, historic Huronia, and the Niagara peninsula. This circuit includes archaeological sites, some of which are marked by the federal and provincial plaquing programs.[113]

Such projects will have to deal with the legacy of the past. Upon hearing of the location of the Mount Slaven site, one Orillia resident remarked to the *Packet and Times* reporter, "'I'd like to get a team in here and root around ... That stuff fascinates me. You never know what you'd find.'" Such a statement prompted the local curator of the Orillia Museum of Art and History to suggest that historical research and its publicity is wonderful for educational purposes but can also lead to looting by those looking for curious objects. As a result, the paper noted, Aboriginal peoples have not wanted the location of such sites to be marked too precisely.[114] Algonquin, Wendat, and other groups across Ontario and Quebec are also in consultation with the creators of these projects and wish to have a say in the excavation process, research into museum collections, and the interpretation of these sites and, as demonstrated by other past and current projects, will likely hold varying opinions. Companies and municipal councillors promoting development are much less interested in, and are even against, protecting and marking such archaeological sites. Discussion about the stewardship of these sites, artifacts, and related intellectual property–both past and future–will likely arise as groups decide how to manage issues of cultural representation, appropriation of voice, access to artifacts, the mandate of the proposed cultural centre, the validity and accuracy of oral knowledge, and the use of anthropological protocol or spirituality in deciding issues around repatriation and interpretation.

# NOTES

## INTRODUCTION

1   *Upper Canada Gazette; or American Oracle*, York, 30 December 1797, 1, and 13 January 1798, 1. For early relations between the Mississauga and settlers, see Smith, "Dispossession of the Mississauga Indians," 67–87.

2   For more about the Scadding family, see Reed, "The Scaddings," 7–20.

3   *CJ* 13, 3 (1872): 267–8; Scadding, *Toronto of Old*, 399–401.

4   Trigger, *Natives and Newcomers*, 8; Trigger, "Indians and Ontario History," 248.

5   Adams to Boyle, 2 April 1901, file 4, box 3, DBP, ROM; Indian Archaeology, note book no. 4, 117, box 1, AFHP, ROM; no. 109, *Packet*, Orillia, 2 December 1892, part 2-94-198, A. F. Hunter, Barrie, ON, Archaelogical Sites in Simcoe County, box 1, AFHP, ROM.

6   Berger, *Science, God and Nature in Victorian Canada*, 10–18.

7   The creation of the historical imagery of Indians as an exotic, extinct, less civilized "other" is ably discussed by Berkhofer, *White Man's Indian*; Francis, *Imaginary Indian*; Trigger, "Archaeology and the Image of the Indian," 662–70.

8   For the paradigm of salvage anthropology, see Gruber, "Ethnographic Salvage and the Shaping of Anthropology," 1289–99.

9   Minister of Education to Duff, 8 January 1906, RG 2-42-0-387, MS 5612, AO.

10  The Haudenosaunee (Five Nations Confederacy) consisted of the Mohawk (Kanienkehaka), the Oneida (Onyot.ka), the Seneca (Onodowahgah), the Onondaga (Onondage'ga'), the Cayuga (Gayogoho:no), and, later, a sixth nation, the Tuscarora (Ska-ru-ren).

11  The inclusiveness of the term Anishinabeg is debated, but I use it to mean the Ojibwa, Ottawa, Potawatomi, Algonquin, and Mississauga.

12  For a summary of the occupation of early Ontario by Algonkian- and Iroquoian-speaking peoples, see Trigger and Day, "Southern

Algonquian Middlemen," in Rogers and Smith, eds, *Aboriginal Ontario*, 64–77; Rogers, "The Algonquian Farmers of Southern Ontario," ibid., 122–66; Trigger, "The Original Iroquoians," ibid., 41–63; Johnston, "The Six Nations in the Grand River Valley," ibid., 167–81; Clifton, *A Place of Refuge*. A detailed archaeological perspective is presented in Ellis and Ferris, eds, *Archaeology of Southern Ontario*.

13  See, for example, Appadurai, ed., *Social Life of Things*; Deetz, *In Small Things Forgotten*; Glassie, *Material Culture*; Lubar and Kingery, eds, *History from Things*; Miller, ed., *Material Cultures*; Pocius, ed., *Living in a Material World*; Schlereth, ed., *Material Culture Studies in America*; Taborsky, "The Discursive Object," 50–77.

14  Clifford, *Routes*, 192 defined museums by using a model of contact zones as expressed in Pratt, *Imperial Eyes*, 6–7.

15  For postmodern literature on museums, see, for example, Beard and Henderson, "Please Don't Touch the Ceiling," in Pearce, ed., *Museums and the Appropriation of Culture*, 5–42; Bennett, *The Birth of the Museum*; Hooper-Greenhill, *Museums and the Shaping of Knowledge*; Price, *Primitive Art in Civilized Places*.

16  For the links between anthropology, museums, and colonialism, see, for example, Asad, ed., *Anthropology and the Colonial Encounter*; Barringer and Flynn, eds, *Colonialism and the Object*; Clifford, *Predicament of Culture*; Clifford and Marcus, eds, *Writing Culture*; Deloria Jr, *Custer Died for Your Sins*, 78–100; Karp and Lavine, eds, *Exhibiting Cultures*; Durrans, "The Future of the Other: Changing Cultures on Display in Ethnographic Museums," 144–69; Riegel, "Into the Heart of Irony: Ethnographic Exhibitions and the Politics of Difference," 83–104; Trigger, "A Present of Their Past?" 71–9. For the construction of the image of the Indian by museums and academics, see, for example, Bieder, *Science Encounters the Indian*; Medicine, "The Anthropologist as the Indian's Image-Maker," 27–9; Trigger, "Archaeology and the Image of the Indian," 662–70; Ames, *Cannibal Tours and Glass Boxes*; McLoughlin, *Museums and the Representation of Native Canadians*; *Muse* 6, 3 (1988), Special Issue, Museums and the First Nations; West, ed., *Changing Presentation of the American Indian*; Simpson, *Making Representations*.

17  Karp, "Introduction," in Karp, Kreamer, and Lavine, eds, *Museums and Communities*, 1; Cameron, "The Museum: A Temple or Forum?" 17.

18  Michaelsen, *Limits of Multiculturism*, xiii, 1–32. Strathern, "The Limits of Auto-Anthropology," 17 defines "auto-anthropology" as "anthropology carried out in the social context of which produced it." In Pratt, *Imperial Eyes*, 7, "autoethnography" is writing by the colonized to respond to the colonizer's representations of indigenous cultures. For a brief overview of the historiography of these terms see Reed-Danahay, ed., *Auto/Ethnography*, 4–9.

19 For anthropologists or informants as cultural brokers, see Karttunen, *Between Worlds*, 171–240; Parker, "D'Arcy McNickle," in Szasz, ed., *Between Indian and White Worlds*, 240–54; Iverson, "Speaking Their Language," ibid., 255–72; Medicine, "Ella C. Deloria," 269–88; Pavlik, ed., *A Good Cherokee, a Good Anthropologist*.

20 Hancock, "Toward a Historiography of Canadian Anthropology," in Harrison and Darnell, eds, *Historicizing Canadian Anthropology*, 32.

21 Abler, "A Mi'kmaq Missionary among the Mohawks: Silas T. Rand," in Haig-Brown and Nock, eds, *With Good Intentions*, 72–86; Black, *Bella Bella*; Black, "Looking for Bella Bella," 273–92; MacDonald, "From Ceremonial Object to Curio," 193–217; Miller, "Silas T. Rand," 235–50; Nock, "Aboriginals and Their Influence on E.F. Wilson's Paradigm Revolution," in Haig-Brown and Nock, eds, *With Good Intentions*, 158–78; Nock, "A Chapter in the Amateur Period," 249–67; Smith, "Missionary as Collector," 96–111; Duncan, "A.J. Clark," 25–33; Kapches, "Antiquarians to Archaeologists," 88, 92–4; McCaffrey, "Rononshonni–The Builder," 43–62; Phillips, "Jasper Grant and Edward Walsh," 56–71; Pilon, "Passions and Pastimes: Thomas Walter Edwin Sowter," in Wright and Pilon, eds, *A Passion for the Past*, 49–58; Williamson et al., "Ruthven and the Collection of Andrew Thompson," 7–34.

22 Avrith-Wakeam, "George Dawson, Franz Boas and the Origins of Professional Anthropology in Canada," 185–203; Barkhouse, *George Dawson*; Chalmers, *George Mercer Dawson*; Darnell, *Edward Sapir*; Gruber, "Horatio Hale," 5–37; Nock, "The Erasure of Horatio Hale's Contributions," in Harrison and Darnell, eds, *Historicizing Canadian Anthropology*, 44–51; Nock, "Horatio Hale," in Haig-Brown and Nock, eds, *With Good Intentions*, 32–50; Nowry, *Man of Mana, Marius Barbeau*; Nurse, "'But Now Things Have Changed': Marius Barbeau and the Politics of Amerindian Identity," 433–72; Nurse, "Marius Barbeau," in Harrison and Darnell, eds, *Historicizing Canadian Anthropology*, 52–64; Preston, "C. Marius Barbeau and the History of Canadian Anthropology," in Freedman, ed., *History of Canadian Anthropology*, 122–35; Morrison, *Arctic Hunters*; Richling, "Diamond Jenness," 245–60; Russell, *National Museum of Canada*; Swayze, *Man-Hunters*, 39–97, 101–40. Also associated with the BAAS was Charles Hill-Tout; see Maud, ed., *The Salish People*, vol. 1, 11–19, vol. 2, 11–17, vol. 3, 11–19, and vol. 4, 9–34. For James Teit, who also worked for the Geological Survey, see Wickwire, "'They wanted … me to help them,'" in Haig-Brown and Nock, eds, *With Good Intentions*, 297–320, and Campbell, "'Not as a White Man, Not as a Sojourner,'" 37–57.

23 McFeat, "The National Museum and Canadian Anthropology," in Freedman, ed., *History of Canadian Anthropology*, 148–74; Richling, "Archaeology, Ethnology and Canada's Public Purse, 1910–1921," in Smith and Mitchell, eds, *Bringing Back the Past*, 103–14; Dyck,

"Toward a History of Archaeology in the National Museum of Canada: the Contributions of Harlan I. Smith and Douglas Leechman," ibid., 114–33. For Wintemberg, see also Trigger, "William J. Wintemberg: Iroquoian Archaeologist," 5–21; Swayze, *Man-Hunters*, 143–78.

24 For the influence of Franz Boas and others who collected in Canada for US institutions, see Cole, *Captured Heritage*; Cole, "Anthropological Exploration in the Great Northwest," 149–64; Darnell, "The Boasian Text Tradition," 39–48; Darnell, *Invisible Genealogies*; Jacknis, *Storage Box of Tradition*; Joyce, *The Shaping of American Ethnography: The Wilkes Exploring Expedition*; Kendall et al., *Drawing Shadows to Stones: The Photography of the Jesup North Pacific Expedition*; Kendall and Krupnik, eds, *Constructing Cultures Then and Now: Celebrating Franz Boas and the Jesup North Pacific Expedition*; Krupnik and Fitzhugh, eds, *Gateways: Exploring the Legacy of the Jesup North Pacific Expedition*.

25 Dawson, "A History of Archaeology in Northern Ontario," 27–32, 37; Pearce, "Prehistory and Native Settlement," 1–10; Mann, *Native Americans, Archaeologists, and the Mounds*, 90–104; St Denis, *Tecumseh's Bones*; La Vere, *Looting Spiro Mounds*, 3–15.

26 For the Canadian Institute, see Killan, "The Canadian Institute," 3–16, and Killan, *David Boyle*. Self-published works include Cook, *Women's Canadian Historical Society of Toronto*; Foster, "Pioneers in History," 11–61; Hamilton Association, *100th Anniversary, 1857–1957*; Hamilton Association, *Proceedings of the Jubilee Celebration*; Hutchison, "Introduction," 5–10; Wallace, ed., *Royal Canadian Institute Centennial Volume*. General surveys include Doherty, "The Common Thread: One Hundred and Fifty Years of Museums in Peterborough," 133–48; Farrell, *History of the London and Middlesex Historical Society*; Garrad, *The Huron Institute and the Petun*; Killan, *Preserving Ontario's Heritage*; Key, *Beyond Four Walls*, 138–49; Stevenson, "James H. Coyne," 25–42.

27 For Hunt, see Berman, "'The Culture as It Appears to the Indian Himself,'" 215–56; Briggs and Bauman, "'The Foundation of all Future Researches,'" 479–528; Cannizzo, "George Hunt," 44–58; Jacknis, "George Hunt, Kwakiutl Photographer," 143–51; Jacknis, "George Hunt, Collector," 177–224; Jonaitis, *Yuquot Whalers' Shrine*. Hunt, among others, is discussed throughout Cole, *Captured Heritage* and Jacknis, *Storage Box of Tradition*. For Beynon, see Anderson and Halpin, "Introduction," in *Potlatch at Gitsegukla*, 3–52; Halpin, "William Beynon," in Liberty, ed., *American Indian Intellectuals*, 157–76; Winter, "William Beynon," 279–92. For Francis LaFlesche, an Omaha who assisted Alice Fletcher of the Bureau of American Ethnology, see Mark, "Francis La Flesche," 497–510; Liberty, "Francis La Flesche," in Liberty, ed., *American Indian Intellectuals*, 51–69; Smith, "Francis LaFlesche," 579–603.

28  Abrams, "The Case for Wampum," in Kaplan, ed., *Museums and the Making of "Ourselves,"* 368–72; Bieder, *Brief Historical Survey of the Expropriation of American Indian Remains*; Ortner, "Scientific Policy and Public Interest," in Bray and Killion, eds, *Reckoning with the Dead*, 11; Pullar, "The Qikertarmiut and the Scientist," in ibid., 21; Loring and Prokopec, "A Most Peculiar Man," in ibid., 31; Echo-Hawk and Echo-Hawk, *Battlefields and Burial Grounds*; Fenton, "Return of Eleven Wampum Belts," 392–411; Gulliford, *Sacred Objects and Sacred Places,* 20; Hill, "Sacred Trust: Cultural Obligations of Museums to Native Peoples," *Muse* 6, 3 (1988): 32; MacDonald, "From Ceremonial Object to Curio," 200–1, 203; Mihesuah, "Introduction," in Mihesuah, ed., *Repatriation Reader*, 3; Nurse, "'But Now Things Have Changed': Marius Barbeau and the Politics of Amerindian Identity," 440; Riding In, "Without Ethics and Morality," *Arizona State Law Journal* 24, 1 (1992): 23; Ridington and Hastings, *Blessing for a Long Time*, 4–5; Thomas, *Skull Wars*, 59–60, 63, 82; Winter, "William Beynon," 286–7; Cole, "Tricks of the Trade," 449–52, 456–7.

29  Michaelsen, *Limits of Multiculturalism*, xiii. For Iroquoian independent scholars, see Weaver, "Seth Newhouse," 165–82; Campbell, "Seth Newhouse," 183–202; Nicks, "Dr. Oronhyatekha's History Lessons," in Brown and Vibert, eds, *Reading beyond Words,* 459–89; Porter, *To Be Indian: The Life of Iroquois-Seneca Arthur Caswell Parker*; Kreis, "John O. Brant-Sero's Adventures in Europe," 27–30; Petrone, "John Ojijatekha Brant-Sero," 137–9. For Anishinabeg examples, see Smith, *Sacred Feathers*; Smith, "The Life of George Copway," 5–38; Michaelsen, *Limits of Multiculturalism*, 107–38.

30  Other informants are discussed in Brown, "'A Place in Your Mind for Them All': Chief William Berens," 204–25; Liberty, ed., *American Indian Intellectuals*; Fenton, *False Faces of the Iroquois*; Killan, *David Boyle*; Nurse, "'But Now Things Have Changed': Marius Barbeau and the Politics of Amerindian Identity," 441; Strong-Boag and Gerson, *Paddling Her Own Canoe*, 40–1.

31  For Lighthall, and McCord and his museum, see Wright, "W.D. Lighthall and David Ross McCord," 134–53; Miller et al., *The McCord Family*; Miller, *The McCord Museum Archives*; McCaffrey, "Rononshonni–The Builder," 43–62; McCaffrey et al., *Wrapped in the Colours of the Earth*; Young, *The Making and Unmaking of a University Museum*; Harvey, "Location, Location, Location: David Ross McCord and the Makings of Canadian History," 57–81. For societies in other provinces, see Connolly, "Archeology in Nova Scotia and New Brunswick," 3–34; Davis, "History of Archaeology in Nova Scotia," in Smith and Mitchell, eds, *Bringing Back the Past*, 153–62; Mak, "Ward of the Government," 7–32; McTavish and Dickison, "William Macintosh, Natural History and the Professionalization of the New Brunswick Museum," 72–90; Squires, *History and*

*Development of the New Brunswick Museum*; Friesen, "The Manitoba
Historical Society," 2–9; Blanchard, ed., *A Thousand Miles of
Prairie*; Rempel, "The Manitoba Mound Builders," 12–18; McTavish,
"Learning to See in New Brunswick," 553–81; Lawson, "Exhibiting
Agendas: Anthropology at the Redpath Museum (1882–99)," 53–65;
Martijn, "Bits and Pieces, Glimpses and Glances," in Smith and
Mitchell, eds, *Bringing Back the Past*, 163–90; Sheets-Pyenson, "'Stones
and Bones and Skeletons': The Origins and Development of the Peter
Redpath Museum," 45–64; Sheets-Pyenson, "Better than a Travelling
Circus: Museums and Meetings in Montreal," 599–618; Frost,
"Science Education in the Nineteenth Century: The Natural History
Society of Montreal," 31–43; Gagnon, "The Natural History Society
of Montreal's Museum," 103–35; Literary and Historical Society of
Quebec, *Centenary Volume of the Literary and Historical Society of
Quebec*; Bernatchez, "La Société Littéraire et Historique de Québec,"
179–92; Duchesne and Carle, "L'ordre des Choses: Cabinets et Musées
d'Histoire Naturelle au Québec," 3–30.

32  Darnell, *And Along Came Boas*.
33  Darnell, "The Uniqueness of Canadian Anthropology," 406; Epp
and Sponsel, "Major Personalities and Developments in Canadian
Anthropology," 7–13; Van West, "George Mercer Dawson," 8;
Hancock, "Toward a Historiography," in Harrison and Darnell,
eds, *Historicizing Canadian Anthropology*, 31–3; Cole, "Origins of
Canadian Anthropology," 40, sees 1884 and the establishment of the
BAAS Committee on the North-western Tribes of Canada as the pivotal
point because it began Boas's influence on Canadian anthropology.
34  Cole, "Origins of Canadian Anthropology," 33–45, and Ames,
"Introduction," in Freedman, ed., *History of Canadian Anthropology*,
1–5, considered these individuals to be dilettantes, hobbyists, or at best
semiprofessional.
35  Hulse, ed., *Thinking with Both Hands*; Kapches, "Antiquarians to
Archaeologists," 87–97; Kidd, "Sixty Years of Ontario Archeology,"
71–82; Killan, *David Boyle*; Killan, "Towards a Scientific
Archaeology," in Smith and Mitchell, eds, *Bringing Back the Past*,
15–24; Noble, "One Hundred and Twenty-Five Years of Archaeology
in the Canadian Provinces," 1–78; Kapches, "Henry Montgomery,"
29–37; Sheets-Pyenson, *John William Dawson*; Trigger, "Sir Daniel
Wilson," 3–28; Trigger, "Sir John William Dawson," 351–9; Trigger,
"Giants and Pygmies," 69–84.
36  For gender and historical work, see Morgan, "History, Nation and
Empire," 491–528; Wright, *Professionalization of History*, 97–120;
Boutilier and Prentice, "Introduction," in Boutilier and Prentice,
eds, *Creating Historical Memory*, 3–21. Specific women in historical
societies and collecting have been treated by Latta, Martelle-Hayter,
and Reed, "Women in Early Ontario Archaeology," in Smith and

Mitchell, eds, *Bringing Back the Past*, 25–38; Fingard, "From Eliza Frame to Phyllis Blakeley," 1–16; Boutilier, "Women's Rights and Duties: Sarah Anne Curzon," in Boutilier and Prentice, eds, *Creating Historical Memory*, 51–74.

37 For a profile of Laidlaw, see Noble, "Laidlaw," 73–5.

38 Hulse, ed., *Thinking with Both Hands*, 293; Averill and Keith, "Daniel Wilson and the University of Toronto," in ibid., 187. For those papers that do survive, see the comprehensive bibliography in *Thinking with Both Hands*, 289–97. The burning of Hale's study is noted by Fenton, "The New York State Wampum Collection," 448.

39 Trigger, "A Present of Their Past?" 76; Benedict, "Made in Akwesasne," in Wright and Pilon, eds, *A Passion for the Past*, 444.

40 Brown and Vibert, "Introduction," in Brown and Vibert, eds, *Reading beyond Words*, xi–xxv.

41 For my original declined application to the Six Nations elected council, see Tremblay to author, 7 October 2003, Six Nations Ethics Committee, Six Nations Council, Ohsweken, ON, author's personal files. In the absence of an official way to return research to the community, I have provided all relevant information to the Haudenosaunee Standing Committee on Burial Rules and Regulations, which is active in museum repatriation requests across North America.

## CHAPTER ONE

1 "Dug Up Hundreds of Human Bones," *Toronto Daily Star*, 8 April 1902, 1.

2 *AARO 1902*, 35.

3 "That Pit of Indian Bones," *Bradford Witness and South Simcoe News*, 17 April 1902, 5.

4 *AARO 1907*, 19.

5 "That Pit of Indian Bones," *Bradford Witness and South Simcoe News*, 17 April 1902, 5.

6 Garrett to Boyle, 2 May 1902, file 9, box 3, DBP, ROM; *AARO 1907*, 19.

7 For these definitions of local knowledge, which most often refer to indigenous societies, see Cruikshank, *Do Glaciers Listen?* 9–10; Krupnik, "'When Our Words Are Put to Paper,'" 67, 70; and Antweiler, "Local Knowledge Theory and Methods," in Bicker, Sillitoe, and Pottier, eds, *Investigating Local Knowledge*, 3. For distinctions between local knowledge and other related terms, see ibid., 3–6.

8 The Canadian Institute was conceived in 1849 but not chartered until 1851. See Wallace, "A Sketch of the History of the Royal Canadian Institute, 1849–1949," in Wallace, ed., *Centennial Volume*, 127–36.

9 The circular was reproduced in *CJ* 1, 2 (1852): 25. Boyle stated that Fleming had issued the original circular in *AARO 1907*, 12.

10  For Boyle's early career and transformation into an archaeologist, see
    Killan, *David Boyle*.
11  *PCI* 4, 1 (1886–7): 3.
12  Archaeologists debate whether the Western Basin peoples were
    Algonkian or Iroquoian. See Murphy and Ferris, "The Late Woodland
    Western Basin Tradition," in Ellis and Ferris, eds, *Archaeology of
    Southern Ontario*, 271–7.
13  Archaeological information has been summarized from Wright,
    "Before European Contact," in Rogers and Smith, eds, *Aboriginal
    Ontario*, 24–36, and from McMillan and Yellowhorn, *First Peoples in
    Canada*, 68–73, 103–8. More detailed archaeological information can
    be obtained from Wright, *History of the Native People of Canada*,
    and Ellis and Ferris, eds, *Archaeology of Southern Ontario*. For a
    general overview of early historic Iroquoian and Algonkian peoples,
    society, and material culture, see Trigger, "The Original Iroquoians," in
    Rogers and Smith, eds, *Aboriginal Ontario*, 41–7, and Trigger and Day,
    "Southern Algonquian Middlemen," in ibid., 64–7.
14  Trigger, *Natives and Newcomers*, 8.
15  *Four Years on the Georgian Bay*, 45.
16  Hunter, *History of Simcoe County*, vol. 1, 4.
17  For ploughing and gardening, see for example, Guest, "Ancient Indian
    Remains," 274; *CJ* 1, 6 (1856): 511; "Our Illustrations," 39; Matheson-
    Moorhouse, "William Matheson," 11; "Omemee," *The Canadian
    Post*, Lindsay, 29 November 1889, 6; *Galt Reformer*, 2 October 1878,
    GELS 1877, 7, ROM; "Big Injun Me," *Post*, nd, GELS 1877, 82, ROM;
    "An Indian Battlefield," *Mail and Empire*, Toronto, 1 September 1896,
    GELS 1877, 100, ROM; *Watchman-Warder*, Lindsay, 12 September
    1901, GELS 3, 93, ROM; *Watchman-Warder*, Lindsay, 18 December
    1902, GELS 3, 108, ROM; Hunter, *Notes on Sites of Huron Villages
    in the Township of Tay*, 20; Hunter, *Notes on Sites of Indian Villages,
    Townships of North and South Orillia*, 7, 14; Hunter, *Notes of Sites of
    Huron Villages in the Township of Tiny*, 26, 33, 40; Hunter, *Notes on
    Sites of Huron Villages in the Township of Oro*, 25, 32; Hunter, *Notes
    on Sites of Huron Village in the Township of Medonte*, 75; Duncan,
    "A.J. Clark," 25, 32; "Discovers Old Indian Relic while Ploughing on
    Farm," *London Advertiser*, nd, scrapbook, np, box X1502, Woolverton
    Papers, UWO Archives and Research Collections Centre; *AARO 1888–
    89*, 19; *AARO 1896–97*, 29, 46, 80; *AARO 1897–98*, 51; *AARO 1899*, 42,
    87, 89; *AARO 1901*, 23. For digging holes for fence posts, see "The Red
    Man," *Globe*, Toronto, 24 May 1881, 6; "Fleetwood," *Lindsay Post*, 30
    September 1898, GELS 3, 35, ROM; Hunter, *Notes of Sites of Huron
    Villages in the Township of Tiny*, 27; *AARO 1890–91*, 17. For forest and
    field clearing, see Bonnycastle, *Canadas in 1841*, vol.1, 287; *History of
    the County of Middlesex*, 620; Conant, *Life in Canada*, photo caption

between 66–7; Canniff, *History of the Settlement of Upper Canada*, 367; "The Red Man's Corn Pits," *World*, Toronto, 29 August 1888, GELS 1877, 82, ROM; Hunter, *Notes of Sites of Huron Villages in the Township of Tiny*, 10, 40; Hunter, *Notes on Sites of Huron Villages in the Township of Oro*, 18, 21; Hunter, *Huron Village Sites*, 30; *AARO 1899*, 43, 83, 86; *AARO 1902*, 87. For pond draining, see *AARO 1896–97*, 71; *AARO 1899*, 87; *AARO 1901*, 35.

18  *AARO 1902*, 37.

19  Kaye, *Hiding the Audience*, 103.

20  Killan, *David Boyle*, 56.

21  For Storry, see *AARO 1903*, 19; Statistics Canada, North Simcoe District, Nottawasaga Sub-district e-8, schedule 2, p1, line 1, T-6496 and schedule 1, p1, line 8, T-6496. For the McPhees, see *AARO 1904*, 12–13; Statistics Canada, Simcoe East District, Orillia Sub-district h-1, schedule 2, p1, line 13, T-6495, and schedule 1, p2, lines 13, 14, T-6495.

22  Kelcey to Boyle, 15 January 1903, box 2, DBC, ROM; *AARO 1903*, 7; *AARO 1904*, 10.

23  "Elgin Historic and Scientific Institute," *Times*, St Thomas, 7 July 1891, file 11, box 52, miscellaneous historical records, Elgin County clippings, 1900–40, Elgin County Archives.

24  Laidlaw to Wintemberg, 26 July 1915, box 2, general correspondence, Wintemberg Papers, Canadian Museum of Civilization Archives; Swayze, *Man-Hunters*, 144; Hammond to Holmes, 22 January 1907, box 3, correspondence, letters received 1907, Records of the Bureau of American Ethnology, NAA; Hunter, *Notes on Sites of Indian Villages in the Townships of North and South Orillia*, 17.

25  For road workers, including statute labourers, see Hunter, *Notes on Sites of Huron Villages in the Township of Medonte*, 76; no. 413, part 6, Archaeological Sites of Simcoe County, box 1, AFHP, ROM; *AARO 1901*, 76; no. 2, Archaeological Sites of York County, box 1, AFHP, ROM; "A Strange Find," *The Newmarket Era*, 27 June 1890, 1; "The Bones of Dead Men," *Watchman-Warder*, Lindsay, 23 July 1903, GELS 3, 119, ROM; "Dominion News," *Globe*, Toronto, 12 January 1882, 5; Jones, *"8endake Ehen,"* 257; *AARO 1896–97*, 80; *AARO 1902*, 37, 65, 80–1; Morden, *Historic Niagara Falls*, 42. For canal workers, see Squier and Davis, *Ancient Monuments of the Mississippi Valley*, 201–2. For loggers, see *Orillia Packet*, 5 September 1879, 2; Strickland, *Twenty-Seven Years in Canada West*, vol. 2, 81; Hunter, *Huron Village Sites*, 31. For sites found during ditch digging, see *AARO 1899*, 91; *AARO 1902*, 65; clipping, *Chatham Planet*, June 1897, David Boyle scrapbook 2, np, Toronto Reference Library. For sites found while digging drains, see no. 39, Archaeological Sites of York County, box 1, AFHP, ROM. For sites found while gravedigging, see Hunter, *Notes on Sites in the Township of Oro*, 17. For brickyard workers, see Hunter, *Notes on Sites of Huron Villages in the Township of Oro*, 18. For removing gravel and

sand, see Carter, *Story of Dundas*, 19–20; Morden, *Historic Niagara Falls*, 42; Thompson, *Reminiscences of a Canadian Pioneer*, 286–7; "Dug Up a Skeleton," *Mail and Empire*, Toronto, 26 June 1901, GELS 3, 90, ROM; "Indian Relics Found," *Mail and Empire*, Toronto, nd, GELS 3, 142, ROM; "Indian Relics at Peterboro," *Lindsay Post*, 23 September 1910, GELS 4, 9, ROM; *CJ* 1, 7 (1853): 160; Bond, *Peninsula Village*, 9. For gas-pipe layers, see *AARO 1901*,12. For construction and building, see *AARO 1887–88*, 41; *AARO 1896–97*, 28; *AARO 1902*, 35, 37; *AARO 1908–11*, 9; Pearce, "Prehistory and Native Settlement," 5; Hunter, *Notes on Sites of Huron Villages in the Township of Tay*, 19; Hunter, *Notes on Sites of Indian Villages, Townships of North and South Orillia*, 9; Hunter, *Notes of Sites of Huron Villages in the Township of Tiny*, 26–7; Hunter, *Notes on Sites of Huron Villages in the Township of Medonte*, 75; Hunter, *Huron Village Sites*, 35; Laidlaw, "Aboriginal Remains of Victoria County," 31; "Seventeen Skeletons Exhumed," *Ottawa Free Press*, 10 September 1898, GELS 3, 26, ROM; "Skeletons Unearthed," *Mail and Empire*, Toronto, 27 June 1907, GELS 3, 140, ROM; Hunter to Laidlaw, 2 January 1906, box 2, Laidlaw file, AFHP, ROM. For sawmill workers, and points found in trees, see Boyle, ed., *Township of Scarboro*, 24; "Struck a Snag," *Watchman*, Lindsay, 30 September 1897, GELS 3, 26, ROM; *Watchman-Warder*, Lindsay, 10 August 1899, GELS 3, 51, ROM; *AARO 1899*, 87.

26  Hamil, *Valley of the Lower Thames*, 6.
27  Pearce, "Prehistory and Native Settlement," 5. This was likely part of the Shaw-Wood (now Lawson) site.
28  *AARO 1898*, 5.
29  Bazely, "History Beneath Our Feet," 25; *CJ* 1, 2 (1852): 25; *JPHA* (1890–1): 132.
30  *AARO 1899*, 85.
31  "The Bones of Indians," *Watchman-Warder*, Lindsay, 15 September 1904, GELS 3, 131, ROM; "Unearthed Hundred Skulls," *Mail and Empire*, Toronto, 7 June 1905, GELS 3, 131, ROM; loose notes, Archaeological Sites of Ontario County, box 1, AFHP, ROM.
32  *CJ* 1, 2 (1852): 25.
33  HA, 1857–1932, 75th Anniversary Meeting Held in the Bruce Room, Hamilton Art Gallery, 29 April 1932, 23, file 3, box 121, RCIP, TFRBL.
34  Littlehales, *Journal*, 10. This was again noted by Jones, *Recollections*, 43.
35  "Indian Relics," *Globe*, Toronto, 15 August 1889, 2.
36  Kirkconnell, *Victoria County*, 132; "Seventeen Skeletons Exhumed," *Ottawa Free Press*, 10 September 1898, GELS 3, 26, ROM; *AARO 1893–94*, 15; *AARO 1894–95*, 53; *AARO 1903*, 121.
37  "Massanoga, or Picture Lake," 2.
38  Bond, *Peninsula Village*, 9. This may also be the site recorded by Dwight, *Northern Traveller*, 82–3; Schoolcraft, *Indian in His Wigwam*, 325.

39  Bycraft, "Catalogue of Relics," np, Museum of Ontario Archaeology; *JPHA* 1, 1 (1882–83): 53; Brown, *America: A Four Year's Residence in the United States and Canada*, 79–80; no. 455, part 6, box 1, AFHP, ROM. Boys unearthing a woodchuck found the Seeley ossuary as recorded by *AARO 1902*, 70.

40  Leacock, *Sunshine Sketches of a Little Town*, 77–9, 90, 97.

41  *AARO 1890–91*, 6.

42  Squier and Davis, *Ancient Monuments of the Mississippi Valley*, 201–2.

43  Bawtree, "A Brief Description of some Sepulchral Pits of Indian Origin Lately Discovered near Penetanguishene," file 15, MU 2563, RCIP, AO.

44  Williamson et al., "Ruthven and the Collection of Andrew Thompson," 27; Dick-Lauder et al., *Pen and Pencil Sketches of Wentworth Landmarks*, 84; Wintemberg, *Lawson Prehistoric Village Site*, 55n5; Willson to Boyle, 14 May 1898, file 1, box 2, DBP, ROM; Hunter to Boyle, 26 July 1897, file 6, box 2, DBP, ROM; *AARO 1894–95*, 11; *AARO 1888–89*, 19; Hunter, *Notes on Sites of Indian Villages, Townships of North and South Orillia*, 14; *AARO 1899*, 12; *AARO 1903*, 22; Judd, *Early Naturalists*, 130–2.

45  Hunter, *Notes on Sites of Huron Villages in the Township of Oro*, 20; Lauriston, *Romantic Kent*, 18.

46  Jones, *Recollections*, 45.

47  McKeough, "Early Indian Occupation of Kent," 13–14.

48  Hunter, *Notes on Sites of Huron Villages in the Township of Medonte*, 80.

49  Brock to Macculloch, 22–27 September 1817, Tupper Papers, AO.

50  Hay to Boyle, 13 August 1897, box 1, DBC, ROM.

51  Hunter, *Notes on Sites of Huron Villages in the Township of Medonte*, 65.

52  *AARO 1919*, 75. See also Hunter, *Notes on Sites of Huron Villages in the Township of Medonte*, 80. For a newspaper reporter's visit to and excavation of the Kinghorn pit, see "The County–The People–The Crops," *Northern Advance and County of Simcoe General Advertiser*, Barrie, 10 August 1859, 2.

53  Hunter, *Notes on Sites of Huron Villages in the Township of Oro*, 14.

54  "Human Skeletons," *Empire*, Toronto, 24 February 1894, GELS 1, 23, ROM.

55  Johnson, *Arkona through the Years*, 60.

56  *AARO 1894–95*, 35.

57  Dick-Lauder et al., *Pen and Pencil Sketches of Wentworth Landmarks*, 76–8, 83; Mills, *Lake Medad and Waterdown*, 7, 11.

58  Thorold and Beaverdams Historical Society, *Jubilee History*, 7; Canniff, *History of the Settlement of Upper Canada*, 368.

59  Adam et al., *History of Toronto and County of York*, vol. 1, part 2, 107, 148.

60  Adam et al., *History of Toronto and County of York*, vol. 1, part 2, 107, 148–50; *History of the County of Middlesex*, 620; Canniff, *History of the Settlement of Upper Canada*, 367–8; Carter, *Story of Dundas*,

19–22; *Illustrated Historical Atlas of Elgin County*, xi; *Illustrated Atlas of the County of Simcoe*, 3–4; Kirkconnell, *Victoria County*, 123–33; Mulvaney et al., *History of the County of Peterborough*, 5; Mulvaney et al., *History of the County of Brant*, 411; *Our Holiday Annual and Kent County Almanac*, 86; Scadding, *Toronto of Old*, 399–400; Slight, *Indian Researches*, 20; Smith, *Point Au Pelee Island*, 8–9, 46; Thorold and Beaverdams Historical Society, *Jubilee History*, 4–8. Smith, *Historical Sketch of the County of Wentworth*, 29–41, reported numerous sites, including those now known as the Snider, Mcdonald, Hood, and probably Dwyer sites. Harris, *Catholic Church in the Niagara Peninsula*, 75–112, discusses Neutral material culture, much of which comes from Boyle's reports. Community memories of finds continued to be recorded in later histories such as Bell, "Pre-History of Binbrook Township," in Bell, ed., *Tweedsmuir History*, 5–6; Bond, *Peninsula Village*, 9; Chant, *Beautiful Charleston*, 183; Johnston, *Aurora*, 1–2; Lauriston, *Romantic Kent*, 16–18; Marsh et al., *History of the County of Grey*, 17; Morden, *Historic Niagara Falls*, 42–3; Moyer, *This Unique Heritage*, 5; Weir, *Scugog and Its Environs*, 127–8.

61  Copway, *Indian Life and Indian History*, 92–3; Copway, *The Life, Letters and Speeches of Kah-ge-ga-gah-bowh*, 15–16.

62  Jones, *History of the Ojebway Indians*, 112–13. See also pages 32 and 74. Illustrations are located between pages 72–3 and 130–1.

63  Carroll, *Case and His Cotemporaries* [sic], vol. 1, 165.

64  Parkman, *The Jesuits in North America in the Seventeenth Century*, 78–9n2.

65  Thwaites, ed., *Jesuit Relations and Allied Documents*, vol. 5, 279, 292–4; Hunter, "Archaeological Research in the Huron Country," in ibid., vol. 5, 295–8; ibid., vol. 8, 303–5; ibid., vol. 10, 318–9, 328; ibid., vol. 13, 269–70; ibid., vol. 18, 258–9; ibid., vol. 19, 269–72; ibid., vol. 20, 305–6; ibid., vol. 21, 316–18; ibid., vol. 33, 273–4; ibid., vol. 34, 247–8; ibid., vol. 36, 245–6.

66  Thompson, *Reminiscences of a Canadian Pioneer*, 286–7; Conant, *Life in Canada*, 66, photo caption between 66–7; Carruthers, *Retrospect of Thirty-Six Years' Residence in Canada West*, 231; Need, *Six Years in the Bush*, 95.

67  Strickland, *Twenty Seven Years in Canada West*, vol. 2, 81.

68  Brown, *America: A Four Years' Residence in the United States and Canada*, 79–80.

69  Dwight, *Northern Traveller*, 82–3.

70  Grant, ed., *Picturesque Canada*, vol. 2, 442, 478–9.

71  *Fenelon Falls*, np.

72  Smily, ed., *Canadian Summer Resort Guide*, 65.

73  Todd, *Notes upon Canada*, 93.

74  Jameson, *Winter Studies and Summer Rambles*, vol. 1, 296; ibid., vol. 3, 175–6, 181–2, 324, 327.

75  Kane, *Wanderings of an Artist*, 3; Grand Trunk Railway Company of Canada, Hamilton to Belleville via Woodstock, 14 October, *Annotated Time Table of the Tour through Canada of Their Royal Highnesses*, np.

76  See, for example, Jasen, *Wild Things*, 105–32.

77  "Massanoga, or Picture Lake," 1; Cotton, "Mississauga," 451–2; Adams, *Ten Thousand Miles through Canada*, 106; *Four Years on the Georgian Bay*, 36, 44–5, 71.

78  McIntosh, *Discovery of America*, 135.

79  *CJ* 1, 1 (1852–3): 6.

80  Schoolcraft, *Indian in His Wigwam*, 324–7; Schoolcraft, *Historical and Statistical Information*, vol. 1, 75, 103–4; *CJ* 3, 7 (1855): 156; *CJ* 3, 17 (1858): 401–2.

81  Bagg, *Canadian Archaeology*, 3; Ryerson, "Canadian Archology," [*sic*], 3.

82  "The Neutral Nation," *Toronto Daily Mail*, 24 October 1885, 7; "The Canadian Institute," *Toronto Daily Mail*, 23 November 1885, 8; "A Valuable Archaeological Find," *Globe*, Toronto, 5 October 1885, 6.

83  Harris, *Catholic Church in the Niagara Peninsula*, 83; Smith, *Historical Sketch of the County of Wentworth*, 29–33.

84  Tweedale to Powell, 3 April 1886, file Twa-Twe, box 79, correspondence, letters received 1879–88, Records of the Bureau of American Ethnology, NAA.

85  "Canadian Items," *The Mail*, Toronto, 10 October 1879, 4.

86  Ackerman to Boyle, 15 March 1898, box 1, DBC, ROM.

87  Jackson to Boyle, 23 February 1900, box 1, DBC, ROM; Boyle to Miller, 24 February 1900, box 1, DBC, ROM.

88  No. 14, part 1 - 1-93 A.F. Hunter, Barrie, Archaeological Sites in Simcoe Co., box 1, AFHP, ROM; no. 163, part 2-94-198, A.F. Hunter, Barrie, Ont., Archaeological Sites in Simcoe Co., box 1, AFHP, ROM.

89  Mackenzie, *Sketches of Canada and the United States*, 92–3.

90  "Londoners and their Hobbies," scrapbook, 111, box 4315, Woolverton Papers, UWO Archives and Research Collections Centre.

91  "Village Sites South Orillia," box 1, JHHP, ROM.

92  Leigh to Boyle, 23 January 1904, MU 5423, F 1139, OHSP, AO.

93  *AARO 1908–11*, 99; *Orillia Times*, 26 June 1890, file A-B, box 2, AFHP, ROM; Dryden to Hunter, 14 September 1903, file D-J, box 2, AFHP, ROM; Blair to Hunter, 2? July 1903, file A-B, box 2, AFHP, ROM; "Thomas Wilson," *Kingston Gazette*, 14 November 1835, 3; Alber et al., *From Relics to Research*, 7.

94  Jones, *Recollections*, 32, 33.

95  Trigger, "William Wintemberg," 7.

96  Laidlaw, "Aboriginal Remains of Victoria County."

97  *CJ* 1, 2 (1852): 25.

98  See, for example, the brief notations Wilson made about his fieldwork in *CJ* 1, 6 (1856): 511, and *CJ* 2, 12 (1857): 416, and in his journal, 27

September 1876, 36, and 25 October 1876, 47, file 1, box 4, Langton Family Papers, University of Toronto Archives. See also "Regular Fortnightly Meeting–An Interesting Relic," *Globe*, Toronto, 3 November 1879, GELS 1, 2, ROM; "Professor Wilson on the Early Indian Tribes of Ontario," *Mail*, Toronto, 3 November 1879, GELS 1, 2, ROM.

99  "Report of the Curator of Canadian Institute for 1885–86," minutes, 5 December 1863 to 1 May 1886, 725, box 37, RCIP, TFRBL.

100 Boyle, *Notes on Primitive Man*, 4.

101 *AARO 1886–87*, 9–14.

102 This included the See Mound.

103 *AARO 1886–87*, 11.

104 *AARO 1896–97*, 13; *AARO 1899*, 4.

105 *AARO 1886–87*, 14.

106 Indian Archaeology. Note book no. 4, 116, box 1, AFHP, ROM; Morrison to Boyle, April 1901, file 12, box 2, DBP, ROM; Meyer to Boyle, 22 May 1900, file 13, box 2, DBP, ROM; no. 118, part 2, box 1, AFHP, ROM; *AARO 1894–95*, 39.

107 Unlabelled clipping, "Mysteries of Southwold Indian Village Solved," file 30, box 46, Thorman Papers, Elgin County Archives; Boyle, *Notes on Primitive Man*, 21.

108 "Massanoga, or Picture Lake," 1.

109 No. 378, part 5, Archaeological Sites of Simcoe County, box 1, AFHP, ROM; CJ 1, 7 (1853): 160; Squier and Davis, *Ancient Monuments of the Mississippi Valley*, 202; "An Indian Burying Ground," *Mail and Empire*, Toronto, 27 March 1899, GELS 3, 41, ROM.

110 Hunter, *Notes of Sites of Huron Villages in the Township of Tiny*, 35, 41; *Huron Village Sites*, 51; Hunter, *Notes on Sites of Huron Villages in the Township of Tay*, 23; *AARO 1919*, 75.

111 *AARO 1896–97*, 29.

112 OFNC, *Ottawa Naturalist* 23, 4–5 (1909–10): 64.

113 Hunter, *Huron Village Sites*, 31, 33–4.

114 *AARO 1901*, 23.

115 *AARO 1899*, 85.

116 Grant, ed., *Picturesque Canada*, vol. 2, 480.

117 "Another Rice Lake Mound," *Examiner*, Peterborough, 5 September 1896, 5; Carter, *Story of Dundas*, 21.

118 No. 269, part 3. Archaeological Sites of Simcoe County, box 1, AFHP, ROM; no. 288, part 4. Archaeological Sites of Simcoe County, box 1, AFHP, ROM.

119 Hunter, "New Aspects of the Old Huron Missions," 353.

120 Chisholm and Co., *Chisholm's All Round Route and Panoramic Guide*, 54.

121 Hunter, *Notes on Sites of Indian Villages in the Townships of North and South Orillia*, 19.

122 Hunter, *Notes on Sites of Huron Villages in the Township of Tay*, 12.

123 Hunter, *Notes on Sites of Huron Villages in the Township of Medonte*, 67.

124 Hunter, *Notes of Sites of Huron Villages in the Township of Tiny*, 9.

125 Hunter, *Notes on Sites of Huron Villages in the Township of Tay*, 8–9.

126 *CJ* 3, 15 (1855): 346–7; *CJ* 1, 6 (1856): 516–9.

127 *CJ* 1, 2 (1852): 25.

128 *CJ* 6, 1 (1856): 519.

129 *CJ* 3, 15 (1855): 346–7; *CJ* 1, 6 (1856): 516–9.

130 *AARO 1888–89*, 2.

131 *CJ* 1, 5 (1852): 98, 99.

132 *AARO 1892–93*, 1.

133 *AARO 1907*, 12.

134 "Indian Relics," *Mail*, Toronto, 14 January 1886, GELS 1, 13, ROM.

135 *AARO 1886–87*, 9; "Canada's Great Fair," *Globe*, Toronto, 13 September 1886, 8.

136 *AARO 1886–87*, 9.

137 "Proposed Archaeological Museum," *Mail*, Toronto, 25 April 1885, GELS 1, 10, ROM; "The Proposed Archaeological Museum," *Globe*, Toronto, 25 April 1885, GELS 1, 10, ROM; "Archaeological Find," *Mail*, Toronto, 16 May 1887, GELS 1, 18, ROM.

138 *PCI* 4, 1 (1886–7): 77, 79–80.

139 Hammond to Boyle, received 15 December 1904, 24 August 1905, box 2, DBC, ROM.

140 See, for example, "Indian Relics," *Warder*, Lindsay, 14 August 1896, GELS 1, 24, ROM.

141 GELS 1, 32–9, 45–6, ROM.

142 *AARO 1887–88*, 10–11.

143 *AARO 1886–87*, 9, 10, 11, 14.

144 *AARO 1887–88*, 14; Killan, *David Boyle*, 146; Boyle, *Notes on Primitive Man*, 3.

145 Hunter, "A Public Museum for Barrie," env. 12, notebook 12, 58–9, box 4, AFHP, Simcoe County Archives.

146 "Elgin's Earlier Days," unlabelled clipping, file 11, box 52, miscellaneous historical records, Elgin County clippings, 1900–40, Elgin County Archives.

147 *AARO 1891*, 15; *AARO 1894–95*, 52.

148 *AARO 1886–87*, 48.

149 Boyle, "History Taught by Museums," NHS *Transactions* 4 (1898): 33.

150 No. 224, *Midland Free Press*, 3 October 1889, part 3, box 1, AFHP, ROM; no. 224, *Penetang Herald*, 10 October 1889, part 3, box 1, AFHP, ROM.

151 Koch to Deacon, 25 November 1905, file 3, MU 7260, F 1139, OHSP, AO.

152 Carscallen and Cahiel to Boyle, 23 November 1901, file 4, box 3, DBP, ROM.

153 Bradt v. Boyle, Hamilton, 1902, RG 2-42-0-808, Department of Education, AO.

154 *AARO 1886–87*, 15.

155 Birch to Boyle, 13 May 1903, box 2, DBC, ROM.

156 Salisbury to Boyle, 14 October 1905, file 3, MU 7260, F 1139, OHSP, AO.

157 Laidlaw to Hunter, 5 May 1902, box 2, file Laidlaw, AFHP, ROM.

158 Elgin Historical and Scientific Institute, "Preface," in *Historical Sketches of the County of Elgin*, np.

159 *JPHA* 9 (1892–3): 109–10.

160 No. 112, "From Letter of J.H. Hammond, Orillia, November 3, 1903," part 2, box 1, AFHP, ROM.

161 *AARO 1902*, 69.

162 Hunter, *Notes of Sites of Huron Villages in the Township of Tiny*, 41; Hunter, *Notes on Sites of Indian Villages in the Townships of North and South Orillia*, 14; no. 112, part 2, box 1, AFHP, ROM; Hunter, *Huron Village Sites*, 32; Beacock to Boyle, 3 March 189?, file January–December 1902, box 2, DBC, ROM; no. 176, no. 183, part 2, box 1, AFHP, ROM; Kapches, "Toronto's Hidden Past: The Archaeological Story," 5.

163 "Catalogue of Indian Relics," box 1, AFHP, ROM.

164 "Catalogue of old relicks gathered up by 'me,'" 1890–97, Leighton Papers, Walker Papers, AO.

165 Indian Archaeology, note book no. 4, 77, box 1, AFHP, ROM; Adams to Boyle, 2 April 1901, file 4, box 3, DBP, ROM.

166 Hunter to Laidlaw, 13 February 1912, file K-Lai, box 3, AFHP, ROM; Jury, *Preliminary Report on the Train Farm Site*, 4. See also "Antiquities of America," *Mail*, Toronto, ? June 1881, GELS 1, 4, ROM.

167 Hunter, *Notes on Sites of Huron Villages in the Township of Oro*, 21.

168 WHS, *Transactions* 6 (1915): 13; Mills, *Lake Medad and Waterdown*, 12.

169 "Trip Georgian Bay, Owen Sound, August 1905," 2A-3A, enc. 2, env. 2, box 7, AFHP, Simcoe County Archives.

170 No. 413, part 6, box 1, AFHP, ROM; no. 47, part 1, box 1, AFHP, ROM.

171 Indian Archaeology, note book no. 4, 117, box 1, AFHP, ROM; no. 109, *Packet*, Orillia, 2 December 1892, part 2, box 1, AFHP, ROM; Trigger, "Foreword," in Tooker, ed., *Ethnography of the Huron Indians*, np; Hunter, *Notes on Sites of Huron Villages in the Township of Medonte*, 73; Jury and Jury, *Sainte-Marie Among the Hurons*, 53.

172 *PCI* 4, 1 (1886–7): 4.

173 Matheson to Boyle, 12 May 1899, file 15, box 2, DBP, ROM.

174 Hunt to Boyle, 21 February 1902, box 2, DBC, ROM.

175 No. 97, Hill to Hunter, 19 June 1901 and Hunter to Hill, 24 June 1901, part 2, box 1, AFHP, ROM. .

176 No. 378, part 4, box 1, AFHP, ROM.

177 Hirschfelder, "The Alleged Archaeological Fizzle," *Toronto Daily Mail*, 4 January 1886, 5.

178 "Archaeological Fizzle," *Mail*, Toronto, 13 December 1885, GELS 1877, 59, ROM.

179 Pickwick, "Toronto Aborigines," *Toronto Daily Mail*, 28 December 1885, 5; see also Kapches, "What the People Said," 1–4.

180 *AARO 1902*, 89; *AARO 1899*, 89.

181 Hunter, *Notes on Sites of Indian Villages in the Townships of North and South Orillia*, 8; Birch to Hunter, 10 May 1904, file A-B, box 2, AFHP, ROM.

182 Cruikshank, *Do Glaciers Listen?* 18.

183 Jury, *Preliminary Report on the Train Farm Site*, 3.

184 Wintemberg, "Preliminary Report on the Exploration of the Southwold Earthworks," 6, 8; Wintemberg, *Roebuck Prehistoric Village Site*, 1; Wintemberg, *Lawson Prehistoric Village Site*, 1.

## CHAPTER TWO

1 Hunter to Laidlaw, 2 January 1906, file Laidlaw, box 2, AFHP, ROM.

2 *PCI* 4, 1 (1886–7): 1–3.

3 The Pioneer and Historical Association of Ontario was originally founded in 1888 as the Pioneer Association of Ontario. For earlier museums and societies, see Duncan, "From Mausoleums to Malls," 107–8; Talman, "Some Precursors of the Ontario Historical Society," 13–21; Killan, *Preserving Ontario's Heritage*, 4–15. For the university museums in Toronto, see Teather, *Royal Ontario Museum* and Teather, "Universities, Museums and Civic Formation," 181–209. For an overview of the philosophy of natural science societies, see Berger, *Science, God and Nature*, 3–27.

4 OHS, *Constitution and By-Laws*, 5–6.

5 Ibid., 3.

6 See, for example, *Niagara Historical Society: Motto, Ducit amor Patriae, Constitution*, np; HA, *Constitution and By-Laws*, 3; WHS, *Journal and Transactions* 1 (1892): 7; "A New Society," file 11, box 52, miscellaneous historical records, Elgin County clippings, 1900–40, Elgin County Archives; "Address of Miss Fitzgibbons before Newly Organized Historical Society," 22 October 1901, LMHS scrapbook, 1, LMHS Papers, London Room, London Public Library; "County of Oxford Historical Society," OxHS minute book, 15 January 1897–1 November 1957, 2, OxHS Papers, Oxford Historical Society; WCHST, *Transaction* 1 (1896): 5; Foster, "Pioneers in History," 12–13; "Prefatory Note," HI, *Papers and Records* 1 (1909): np, 94, 96; "Society

Organized," *Stratford Daily Beacon*, 6 December 1899, 5; OLSS, minutes, vol. 1, np, OFNC Papers, LAC; York Pioneers, *Constitution and By-Laws*, 3.

7 Wright, *Professionalization of History*, 8, 20.
8 *CJ* 5, 29 (1860): 409–17.
9 Hunter to Heyden, 12 July 1889, box 2, AFHP, ROM.
10 Hunter, *Huron Village Sites*, 20.
11 Hunter, *Notes on Sites of Huron Villages in the Township of Medonte*, 65.
12 Hunter, *Notes on Sites of Huron Villages in the Township of Oro*, 9.
13 Hunter, *Notes on Sites of Huron Villages in the Township of Medonte*, 65.
14 Hunter to Laidlaw, 4 December 1899, file Laidlaw 1897–99, box 4, AFHP, ROM.
15 *AARO 1898*, 5; *AARO 1890–91*, 5, 13.
16 Laidlaw, "Teeth Tools in Canada," 236–8; Laidlaw, "Some Copper Implements from the Midland District, Ontario," 83–90; Laidlaw, "Horn Relics – Ontario," 65–71; Laidlaw, "Miniatures, or Dimunitive Relics," 37–44; Laidlaw, "The Aboriginal Remains of Balsam Lake, Ontario," 68–72; Laidlaw, "Aboriginal Remains of Balsam Lake, Ontario," 138–45; Laidlaw, "Remains in Ash Beds at Balsam Lake," 271–5; *AARO 1890–1*, 73–7; *AARO 1893–4*, 17–22; *AARO 1901*, 100–8.
17 Laidlaw, "Remains in Ash Beds at Balsam Lake," 274.
18 Laidlaw, "Aboriginal Remains of Victoria County," 87, MS 165, AO.
19 *AARO 1902*, 69.
20 Swayze, *Man-Hunters*, 150–1; Killan, *David Boyle*, 206.
21 OFNC, *Ottawa Naturalist* 23, 4–5 (1909–10): 63–4.
22 "Ottawa Field-Naturalists' Club," *Ottawa Free Press*, 26 June 1883, scrapbook, 1879–88, 94–95, OFNC Papers, LAC; *Ottawa Free Press*, 22 August 1884, scrapbook, 1879–88, 118, OFNC Papers, LAC; OFNC, *Ottawa Naturalist* 13, 5 (1899): 132.
23 OFNC, *Ottawa Naturalist* 18, 4 (1904): 89.
24 HA, 1857–1932, 75th Anniversary Meeting Held in the Bruce Room, Hamilton Art Gallery, 29 April 1932, 9, file 3, box 121, RCIP, TFRBL.
25 "Historical Society's Picnic," *St Thomas Daily Times*, 1 August 1891, 5.
26 "The Rock that Stands Out," *Enterprise-Messenger*, Collingwood, 26 September 1907, 1.
27 "Many Sites of Indian Villages," *Saturday News*, Collingwood, 20 June 1908, 2.
28 HI, *Papers and Records* 1 (1909): 12–13.
29 Hammond to Boyle, 13 May 1904, 8 December 1904, file 2, box 2, DBP, ROM.
30 "Ossuary Burial Hurons Mound Exploration," box 1, JHHP, ROM; Hammond to Boyle, 27 July 1904, file 1, box 2, DBP, ROM.

31 Hammond to Boyle, 11 May 1904, box 2, DBC, ROM.

32 Hammond to Holmes, 2 February 1907, box 3, correspondence, letters received, 1907, Records of the Bureau of American Ethnology, NAA.

33 Hammond, Notebook Archaeological and Ethnological, np, box 4, AFHP, ROM.

34 Hammond to Holmes, 18 February 1907, box 3, correspondence, letters received, 1907, Records of the Bureau of American Ethnology, NAA; Hammond to Boyle, 30 March 1906, file 4, MU 7260, OHSP, AO.

35 Secord to Hunter, 11 May 1904, env. 6 , correspondence 1904, box 3, AFHP, Simcoe County Archives.

36 Extracts from Minute Book, 20 April 1910, Essex Historical Society Papers, Hiram Walker Historical Museum Papers, AO; Foster, "Pioneers in History," 18; Peterborough Historical Society, 11 January 1897, 14 April 1897, minute book, 15, 39, 71–026/2, and file acc. 71–026, Victoria Museum Fonds, Peterborough Centennial Museum and Archives; Elgin Historical and Scientific Institute, "Preface," *Historical Sketches of the County of Elgin*, np; WHS, *Journal and Transactions* 1 (1892): 190–1.

37 "First Anniversary," *Times*, Niagara-on-the-Lake, 24 September 1896, 8.

38 "40th Anniversary of the Elgin Historical," *Times-Journal*, St Thomas, 30 April 1931, file 11, box 52, miscellaneous historical records, Elgin County clippings, Elgin County Archives.

39 Pamphlet, *Lundy's Lane Observatory, Niagara Falls* and *Annual Report of the Lundy's Lane Historical Society 1893*, LLHS correspondence, MN 130, RG 38-4-0-83, Niagara Parks Commission Papers, AO.

40 "The Lundy's Lane Observatory Company in Liquidation," *Niagara Falls Record*, 13 November 1896, LLHS correspondence, MN 130, RG 38-4-0-83, Niagara Parks Commission Papers, AO.

41 Secretary-Treasurer to Leask, 13 August 1910 and "Lundy's Lane Historical Society Niagara Falls," 12 October 1910, LLHS correspondence, MN 131, RG 38-4-0-87, Niagara Parks Commission Papers, AO.

42 An Act to Provide for the Establishment of Free Libraries, (1882), 45 Vict., ch. 22.

43 Stratford-Perth Museum, accession/registration register, Perth County Historical Collection, 1, Stratford-Perth Museum, 1.

44 "Historical Soc. Formed in City," *Stratford Daily Beacon*, 30 June 1922, 4.

45 Anderson, *Stratford: Library Services Since 1846*, 19. For Nichol's catalogue, see Nichol's accession notebook, Nichol Papers, Stratford-Perth Archives.

46 OHS, *Annual Report 1900*, 35.

47   OxHS, 8 December 1899, minute book, 15 January 1897–1 November
     1957, 33, OxHS Papers, Oxford Historical Society; "From the Sentinel
     Review Illustrated Supplement Nos. 120, February 4, 1899," file
     Museum Curators–Hill, Louise, Woodstock Museum.
48   OHS, *Annual Report 1905 and 1906*, 55.
49   "In and Around the City," *Daily Sentinel-Review*, Woodstock, 19
     November 1902, 5.
50   Report of the Minister of Education Province of Ontario for the Year
     1909, 420; "Beginnings of a Local Museum," *Daily Sentinel-Review*,
     Woodstock, 4 June 1910, 4.
51   The museum still housed in the library consisted of two glass cases, one
     of Aboriginal stone tools, amulets, and pottery fragments and another
     of geological and zoological specimens. Pioneer relics were also
     discovered by the former secretary of the society. See "Relics of Early
     Oxford Stored in Public Library," *Daily Sentinel-Review*, Woodstock,
     21 February 1930, 2, and "Inventory of Articles Moved from the
     Basement of the Public Library to Room in Court House," OxHS
     accession records 1933–34, 3–31, Woodstock Museum.
52   Spicer, *History of the London Public Library*, 8.
53   Ami to Woolverton, 11 May 1904, scrapbook, 164–5, box 4315,
     Woolverton Papers, UWO Archives and Research Collection Centre.
54   "Annual Meeting of Historical Society," unlabelled clipping, LMHS
     scrapbook, 58, LMHS papers, London Room, London Public Library.
55   Unlabelled clipping, LMHS scrapbook, 69, LMHS Papers, London
     Room, London Public Library.
56   "Londoners and Their Hobbies," unlabelled clipping, Woolverton
     scrapbook, 111, box 4315, Woolverton Papers, UWO Archives and
     Research Collections Centre.
57   D.H. Price, … *For Sale Specimens Illustrative of Aboriginal Life in
     Western Ontario. Chiefly Collected in the Country of the Neuters,
     or Attiwandarons (A Branch of the Huron-Iroquois)*, file 3, box 7,
     Peabody Museum Director Papers, Frederick W. Putnam, Harvard
     University, Peabody Museum of Archaeology and Ethnology; Zaslow,
     *Reading the Rocks*, 210; Geological Survey to purchase Mr D.H.
     Price's collection of Canadian archaeological specimens, about 9,000
     specimens, $5,949, *Debates*, House of Commons, 1904, 4 Edward VII,
     vol. 5, 9015–16.
58   18 November 1882, minutes, 5 December 1863–1 May 1886, 530, box
     37, RCIP, TFRBL; 2 December 1882, minutes, 5 December 1863–1
     May 1886, 535, box 37, RCIP, TFRBL.
59   "The Indian Tribes," *Toronto Daily Mail*, 11 November 1885, GELS 1,
     10, ROM.
60   16 December 1885, minutes of council, 9 February 1861–1 April 1887,
     300–1, box 19, RCIP, TFRBL.

61 "Deputations to Government," *Globe*, Toronto, 21 January 1886, 8.

62 *AARO 1886–87*, 1; Killan, *David Boyle*, 99.

63 *PCI* 4, 1 (1886–7): 3–4.

64 Boyle to Goode, 28 July 1891, file 6, box 12, assistant secretary in charge of the United States National Museum, correspondence and memoranda, 1860–1908, Smithsonian Institution Archives.

65 *AARO 1892–3*, 2.

66 Beeman to Ross, 2 August 1894, RG 2-42-0-3586, Department of Education, AO.

67 Pioneer and Historical Association of Ontario, *Annual Report 1891*, 6; Pioneer and Historical Association of Ontario, *Annual Report 1893*, 10.

68 Files 4–18, box 3, RCIP, TFRBL.

69 25 November 1893, minutes, 6 November 1886–5 May 1894, 614, box 38, RCIP, TFRBL.

70 22 February 1890, minutes, 6 November 1886–5 May 1894, 250–1, box 38, RCIP, TFRBL; Vankoughnet to Dewdney, 18 February 1890, deputy superintendent-general's letterbook, 21 January 1890–1 May 1890, vol. 1102, C-8627, RG 10, DIA, LAC; Canadian Institute Historical Section, 6 March 1890, minute book, 15 February 1890–23 April 1896, 3–4, box 10, RCIP, TFRBL; memo, 18 February 1890, Hamilton to DIA, 2 April 1890, correspondence, memoranda and report of archaeological, anthropological and ethnological research by the Department of Mines and various universities and museums, file 486-6-1, part 1, vol. 6816, C-8538, Central Registry Files, RG 10, DIA, LAC.

71 Vankoughnet to Dewdney, 7 April 1891, correspondence, Memoranda and report of archaeological, anthropological and ethnological research by the Department of Mines and various universities and museums, file 486-6-1, part 1, vol. 6816, C-8538, Central Registry Files, RG 10, DIA, LAC.

72 2 May 1891, minutes, 6 November 1886–5 May 1894, 372, box 38, RCIP, TFRBL; memorial to the minister of the interior, 6 October 1892, file 20, box 2, RCIP, TFRBL.

73 Teather, *Royal Ontario Museum*, 187.

74 Killan, *David Boyle*, 211–15.

75 Beeman to Boyle, 5 October 1906, file NS (D. Boyle) North America–mainly proveniences, Normal School, ROM; Wintemberg to Colquhoun, 1 September 1908, RG 2-42-0-3580, Department of Education, AO; *AARO 1902*, 69–70.

76 Killan, *Preserving Ontario's Heritage*, 54.

77 WCHST, *Annual Report 1898–99*, 2–4; Killan, *Preserving Ontario's Heritage*, 106–10; WCHST, *First Canadian Historical Exhibition*, 3–4.

78 Ontario, An Act Respecting the Canadian Historical Exhibition, 1896, 59 Vict., ch. 16, s.3, s.10, s.14.

79  Ibid., preamble, s.27.
80  WCHST, *First Canadian Historical Exhibition*, 11.
81  Ibid., 9–10.
82  Cook, *Women's Canadian Historical Society of Toronto*, 28.
83  "Record Broken for First Week," *Globe*, Toronto, 3 September 1906, 8.
84  "The Canadian Institute," *Toronto Daily Mail*, 23 November 1885, 8.
85  Arthur Harvey, "The Neutral Nation," *Toronto Daily Mail*, 24 October 1885, 7; Arthur Harvey, "Indian Tombstones," *Toronto Daily Mail*, 30 December 1885, 6.
86  20 October 1886, minutes of council, 9 February 1861–1 April 1887, 312, box 19, RCIP, TFRBL.
87  *AARO 1886–87*, 1.
88  *AARO 1901*, 35.
89  OHS, *Annual Report 1910*, 61.
90  *AARO 1890–91*, 10.
91  Boyle, *Notes on Primitive Man*, 21.
92  OHS, *Annual Report 1903*, 28; *Proceedings and Transactions of the Royal Society of Canada* 12, series 2 (1906): cx.
93  "Prehistoric Earthworks are Presented to Dominion," *Border Cities Star*, Windsor, 16 September 1930, 9.
94  Taylor, *Negotiating the Past*, 71.
95  *AARO 1896–97*, 26.
96  Strickland to Boyle, nd, RG 2-42-0-3618, Department of Education, AO; Boyle to Ross, 8 October 1896, RG 2-42-0-3618, Department of Education, AO.
97  Hay to Boyle, 13 August 1897, box 1, DBC, ROM; Drummond to Boyle, 18 December 1897, box 1, DBC, ROM; Anderson to Boyle, 21 December 1897, box 1, DBC, ROM.
98  4 February 1897, minute book, 20–1, file acc. 71-026/2, Victoria Museum Fonds, Peterborough Centennial Museum and Archives.
99  Dawson to Boyle, 2 October 1897, 13 October 1897, box 1, DBC, ROM; Pearse to Boyle, 21 October 1897, box 1, DBC, ROM; Boyle to Hay, February 1897, file acc. 71-026/5, Victoria Museum Fonds, Peterborough Centennial Museum and Archives.
100 OHS, *Annual Report 1907*, 46.
101 Boyle to Millar, 22 March 1902, RG 2-42-0-3541, Department of Education, AO; Boyle, "History Taught by Museums," NHS *Transactions* 4 (1898): 33; "Historical Anniversary," 17 September 1897, minute book, vol. 1, 1895–1909, 34, NHSP, AO.
102 *AARO 1904*, 101.
103 *TCI* 1, 1 (1889–90): 70.
104 Killan, *David Boyle*, 25.
105 For more on this system, see Willey and Sabloff, *A History of American Archaeology*, 34–57.
106 *AARO 1886–87*, 16.

107 *AARO 1894–95*, 29; Boyle, "Introduction," in *Catalogue of Specimens in the Ontario Archaeological Museum*, np.

108 *AARO 1888–89*, 47–101.

109 Ibid.

110 *AARO 1886–87*, 16.

111 *AARO 1893–94*, 6; Report of the Ontario Commissioner to the World's Columbian Exposition, 1893, Sessional Papers, no. 98, 57 Vict., 1894, 42.

112 Report of the Ontario Commissioner to the World's Columbian Exposition, 1893, Sessional Papers, no. 98, 57 Vict., 1894, 42.

113 *AARO 1892–93*, 7–14.

114 Boyle, *Notes on Primitive Man*, 73.

115 Boyle, "Archaeological Remains as a Factor in the Study of History read July 3, 1890," 16, file 9, box 1, DBP, ROM.

116 *AARO 1896–97*, 1.

117 For more, see Willey and Sabloff, *A History of American Archaeology*, 83–129.

118 *AARO 1890–91*, 5–6.

119 Goode to Boyle, 25 November 1895, 474–5, vol. L109, assistant secretary in charge of the United States National Museum, correspondence and memoranda, 1879–1907, Smithsonian Institution Archives.

120 *AARO 1900*, 1; *AARO 1908–11*, 84–5; *AARO 1926–28*, 82, 83. According to ROM staff, the photo titles are misleading as the artifacts pictured are not just from the Laidlaw collection.

121 Laidlaw, "The Aboriginal Remains of Balsam Lake, Ontario, 68–72"; Laidlaw, "Miniatures, or Diminutive Relics, 37–44"; *AARO 1902*, 37–57; Hammond, "Pottery–its Making and Use–and Pipe Making and Use of the Aboriginal Nations of the Province of Ontario, Canada, by J. Hugh Hammond–Orillia Ontario," box 1, JHHP, ROM.

122 *AARO 1902*, 37.

123 "Descriptive List of Collection," notebook 12, North American Indian Archaeology, History, and Ethnology, 11–15, 168–9, 211, 218–19, box 1, AFHP, ROM; Hunter, notebook 12, 68, box 1, AFHP, ROM.

124 "Historical Anniversary," 17 September 1897, minute book, vol. 1, 1895–1909, NHSP, AO; Boyle, "History Taught by Museums," NHS *Transactions* 4 (1898): 32–3.

125 Boyle to Harcourt, 31 July 1902, RG 2-42-0-3639, Department of Education, AO; NHS, *Seventh Annual Report*, 1.

126 NHS, *Catalogue of Articles in Historical Room*, 10.

127 NHS, *Transactions* 24 (1911): 33–5, 51.

128 Entry form, 1899, file 16, MU 7843, WCHSTP, AO.

129 OHS, *Annual Report 1899*, 33–4.

130 OHS, *Catalogue, Canadian Historical Exhibition*, 90–7.

131 OHS, *Catalogue, Canadian Historical Exhibition*, passim.

132 Tivy, "The Local History Museum in Ontario," 93.

133 HA, 5 November 1896, minute book, 1895–1907, 17, HAP, Hamilton Public Library.

134 "Dundurn Castle and Park," *Herald*, Hamilton, 23 May 1902, Dundurn Castle, scrapbook of clippings, 1849–1925, vol. 1, p. 8j-k, Hamilton Public Library; HA, Hamilton Literary and Scientific Association museum and librarian and curator book 1886–7, 94, HAP, Hamilton Public Library.

135 "Dundurn Castle and Park," *Herald*, Hamilton, 23 May 1902, Dundurn Castle, scrapbook of clippings, 1849–1925, vol. 1, 8k, Hamilton Public Library.

136 Bailey, *History of the Dundurn Castle*, 33.

137 "Historic Dundurn Has Rare Treasures," *Spectator*, Hamilton, 26 November 1924, Dundurn Castle, scrapbook of clippings, 1849–1925, vol. 1, 5–6, Hamilton Public Library.

138 "Display Relics to Tell Indian Story," *Globe and Mail*, Toronto, 4 January 1958, Dundurn Castle, scrapbook of clippings, 1849–1925, vol. 1, 87, Hamilton Public Library.

139 Wright, *Professionalization of History*, 26–7.

## CHAPTER THREE

1 Mulvaney et al., *History of the County of Brant*, 411.

2 The history of collecting Native American human remains in the United States has been documented by Bieder, "The Collecting of Bones for Anthropological Narratives," 21–35.

3 *CJ* 13, 3 (1872): 268.

4 Canada West, An Act Respecting the Municipal Institutions of Upper Canada, chapter 54, s266, no. 12, *Consolidated Statutes for Upper Canada* (1859), 22 Vict.

5 British Columbia, An Ordinance to Prevent the Violation of Indian Graves, no. 19, 1865; "The Indian Graves Ordinance," *British Columbian*, New Westminster, 30 March 1865, 2; British Columbia, An Ordinance to Prevent the Violation of Indian Graves, *Laws of British Columbia since the Union of the Two Formerly Separate Colonies of Vancouver Island and British Columbia*, no. 69, 30 Vict., 1867.

6 Canada, An Act Respecting Larceny and Similar Offences, *Revised Statutes of Canada*, vol. 2 (1886), 49 Vict., chapter 164, s98, 1924–5.

7 Canada, An Act Respecting the Criminal Law, *Statutes of Canada*, vol. 1 (1892), 55–6 Vict., chapter 29, part 1, s206, 89; Canada, An Act Respecting the Criminal Law, *Revised Statutes of Canada*, vol. 3 (1906), 3 Edward VII, part 7, chapter 146, s385, 2518.

8 Hammond to Holmes, 18 February 1907, box 3, correspondence, letters received, 1907, Records of the Bureau of American Ethnology, NAA.

9 Strickland, *Twenty Seven Years in Canada West*, vol. 2, 82–4.

10 Cole, *Captured Heritage*, 175.

11  "What the People Say," *Victoria Daily Colonist*, 31 October 1897, 8.

12  Cole, *Captured Heritage*, 175–6; Cole, "Tricks of the Trade," 456.

13  Cole, *Captured Heritage*, 176.

14  Martin to Vowell, 13 October 1898, Vowell to ?, 14 October 1898, West Coast Agency - correspondence regarding the prosecution of A.J. McCordie for removing a skull from an Indian grave near Alberni, file 176 734, vol. 3990, C-10202, RG 10, DIA, LAC.

15  Pass, "'The Wondrous Story and Traditions of the Country,'" 10-11.

16  *CJ* 13, 3 (1872): 268.

17  *CJ* 1, 2 (1852): 25; *PCI* 4, 1 (1886-87): 2.

18  "Grant Asked for a Provincial Museum," *The Indian*, Hagersville, 17 February 1886, 35; "The Neutral Nation," *Toronto Daily Mail*, Toronto, 24 October 1885, 7.

19  Bruce to Duff, 18 January 1906, RG 2-42-0-387, Department of Education, AO.

20  Gidney and Millar, *Professional Gentlemen*, 152–9, 354–68.

21  Highet, "Body Snatching and Grave Robbing," 417.

22  Berkhofer, *White Man's Indian*, 44–69.

23  Highet, "Body Snatching and Grave Robbing," 415; Blakely and Harrington, eds, *Bones in the Basement*; Gidney and Millar, "'Beyond the Measure of the Golden Rule,'" 219–35.

24  Brown, "Victorian Visual Memory and the 'Departed' Child," 22–31; Jalland, *Death in the Victorian Family*, 288–91, 295–317.

25  Jalland, *Death in the Victorian Family*, 265, 205–6.

26  Thwaites, ed., *Jesuit Relations*, vol. 10, 143, 287; Sagard, *Long Journey*, 209.

27  Trigger and Day, "Southern Algonquian Middlemen," in Rogers and Smith, eds, *Aboriginal Ontario*, 67.

28  Fenton and Kurath, "The Feast of the Dead," 143-5.

29  Shimony, *Conservatism among the Iroquois*, xxxi; see also 231–56.

30  Fenton and Kurath, "The Feast of the Dead," 145.

31  Johnson, *Legends, Traditions and Laws, of the Iroquois*, 35, 37–8.

32  Johnston, *Ojibway Ceremonies*, 131–51.

33  See for example, Danziger, *Chippewas of Lake Superior*, 1.

34  Jones, *History of the Ojebway Indians*, 98–101.

35  Densmore, *Chippewa Customs*, 73–8.

36  Jenness, *Ojibwa Indians of Parry Island*, 104–8.

37  Jones, *History of the Ojebway Indians*, 99-100.

38  Hallen, Diary of Reverend George Hallen, January-August 1835, 80–1, acc. 975–64, Simcoe County Archives.

39  Unlabelled note, file 5, MU 57, Barnett Papers, AO; "Visitors to Niagara," pamphlet, file 10, MU 57, Barnett Papers, AO; "Interesting Indian Ceremony at the Falls," *St. Catharines Constitutional*, 9 June 1870, 2. See also Teather, "'Delighting the Eye and Mending the Heart,'" 64.

40  Garrad, *Andrew F. Hunter and the Petun*, 3; Hunter, Indian Archaeology, notebook 4, 146–7, box 1, AFHP, ROM.

41  *AARO 1890-91*, 15–17.

42  *AARO 1890-91*, 11–12.

43  Coyne to Barber, 12 July 1937, William A. Elias, box E3, Biographical Files, United Church Archives.

44  Coyne to Barber, 12 July 1937, William A. Elias, Biographical Files, box E3, United Church Archives; Ashkebee and Yakmodt to superintendent general, nd, Walpole Island Agency – complaint of Chief Ashkebee and John Yakmodt that certain persons have dug up remains of Indians at the burial places on Walpole Island, file 128 246, vol. 2632, C-11253, DIA, RG 10, LAC. The file title mistakenly spells Yahnodt as Yakmodt.

45  McKelvey to superintendent general, 29 July 1892, file 129 116, vol. 2632, C-11253, DIA, RG 10, LAC; Elias to Vankoughnet, 14 August 1892, file 129 337, DIA, RG 10, LAC.

46  Annis to DIA, excerpt from letter dated Chatham July 30, 1892, file 129 118, vol. 2632, C-11253, DIA, RG 10, LAC.

47  Coyne to DIA, 20 August 1892, file 129 337, vol. 2632, C-11253, DIA, RG 10, LAC.

48  Coyne to Ross, 1897, letterbook, 1888–1917, 223, file 319, box 4020, Coyne Papers, UWO Archives and Research Collections Centre.

49  Coyne to DIA, 20 August 1892, file 129 337, DIA, RG 10, LAC; Coyne to Ross, 1897, letterbook, 1888–1917, 223, file 319, box 4020, Coyne Papers, UWO Archives and Research Collections Centre.

50  Ashkebee and Yakmodt to superintendent general, file 128 246, vol. 2632, C-11253, DIA, RG 10, LAC; Elias to Vankoughnet, 14 August 1892, file 129 337, vol. 2632, C-11253, DIA, RG 10, LAC.

51  Coyne to Barber, 12 July 1937, William A. Elias, Biographical Files, box E3, United Church Archives.

52  Annis to DIA, file 129 118, vol. 2632, C-11253, DIA, RG 10, LAC; Elias to Vankoughnet, 14 August 1892, file 129 337, vol. 2632, C-11253, DIA, RG 10, LAC; Annis to Sinclair, 12 August 1892, file 129 768, vol. 2632, C-11253, DIA, RG 10, LAC.

53  Coyne to DIA, 20 August 1892, file 129 337, vol. 2632, C-11253, DIA, RG 10, LAC.

54  Annis to DIA, file 129 118, vol. 2632, C-11253, DIA, RG 10, LAC; Coyne to DIA, 20 August 1892, file 129 337, vol. 2632, C-11253, DIA, RG 10, LAC; Elias to Vankoughnet, 14 August 1892, file 129 337, vol. 2632, C-11253, DIA, RG 10, LAC; Annis to Sinclair, 12 August 1892, file 129 768, vol. 2632, C-11253, DIA, RG 10, LAC.

55  Coyne to DIA, 20 August 1892, file 129 337, vol. 2632, C-11253, DIA, RG 10, LAC; Annis to Sinclair, 12 August 1892, file 129 768, vol. 2632, C-11253, DIA, RG 10, LAC.

56  Annis to Sinclair, 12 August 1892, file 129 768, vol. 2632, C-11253, DIA, RG 10, LAC.

57  McKelvey to Annis, 6 August 1892, file 128 240, vol. 2632, C-11253, RG 10, LAC; McKelvey to DIA, 4 July 1892, file 128 246, vol. 2632, C-11253, RG 10, LAC.

58  Coyne to DIA, 20 August 1892, file 129 337, vol. 2632, C-11253, DIA, RG 10, LAC; Annis to Sinclair, 12 August 1892, file 129 768, vol. 2632, C-11253, DIA, RG 10, LAC.

59  Coyne to Ross, 1897, letterbook, 1888–1917, 223, file 319, box 4020, Coyne Papers, UWO Archives and Research Collections Centre.

60  McKelvey to DIA, McKelvey to Annis, 26 August 1892, file 129 768, vol. 2632, C-11253, DIA, RG 10, LAC.

61  Strickland, *Twenty Seven Years in Canada West*, vol. 2, 81.

62  Traill, *Pearls and Pebbles*, xxxii-xxxiii; Strickland, *Twenty Seven Years in Canada West*, vol. 2, 82; letter, to C.J. Bloomfield, Indian Land Agent, Alnwick Agency, 30 June 1893 and memorandum, 6 July 1893, correspondence regarding the sale to Catherine Parr Traill of Polly Cows Island in the Otonabee River, file 139 410, vol. 2690, C-11264, DIA, RG 10, LAC. The deed itself is at vol. 11, file 12, 1893, reel H-12, Traill Collection, LAC; Traill, "The Indian Maiden's Grave," 280.

63  Ke-Che-Ah-Gah-Me-Qua, *Life of Captain Joseph Brant*, 29–30; Jones, *History of the Ojebway Indians*, 209–10.

64  Evelyn Johnson, "The Land Thou Gave Us," 4, file 4, box 1, Johnson Papers, Trent University Archives; Six Nations Council minutes, 28 November 1879, vol. 874, C-15120, RG 10, DIA, LAC; Caswel, "Canoeing on the Grand River," 96. In 1886 a memorial statue of Brant was erected in Brantford. See "Brant," *Brantford Expositor*, 13 October 1886, 1.

65  The following material is derived from St Denis, *Tecumseh's Bones*, which details the full and highly complicated story of the search for Tecumseh's grave.

66  WHS, 6 June 1910, minute book 1908-26, 24, M122, WHSP, Hamilton Public Library.

67  St Denis, *Tecumseh's Bones*, 70.

68  St Denis, *Tecumseh's Bones*, 36.

69  *AARO 1896-97*, 6; Normal School Catalogue, 75, ROM; *AARO 1897–98*, 6, 8; *AARO 1901*, 4; Normal School Catalogue, 89, ROM; *AARO 1906*, 5; *AARO 1904*, 15; *AARO 1908–11*, 95.

70  For descriptions of these items, see, for example, "The Indian Day," *Free Press*, London, 28 September 1888, 5; "A Wet Wind Up," *Free Press*, London, 27 September 1890, 3; "'Twas Germania Day," *Free Press*, London, 20 September 1893, 6; "Practically Begun," *London Advertiser*, 14 September 1894, 4. For a fuller account of the Indians of Ontario exhibit, see Hamilton, "Primitivism and Progress," unpublished paper.

71 Six Nations Agricultural Society, prize lists, 1892–1942, reel 193, Records Management Office, Ohsweken, ON.
72 Six Nations Agricultural Society, *Six Nations Indians*, 11.
73 Maracle to Boyle, nd, file 1903 July-December and undated, box 2, DBC, ROM.
74 Johnson, "Chiefswood," chapter 11, 18, MS 4, MU 4642, Miscellaneous Indian Manuscripts, AO.
75 Hale, *An Iroquois Condoling Council*, 49.
76 WHS, annual meeting, 6 June 1895, minute book 1888–1908, 227, 231, M122, WHSP, Hamilton Public Library.
77 Canada, DIA, *Annual Report 1893*, 1.
78 *AARO 1886-87*, 39; *AARO 1892–93*, 16, 20; *AARO 1894–95*, 55, 62; *AARO 1905*, 19; Normal School Catalogue, 3, 19, 20, 52, 102, ROM; "The Canadian Institute. Forty-Fourth Annual Report," minutes 6 November 1886 to May 5 1894, 584, box 38, RCIP, TFRBL.
79 Canada, DIA, *Annual Report 1893*, 1.
80 Cumberland, *Catalogue and Notes of the Oronhyatekha Historical Collection*, 30, 33, 48, 14.
81 Ibid., 25, 35, 51, 31, 41, 52, 75, 45, 67.
82 Nicks, "Dr Oronhyatekha's History Lessons," in Brown and Vibert, eds, *Reading beyond Words*, 475.
83 Paudash to McClurg, 3 May 1904, file 4337-1-0-12, McClurg Correspondence, United Indian Bands of the Chippewas and the Mississaugas Papers, MS 2604, AO.
84 Montague to McClurg, 5 December 190?, file 4337-1-0-6, McClurg Correspondence, United Indian Bands of the Chippewas and the Mississaugas Papers, MS 2604, AO.
85 Holden to Boyle, 23 October 1900, box 1, DBC, ROM.
86 "Historic Room in Forester's Temple," *Toronto Daily Star*, 10 September 1902, 7.
87 Nicks, "Dr Oronhyatekha's History Lessons," in Brown and Vibert, eds, *Reading beyond Words*, 474.
88 Cumberland, *Catalogue and Notes of the Oronhyatekha Historical Collection*, 10.
89 "Archaeology" case label, *Mohawk Ideals, Victorian Values: Dr Oronhyatekha, MD*, exhibit produced by the Woodland Cultural Centre, 2002.
90 Jones, *History of the Ojebway Indians*, illustrations between 72–3, 130–1.
91 Burkholder, *Hagersville Past and Present*, np.
92 Jones to Draper, 12 November 1882, Brant Papers, Draper Collection, Series F, vol. 13, pages 14²–14³, State of Wisconsin Historical Society, Madison, WI.
93 *AARO 1890-91*, 11-12.

94 Normal School Catalogue, 71, 72, ROM.

95 Cochrane, *The Canadian Album: Men of Canada*, vol. 2, 262.

96 Accession number 33939, AMNH, Smithsonian Institution.

97 Catalogue of Articles Loaned to Canadian Historical Exhibition by Dr P.E. Jones, Hagersville, June 1899, file 8, MU 7844, WCHSTP, AO.

98 Jones to Carnochan, 20 April 1898, box 6, NHSC, Niagara Historical Museum; NHS, *Catalogue of Articles in Memorial Hall, Transactions* 24 (1911): 35.

99 JHPA (1894–95): 100; HA, 28 January 1886, 13 December 1894, minute book 1890–95, np, Hamilton Public Library.

100 Jones, *Prospectus of the "The Indian."*

101 *The Indian*, Hagersville, 30 December 1885, 1, 6.

102 "Grant Asked for a Provincial Museum," *The Indian*, Hagersville, 17 February 1886, 35.

103 Smith, "Jones, Peter Edmund," 530–1; Cochrane, *The Canadian Album: Men of Canada*, vol. 2, 262.

104 Whale to Currelly, 3 March 1943, Whale Papers, ROM.

105 Carruthers, *Retrospect of Thirty-Six Years' Residence in Canada West*, 231. This incident is also likely the one recorded in no. 195, part 2–94–198 A.F. Hunter, Barrie, Ont. Archaeological Sites in Simcoe Co., box 1, AFHP, ROM.

106 Grand General Indian Council, *Minutes of the Eighth Grand General Indian Council*, 19–20.

107 Chamberlain, *Archaeology of Scugog Island*, 1; Chamberlain, *Language of the Mississaga Indians of Skugog*, 52.

108 Chamberlain, *Archaeology of Scugog Island*, 1-3.

109 Chamberlain, *Archaeology of Scugog Island*, 1.

110 Secord to Hunter, 11 May 1904, env. 6, box 3, AFHP, Simcoe County Archives.

111 Jones, *Recollections*, 35.

112 McKeough, "Early Indian Occupation of Kent," 21.

113 Brown, *America: A Four Year's Residence in the United States and Canada*, 80.

114 No. 118, part 2, box 1, AFHP, ROM. See also Morrison to Boyle, April 1901, file 12, box 2, DBP, ROM; Meyer to Boyle, 22 May 1900, file 13, box 2, DBP, ROM. For other examples, see AARO 1899, 89; no. 248, part 3, Archaeological Sites of Simcoe County, box 1, AFHP, ROM; "Seventeen Skeletons Exhumed," *Ottawa Free Press*, 10 September 1898, GELS 3, 26; "A Long Dead Indian," *Mail and Empire*, Toronto, 23 May 1908, GELS 3, 154.

115 AARO 1899, 85.

116 Hammond to Holmes, 18 February 1907, box 3, correspondence, letters received, 1907, Records of the Bureau of American Ethnology, NAA.

117 No. 224, *Penetang Herald*, 10 October 1889, part 3, box 1, AFHP, ROM.

## CHAPTER FOUR

1   David Boyle, "What Is a Savage?" file 18, box 1, DBP, ROM.
2   The English name of Dahkahedondyeh is so far unknown.
3   *AARO 1886–87*, 13; *AARO 1928*, 48–50.
4   23 February 1889, 20 April 1889, minutes, 6 November 1886 to 5 May
    1894, 167, 186, box 38, RCIP, TFRBL. For biographical information
    about Brant-Sero, see Petrone, "John Ojijatekha Brant-Sero," 137–9,
    and Kreis, "John O. Brant-Sero's Adventures in Europe," 27–30.
5   *AARO 1905*, 59.
6   13 June 1892, minutes of council, 29 April 1887–9 March 1908, 137,
    box 20, RCIP, TFRBL; Normal School Museum Catalogue, 1887–, 2–3,
    19–20, 52, 102, ROM.
7   7 January 1895, minutes of council, 29 April 1887–9 March 1908, 197,
    box 20, RCIP, TFRBL; Williams, "Haudenosaunee Wampum at the
    Grand River," unpublished manuscript, nd.
8   *AARO 1896-7*, 14, 61–2. The previous owner was likely Chief Joseph
    Snow; see Hale to Johnson, July 1896, file 6, box 1, Johnson Papers,
    William Ready Division of Archives and Research Collections,
    McMaster University.
9   *AARO 1897–98*, 5.
10  Killan, *David Boyle*, 183.
11  1 June 1898, minute book, 10-11, MS 249, reel 1, OHSP, AO recorded
    four hundred Six Nations attendees. OHS, *Annual Report 1898*, 7,
    recorded the number as two hundred.
12  Brant-Sero to Boyle, 9 December 1899, box 1, DBC, ROM.
13  *AARO 1898*, 6–8, 10; *AARO 1904*, 11.
14  *AARO 1899*, 6, 10, 13.
15  *AARO 1900*, 7; *AARO 1901*, 5, 13; *AARO 1902*, 8, 9.
16  Hess to Boyle, 3 October 1904, 10 October 1904, 25 October 1904, 5
    November 1905, 9 January 1905, 16 January 1905, 30 January 1905, 20
    February 1905, 17 April 1905, 2 June 1905, 14 July 1905, box 2, DBC,
    ROM; Hess to Boyle, 17 October 1904, file 3, box 2, DBP, ROM; Hess
    to Boyle, 23 October 1908, Normal School Accession Files, ROM.
17  *AARO 1905*, 7–8. Many of these pieces had previously belonged to
    Cory W. Hartman of The Indocrafters, a "Self-supporting Indian
    School and Industry" near Gowanda, New York. Hartman had
    organized a production of Hiawatha at Niagara Falls, but it was a
    monetary failure. He owed wages to several individuals, including
    Austin Bill, and, unable to pay, he instead gave items worth more
    than the seventy-five dollars he owed to Bill as security for the debt.
    Hartman had asked Bill to leave the items in Toronto for him, but, at
    some point, Bill sold them to Boyle. See Hartman to Boyle, 18 May

1907, 23 May 1907, Boyle to Hartman, 13 July 19?, Hartman to Pyne, 13 September 1907, Normal School Accession Files, ROM.

18  *AARO 1908–11*, 95; Boyle to Hess, 18 January 1909, Normal School Accession Files, ROM.

19  Killan, *David Boyle*, 227.

20  *AARO 1898*, 1.

21  Killan, *David Boyle*, 181–2.

22  *AARO 1898*, 56.

23  *AARO 1898*, 121.

24  *AARO 1898*, 122.

25  *AARO 1896-97*, 61.

26  *AARO 1898*, 54.

27  Hess to Boyle, 17 October 1904, file 3, box 2, DBP, ROM; 10 October 1904, box 2, DBC, ROM.

28  Johnson to Boyle, 13 July 1896, file 19, box 2, DBP, ROM.

29  Hale to Johnson, July 1896, file 6, box 1, Johnson Papers, William Ready Division of Archives and Research Collections, McMaster University.

30  Johnson to Boyle, 4 August 1897, box 1, DBC, ROM.

31  Johnson to Seton, 2 August 1905, vol. 16, Seton Papers, LAC.

32  Johnson to Harcourt, 6 January 1902, Boyle to Harcourt, 9 January 1902, RG 2-42-0-3549, AO.

33  Evelyn Johnson's anger was not only directed at Boyle. She expressed bitterness over the treatment of her grandfather John Smoke Johnson, once the keeper of a rare copy of the traditional Book of Rites, which described many of the Confederacy's ceremonial procedures. US collector Erminnie A. Smith had visited the family and purchased the manuscript for only ten dollars, turning a generous profit of a few hundred dollars upon its sale to the Smithsonian Institution. The family had tried to repatriate the item from Smith to no avail. See Johnson, "Chief John Smoke Johnson," 112.

34  Brant-Sero to Coyne, 7 March 1911, file 20, box 4018, Coyne Papers, UWO Archives and Research Collections Centre.

35  Boyle to Ross, 5 January 1898, RG 2-42-0-3669, AO; OHS, *Catalogue, Canadian Historical Exhibition*, 94–6. This collection was up for sale after Brant-Sero left for England, presumably leaving his wife in Canada. In 1900, Frances Baynes Kirby wrote to Boyle that "I *must* sell, for I am *really* in need of money to pay for notes on machinery." She also asked him for information about US collector T.R. Roddy and a museologist at the Field Columbian Museum, both who had expressed interest in purchasing her collection. See Brant-Sero to Boyle, 6 February 1900, box 1, DBC, ROM. For more about the Brant-Sero collection, see Brownstone, "Treasures of the Bloods," 22–31.

36  Postcard advertisement, file 1898-June 1900, MU 5422, OHSP, AO.

37   Petrone, ed., *First People, First Voices*, 138; Brant-Sero to Boyle, 26 October 1899, box 1, DBC, ROM; "Germans Hear Mohawk Yell," *New York Times*, 6 May 1910, 4.

38   Brant-Sero to Boyle, 26 October 1899, box 1, DBC, ROM; deputy minister to Brant-Sero, 14 May 1901, RG 2-42-0-3592, AO.

39   Brant-Sero to Boyle, 29 September 1899, 3 October 1899, 5 October 1899, box 1, DBC, ROM.

40   Brant-Sero to Boyle, 9 December 1899, 6 January 1900, 15 February 1900, box 1, DBC, ROM.

41   Brant-Sero to Boyle, 15 February 1900, box 1, DBC, ROM.

42   Ojijatekha to Powell, 13 December 1889, box 17, correspondence, letters received 1888-1906, Records of the Bureau of American Ethnology, NAA.

43   Brant-Sero to Powell, 16 February 1900, box 2, correspondence, letters received 1888–1906, Records of the Bureau of American Ethnology, NAA.

44   Brant-Sero to Mooney, 3 May 1900, Thwaites to Boas, 4 May 1900, Boas to Brant-Sero, 16 May 1900, file 21, box 2, general correspondence, 1894–1907, Division of Anthropology Archives, AMNH; Mooney to Boyle, 20 May 1900, file 3, box 2, DBP, ROM.

45   Brant-Sero to Boas, 20 October 1900, file 21, box 2, general correspondence, 1894–1907, Division of Anthropology Archives, AMNH.

46   Brant-Sero to Boas, 3 May 1900, Brant-Sero to Mooney, 3 May 1900, Brant-Sero to Boas, 20 October 1900, file 21, box 2, general correspondence, 1894–1907, Division of Anthropology Archives, AMNH.

47   Brant-Sero to Carnochan, 19 June 1899, 7 December 1899, box 6, NHSC, Niagara Historical Society Museum.

48   Brant-Sero to Boas, 2 October 1902, file 21, box 2, general correspondence, 1894–1907, Division of Anthropology Archives, AMNH.

49   *AARO 1898*, 85, 87.

50   *AARO 1898*, plates 3, 18.

51   Census of Canada, 1901, South Brant District, Onondaga Sub-District, c-2, schedule 1, p5, lines 18–22, T-6460, RG 31, Statistics Canada, LAC. Although census enumerators were to record the information given by each individual, the use of census data for First Nations, particularly ethnicity, is problematic. In 1911, census instructions explicitly state that First Nations tribal designations should be traced through matrilineal lines, but it is unclear whether this also occurred earlier, or whether enumerators used patrilineal lineages as they did for the rest of those who resided in Canada. The Six Nations were traditionally

matrilineal. See Hamilton, "'Anyone not on the list might as well be dead,'" 66–7.

52  Census of Canada, 1901, South Brant District, Tuscarora Sub-District, e-3, schedule 1, p7, lines 29–30, T-6460, RG 31, Statistics Canada, LAC; *AARO 1898*, plate 8.

53  *AARO 1898*, plate 9; Brownstone, "Treasures of the Bloods," 24.

54  *AARO 1898*, plate 16.

55  Lizzie Davis to Boyle, 25 January 1898, Isaac Davis to Boyle, 25 January 1898, box 1, DBC, ROM.

56  J.R. Davis to Boyle, 7 March 1898, 30 November 1899, box 1, DBC, ROM.

57  *AARO 1898*, 188.

58  J.R. Davis to Boyle, 29 January 1900, box 1, DBC, ROM. Uncle Bill was Kahnishandon or William Williams; see untitled lecture, number II, file 21, 14, DBP, ROM.

59  Mrs Davis to Boyle, 11 September 1899, box 1, DBC, ROM.

60  Killan, *David Boyle*, 182.

61  Brant-Sero to Coyne, 7 March 1911, file 20, box 4018, Coyne Papers, UWO Archives and Research Collections Centre.

62  *AARO 1898*, 82–3.

63  *AARO 1898*, 121.

64  J.R. Davis to Boyle, 29 January 1900, box 1, DBC, ROM.

65  Boyle to Hess, 18 January 1909, Hess to Boyle, 11 January 1909, Normal School Accession Files, ROM.

66  Bowmans to Boyle, 26 April 1899, box 1, DBC, ROM; Elizabeth Brant-Sero to Boyle, 8 September 1899, box 1, DBC, ROM; J.O. Brant-Sero to Boyle, 2 December 1899, box 1, DBC, ROM; J.R. Davis to Boyle, 7 March 1900, box 1, DBC, ROM.

67  "Council Notes," *Indian Magazine*, Ohsweken, January 1896, 12. Others adopted by the Six Nations include Helen Merrill, the secretary of the UEL Association (Kah-ya-tonhs or "one who writes or keeps a record"), at a ceremony conducted by Chief Isaac of the Onyot.ka (Oneida) nation in 1912, presumably for her role in the celebrations for General Brock, and, before 1898, Mary Rose Holden of the Wentworth Historical Society (Ka-rih-wen-ha-wi of the Beaver Clan of the Onondage'ga' nation). See "A Memory of Gen. Brock; A Picturesque Ceremony," *Globe*, Toronto, 14 October 1912, 1, 3; WHS, *Transactions* (1899): 37.

68  Kan, "Introduction," in Kan, ed., *Strangers to Relatives*, 5–12.

69  OHS, *Annual Report 1898*, 35.

70  Killan, *Preserving Ontario's Heritage*, 43.

71  George Buck and other chiefs stating they will follow the ancient laws and not the government laws, 17 August 1876, file 6897, vol. 1995, C-11130, DIA, RG 10, LAC.

72   Dewdney to ?, 19 November 1888, office of the deputy
     superintendent general letterbook, 16 November 1888–11 February
     1889, vol. 1098, C-7223, RG 10, DIA, LAC; Vankoughnet to ?,
     29 September 1890, office of the deputy superintendent general
     letterbook, 5 September 1890–19 January 1891, 59–60, vol. 1104,
     C-8628, RG 10, DIA, LAC.
73   Petition to be allowed to remain under their ancient laws, introduced
     1 September 1890, minutes, 7–13 November 1890, series A-1-a, no.
     1890–2102, RG 2, Privy Council, LAC. The ancient date given to this
     belt by the Haudenosaunee, and thus the British ratification of it, has
     been called into question by Muller, "The Two 'Mystery' Belts of the
     Grand River," 129–64.
74   Petition to be allowed to remain under their ancient laws, introduced
     1 September 1890, minutes, 7–13 November 1890, series A-1-a, no.
     1890-2102, RG 2, Privy Council, LAC; superintendent general to ?, 17
     October 1890, deputy superintendent general letterbook, 5 September
     1890-19 January 1891, 108–11, vol. 1104, C-8628, RG 10, DIA, LAC.
75   Dewdney to ?, unknown date, deputy superintendent general
     letterbook, 14 January 1892–9 April 1920, 427, vol. 1109, reel C-8631,
     RG 10, DIA, LAC; Dewdney to governor general, 9 March 1892,
     ibid., 490–2; superintendent general to governor general, 10 June 1892,
     deputy superintendent general letterbook, 9 April 1892–10 June 1892,
     610–11, vol. 1110, C-8632, RG 10, DIA, LAC.
76   See Weaver, "The Iroquois: The Grand River Reserve in the Late
     Nineteenth and Early Twentieth Centuries," in Rogers and Smith,
     eds, *Aboriginal Ontario*, 233–45; Shimony, *Conservatism among the
     Iroquois at the Six Nations Reserve*, xxxii–xxxiii.
77   Hill, "Through a Haudenosaunee Lens: An Examination of Sally
     Weaver's Six Nations Historical Publications," Paper Presented at
     the 86th Annual Meeting of the Canadian Historical Association
     (2007); Capatano, "The Rising of the Ongwehònwe," 6–9; Williams,
     Haudenosaunee Standing Committee on Burial Rules and Regulations,
     interview with author (March 2004). Further, Raibmon, *Authentic
     Indians*, 12, points out that the different reactions of an Aboriginal
     community to colonialism is usually negatively characterized as
     factionalism.
78   For more about the UEL myth, see Knowles, *Inventing the Loyalists*,
     26–47.
79   Radforth, *Royal Spectacle*, 206–41; Knowles, *Inventing the Loyalists*,
     86–8.
80   "Old Niagara," *Globe*, Toronto, 12 June 1897, 4.
81   "UEL Association," *Globe*, Toronto, 12 May 1898, 12. He is called
     "Chief C.I. Johnson" in "U.E. Loyalist Association," *Globe*, Toronto,

13 May 1898, 5; UEL Association of Ontario," *Annual Transactions,* 1899, 7.

82  UEL Association of Ontario, *Annual Transactions,* 1899, 18, 40–1; UEL Association of Ontario, *Annual Transactions,* 1900, 46–9.

83  OHS, *Annual Report 1898,* 41–2.

84  Macdonald, "Accessing Audiences: Visiting Visitor Books," 119–36.

85  NHS, 2 June 1897, 11–13 June 1898, visitors register, vol. 1, 1896–1907, 57, 67–9, M472, NHSP, AO; "More Uniformity Desired," *Globe,* Toronto, 15 June 1898, 12.

86  NHS, visitors register, vol. 1, 1896–1907, 61, 98, 111, M472, NHSP, AO; NHS, visitors register, vol. 2, 1907–16, 81, 92, 96, M472, NHSP, AO.

87  Coyne to Cameron, 1 November 1898, letterbook, 710, file 320, box 4020, Coyne Papers, UWO Archives and Research Collections Centre.

88  Cameron to Thompson, 23 September 1907, MU 5423, OHSP, AO.

89  Hill to Cumberland, 19 May 1909, Cumberland to Hill, 3 June 1909, MU 5424, OHSP, AO.

90  OHS, *Annual Report 1911,* 43–9.

91  OHS, *Annual Report 1911,* 43–8; "Historical Interest in the Province Is Active," *Saturday News,* Collingwood, 21 October 1911, OHS scrapbook, 1897–1974, MS 259, OHSP, AO; Killan, *Preserving Ontario's Heritage,* 44.

92  Program, Celebration of the One Hundredth Anniversary of the Battle of Lundy's Lane, 25 July 1914, OHS scrapbook, 1897–1974, MS 259, OHSP, AO; "Honours Lundy's Lane Heroes," *Telegram,* 27 July 1914, OHS scrapbook, 1897–1974, MS 259, OHSP, AO.

93  "Rights Claimed by Six Nations," *Mail,* OHS scrapbook, 1897–1974, MS 259, OHSP, AO; "Ontario Historical Society," 11 July 1921, OHS scrapbook, 1897–1974, MS 259, OHSP, AO; OHS, *Annual Report 1921,* 16, 35.

94  For the Newhouse controversy, see Fenton, *The Great Law and the Longhouse,* 80–4, and Weaver, "Seth Newhouse and the Grand River Confederacy at Mid-Nineteenth Century," in Foster, Campisi, and Mithun, eds, *Extending the Rafters,* 165–82; Campbell, "Seth Newhouse, the Grand River Six Nations and the Writing of the Great Laws," 183–202. See also Six Nations Agency – correspondence regarding a request for aid, from Mr S. Newhouse in publishing his book, the original historical narratives of the five Nations Indians Confederation, file 71 043, vol. 2353, C-11206, RG 10, DIA, LAC. For a version transcribed by Indian Agent E.D. Cameron, see "Narrative of the Origins of the Five Nations Confederacy," 31 March 1900, acc. 16397, MS 1, MU 4642, Miscellaneous Indian Manuscripts, AO.

95  Paudash and Paudash, "Coming of the Mississagas," 10.

96  Fenton, *False Faces,* 152–3, and for similar cases outside of Grand River, see 152, 154–5.

97 *AARO 1898*, 157.

98 *AARO 1899*, 27–9.

99 Fenton, *False Faces*, 169, 174.

100 *AARO 1899*, 29.

101 Hess to Boyle, 17 October 1904, file 3, box 2, DBP, ROM; *AARO 1904*, 15.

102 Hess to Boyle, 25 October 1904, 9 January 1905, box 2, DBC, ROM.

103 Brant-Sero to Carnochan, 7 December 1899, NHSC, Niagara Historical Society Museum.

104 Cumberland, *Catalogue and Notes of the Oronhyatekha Historical Collection*, 35–7.

105 Cumberland, *Catalogue and Notes of the Oronhyatekha Historical Collection*, 58.

106 Jones, *Life and Journals*, 217.

107 Jones, *History of the Ojebway Indians*, 87, illustrations between pages 82–3, 84–5, 144–5. Pabookowaih is now in the David Livingstone Centre, Blantyre, Scotland. A mask similar to Pabookowaih, purchased by M.R. Harrington but not pictured in Jones's history, is at the American Museum of Natural History. See Fenton and Smith, "Pabookowaih Unmasked," 279–84. Harrington also purchased Nahneetis. See Harrington, "Vestiges of Material Culture among the Canadian Delawares," 408–18.

108 Secular items included a war club, wampum, invitation quills for notice of ceremonies, a scalping knife, a game, a quilled birchbark mokuk or basket, and a suit of beaded clothing. The list of items is from the catalogue records of the Jones collection purchased from P.E. Jones by the Smithsonian Institution.

109 Harrington, "Vestiges of Material Culture among the Canadian Delawares," 417–18; Jones, *History of Ojebway Indians*, 87.

110 Jones, *Life and Journals*, 217, 324.

111 Jones, *History of the Ojebway Indians*, 91.

112 *AARO 1897–98*, 5.

113 Hale, *Chief George H.M. Johnson, Onwanonsyshon*, 134–5; E.H.C. Johnson, Normal School Accession Files, ROM; Johnson, "The Delaware Idol," in *The Shagganappi*, 180–90; Evelyn Johnson, "Chiefswood," chapter 3, 4, acc. 13601, MS 4, MU 4642, Miscellaneous Indian Manuscripts, AO; Fenton, *False Faces*, 464. The head of this idol was eventually given to the ROM.

114 Hale, *Chief George H.M. Johnson, Onwanonsyshon*, 134; Whale to Currelly, 9 April 1943, file Currelly-R.W. Whale, Whale Papers, ROM.

115 Johnson, "The Delaware Idol," in *The Shagganappi*, 187.

116 The most complete inventory of her collection was in her will. See Kellar, *Pauline*, 272–4.

117 Gray, *Flint and Feather*, 175.

118 Johnson to Heye, 23 March 1906, box V-E.5, Heye Correspondence, NMAI.

119 Strong-Boag and Gerson, *Paddling Her Own Canoe*, 22.

120 *AARO 1898*, plate 18B.

121 Fenton, *False Faces*, 178.

122 Fenton, "Return of Eleven Wampum Belts to the Six Nations Iroquois Confederacy," 403. The Buck family also sold Boyle a mask, two flutes, and a pair of moccasins belonging to Abram Buck. See *AARO 1898*, 10; *AARO 1899*, 6, 10.

123 Joshua Buck to Hewitt, 19 July 1898, box 2, Hewitt Papers, NAA.

124 8 November 1893, 14 November 1893, file 143 692, Six Nations Council minutes, vol. 2712, C-11268, RG 10, LAC.

125 See Fenton, "Return of Eleven Wampum Belts to the Six Nations Iroquois Confederacy," 392–410; Tooker, "A Note on the Return of Eleven Wampum Belts," 219–36.

126 7 January 1895, minutes of council, 29 April 1887 to 9 March 1908, 197, box 20, RCIP, TFRBL; minutes, 2 November 1894–7 May 1910, annual report, 59, box 39, RCIP, TFRBL.

127 6 February 1895, file 63–32, part 3, Six Nations Council minutes, vol. 1739, C-15023, imperial government records, general administration records, RG 10, DIA, LAC.

128 Chadwick, *People of the Longhouse*, 77; Fenton, "Return of Eleven Wampum Belts to the Six Nations Iroquois Confederacy," 404.

129 For Converse, see Johnson to Boyle, 20 August 1906, Normal School Accession Files, ROM; for Leighton, see Leighton to Johnson, 7 July 1894, file 1, Johnson Correspondence, City of Vancouver Archives. Pauline's brother Allan Wawanosh Johnson appears to have purchased a belt from Susan Buck in 1893. See CPR telegraph, 8 May 1893, A.W. Johnson file, Brant Museum and Archives.

130 Kellar, *Pauline Johnson*; Strong-Boag and Gerson, *Paddling Her Own Canoe*; Gray, *Flint and Feather*.

131 Johnson to Boyle, 4 August 1897, box 1, DBC, ROM.

132 Johnson to Seton, 2 August 1905, vol. 16, Seton Papers, LAC.

133 Johnson to Heye, 17 March 1906, 20 March 1906, 23 March 1906, 31 March 1906, 4 April 1906, 10 April 1906, box V-E.5, Heye Correspondence, NMAI; Johnson to Heye, 19 March 1907, box OC137.10, Heye Correspondence, NMAI; contract entered into this twenty-sixth day of March, nineteen hundred and six, between Miss E. Pauline Johnson, of Hamilton, Ontario, and Mr George G. Heye, of New York City, New York, box V-E.5, Heye Correspondence, NMAI. In contrast to Johnson's description, this belt is likely of a more recent origin. For a fuller account of this wampum and its repatriation, see Williams, "Pauline Johnson and the Zigzag Wampum," unpublished paper, nd.

134 Johnson to Lighthall, 7 April 1907, file 19, box 1, Lighthall Papers, Rare Book Room, McGill University. Lighthall noted that he had sent Johnson $50 as a gift, with no artifacts sent as security.

135 Johnson to Boyle, 20 August 1906, Boyle to Johnson, 8 October 1906, Normal School Accession Files, ROM.

136 "Miss Johnson's Relics for Brantford Museum," *Globe*, Toronto, 12 May 1913, 7; OHS, *Annual Report 1914*, 121; "Relics of Indian Poet Offered to Brantford," *Globe*, Toronto, 16 May 1924, 3; Whale to Currelly, 9 April 1943, file Currelly–R.R. Whale, Whale Papers, ROM. Johnson had joined the Brant Historical Society and in 1913 was listed as a "historian" helping to write two books, "Life of Brant" and a "History of the Six Nation Indians of the Grand River Reserve." See OHS, *Annual Report 1913*, 69–70. In 1922, Evelyn Johnson discovered that some of her artifacts given to the Brant Historical Society had been stolen and shipped several pieces, including the Delaware idol head, to the ROM. See Evelyn Johnson to Rowe, 23 April 1924, 27 May 1924, Evelyn Johnson Files, Brant Museum and Archives.

137 Evelyn H.C. Johnson to Currelly, 16 January 1916, Currelly Correspondence, ROM.

138 Evelyn H.C. Johnson to Currelly, 30 January 1916, 10 October 1922, Currelly Correspondence, ROM. For a fuller account, see Williams, "Evelyn H.C. Johnson and the Royal Ontario Museum," unpublished paper, nd.

139 Fenton, "The New York State Wampum Collection," 438.

140 Fenton, "Return of Eleven Wampum Belts to the Six Nations Iroquois Confederacy," 403.

141 Carryer to Boyle, 4 June 1900, box 1, DBC, ROM.

142 Conaty, "Repatriation of Blackfoot Sacred Material," 74–8.

143 *AARO 1898*, 7; *AARO 1899*, 6, 10, 13.

144 Hill to Boyle, 9 December 1899, box 1, DBC, ROM.

145 Maracle to Boyle, nd, file July–December 1903 and undated, box 2, DBC, ROM.

146 Carryer to Boyle, 29 April 1900, 17 May 1900, 4 June 1900, box 1, DBC, ROM.

147 Census of Canada, 1901, South Brant District, Tuscarora Sub-District, e-3, schedule 1, page 7, line 11, T-6460, RG 31, Statistics Canada, LAC; *AARO 1901*, 5; *AARO 1902*, 8.

148 Census of Canada, 1901, South Brant District, Tuscarora Sub-District, e-3, schedule 1, p5, line 32, T-6460, RG 31, Statistics Canada, LAC; *AARO 1899*, 6.

149 Normal School Museum Catalogue, 1887–, 138, ROM.

150 Strong-Boag and Gerson, *Paddling Her Own Canoe*, 40–1.

151 Johnson, "A Red Girl's Reasoning," in Strong-Boag and Gerson, eds, *E. Pauline Johnson Tekahionwake*, 189, 192.

152 Johnson, "Hoolool of the Totem Poles," in ibid., 257–62.
153 Johnson to Seton, 2 August 1905, vol. 16, Seton Papers, LAC.

## CHAPTER FIVE

1   Woolverton, untitled poem, extracts from Dr Woolverton's notebook, papers on geology and mineralogy of Solon Woolverton, DDS, 12, box 4315, Woolverton Papers, UWO Archives and Research Collections Centre.
2   Judd, *Early Naturalists and Natural History Societies*, 48; AARO 1894-55, 35–7.
3   For a history of this imagery, see Berkhofer, *White Man's Indian*.
4   For more on nineteenth-century theories in anthropology, see Harris, *The Rise of Anthropological Theory*, 142–216; Berkhofer, *White Man's Indian*, 44–61.
5   Haycock, *Image of the Indian*; Monkman, *A Native Heritage*, 3–6.
6   Jasen, *Wild Things*, 8-10, 15.
7   Carter, *Story of Dundas*, 19.
8   Gerson, *A Purer Taste*, 52, 92.
9   Lighthall, *The Master of Life*, v, vi.
10  Dickson, *Camping in the Muskoka Region*, 161, 162.
11  McLachan, "To an Indian's Skull," in *Poems and Songs*, 162.
12  Mulvaney et al., *History of the County of Peterborough*, 4–5; Adam et al., *History of Toronto and County of York*, vol. 1, part 2, 150.
13  *History of the County of Middlesex*, 620.
14  *Four Years on the Georgian Bay*, 42.
15  Small, *Canadian Handbook and Tourist's Guide*, 144.
16  Withrow, *Our Own Country*, 489–90.
17  Wall, "Totem Poles, Teepees, and Token Traditions," 522–3, 525–7, 533.
18  Galway, *From Nursery Rhymes to Nationhood*, 95–114.
19  Traill, *Canadian Crusoes*.
20  Ballantyne, *Snowflakes and Sunbeams*, 140–57.
21  Seton, *Two Little Savages*, 22.
22  Ibid., 20.
23  *Ontario Public School History of England and Canada*, part 2, 7–10; Duncan, *Story of the Canadian People*, 6–18; Clement, *History of the Dominion of Canada*, 9-14; Weaver, *A Canadian History for Boys and Girls*, 8–10; Jeffers, *History of Canada for the Use of Schools*, 30–2; Hodgins, *A School History of Canada and of the Other British North American Provinces*, 99–107. Texts authored by Clement, Jeffers, Hodgins, Adam and Robertson, and the *Ontario Public School History* were all approved texts for school use. For specific textbooks and the history of approved and/or commonly used ones, see Parvin, *Authorization of Textbooks for the Schools of Ontario*, especially 145–50.

24  Adam and Robertson, *Public School History of England and Canada*, 143.

25  Hodgins, *A History of Canada and of the Other British Provinces of North America*, 128-30; Clement, *History of the Dominion of Canada*, 127.

26  Hunter, *Notes on Sites of Huron Villages in the Township of Oro*, 9.

27  McIntyre, "Indian Romance," *Poems of James McIntyre*, 92.

28  Wintemberg, "Preliminary Report on the Exploration of the Southwold Earthworks," 5.

29  "Mounds and Dance Circles," *Saturday Night*, Toronto, 28 November 1896, 5.

30  *AARO 1896–97*, 44.

31  Hunter, *Notes on Sites of Huron Villages in the Township of Oro*, 7, 27; Hunter, *Notes on Sites of Indian Villages in the Townships of North and South Orillia*, 13; *AARO 1896–97*, 21.

32  Grant, ed., *Picturesque Canada*, vol. 2, 480.

33  Lauriston, *Romantic Kent*, 17.

34  "A Rice Lake Prehistoric Princess," *Warder*, Lindsay, 18 September 1896, GELS 1, 25, ROM; "Interesting Discovery in an Old Indian Grave," *Weekly News*, Toronto, 6 January 1887, GELS 1877, 77, ROM.

35  "Big Injun Me," *Post*, Lindsay, nd, GELS 1877, 82, ROM; *Packet*, Orillia, 5 October 1903, GELS 3, 123, ROM.

36  Thorold and Beaverdams Historical Society, *Jubilee History*, 9.

37  Carter, *Story of Dundas*, 20.

38  Bonnycastle, *Canadas in 1841*, vol. 1, 286–8.

39  "Our Illustrations," 34; "Pre-historic Canada," 39.

40  *AARO 1896–97*, 38, 14. There seems to have been much less wild speculation and spectacular fakes compared to those documented in the United States. For an analysis of US fakes, see Silverberg, *Mound Builders of Ancient America*, and Williams, *Fantastic Archaeology*. For a brief newspaper argument over whether Jewish people had been in historic Huronia, see "Singular Discovery in Connexion with the Aborigines of this Continent," *Globe*, Toronto, 6 October 1847, 2; "Indian Relics," *Globe*, Toronto, 17 November 1847, 2. See also "Interesting Discovery," *Mail and Empire*, Toronto, 20 November 1897, GELS 3, 26, ROM, for a reference to a human face turned to stone.

41  Hunter, *Huron Village Sites*, 31-2.

42  See, for example, "Indian Remains," *Daily Globe*, Toronto, 20 October 1856, 2; *AARO 1894–95*, 40.

43  "Indian Remains," *Orillia Packet*, 2 October 1902, GELS 3, 105, ROM.

44  Carroll, *Case and His Cotemporaries [sic]*, 165; Wintemberg, *Lawson Prehistoric Village Site*, 32; "Canadian Items," *Mail*, Toronto, 10 October 1879, 4; Adam et al., *History of Toronto and County of York*,

vol. 1, part 2, 149; *Watchman-Warder*, Lindsay, 16 August 1902, GELS 3, 102, ROM; *Mail*, 10 October 1879, GELS 1877, 12, ROM; "Science of Archaeology," *Mail*, Toronto, 18 January 1883, GELS 1877, 25, ROM; "Human Skeletons," *Empire*, Toronto, 24 February 1894, GELS 1, 23, ROM; "Skull Was Perforated," *Mail and Empire*, Toronto, 19 June 1906, GELS 1, 48, ROM; "Indian Remains," *Orillia Packet*, 2 October 1902, GELS 3, 105, ROM.

45  *AARO 1901*, 42; Wintemberg to Boyle, 27 January 1898, box 1, DBC, ROM.

46  "Massanoga, or Picture Lake," 1–2.

47  *AARO 1904*, 76–7, 57–8.

48  Hunter, book 12, North American Indian Archaeology, History, and Ethnology, 78-80, box 1, AFHP, ROM; Hunter, 23 July 1886, Indian Archaeology. notebook no. 4, 116, box 1, AFHP, ROM.

49  Copway, *Indian Life and Indian History*, 91–4.

50  Jones, *History of the Ojebway Indians*, 112–13.

51  Paudash and Paudash, "Coming of the Mississagas," 8–9.

52  Carroll, *Case and His Cotemporaries [sic]*, vol. 1, 165.

53  Hamil, *Valley of the Lower Thames*, 6.

54  Littlehales, *Journal*, 10.

55  Need, *Six Years in the Bush*, 94–5.

56  Jameson, *Winter Studies and Summer Rambles*, vol. 3, 175–6; Henry, *Travels and Adventures in Canada*, 185–6.

57  Kane, *Wanderings of an Artist*, 3.

58  *Four Years on the Georgian Bay*, 44–5, 71.

59  Hamilton, *The Georgian Bay*, 97–8. Assikinack himself told a version of this story in a paper to the Canadian Institute, published in *CJ* 3, 16 (1858): 297–309. For more about Assikinack, see Leighton, "Assikinack, Francis," 10–11.

60  "Anthropological Discoveries," *Toronto Daily Mail*, 2 December 1882, 11.

61  Hunter, *Notes on Sites of Huron Villages in the Township of Oro*, 27; Hunter, *Huron Village Sites*, 33, 45.

62  Coyne, *Country of the Neutrals*, 1.

63  Thorold and Beaverdams Historical Society, *Jubilee History*, 9, 11.

64  OFNC, *Ottawa Naturalist* 23, 4–5 (1909–10): 104.

65  See, for example, "Interesting Paper by Dr Cl. T. Campbell on the Aims and Work of the History Society," *Free Press*, London, 20 November 1901, 3, LMHS scrapbook, 4, LMHS Papers, London Room, London Public Library; Foster, "Pioneers in History," 13; "Society Organized," *Stratford Daily Beacon*, 6 December 1899, 5; OFNC, *Transactions* 6 (1884–85): 168.

66  Thorold and Beaverdams Historical Society, *Jubilee History*, 8–9.

67  Sonley, "Description of the Old Indian Fort Situated on Lot 20 of the Fourth Concession of London Township," 7, file 13, box 4314, Woolverton Papers, UWO Archives and Collections Research Centre.

68  Coyne, *Country of the Neutrals*, 14.

69  Sonley, "Description of the Old Indian Fort Situated on Lot 20 of the Fourth Concession of London Township," 2, file 13, box 4314, Woolverton Papers, UWO Archives and Collections Research Centre.

70  Lauriston, *Romantic Kent*, 17.

71  WHS, *Transactions* 11 (1924): 38–9.

72  JPHA 16 (1899-1900): 46.

73  Thorold and Beaverdams Historical Society, *Jubilee History,* 10.

74  "Interesting Paper by Dr Cl. T. Campbell on the Aims and Work of the Historical Society," *Free Press*, London, 20 November 1901, LMHS scrapbook, 4, LMHS Papers, London Room, London Public Library.

75  Sonley, "Description of the Old Indian Fort Situated on Lot 20 of the Fourth Concession of London Township," 2, file 13, box 4314, Woolverton Papers, UWO Archives and Research Collection Centre.

76  Harris, *The Catholic Church in the Niagara Peninsula*, 23.

77  WHS, *Transactions* 6 (1915): 6.

78  Mills, *Lake Medad and Waterdown*, 9.

79  Boyle, "What Is a Savage?" box 1, file 18, DBP, ROM.

80  Boyle, "Archaeological Remains as a Factor in the Study of History read July 3, 1890," 10, file 9, box 1, DBP, ROM.

81  *AARO 1891*, 9.

82  *AARO 1903*, 69-70.

83  *AARO 1887-88*, 15.

84  Hunter, book 12, 3, 7, AFHP, ROM.

85  Trigger, "Archaeology and the Image of the Indian," 662.

86  Killan, *David Boyle*, 111, 148; Cole, "Origins of Canadian Anthropology," 38-40; Nock, "Horatio Hale," in Haig-Brown and Nock, eds, *With Good Intentions*, 32–50.

87  "Indian Civilization," box 1, JHHP, ROM; Hunter, "New Aspects of the Old Huron Missions," 352–3.

88  Boyle, "Archaeological Remains as a Factor in the Study of History read July 3, 1890," 10, file 9, box 1, DBP, ROM.

89  *AARO 1894-5*, 29–33.

90  *AARO 1900*, 12.

91  Boyle, *Notes on Primitive Man*, 21, 30.

92  Hammond, "Removal of the Flesh from Body before Burial in Ossuary," box 1, JHHP, ROM.

93  Hunter to McGuire, 29 July 1897, file Lar-N, box 3, AFHP, ROM; Waugh, "Indian Art in Pottery," 230–1.

94  "From a Woman's Standpoint," *Globe*, Toronto, 17 February 1894, 7.

95  *AARO 1900*, 18–21.

96  Hunter, *Huron Village Sites*, 9, 11, 14.
97  Hunter, unlabelled note, unlabelled file, box 3, AFHP, ROM.
98  "Professor Wilson on the Early Indian Tribes of Ontario," *Mail*, Toronto, 3 November 1879, GELS 1, 2, ROM.
99  OFNC, *Ottawa Naturalist* 13, 10 (1900): 232.
100  *AARO 1889–90*, 6.
101  *AARO 1886–87*, 13, 16.
102  *TCI* 1 (1889–90): 69.
103  Boyle, *Notes on Primitive Man*, 3-4.
104  *AARO 1896–97*, 20-1.
105  Paudash and Paudash, "Coming of the Mississagas," 9.
106  Paudash and Paudash, "Coming of the Mississagas," 7, 9.
107  Paudash and Paudash, "Coming of the Mississagas," 11.
108  *AARO 1896–97*, 23, 25.
109  *AARO 1896–97*, 21, 25.
110  Johnson, "A Strong Race Opinion," in Gerson and Strong-Boag, eds, *E. Pauline Johnson Tekahionwake*, 177–83.
111  Johnson, "The Iroquois Women of Canada," in ibid., 203; Johnson, "Mothers of a Great Red Race," in ibid., 223–4.
112  WHS, *Transactions* 2 (1899): 62.
113  "Views of a Mohawk Indian," 161.
114  Town and County Historical Society of Peterborough, constitution, 1903, acc. 71-026/3, Victoria Museum Fonds, Peterborough Centennial Museum and Archives; WCHST, *Transaction* 1 (1896): 5; *Niagara Historical Society: Motto, Ducit a Mor Patriae*, np; circular, Niagara Historical Society, 9 November 1903, LLHS correspondence, MN 131, RG 38-4-0-84, Niagara Parks Commission Papers, AO; "An Informal Meeting," *St Thomas Daily Times*, 30 April 1891, 4; "Address of Mrs Fitzgibbons Before Newly Organized Historical Society," 22 October 1901, LMHS scrapbook, 1, LMHS Papers, London Room, London Public Library; "County of Oxford Historical Society," OxHS minute book, 15 January 1897–1 November 1957, 2, OxHS Papers, Oxford Historical Society.
115  *Annual Report of the Lundy's Lane Historical Society 1893*, LLHS correspondence, MN 130, RG 38-4-0-83, Niagara Parks Commission Papers, AO.
116  For the concept of "imagined community," see Anderson, *Imagined Communities*, 6–7.
117  Cumberland, *Catalogue and Notes of the Oronhyatekha Historical Collection*, 135, 21, 23, 87, 133–4.
118  Ibid., 87–9, 83.
119  Ibid., 54–5, 57, 40, 34.
120  Prucha, *Indian Peace Medals*, xiii–xiv, 34.
121  Silverstein-Willmott, "Object Lessons," 79.

242 NOTES TO PAGES 165–73

122 Cumberland, *Catalogue and Notes of the Oronhyatekha Historical Collection*, 21–2, 24, 25, 26.
123 Ibid., 86, 90.
124 Radforth, "Performance, Politics, and Representation," 16.
125 *Mohawk Ideals, Victorian Values: Dr Oronhyatekha, MD*, produced by the Woodland Cultural Centre, Brantford, ON, 2002.
126 Nicks, "Dr Oronhyatekha's History Lessons," in Brown and Vibert, eds, *Reading beyond Words*, 476-7.
127 Unlabelled clipping, vol. 2, 36, box 4, Sproatt Collection, TFRBL.
128 Van Dusen, *Indian Chief*, 147–8. Radforth, "Performance, Politics, and Representation," 2, 5, 18, suggests that the press depicted the presence of Aboriginal peoples at the 1860 visit in stereotypical images, thus confirming the obstacles in obtaining Aboriginal rights and acting as a foil to the "progress" of non-Aboriginal Canadians.
129 See Surtees, "Land Cessions, 1763–1830," in Rogers and Smith, eds, *Aboriginal Ontario*, 92-121.
130 Jones, *History of the Ojebway Indians*, 119.
131 Smith, *Sacred Feathers*, 176. Another version of this council, one devoid of any conflict, is presented by Jones, *History of the Ojebway Indians*, 118–22.
132 *AARO 1886–87*, 13.
133 *AARO 1901*, 55.
134 Beauchamp, "Wampum and Shell Articles," 438.
135 Hale, "Indian Wampum Records," 486.
136 Hale, *Iroquois Book of Rites*, 41, 61.
137 Hale, "Four Huron Wampum Records," 233, 242, 247; Hale to Powell, 14 May 1881, box 64, correspondence, letters received, 1879–1888, Records of the Bureau of American Ethnology, NAA.
138 Lee, "Romantic Nationalism and the Image of Native Peoples," in King, Calver, and Hoy, eds, *The Native in Literature*, 24–5; Goldie, *Fear and Temptation*, 19, 23, 25, 37; Wall, "Totem Poles, Teepees, and Token Traditions," 514–15.
139 *Herald*, Hamilton, 3 June 1901, GELS 1, 41, ROM.

## CONCLUSION

1   "Indian Burying Ground," *Bytown Gazette and Ottawa and Rideau Advertiser*, 15 June 1843, 3. See also Boswell, "How Ottawa's History Took a Wrong Turn," *Ottawa Citizen*, 18 May 2002, B1.
2   *CJ* 1, 7 (1853): 160–1.
3   Boswell, "'Upon Human Bones,'" *Ottawa Citizen*, 1 July 2002, A1.
4   OFNC, *Ottawa Naturalist* 23, 5 (1909): 99–100.
5   Two very useful syntheses of repatriation and the interpretation of associated legislation in Canada are Bell et al., "First Nations Cultural Heritage," 367–414 and Bell, "Restructuring the Relationship," in Bell

and Paterson, eds, *Protection of First Nations Cultural Heritage*, 15–77. For the fuller definition of historicizing as put forth by Harrison and Darnell, see "Historicizing Traditions," in Harrison and Darnell, eds, *Historicizing Canadian Anthropology*, 5.

6   Janes and Conaty, "Introduction," in Janes and Conaty, eds, *Looking Reality in the Eye*, 11–12.

7   The most recent discussion of *The Spirit Sings* is Cooper, *Spirited Encounters*, 21-8. See also Blundell and Grant, "Preserving Our Heritage: Getting beyond Boycotts and Demonstrations," 12–16; Gillam, *Hall of Mirrors*, 101–33; Halpin, "Museum Review: 'The Spirit Sings,'" 89–93; McLoughlin, *Museums and the Representation of Native Canadians*, 3–13; *Muse* 6, 3 (1988), Special Issue, First Nations and Museums; Vogel, "The Glenbow Controversy," 7–11.

8   Harrison, "'The Spirit Sings' and the Future of Anthropology," 6.

9   Harrison, "Introduction," in *The Spirit Sings: Artistic Traditions of Canada's First Peoples*, 11; *Glenbow* 8, 1 (1988), Special Issue, The Spirit Sings: Artistic Traditions of Canada's First Peoples. See also Harrison, "The Great White Coverup," 47–59.

10  AFN and CMA, *Turning the Page*; Canada, *Report of the Royal Commission of Aboriginal Peoples*, vol. 3, Gathering Strength, 587–96, 652–62.

11  There are a number of case studies about such collaborative projects. See, for example, Ames, "Cultural Empowerment and Museums," in Pearce, ed., *Objects of Knowledge*, 158-73; Ames, "How to Decorate a House" and Conaty, "Glenbow's Blackfoot Gallery," in Peers and Brown, eds, *Museums and Source Communities*, 171-80, 227-41; Clavir, *Preserving What Is Valued*; Conaty and Carter, "Our Story in Our Words," in Janes and Conaty, eds, *Looking Reality in the Eye*, 43-58; Conaty, "Canada's First Nations and Museums," 407-13; Hanna, "A Time to Choose," 43–53; Harrison, "Listening for the Conversation," 293–9; Holm and Pokotylo, "From Policy to Practice," 33–43; Janes, "Personal, Academic and Institutional Perspectives," 147–56; Phillips and Phillips, "Double Take," 694–704; Harrison, "Shaping Collaboration," 195–212; Rowley and Hausler, "The Journey Home," in Gabriel and Dahl, eds, *Utimut*, 202–12.

12  Clarke-Hazlett, "Communicating Critical Historical Scholarship Through Museum Exhibition," in Rider, ed., *Studies in History and Museums*, 73.

13  Tivy, "Quality of Research," 61–8.

14  Tivy, "Museums, Visitors and the Reconstruction of the Past in Ontario," 35–51.

15  CAA, *Statement of Principles* and *A Report from the Aboriginal Heritage Committee*.

16  Parks Canada, *Human Remains, Cemeteries and Burial Grounds*.

17  Carter, "Museums and Indigenous Peoples in Canada," in Pearce, ed., *Museums and the Appropriation of Culture*, 222–4.

18  AAA, *Code of Ethics*.

19  For the history and background of NAGPRA see Trope and Echo-Hawk, "Native American Graves Protection and Repatriation Act," in Mihesuah, ed., *Repatriation Reader*, 123-68.

20  Ferguson, Watkins, and Pullar, "Native Americans and Archaeologists," in Swidler et al., eds, *Native Americans and Archaeologists*, 240–1; Nicholas, "Education and Empowerment," in Nicholas and Andrews, eds, *At a Crossroads*, 93.

21  Powell, Garza, and Hendricks, "Ethics and Ownership of the Past," 2.

22  Smith and Wobst, "Decolonizing Archaeological Theory and Practice," in Smith and Wobst, eds, *Indigenous Archaeologies*, 15.

23  Kerber, "Introduction," in Kerber, ed., *Cross-Cultural Collaboration*, xxi.

24  Blume, "Working Together," in Kerber, ed., *Cross-Cultural Collaboration*, 210. See also Colwell-Chanthaphonh and Ferguson, "Introduction," in Colwell-Chanthaphonh and Ferguson, eds, *Collaboration in Archaeological Practice*, 7–14.

25  Watkins, *Indigenous Archaeology*, 171–2, 178.

26  TwoBears, "A Navajo Student's Perception," in Dongoske, Aldenderfer, and Dochner, eds, *Working Together*, 16–17.

27  For a variety of case studies in which archaeologists and Aboriginal groups have collaborated, see Dongoske, Aldenderfer, and Doehner, eds, *Working Together*; Kerber, ed., *Cross-Cultural Collaboration*; Killion, ed., *Opening Archaeology*; Nicholas and Andrews, eds, *At a Crossroads*; Colwell-Chanthaphonh and Ferguson, eds, *Collaboration in Archaeological Practice*.

28  Wakeham, *Taxidermic Signs*, 172–4.

29  Ferguson, "NHPA," in Dongoske, Aldenderfer, and Doehner, eds, *Working Together*, 27.

30  For a history and analysis of the projects of the Zuni Archaeology Program, see Mills and Ferguson, "Preservation and Research of Sacred Sites by the Zuni," 30–43; Anyon and Ferguson, "Cultural Resources Management at the Pueblo of Zuni," 913–30.

31  For the Navajo program, see Klesert and Downer, eds, *Preservation on the Reservation* and Carmean, *Spider Woman Walks This Land*. For others, see Ferguson, Dongoske, Yeatts, and Kuwanwisiwma, "Hopi Oral History and Archaeology"; Welch, "The White Mountain Apache Tribe Heritage Program," in Dongoske, Aldenderfer, and Doehner, eds, *Working Together*, 45–60, 67–83; and Stapp and Burney, *Tribal Cultural Resource Management*. For a list of Native American tribes engaged in archaeology and heritage preservation, see Ferguson,

"NHPA," in Dongoske, Aldenderfer, and Doehner, eds, *Working Together*, 28–9.

32  Budhwa, "An Alternative Model for First Nations Involvement in Resource Management Archaeology," 20–45.

33  Roy, "'Who Were these Mysterious People?'" 94–5.

34  Paul O'Neal, chief archaeologist, Mayer Heritage Consultants, London, interview with author, 18 September 2002.

35  Johnson and Jones, "The Saskatchewan Archaeological Society and the Role of Amateur Societies," in Smith and Mitchell, eds, *Bringing Back the Past*, 249–57.

36  Johnson and Jones, "The Saskatchewan Archaeological Society and the Role of Amateur Societies," in Smith and Mitchell, eds, *Bringing Back the Past*, 255; Kenyon, "Afterword," in *Avocational Archaeologists*, 32–5. See also Hyder and Loendorf, "Role of Avocational Archaeologists," 234–9.

37  The problems of looting are discussed in Messenger, ed., *Ethics of Collecting Cultural Property*; Zimmerman, Vitelli, and Hollowell-Zimmer, eds, *Ethical Issues in Archaeology*; Davis, "Looting Graves/Buying and Selling Artefacts," 235–40; Vitelli, ed., *Archaeological Ethics*, 29–110.

38  Pokotylo and Guppy, "Public Opinion and Archaeological Heritage," 409–10.

39  Marron, "Nearby Graves Also Desecrated, Men Fined for Looting Indian Site," *Globe and Mail*, Toronto, 2 May 1985, M3; Fox, "The Freelton/Misner Site Looting and Prosecution," 31–9.

40  Bourrie, "Archeologists Losing Battle with Site Looters," *Toronto Star*, 2 July 1989, F7.

41  Fournier, "Desecration of Human Remains Angers Natives," *The Province*, Vancouver, 12 December 2003, A25.

42  Bourrie, "Archeologists Losing Battle with Site Looters," *Toronto Star*, 2 July 1989, F7.

43  Mallouf, "An Unraveling Rope," 202–3, 205, 207.

44  Ames, "Are Changing Representations of First Peoples in Canadian Museums and Galleries Challenging the Curatorial Prerogative?" in West, ed., *Changing Presentation of the American Indian*, 79.

45  Doxtator, "Implications of Canadian Nationalism for Aboriginal Cultural Autonomy," 63–4.

46  For other examples, see Cooper and Sandoval, eds, *Living Homes for Cultural Expression;* Lawlor, *Public Native America;* Stanley, ed., *The Future of Indigenous Museums.*

47  NMAI, *Facts and Figures from the Grand Opening of the Smithsonian's National Museum of the American Indian.*

48  For a history of the Heye collection, see Jacknis, "A New Thing?" 511–42.

49   Horse Capture, "Way of the People," Blue Spruce, ed., *Spirit of a Native Place*, 42–3.

50   Evelyn, "Launching an International Institution of Living Cultures," 9; NMAI, "About the National Museum of the American Indian."

51   Cobb, "The National Museum of the American Indian as Cultural Sovereignty," 485–506.

52   Cobb, "The National Museum," 367.

53   Volkert, Martin, and Pickworth, *National Museum of the American Indian*, 44–61.

54   Blue Spruce, ed., *Spirit of a Native Place*; Cobb, "The National Museum," 369–71.

55   Hill, "A Home for the Collections," in Blue Spruce, ed., *Spirit of a Native Place*, 125–30.

56   Jacobson, ed., "Review Roundtable," 45–90; Ruffins, "Culture Wars Won and Lost," 79–100; *American Indian Quarterly* 30, 3–4 (2006) Special Issue, Critical Engagements with the National Museum of the American Indian; Evelyn, "Launching an International Institution," 10; Ringle, "Where's Tonto?" *Weekly Standard*, Washington, DC, 4 April 2005, 31–4; Rothstein, "Museum with an American Indian Voice," *New York Times*, 21 September 2004, E1; Rothstein, "Who Should Tell History: The Tribes or the Museums," *New York Times*, 21 December 2004, E1; Shea, "Nonhegemonic Curating," *New York Times*, 12 December 2004, 84; Stewart, "Pricey Gift Shops Obscure Museum of the American Indian's Message," *Dayton Daily News*, 21 November 2004, K1; Basen, "National Museum of the American Indian," *Roanoke Times*, 7 November 2004, 5; Quattlebaum, "Through Native Eyes," *Washington Post*, 5 November 2004, T57; Jenkins, "The Museum of Political Correctness," *The Independent*, London, 25 January 2005, 15; Richard, "Shards of Many Untold Stories," *Washington Post*, 21 September 2004, C01; Fisher, "Indian Museum's Appeal, Sadly, Only Skin-Deep," *Washington Post*, 21 September 2004, B01.

57   Biolsi and Zimmerman, "What's Changed, What Hasn't," in Biolsi and Zimmerman, eds, *Indians and Anthropologists*, 11; Landau and Steele, "Why Anthropologists Study Human Remains"; and Crawford, "(Re) Constructing Bodies," in Mihesuah, ed., *Repatriation Reader*, 74–94, 220.

58   "The County–The People–The Crops," *Northern Advance and County of Simcoe General Advertiser*, Barrie, 10 August 1859, 2.

59   Price, *Disputing the Dead*, 2.

60   See, for example, White Deer, "From Specimens to SAA Speakers," in Dongoske, Aldenderfer, and Doehner, eds, *Working Together*, 14.

61   Mihesuah, "American Indians, Anthropologists, Pothunters, and Repatriation," in Mihesuah, ed., *Repatriation Reader*, 93–105.

62 See, for example, Arkeketa, "Repatriation," 239; Echo-Hawk and Echo-Hawk, "Repatriation, Reburial, and Religious Rights," 181.

63 Sampson, "Ancient One/Kennewick Man," in Burke et al., eds, *Kennewick Man*, 41.

64 Killion, "A View from the Trenches," in Killion, ed., *Opening Archaeology*, 137.

65 Downey, *Riddle of the Bones*, ix.

66 Fitzhugh, "Foreword," in Bray and Killion, eds, *Reckoning with the Dead*, vii. For Aboriginal understandings of repatriation see, for example, Echo-Hawk and Echo-Hawk, *Battlefields and Burial Grounds*; Russell, "Law and Bones," 214–26; Mihesuah, "American Indians, Anthropologists, Pothunters, and Repatriation," 95–105; Riding In, "Repatriation: A Pawnee's Perspective," 106-20; and Deloria Jr, "Secularism, Civil Religion, and the Religious Freedom of American Indians," 169–89, all in Mihesuah, ed., *Repatriation Reader*; Weaver, "Indian Presence with no Indians Present," 13–30.

67 Zimmerman, "Anthropology and Responses to the Reburial Issue," in Biolsi and Zimmerman, eds, *Indians and Anthropologists,* 103.

68 Dumont, Jr, "The Politics of Scientific Objections to Repatriation," 109–28; Watkins, "Who's Right and What's Left on the Middle Ground?" in Gabriel and Dahl, eds, *Utimut*, 105; Fish, "Indigenous Bodies in Colonial Courts," 80–9.

69 Klesert and Powell, "A Perspective on Ethics and the Reburial Controversy," in Mihesuah, ed., *Repatriation Reader*, 204. See also Knudson and Keel, eds, *Public Trust and the First Americans*.

70 SAA Repatriation Policy.

71 Dongoske, Aldenderfer, and Doehner, eds, *Working Together*. For the SAA and NAGPRA, see Lovis et al., "Archaeological Perspectives on NAGPRA," 165–84.

72 Meighan, "Another View on Repatriation," 39–45; Meighan, "Some Scholars' Views on Reburial," in Mihesuah, ed., *Repatriation Reader*, 190–9; Meighan, "Burying American Archaeology," in Vitelli and Colwell-Chanthaphonh, eds, *Archaeological Ethics*, 167–70.

73 Clark, "NAGPRA and the Demon-Haunted World," 3.

74 See, for example, Killion and Molloy, "Repatriation's Silver Lining," in Dongoske, Aldenderfer, and Doehner, eds, *Working Together,* 111-7.

75 See Kakaliouras, "Toward a 'New and Different' Osteology," 109–29; Killion, "Opening Archaeology," 10; Bray, "Repatriation and Archaeology's Second Loss of Innocence," 79–81, all in Killion, ed., *Opening Archaeology*; Dongoske, "NAGPRA: A New Beginning, Not the End, for Osteological Analysis," in Mihesuah, ed., *Repatriation Reader*, 282–93.

76  For more information on the Kennewick Man case and how it has
    affected NAGPRA, see Benedict, *No Bone Unturned*; Chatters, *Ancient
    Encounters*; Dewar, *Bones*; Downey, *Riddle of the Bones*; Thomas,
    *Skull Wars*; Owsley and Jantz, "Kennewick Man – A Kin? Too
    Distant," and Gerstenblith, "Cultural Significance and the Kennewick
    Skeleton," in Barkan and Bush, eds, *Claiming the Stones/Naming
    the Bones*, 141–61, 162–97; Johansen, "Kennewick Man," 283–303;
    Powell, *The First Americans*; Wakeham, *Taxidermic Signs*, 165–202;
    Owsley and Jantz, "Archaeological Politics and Public Interest in
    Paleoamerican Studies," 565–75; Bruning, "Complex Legal Legacies,"
    501–21; Burke et al., *Kennewick Man*.
77  Dunn, "'My Grandfather Is Not an Artifact'"; Dunn, "A National
    Overview of the Department of Communications Consultation with
    Aboriginal Peoples on Canadian Archaeological Heritage."
78  Assembly of First Nations, Resolution no. 27/99.
79  CAA, *Statement of Principles*.
80  Hanna, "Old Bones, New Reality," 242–5.
81  Cybulski et al., "Committee Report: Statement on the Excavation,
    Treatment, Analysis and Disposition of Human Skeletal Remains from
    Archaeological Sites in Canada," 32–6; Richard Lazenby, president of
    CAPA, email communication with author.
82  Avery, "Gathering Reunites a Once Powerful Nation," *Windspeaker*,
    Edmonton, October 1999, 6; Avery, "Ancestors Laid to Rest in
    Ontario Homeland," in ibid.; Withers, "Hurons Reunite after 350
    Years," *The Gazette*, Montreal, 30 August 1999, A9.
83  Warrick, *Population History of the Huron-Petun*, 144–5.
84  Humphreys, "Workers at Burial Site Warned of Spirits," *National Post*,
    Don Mills, 3 June 2003, A2. See also Avery, "Wendat Woman Vows to
    Watch Over Remains," *Windspeaker*, Edmonton, July 2003, 25.
85  Interview with Jamie Hunter, director, Huronia Museum, 7 December
    2009.
86  Bethune, "Bones of Contention," *Macleans*, 19 March 2001, 30.
87  Boswell, "Reburial of Aboriginal Bones a Grave Loss to Science,"
    *Edmonton Journal*, 21 June 2005, A2; Boswell, "Scientists Mourn
    Reburial of 5,000-year-old Bones, Artifacts," *The Gazette*, Montreal,
    21 June 2005, A13; Boswell, "Museum Returns Ancient Native Bones,"
    *Edmonton Journal*, 31 December 2002, A12.
88  "Boning Up on the Past," *Ottawa Citizen*, 21 January 2003, C4.
89  For the full story, see also Boswell, "Solved," *Ottawa Citizen*, 18 May
    2002, A1; Boswell, "Museum to Return Indian Bones," *The Gazette*,
    Montreal, 31 December 2002, A4; Boswell, "Bones of Contention,"
    *Ottawa Citizen*, 31 December 2002, A1; "Museum Preparing to
    Repatriate Native Bones," *Globe and Mail*, Toronto, 1 January 2003,
    A4; Boswell, "Museum to Get Petition over Return of Bones," *Ottawa*

*Citizen*, 12 January 2003, A3; Boswell, "Museum Asked to Give Up Indian Skeletons," *The Gazette*, Montreal, 13 January 2003, A9; Boswell, "Return Our Ancestors' Bones within 2 Years, Algonquin Demand," *Ottawa Citizen*, 16 January 2003, A5; Boswell, "Scientists to Canada," *Ottawa Citizen*, 18 January 2003, A1; Boswell, "Boyhood Adventure Unravels Puzzle," *Ottawa Citizen*, 23 January 2003, C1; Boswell, "Bridge over Ancient Waters," *Edmonton Journal*, 1 February 2003, A17; Heller, "Bones Returned to Aboriginals," *Leader Post*, Regina, 20 June 2005, D7; Boswell, "Reburial of 5,000-Year-Old Remains a 'terrific loss,' Scholar Says," *Ottawa Citizen*, 21 June 2005, C1.

90  Bray and Grant, "The Concept of Cultural Affiliation," in Bray and Killion, eds, *Reckoning with the Dead*, 157.

91  Hill, "Repatriation Must Heal Old Wounds," in ibid., 185.

92  Riding In, Seciwa, Shown Harjo, and Echo-Hawk, "Protecting Native American Human Remains, Burial Grounds, and Sacred Places," 171–5.

93  Pensley, "The Native American Graves Protection and Repatriation Act," 52.

94  Sioui, *For an Amerindian Autohistory*, 105, x.

95  Echo-Hawk, "Ancient History in the New World," 267.

96  Mason, "Archaeology and Native North American Oral Traditions," 239–66; Whiteley, "Archaeology and Oral Tradition: The Scientific Importance of Dialogue," 405–15.

97  Nabokov, *A Forest of Time*, 5; Meyer and Klein, "Native American Studies and the End of Ethnohistory," in Thornton, ed., *Studying Native America*, 203; Krupat, *Ethnocriticism*, 3–45; Michaelsen, *Limits of Multiculturalism*, xiii.

98  Roness and McNeil, "Legalizing Oral History," 66–74.

99  For an overview of these concerns, see Gulliford, "Curation and Repatriation of Sacred and Tribal Objects," 23–38.

100  Arkeketa, "Repatriation," 239; Echo-Hawk and Echo-Hawk, "Repatriation, Reburial, and Religious Rights," 177–93; Noble, "Niitooii: 'the same that is real,'" 113–30.

101  Simpson, "Indigenous Heritage and Repatriation – A Stimulus for Cultural Renewal," in Gabriel and Dahl, eds, *Utimut*, 64.

102  For examples of repatriation of sacred items and those of cultural patrimony, see Jonaitis, *Yuquot Whalers' Shrine*; Ridington and Hastings, *Blessing for a Long Time*; Ferguson, Anyon, and Ladd, "Repatriation at the Pueblo of Zuni," and Jacknis, "Repatriation as Social Drama," in Mihesuah, ed., *Repatriation Reader*, 239–65, 266–81; Merrill et al., "The Return of the Ahayu: da," 523–67.

103  The First Nations Sacred Ceremonial Objects Repatriation Act is provincial legislation that applies to the Royal Alberta Museum

and the Glenbow Museum. For legislation in other provinces, see
Carter, "Museums and Indigenous People in Canada," in Pearce, ed.,
*Museums and the Appropriation of Culture*, 214–20, and Ziff and
Hope, "Unsitely," in Bell and Paterson, eds, *Protection of First Nations
Cultural Heritage*, 181–202.

104 Parks Canada, *Repatriation of Moveable Cultural Resources of
Aboriginal Affiliation*. Parks Canada has also taken steps to increase the
documentation, preservation, and commemoration of archaeological
sites in their national inventory, as designated by Aboriginal groups.
See Fox, "Aboriginal Peoples, Archaeology, and Parks Canada," 35–42.

105 GRASAC, Great Lakes Research Alliance for the Study of Arts and
Cultures; Museum of Anthropology, Reciprocal Research Network.

106 Kathy Walker, "Cree Want 'Spiritual' Meteorite Returned," *Edmonton
Journal*, 26 May 2003, B1.

107 Fenton, *False Faces*, 455–8.

108 Haudenosaunee Standing Committee on Burial Rules and Regulations,
Haudenosaunee Policy on Wampum; Grand Council of the
Haudenosaunee, *Haudenosaunee Confederacy Policy on False Face
Masks*.

109 Bourette, "ROM to Return Five Wampum Artifacts to Iroquois,"
*Globe and Mail*, Toronto, 12 November 1999, A11; Chung, "Six
Nations Plans Ceremony to Welcome Back Its Artifacts: ROM Will
Return Five Iroquois Wampum Items," *Toronto Star*, 12 November
1999, 1; Kapches, Department of Anthropology, ROM, communication
with author.

110 Fenton, "The New York State Wampum Collection," 438. See also
Sullivan, "Return of the Sacred Wampum Belts," 7–14.

111 Fenton, "The New York State Wampum Collection," 437–61.

112 Fenton, "Return of Eleven Wampum Belts," 408. See also Abrams,
"The Case for Wampum," 351–84.

113 See their *Guide du Circuit Champlain*.

114 "Huronia Museum Aims to Map Out Champlain's Route and Create
Series of Walking Tours," *Orillia Packet and Times*, 1 October 2008,
A6; "City of Bones," *Orillia Packet and Times*, 1 October 2008; A6.

# BIBLIOGRAPHY

## ARCHIVAL SOURCES

*American Museum of Natural History, Division of Anthropology Archives, New York, New York*
General Correspondence. 1894–1907.

*Archives of Ontario, Toronto, Ontario*
Sidney Barnett Papers. 1838–1904. F 684.
Department of Education Records. Select Subject Files. 1885–1964. RG 2.
Andrew F. Hunter Papers. 1863–1912. F 1084.
George Laidlaw. "Aboriginal Remains of Victoria County." 10 June 1912. Acc. 6175. MS 165.
Perry B. Leighton Papers. 1838–97. Hiram Walker Historical Museum Collection. F 378.
Lennox and Addington Historical Society Papers. 1898–1922. D 59. M 225.
Lundy's Lane Historical Society Correspondence. 1888–1911. Niagara Parks Commission Papers. RG 38.
Lundy's Lane Historical Society Papers. 1888–1947. F 1137.
George H. Mills Papers. 1887–9. F 83.
G. Mills McClurg Correspondence. A.E. Williams / United Indian Bands of the Chippewas and the Mississaugas Papers. F 4337.
Miscellaneous Indian Manuscripts. MU 4642.
Niagara Historical Society Papers. 1727–1964. F 1138.
Ontario Historical Society Papers. 1895–1974. F 1139.
Royal Canadian Institute Papers. 1848–1919. F 1052.
Simcoe Pioneer and Historical Society Papers. 1873–1911. F 1141.
Ferdinand Brock Tupper Papers. 1804–1950. F 1081.
Women's Canadian Historical Society of Toronto Papers. 1794–1983. F 1180.

York Pioneer and Historical Society Papers. 1899–1987. F 1143.

*Brant Museum and Archives, Brantford, Ontario*
Allan Wawanosh Johnson Files.
Evelyn H.C. Johnson Files.
Pauline Johnson Files.

*Canadian Museum of Civilization Archives, Gatineau, Quebec*
Van West, John. "The History of Anthropology in Canada." 1974.
   I-A-177M.
William J. Wintemberg Papers. 1907–39. I-A-242M.

*City of Vancouver Archives, Vancouver, British Columbia*
E. Pauline Johnson Papers. 1890–1962. Add. MSS 1102. 579–6-4.

*Elgin County Archives, St Thomas, Ontario*
Elgin Historical Society Papers. 1891–3.
Miscellaneous Historical Records, Elgin County Clippings. 1900–40.
George Thorman Papers.

*Hamilton Public Library Special Collections, Hamilton, Ontario*
Dundurn Castle Scrapbook of Clippings. 1849–1925.
Hamilton Association for the Advancement of Literature, Science and Art
   Papers. 1857–1929.
Wentworth Historical Society Papers. 1888–1926.

*Harvard University, Peabody Museum of Archaeology and Ethnology,*
*Boston, Massachusetts*
Director Records, Frederick W. Putnam. 1870–1923.

*Library and Archives Canada, Ottawa, Ontario*
Department of Indian Affairs Records. RG 10.
Ottawa Field-Naturalists' Club Papers. 1863–1977. R5475-0-0-E.
Privy Council Minutes. RG 2.
Ernest Thompson Seton Papers. 1792–1983. R7616-0-7-E.
Statistics Canada. Census of Canada. 1901. RG 31.
Traill Family Papers. 1816–1997. R5652-0-0-E.

*London Public Library, London Room, London, Ontario*
London and Middlesex Historical Society Papers. 1902–75.

*McGill University Rare Books and Special Collections, Montreal, Quebec*
William Douw Lighthall Papers. 1886–1924. MS 216.

*McMaster University William Ready Division of Archives and Research Collections, Hamilton, Ontario*
E. Pauline Johnson Papers. 1870–2003.

*Museum of Ontario Archaeology, London, Ontario*
John Bycraft Papers.

*Museum at the Station, Collingwood, Ontario*
Huron Institute Papers. 1904–10.

*National Anthropological Archives, Smithsonian Institution, Suitland, Maryland*
Bureau of American Ethnology. Correspondence, Letters Received. 1879–88; 1888–1906; 1907.
J.N.B. Hewitt Papers.

*National Museum of the American Indian, Smithsonian Institution, Washington, DC*
George G. Heye Correspondence.

*Niagara Historical Society Museum, Niagara-on-the-Lake, Ontario*
Niagara Historical Society Correspondence. 1891–1930.

*Oxford Historical Society, Woodstock, Ontario*
Oxford Historical Society Papers. 1897–1910.

*Peterborough Centennial Museum and Archives, Peterborough, Ontario*
Victoria Museum Fonds. 1897–1914.

*Royal Ontario Museum Archives, Toronto, Ontario*
David Boyle Correspondence. 1893–1906.
David Boyle Papers. SCI. 1887–1950.
David Boyle Scrapbooks. Vols 1–2. 1870–1902.
Charles Trick Currelly Correspondence.
J. Hugh Hammond Papers.
Andrew F. Hunter Papers. 1887–1912.
George E. Laidlaw Scrapbooks. Vols 1877 and 1, 3, 4. 1877–1912.
Normal School Accession Files.
Normal School File N.S. (D. Boyle) North America–Mainly Proveniences. 1906–34.
Normal School Museum Catalogue. 1887–.
Normal School Visitors' Register. 1889–96.
Reginald W. Whale Papers.

*Simcoe County Archives, Minesing, Ontario*
Reverend George Hallen Diary. 1835.
Andrew F. Hunter Papers. 1881–1957.


*Six Nations Records Management Office, Ohsweken, Ontario*
Six Nations Agricultural Society Prize Lists. 1892–1942. Film 193.


*Smithsonian Institution Archives, Washington, DC*
United States National Museum. Assistant Secretary in Charge of the
    United States National Museum. Correspondence and Memoranda.
    1879–1907. RU 112.
United States National Museum. Assistant Secretary in Charge of the
    United States National Museum. Correspondence and Memoranda.
    1860–1908. RU 189.


*State Historical Society of Wisconsin, Madison, Wisconsin*
Lyman C. Draper Papers. Joseph Brant Papers.


*Stratford-Perth Archives, Stratford, Ontario*
Hugh Nichol Papers.
Stratford Perth Historical Society Papers. 1922–30.


*Stratford-Perth Museum, Stratford, Ontario*
Stratford-Perth Museum Accession/Registration Records.


*Toronto Reference Library, Baldwin Room, Toronto, Ontario*
David Boyle Scrapbooks. Vols 1–7. 1859–82. S166.
Matheson-Moorhouse, Elena Bell. "William Matheson: Watchmaker,
    Lucan, Ontario." c1940. File 31. B5582–3.
Henry Scadding Papers. 1833–1900. S98. S99.
Daniel Wilson Scrapbooks. Vols 1–7. 1854–98. S65.


*Trent University Archives, Peterborough, Ontario*
E. Pauline Johnson Papers. 1870–1937. 89-013.


*United Church Archives, Toronto, Ontario*
Jeremiah W. Annis Biographical Files. A4.
William A. Elias Biographical Files.


*University of Toronto Archives, Toronto, Ontario*
Daniel Wilson Correspondence. 1859–92. B93-0022/001.
Daniel Wilson Journal. John Langton Family Papers. B-1965-0014.

*University of Toronto Thomas Fisher Rare Book Library, Toronto, Ontario*
Royal Canadian Institute Papers. 1849–1985. MS 193.
Thomas Sproatt Collection. MS 47.

*The University of Western Ontario Archives and Research Collections*
*Centre, London, Ontario*
James H. Coyne Papers. 1843–1942.
London and Middlesex Historical Society Papers. 1900–74.
Wintemberg, William J. "Preliminary Report on the Exploration of the
    Southwold Earthworks, Elgin County, Ontario."
Solon Woolverton Papers. 1832–1937.

*Woodstock Museum, Woodstock, Ontario*
Oxford Historical Society Papers.

## GOVERNMENT DOCUMENTS

Boyle, David. *Catalogue of Specimens in the Ontario Archaeological*
    *Museum Toronto.* Toronto: Warwick Bros and Rutter, 1897.
– *Notes on Primitive Man in Ontario. Being an Appendix to the Report*
    *of the Minister of Education for Ontario.* Toronto: Warwick Bros and
    Rutter, 1895.
British Columbia. *The Laws of British Columbia Since the Union of*
    *the Two Formerly Separate Colonies of Vancouver Island and British*
    *Columbia.* 1867.
– An Ordinance to Prevent the Violation of Indian Graves. No. 19. 1865.
Canada. *Report of the Royal Commission of Aboriginal Peoples,* vol. 3.
    *Gathering Strength.* Ottawa: Canada Communication Group
    Publishing, 1996.
– An Act Respecting the Criminal Law. 6 Edward VII. 1906.
– House of Commons. *Debates.* Vol. 5. 4 Edward VII. 1904.
– An Act Respecting the Criminal Law. 55–6 Vict. 1892.
– An Act Respecting Larceny and Similar Offences. 49 Vict. 1886.
Canada, Department of Indian Affairs. *Annual Report of the Department of*
    *Indian Affairs for the Year Ended 20th June 1893.* Sessional Paper 14. 57
    Vict. 1894.
Canada West. An Act Respecting the Municipal Institutions of Upper
    Canada. 22 Vict. 1859.
Canadian Institute. *Archaeological Report 1894–95. By David Boyle.*
    *Appendix to the Report of the Minister of Education Ontario.* Toronto:
    Warwick Bros and Rutter, 1896.
– *Seventh Annual Report of the Canadian Institute. Session 1893–4. Being*
    *Part of Appendix to the Report of the Minister of Education, Ontario.*
    Toronto: Warwick Bros and Rutter, 1894.

– *Fifth Annual Report of the Canadian Institute, Session 1892–3, Being an
  Appendix to the Report of the Minister of Education, Ontario.* Toronto:
  Warwick and Sons, 1893.
– *Annual Archaeological Report and Canadian Institute, (Session 1891),
  Being an Appendix to the Report of the Minister of Education, Ontario.*
  Toronto: Warwick and Sons, 1892.
– *Fourth Annual Report of the Canadian Institute, (Session of 1890–91.)
  Being an Appendix to the Report of the Minister of Education, Ontario.*
  Toronto: Warwick and Sons, 1891.
– *Annual Report of the Canadian Institute, Session 1888–9. Being Part of
  Appendix to the Report of the Minister of Education, Ontario, 1889.*
  Toronto: Warwick and Sons, 1889.
– *Annual Report of the Canadian Institute Session 1887–8. Being Part of
  Appendix L to the Report of the Minister of Education, Ontario, 1888.*
  Toronto: Warwick and Sons, 1889.
– *Annual Report of the Canadian Institute, Session 1886–87, Being Part
  of Appendix to the Report of the Minister of Education, Ontario 1887.*
  Toronto: Warwick and Sons, 1888.
Dunn, Martin. "'My Grandfather Is Not an Artifact': A Report on the
  Aboriginal Archaeological Heritage Symposium February 17–18,
  1991." Prepared for the Department of Communications, Archaeology
  Heritage Branch, Government of Canada, 1991.
– "A National Overview of the Department of Communications
  Consultation with Aboriginal Peoples on Canadian Archaeological
  Heritage." Ottawa: Canadian Department of Communications, 1991.
Jones, Arthur Edward. *"8endake Ehen" or Old Huronia.* Fifth Report
  of the Bureau of Archives for the Province of Ontario. Ed. Alexander
  Fraser. Toronto: L.K. Cameron, 1909.
Ontario. *Report of the Minister of Education (Ontario).* 1886–1910.
– An Act Respecting the Canadian Historical Exhibition. Ch. 16. 59 Vict.
  1896.
– *Report of the Ontario Commissioner to the World's Columbian
  Exposition, 1893.* 57 Vict. 1894.
– An Act to Provide for the Establishment of Free Libraries. Ch. 22. 45
  Vict. 1882.
Ontario Provincial Museum. *Thirty-Sixth Annual Archaeological Report,
  1928, Including 1926–1927 Being Part of Appendix to the Report of the
  Minister of Education, Ontario.* Toronto: Clarkson W. James, 1928.
– *Thirty-Fifth Annual Archaeological Report, 1924–1925 Being Part of
  Appendix to the Report of the Minister of Education, Ontario.* Toronto:
  Clarkson W. James, 1925.
– *Thirty-Fourth Annual Archaeological Report, 1923 Being Part of
  Appendix to the Report of the Minister of Education, Ontario.* Toronto:
  Clarkson W. James, 1924.

– *Thirty-Third Annual Archaeological Report, 1921–2 Being Part of Appendix to the Report of the Minister of Education, Ontario.* Toronto: Clarkson W. James, 1922.

– *Thirty-Second Annual Archaeological Report, 1920 Being Part of Appendix to the Report of the Minister of Education, Ontario.* Toronto: Clarkson W. James, 1920.

– *Thirty-First Annual Archaeological Report, 1919 Being Part of Appendix to the Report of the Minister of Education, Ontario.* Toronto: A.T. Wilgress, 1919.

– *Thirtieth Annual Archaeological Report, 1918 Being Part of Appendix to the Report of the Minister of Education, Ontario.* Toronto: A.T. Wilgress, 1918.

– *Twenty-Ninth Annual Archaeological Report, 1917 Being Part of Appendix to the Report of the Minister of Education, Ontario.* Toronto: A.T. Wilgress, 1917.

– *Twenty-Eighth Annual Archaeological Report, 1916 Being Part of Appendix to the Report of the Minister of Education, Ontario.* Toronto: A.T. Wilgress, 1916.

– *Twenty-Seventh Annual Archaeological Report, 1915 Being Part of Appendix to the Report of the Minister of Education, Ontario.* Toronto: A.T. Wilgress, 1915.

– *Annual Archaeological Report, 1914 Being Part of Appendix to the Report of the Minister of Education, Ontario.* Toronto: L.K. Cameron, 1914.

– *Annual Archaeological Report, 1913 Being Part of Appendix to the Report of the Minister of Education, Ontario.* Toronto: L.K. Cameron, 1913.

– *Annual Archaeological Report, 1912 Being Part of Appendix to the Report of the Minister of Education, Ontario.* Toronto: L.K. Cameron, 1912.

– *Annual Archaeological Report, 1911, Including 1908-9-10. Being Part of Appendix to the Report of the Minister of Education, Ontario.* Toronto: L.K. Cameron, 1911.

– *Annual Archaeological Report, 1907. Being Part of Appendix to the Report of the Minister of Education, Ontario.* Toronto: L.K. Cameron, 1908.

– *Annual Archaeological Report 1906. Being Part of Appendix to the Report of the Minister of Education Ontario.* Toronto: L.K. Cameron, 1907.

– *Annual Archaeological Report 1905 Being Part of Appendix to the Report of the Minister of Education Ontario.* Toronto: L.K. Cameron, 1906.

– *Annual Archaeological Report 1904 Being Part of Appendix to the Report of the Minister of Education Ontario.* Toronto: L.K. Cameron, 1905.

– *Annual Archaeological Report 1903 Being Part of Appendix to the Report of the Minister of Education Ontario.* Toronto: L.K. Cameron, 1904.

– *Annual Archaeological Report 1902. Being Part of Appendix to the Report of the Minister of Education Ontario.* Toronto: L.K. Cameron, 1903.

– *Annual Archaeological Report 1901. Being Part of Appendix to the Report of the Minister of Education Ontario.* Toronto: L.K. Cameron, 1902.

– *Annual Archaeological Report 1900. Being Part of Appendix to the Report of the Minister of Education Ontario*. Toronto: Warwick Bros and Rutter, 1901.
– *Archaeological Report 1899. Being Part of Appendix to the Report of the Minister of Education Ontario*. Toronto: Warwick Bros and Rutter, 1900.
– *Archaeological Report 1898 Being Part of Appendix to the Report of the Minister of Education Ontario*. Toronto: Warwick Bros and Rutter, 1898.
– *Annual Archaeological Report 1897–98. Being Part of Appendix to the Report of the Minister of Education Ontario*. Toronto: Warwick Bros and Rutter, 1898.
– *Annual Archaeological Report, 1896–97, Being Part of Appendix to the Report of the Minister of Education Ontario*. Toronto: Warwick Bros and Rutter, 1897.
Parks Canada. *Human Remains, Cemeteries and Burial Grounds.* Management Directive 2.3.1., File C-8412. June 2000.
– *Repatriation of Moveable Cultural Resources of Aboriginal Affiliation.* Management Directive 2.3.4., File 8800-82/P3. June 2000.

## NEWSPAPERS AND MAGAZINES

*Bradford Witness and South Simcoe News.*
*Brantford Expositor.*
*Border Cities Star.* Windsor.
*British Columbian.* New Westminster.
*Bytown Gazette and Ottawa and Rideau Advertiser.*
*Canadian Illustrated News.*
*Daily Globe.* Toronto.
*Daily Sentinel-Review.* Woodstock.
*Dayton Daily News.*
*Edmonton Journal.*
*Enterprise-Messenger.* Collingwood.
*Examiner.* Peterborough.
*Free Press.* London.
*The Gazette.* Montreal.
*Globe.* Toronto.
*Globe and Mail.* Toronto.
*The Independent.* London.
*The Indian.* Hagersville.
*The Indian Magazine.* Ohsweken.
*Kingston Gazette.*
*Leader Post.* Regina.
*London Advertiser.*
*Macleans.*
*National Post.* Don Mills.
*New York Times.*

*Northern Advance and County of Simcoe General Advertiser.*
*Orillia Packet and Times.*
*Ottawa Citizen.*
*The Province.* Vancouver.
*Roanoke Times.*
*St Thomas Daily Times.*
*Saturday News.* Collingwood.
*Saturday Night.* Toronto.
*Stratford Daily Beacon.*
*Times.* Niagara-on-the-Lake.
*Toronto Daily Mail.*
*Toronto Star.*
*Upper Canada Gazette; or American Oracle.* York.
*Victoria Daily Colonist.*
*Washington Post.*
*Weekly Standard.* Washington, DC.
*Windspeaker.* Edmonton.

## UNPUBLISHED SECONDARY SOURCES

Hamilton, Michelle A. "Primitivism and Progress: The Indians of Ontario
    Exhibit at the Western Fair, 1888–1901." Unpublished paper. 2006.
Hill, Susan M. "Through a Haudenosaunee Lens: An Examination of Sally
    Weaver's Six Nations Historical Publications." Paper Presented at the
    86th Annual Meeting of the Canadian Historical Association. 2007.
Kapches, Mima. "Toronto's Hidden Past: The Archaeological Story."
    Unpublished MS. Royal Ontario Museum, Toronto. 2001.
Williams, Paul. "Evelyn H.C. Johnson and the Royal Ontario Museum."
    Unpublished paper. Nd.
– "Haudenosaunee Wampum at the Grand River." Unpublished paper. Nd.
– "Pauline Johnson and the Zigzag Wampum." Unpublished paper. 2004.

## BOOKS, ARTICLES, AND THESES

Abrams, George H.J. "The Case for Wampum: Repatriation from the
    Museum of the American Indian to the Six Nations Confederacy,
    Brantford, Ontario, Canada." *Museums and The Making of Ourselves:
    The Role of Objects in National Identity.* Flora E.S. Kaplan, ed., 351–84.
    London and New York: Leicester University Press, 1994.
Adam, G. Mercer and W.J. Robertson. *Public School History of England
    and Canada; with Introduction, Hints to Teachers, and Brief
    Examination Questions.* Toronto: Copp, Clark Company, 1886.
Adam, G. Mercer et al. *History of Toronto and County of York Ontario;
    Containing an Outline of the History of the Dominion of Canada;
    a History of the City of Toronto and the County of York, With the*

*Townships, Towns, Villages, Churches, Schools; General and Local Statistics; Biographical Sketches, etc., etc.* Toronto: C. Blackett Robinson, 1885.

Adams, Joseph. *Ten Thousand Miles through Canada: The Natural Resources, Commercial Industries, Fish and Game, Sports and Pastimes of the Great Dominion.* Toronto: McClelland and Goodchild, 1912?

Alber, Melissa et al. *From Relics to Research: A 60 Year Retrospective of the London Museum of Archaeology.* London, 1993.

American Anthropological Association. *Code of Ethics.* June 1998. www.aaanet.org/committees/ethics/ethcode.htm (31 July 2009).

*American Indian Quarterly* 30, 3–4 (2006). Special Issue. Critical Engagements with the National Museum of the American Indian.

*American Indian Quarterly* 20, 2 (1996). Special Issue. Repatriation: An Interdisciplinary Dialogue.

Ames, Michael M. *Cannibal Tours and Glass Boxes: The Anthropology of Museums.* Vancouver: University of British Columbia Press, 1992.

– "The Liberation of Anthropology: A Rejoinder to Professor Trigger's 'A Present of Their Past?'" *Culture* 8, 1 (1988): 81–5.

Anderson, Benedict R. *Imagined Communities: Reflections on the Origin and Spread of Nationalism.* Rev. Ed. London and New York: Verso, 2006.

Anderson, James. *Stratford: Library Services Since 1846.* Stratford, 1975.

Anderson, Margaret and Marjorie Halpin, eds. *Potlatch at Gitsegukla: William Beynon's 1945 Notebooks.* Vancouver: University of British Columbia Press, 2000.

Antweiler, Christoph. "Local Knowledge Theory and Methods: An Urban Model from Indonesia." *Investigating Local Knowledge: New Directions, New Approaches.* Alan Bicker, Paul Sillitoe, and Johan Pottier, eds, 1–34. Aldershot and Burlington: Ashgate Publishing, 2004.

Anyon, Roger and T.J. Ferguson. "Cultural Resources Management at the Pueblo of Zuni, New Mexico, USA." *Antiquity* 69, 266 (1995): 913–30.

Appadurai, Arjun, ed. *The Social Life of Things: Commodities in Cultural Perspective.* Cambridge: Cambridge University Press, 1986.

Arkeketa, Annette. "Repatriation: Religious Freedom, Equal Protection, and Institutional Racism." *American Indian Thought: Philosophical Essays.* Anne Waters, ed., 239–48. Malden: Blackwell Publishing, 2004.

Asad, Talal, ed. *Anthropology and the Colonial Encounter.* London: Ithaca Press, 1973.

Assembly of First Nations. Resolution No. 27/99. Aboriginal Graves and Burial Sites in Canada. 1999. www.afn.ca/article.asp?id=988 (31 July 2009).

Assembly of First Nations and the Canadian Museums Association. *Turning the Page: Forging New Partnerships between Museums and First Peoples.* Ottawa, 1992.

Atleo, E. Richard. "Policy Development for Museums: A First Nations Perspective." *BC Studies* 89 (1991): 48–61.

Avrith-Wakeam, Gail. "George Dawson, Franz Boas and the Origins of Professional Anthropology in Canada." *Scientia Canadensis* 17 (1994): 185–203.

Bagg, Stanley Clark. *Canadian Archaeology*. Montreal: Daniel Rose, 1864.

Bailey, Melville. *The History of the Dundurn Castle and Sir Allan MacNab*. Hamilton: Hughes and Wilkins, 1943.

Ballantyne, R.M. *Snowflakes and Sunbeams, or, The Young Fur Traders, a Tale of the Far North*. London: T. Nelson, 1856.

Barkan, Elazar and Ronald Bush, eds. *Claiming the Stones/Naming the Bones: Cultural Property and the Negotiation of National and Ethnic Identity*. Los Angeles: Getty Research Institute, 2002.

Barkhouse, Joyce C. *George Dawson, The Little Giant*. Toronto: Clarke, Irwin and Company Limited, 1974.

Barringer, Tim and Tom Flynn, eds. *Colonialism and the Object: Empire, Material Culture, and the Museum*. London and New York: Routledge, 1998.

Bazely, Susan M. "History Beneath our Feet: Exploring Kingston's Archaeological Past." *Historic Kingston* 49 (2001): 23–31.

Beauchamp, William M. "Wampum and Shell Articles Used by the New York Indians." *Bulletin of the New York State Museum* 8, 41 (1901): 320–480.

Bell, Catherine and Robert K. Paterson, eds. *Protection of First Nations Cultural Heritage: Laws, Policy, and Reform*. Vancouver: University of British Columbia Press, 2009.

Bell, Catherine et al. "First Nations Cultural Heritage: A Selected Survey of Issues and Initiatives." *First Nations Cultural Heritage and Law: Case Studies, Voices, and Perspectives*. Catherine Bell and Val Napoleon, eds, 367–414. Vancouver: University of British Columbia Press, 2008.

Bell, Louise, ed. *Tweedsmuir History. Binbrook Township*. Caledonia: Sachem Print, 1948.

Benedict, Jeff. *No Bone Unturned: The Adventures of a Top Smithsonian Forensic Scientist and the Legal Battle for America's Oldest Skeletons*. New York: HarperCollins, 2003.

Bennett, Tony. *The Birth of the Museum: History, Theory, Politics*. London and New York: Routledge, 1995.

Berger, Carl. *Science, God and Nature in Victorian Canada*. Toronto: University of Toronto Press, 1983.

– *The Writing of Canadian History: Aspects of English-Canadian Historical Writing, 1900–1970*. Toronto: Oxford University Press, 1976.

Berkhofer, Robert. *White Man's Indian: Images of the American Indian from Columbus to the Present*. New York: Alfred A. Knopf, 1978.

Berman, Judith. "'The Culture as It Appears to the Indian Himself':
    Boas, George Hunt, and the Methods of Ethnography." *Volksgeist As
    Method and Ethic: Essays on Boasian Ethnography and the German
    Anthropological Tradition.* George W. Stocking, Jr, ed., 215–56. Madison:
    University of Wisconsin Press, 1996.
Bernatchez, Ginette. "La Société Littéraire et Historique de Quebec, 1824–
    1890." *Revue d'Histoire de L'Amérique Française* 35, 2 (1981): 179–92.
Bieder, Robert E. "The Collecting of Bones for Anthropological
    Narratives." *American Indian Culture and Research Journal* 16, 2 (1992):
    21–35.
– *A Brief Historical Survey of the Expropriation of American Indian
    Remains.* Bloomington: Native American Rights Fund, 1990.
– *Science Encounters the Indian, 1820–1880: The Early Years of American
    Ethnology.* Norman: University of Oklahoma Press, 1986.
Biolsi, Thomas and Larry J. Zimmerman, eds. *Indians and Anthropologists:
    Vine Deloria Jr and the Critique of Anthropology.* Tucson: University of
    Arizona Press, 1997.
Black, Martha. *Bella Bella: A Season of Heiltsuk Art.* Toronto, Vancouver
    and Seattle: Royal Ontario Museum, Douglas & McIntyre, and
    University of Washington Press, 1997.
– "Looking for Bella Bella: The R.W. Large Collection and Heiltsuk Art
    History." *Canadian Journal of Native Studies* 9, 2 (1989): 273–92.
Blakely, Robert L. and Judith M. Harrington, eds. *Bones in the Basement:
    Postmortem Racism in Nineteenth-Century Medical Training.*
    Washington, DC, and London: Smithsonian Institution Press, 1997.
Blanchard, Jim, ed. *A Thousand Miles of Prairie: The Manitoba Historical
    Society and the History of Western Canada.* Winnipeg: University of
    Manitoba Press, 2002.
Blue Spruce, Duane, ed. *Spirit of a Native Place: Building the National
    Museum of the American Indian.* Washington, DC: Smithsonian
    Institution and National Geographic, 2004.
Blundell, Valda and Laurence Grant. "Preserving Our Heritage: Getting
    beyond Boycotts and Demonstrations." *Inuit Art Quarterly* 4, 1 (1989):
    12–16.
Bond, Ray Corry. *Peninsula Village: The Story of Chippawa.* Chippawa,
    1964.
Bonnycastle, Sir Richard Henry. *The Canadas in 1841.* Vols 1–2. London:
    H. Colburn, 1842.
Boutilier, Beverly and Alison Prentice, eds. *Creating Historical Memory:
    English-Canadian Women and the Work of History.* Vancouver:
    University of British Columbia Press, 1997.
Boyle, David, ed. *The Township of Scarboro, 1796–1896.* Toronto: William
    Briggs, 1896.
Bray, Tamara L. *The Future of the Past: Archaeologists, Native Americans,
    and Repatriation.* New York and London: Garland Publishing, 2001.

– and Thomas W. Killion, eds. *Reckoning with the Dead: The Larsen Bay Repatriation and the Smithsonian Institution*. Washington, DC, and London: Smithsonian Institution Press, 1994.

Briggs, Charles and Richard Bauman. "'The Foundation of all Future Researches': Franz Boas, George Hunt, Native American Texts, and the Construction of Modernity." *American Quarterly* 51, 3 (1999): 479–528.

Brown, Eleanor. "Victorian Visual Memory and the 'Departed' Child." *Archivist* 115 (1997): 22–31.

Brown, Jennifer S.H. and Elizabeth Vibert, eds. *Reading beyond Words: Contexts for Native History*. Peterborough: Broadview Press, 2003.

Brown, Jennifer S.H. "'A Place in Your Mind for Them All': Chief William Berens." *Being and Becoming Indian: Biographical Studies of North American Frontiers*. James A. Clifton, ed., 204–25. Chicago: Dorsey Press, 1989.

Brown, William. *America: A Four Years' Residence in the United States and Canada: Giving a Full and Fair Description of the Country, As it Really is, with the Manners, Customs and Character of the Inhabitants, Anecdotes of Persons and Institutions, Prices of Land and Produce, State of Agriculture and Manufactures*. Leeds: Kemplay and Bolland, 1849.

Brownstone, Arni. "Treasures of the Bloods." *Rotunda* 38, 2 (2005): 22–31.

Bruning, Susan B. "Complex Legal Legacies: The Native American Graves Protection and Repatriation Act, Scientific Study, and Kennewick Man." *American Antiquity* 71, 3 (2006): 501–21.

Budhwa, Rick. "An Alternative Model for First Nations Involvement in Resource Management Archaeology." *Canadian Journal of Archaeology* 29, 1 (2005): 20–45.

Burke, Heather, Claire Smith, Dorothy Lippert, Joe Watkins, and Larry Zimmerman, eds. *Kennewick Man: Perspectives on the Ancient One*. Walnut Creek: Left Coast Press, 2008.

Burkholder, Mabel. *Hagersville Past and Present*. Hagersville, 1950.

Burley, D.V. "The Never Ending Story: Historical Developments in Canadian Archaeology and the Quest for Heritage Legislation." *Canadian Journal of Archaeology* 18, 1 (1994): 77–98.

Cameron, Duncan. "The Museum: A Temple or Forum?" *Curator* 14, 1 (1971): 11–24.

Campbell, Peter. "'Not as a White Man, Not as a Sojourner': James A. Teit and the Fight for Native Rights in British Columbia, 1884–1922." *Left History* 2, 2 (1994): 37–57.

Campbell, William J. "Seth Newhouse, the Grand River Six Nations and the Writing of the Great Laws." *Ontario History* 96, 2 (2004): 183–202.

Canadian Archaeological Association. *Statement of Principles for Ethical Conduct Pertaining to Aboriginal Peoples*. 1996. www.canadianarchaeology.com/ethical.lasso (31 July 2009).

– *A Report from the Aboriginal Heritage Committee.* Bev Nicholson, David Pokotylo, and Ron Williamson, eds. www.canadianarchaeology.com/aboriginal.lasso (31 July 2009).

Canadian Indian Research and Aid Society. *The Canadian Indian.* Vol. 1. 1890–91.

Canadian Institute. *Transactions of the Canadian Institute.* Vols 1–10. 1889–1914.

– *Proceedings of the Canadian Institute.* Vols 1–7. 1879–90.

– *The Canadian Journal of Science, Literature, and History.* Vols 12–15. 1868–78.

– *The Canadian Journal of Industry, Science, and Art.* Vols 1–11. 1856–67.

– *The Canadian Journal: A Repertory of Industry, Science and Art, and a Record of the Proceedings of the Canadian Institute.* Vols 1–3. 1852–55.

Canniff, William. *History of the Settlement of Upper Canada, (Ontario,) with Special Reference to the Bay of Quinte.* Toronto: Dudley and Burns, 1869.

Cannizzo, Jeanne. "George Hunt and the Invention of Kwakiutl Culture." *Canadian Review of Sociology and Anthropology* 20, 1 (1983): 44–58.

Carmean, Kelli. *Spider Woman Walks This Land: Traditional Cultural Properties and the Navajo Nation.* Walnut Creek: AltaMira Press, 2002.

Carroll, John. *Case and His Cotemporaries [sic]; or, the Canadian Itinerants' Memorial: Constituting a Biographical History of Methodism in Canada, from Its Introduction into the Province, till the Death of the Reverend William Case in 1855.* Vol. 1. Toronto: Samuel Rose, 1867.

Carruthers, John. *Retrospect of Thirty-Six Years' Residence in Canada West: Being A Christian Journal and Narrative.* Hamilton: T.L. M'Intosh, 1861.

Carter, J. Smyth. *The Story of Dundas: Being a History of the County of Dundas from 1784 to 1904.* Iroquois: St Lawrence News Publishing House, 1905.

Caswel, A.B. "Canoeing on the Grand River." *Rod and Gun in Canada* (October 1899): 96–7.

Catapano, Andrea C. "The Rising of the Ongwehònwe: Sovereignty, Identity, and Representation on the Six Nations Reserve." PhD dissertation, Stonybrook University, 2007.

*Celebrating One Thousand Years of Ontario's History.* Willowdale: Ontario Historical Society, 2000.

Chadwick, Edward M. *The People of the Longhouse.* Toronto: Church of England Publishing, 1897.

Chalmers, William. *George Mercer Dawson: Geologist, Scientist, Explorer.* Montreal: XYZ Publishing, 2000.

Chamberlain, A.F. *The Language of the Mississaga Indians of Skugog: A Contribution to the Linguistics of the Algonkian Tribes of Canada.* Philadelphia: MacCalla and Company, 1892.

– *The Archaeology of Scugog Island*. 1889.

Chant, Edna B. *Beautiful Charleston*. Belleville: Mika Publishing Company, 1975.

Chatters, James C. *Ancient Encounters: Kennewick Man and the First Americans*. New York: Simon and Schuster, 2001.

Chisholm and Co. *Chisholm's All Round Route and Panoramic Guide of the St Lawrence: The Hudson River; Trenton Falls; Niagara; Toronto; The Thousand Islands and the River St Lawrence; Ottawa; Montreal; Quebec; the Lower St Lawrence and the Saguenay Rivers; the White Mountains; Portland; Boston; New York*. Montreal: John Lovell, 1872.

Clark, G.A. "NAGPRA and the Demon-Haunted World." *Society for American Archaeology Bulletin* 14, 5 (1996): 3.

Clavir, Miriam. *Preserving What Is Valued: Museums, Conservation, and First Nations*. Vancouver: University of British Columbia Press, 2002.

Clement, W.H.P. *The History of the Dominion of Canada*. Toronto: William Briggs and Copp, Clark Company, 1897.

Clifford, James. *Routes: Travel and Translation in the Late Twentieth Century*. Cambridge: Harvard University Press, 1997.

Clifton, James A. *A Place of Refuge for All Time: Migration of the American Potawatomi into Upper Canada, 1830 to 1850*. Canadian Ethnology Service Paper 26. Mercury Series. Ottawa: National Museums of Canada, 1975.

Cobb, Amanda J. "The National Museum of the American Indian as Cultural Sovereignty." *American Quarterly* 57, 2 (2005): 485–506.

– "The National Museum of the American Indian: Sharing the Gift." *American Indian Quarterly* 29, 3–4 (2005): 361–83.

Cochrane, William. *The Canadian Album. Men of Canada; or, Success by Example, in Religion, Patriotism, Business, Law, Medicine, Education and Agriculture; Containing Portraits of Some of Canada's Chief Business Men, Statesmen, Farmers, Men of the Learned Professions, and Others, Also, An Authentic Sketch of their Lives*. Vol. 2. Brantford: Bradley, Garretson and Co., 1893.

Cole, Douglas. "Anthropological Exploration in the Great Northwest, 1778–1889 and After." *Encounters with a Distant Land: Exploration and the Great Northwest*. Carlos A. Schwantes, ed., 149–64. Moscow, Idaho: University of Idaho Press, 1994.

– *Captured Heritage: The Scramble for Northwest Coast Artifacts*. Seattle: University of Washington Press, 1985.

– "Tricks of the Trade: Northwest Coast Artifact Collecting, 1875–1925." *Canadian Historical Review* 63, 4 (1982): 439–60.

– "The Origins of Canadian Anthropology, 1850–1910." *Journal of Canadian Studies* 8, 1 (1973): 33–45.

Coleman, Thelma. *The Canada Company*. Stratford: County of Perth Historical Board and Cumming Publishers, 1978.

Colwell-Chanthaphonh and T.J. Ferguson, eds. *Collaboration in Archaeological Practice: Engaging Descendant Communities*. Lanham: AltaMira Press, 2008.

Conant, Thomas. *Life in Canada*. Toronto: William Briggs, 1903.

Conaty, Gerald T. "The Repatriation of Blackfoot Sacred Material: Two Approaches." *Anthropologie et Sociétés* 28, 2 (2004): 63–81.

– "Canada's First Nations and Museums: A Saskatchewan Experience." *International Journal of Museum Management and Curatorship* 8 (1989): 407–13.

– and Janes, Robert R. "Issues of Repatriation: A Canadian View." *European Review of Native American Studies* 11, 2 (1997): 31–7.

Connolly, John. "Archeology in Nova Scotia and New Brunswick Between 1863 and 1914 and Its Relationship to the Development of North America Archeology." *Man in the Northeast* 13 (1977): 3–34.

Cook, Stella M. *The Women's Canadian Historical Society of Toronto: Seventy Years of History, 1895–1965*. Transaction 29. Toronto: The Women's Canadian Historical Society of Toronto, 1970.

Cooper, Karen Coody. *Spirited Encounters: American Indians Protest Museum Policies and Practices*. Lanham: AltaMira Press, 2008.

– and Nicolasa I. Sandoval, eds. *Living Homes for Cultural Expression: North American Native Perspectives on Creating Community Museums*. Washington, DC, and New York: National Museum of the American Indian, 2006.

Copway, George. *Indian Life and Indian History by an Indian Author: Embracing the Traditions of the North American Indians Regarding Themselves, Particularly of that most Important of all the Tribes, the Ojibways, by the Celebrated Kah-ge-ga-gah-bowh; Known also by the English name of George Copway*. Boston: A. Colby, 1858.

– *The Life, Letters, and Speeches of Kah-ge-ga-gah-bowh, or G. Copway, Chief, Ojibway Nation*. New York: S.W. Benedict, 1850.

Cotton, George G. "Mississauga." *Rod and Gun in Canada* (February 1904): 449–59.

Coyne, James H. *The Country of the Neutrals (as Far as Comprised in the County of Elgin) from Champlain to Talbot*. St Thomas: Times Print, 1895.

Cruikshank, Julie. *Do Glaciers Listen? Local Knowledge, Colonial Encounters, and Social Imagination*. Vancouver: University of British Columbia Press, 2005.

Cumberland, F. Barlow. *Catalogue and Notes of the Oronhyatekha Historical Collection*. Toronto: Hunter, Rose Company, 1904.

Cybulski, J.S. et al. "Committee Report: Statement on the Excavation, Treatment, Analysis and Disposition of Human Skeletal Remains from Archaeological Sites in Canada." *Canadian Review of Physical Anthropology* 1, 1 (1979): 32–6.

Danziger, Jr, Edmund Jefferson. *The Chippewas of Lake Superior*. Norman: University of Oklahoma Press, 1978.

Darnell, Regna. *Invisible Genealogies: A History of Americanist Anthropology*. Lincoln and London: University of Nebraska Press, 2001.

– *And Along Came Boas: Continuity and Revolution in Americanist Anthropology*. Amsterdam and Philadelphia: J. Benjamins, 1998.

– "The Boasian Text Tradition and the History of Canadian Anthropology." *Culture* 17 (1992): 39–48.

– *Edward Sapir: Linguist, Anthropologist, Humanist*. Berkeley: University of California Press, 1990.

– "The Uniqueness of Canadian Anthropology: Issues and Problems." *Proceedings of the Second Congress, Canadian Ethnology Society*. Jim Freedman and Jerome H. Barkow, eds, vol. 2, 399–416. Canadian Ethnology Service Paper 28. Mercury Series. Ottawa: National Museums of Canada, 1975.

Davis, Hester A. "Looting Graves/Buying and Selling Artefacts: Facing Reality in the US." *Illicit Antiquities: The Theft of Culture and the Extinction of Archaeology*. Neil Brodie and Kathryn Walker Tubb, eds, 235–40. London and New York: Routledge, 2002.

Dawson, K.C.A. "A History of Archaeology in Northern Ontario to 1983 with Bibliographic Contributions." *Ontario Archaeology* 42 (1984): 27–92.

Deetz, James. *In Small Things Forgotten: The Archaeology of Early American Life*. New York: Doubleday, 1996.

Deloria, Philip J. *Playing Indian*. New Haven: Yale University Press, 1998.

Deloria, Jr, Vine. *Evolution, Creationism, and Other Modern Myths: A Critical Inquiry*. Golden: Fulcrum, 2002.

– *Red Earth, White Lies: North America and the Myth of Scientific Fact*. New York: Scribner, 1995.

Densmore, Frances. *Chippewa Customs*. Smithsonian Institution, Bureau of American Ethnology Bulletin 86. Washington, DC: Government Printing Office, 1929.

Destination Nord. *Guide du Champlain Circuit: Commémoration de Nouvelle-France*. 2004. www.circuitchamplain.com/doc_pdf/guide_400.pdf (31 July 2009).

Dewar, Elaine. *Bones: Discovering the First Americans*. Toronto: Random House Canada, 2001.

Dick-Lauder, Mrs et al. *Pen and Pencil Sketches of Wentworth Landmarks: A Series of Articles Descriptive of Quaint Places and Interesting Localities in the Surrounding County*. Hamilton: Spectator Printing Co., 1897.

Dickson, James. *Camping in the Muskoka Region*. Toronto: C. Blackett Robinson, 1886.

Dickson, Lovat. *The Museum Makers: The Story of the Royal Ontario Museum*. Toronto: Royal Ontario Museum, 1986.

Doherty, Ken. "The Common Thread: One Hundred and Fifty Years of Museums in Peterborough." *Ontario History* 86, 2 (1994): 133–48.

Dongoske, Kurt E., Mark Aldenderfer, and Karen Doehner, eds. *Working Together: Native Americans and Archaeologists*. Washington, DC: Society for American Archaeology, 2000.

Downey, Roger. *Riddle of the Bones: Politics, Science, Race, and the Story of Kennewick Man*. New York: Copernicus, 2000.

Doxtator, Deborah. "The Implications of Canadian Nationalism for Aboriginal Cultural Expression." *Curatorship: Indigenous Perspectives in Post-Colonial Societies*. Directorate Paper 8. Mercury Series. Hull: Canadian Museum of Civilization, with the Commonwealth Association of Museums, and the University of Victoria, 1996.

– "The Idea of the Indian and the Development of Iroquoian Museums." *Museum Quarterly* 14, 2 (1985): 20–6.

Duchesne, Raymond and Paul Carle. "L'ordre des Choses: Cabinets et Musées d'Histoire Naturelle au Québec (1824–1900)." *Revue d'Histoire de l'Amérique Française* 41, 1 (1990): 3–30.

Dumont Jr, Clayton W. "The Politics of Scientific Objections to Repatriation." *Wicazo Sa Review* 18, 1 (2003): 109–28.

Duncan, David M. *The Story of the Canadian People*. Toronto: Morang and Company, 1905.

Duncan, Dorothy. "From Mausoleums to Malls: What Next?" *Ontario History* 86, 2 (1994): 107–18.

Duncan, George W.J. "A.J. Clark (1876–1934) Artist, Historian and Avocational Archaeologist." *The York Pioneer* 97 (2002): 25–33.

Durrans, Brian. "The Future of the Other: Changing Cultures on Display in Ethnographic Museums." *The Museum Time Machine: Putting Cultures on Display*. Robert Lumley, ed., 144–68. London and New York: Routledge, 1988.

Dwight, Theodore. *The Northern Traveller, Containing the Routes to Niagara, Quebec, and the Springs, with the Tour of New-England and the Route to the Coal Mines of Pennsylvania*. New York: A.T. Goodrich, 1826.

Echo-Hawk, Roger C. "Ancient History in the New World: Integrating Oral Traditions and the Archaeological Record in Deep Time." *American Antiquity* 65, 2 (2000): 267–90.

– and Walter R. Echo-Hawk. *Battlefields and Burial Grounds: The Indian Struggle to Protect Ancestral Graves in the United States*. Minneapolis: Lerner Publications, 1994.

Echo-Hawk, Walter R. and Roger C. Echo-Hawk. "Repatriation, Reburial, and Religious Rights." *American Indians in American History, 1870–2001*. Sterling Evans, ed., 177–93. Westport: Praeger Publishers, 2002.

Elgin Historical and Scientific Institute. *Historical Sketches of the County of Elgin*. St Thomas: Times Print, 1895.

Ellis, Chris J. and Neal Ferris, eds. *The Archaeology of Southern Ontario to A.D. 1650.* Occasional Publications of the London Chapter No. 5. London: Ontario Archaeological Society Inc., 1990.

Epp, Henry T. and Leslie E. Sponsel. "Major Personalities and Developments in Canadian Anthropology, 1860–1940." *Na'páo* 10, 1–2 (1980): 7–13.

Evelyn, Douglas E. "Launching an International Institution of Living Cultures: The Smithsonian's National Museum of the American Indian." *History News* 60, 3 (2005): 7–11.

Farrell, Wilfrid. *The History of the London and Middlesex Historical Society.* London: Farrell Publishing, 1992.

*Fenelon Falls: Prettiest Summer Resort on Kawartha Lakes: 1,000 Feet above Sea Level, Absolutely No Hay Fever, Boating, Fishing and Hunting Unexcelled.* Fenelon Falls: Gazette Print, 190?.

Fenton, William N. and Donald B. Smith. "Pabookowaih Unmasked." *Anthropology, History, and American Indians: Essays in Honor of William Curtis Sturtevant.* William L. Merrill and Ives Goddard, eds, 279–84. Smithsonian Contributions to Anthropology 44. Washington, DC: Smithsonian Institution, 2002.

Fenton, William N. *The Great Law and the Longhouse: A Political History of the Iroquois Confederacy.* Norman: University of Oklahoma Press, 1998.

– "Return of Eleven Wampum Belts to the Six Nations Iroquois Confederacy on Grand River, Canada." *Ethnohistory* 36, 4 (1989): 392–410.

– *The False Faces of the Iroquois.* Norman: University of Oklahoma Press, 1987.

– "The New York State Wampum Collection: The Case for the Integrity of Cultural Treasures." *Proceedings of the American Philosophical Society* 115, 6 (1971): 437–61.

– and Gertrude P. Kurath. "The Feast of the Dead, or Ghost Dance at Six Nations Reserve, Canada." *Symposium on Local Diversity in Iroquois Culture.* William N. Fenton, ed. *Bureau of American Ethnology Bulletin* 149 (1951): 139–65.

Ferris, Neal. "Between Colonial and Indigenous Archaeologies: Legal and Extra-Legal Ownership of the Archaeological Past in North America." *Canadian Journal of Archaeology* 27, 2 (2003): 154–90.

Fine-Dare, Kathleen S. *Grave Injustice: The American Indian Repatriation Movement and NAGPRA.* Lincoln: University of Nebraska Press, 2002.

Fingard, Judith. "From Eliza Frame to Phyllis Blakeley: Women and the Nova Scotia Historical Society." *Journal of the Royal Nova Scotia Historical Society* 8 (2005): 1–16.

Fish, Adam. "Indigenous Bodies in Colonial Courts: Anthropological Science and the (Physical) Laws of the Remaining Human." *Wicazo Sa Review* 21, 1, (2006): 77–95.

Fitting, J.E., ed. *The Development of North American Archaeology: Essays in the History of Regional Traditions*. Garden City: Anchor Press, 1973.

Foster, W. Jane. "Pioneers in History: The Story of the Lennox and Addington Historical Society from 1907–1977." *Lennox and Addington Historical Society Papers and Records* 16 (1978): 11–61.

Foster, Mrs W. Garland. *The Mohawk Princess: Being Some Account of the Life of Tekahion-Wake* (E. Pauline Johnson). Vancouver: Lion's Gate Publishing Company, 1931.

*Four Years on the Georgian Bay: Life among the Rocks, Information for Tourists, Campers, and Prospective Settlers. Portraying the Fishing and Hunting Grounds, Islands and Summer Resorts, to French River, with Scenic Views and Descriptions*. Toronto: Copp, Clark Company, 1888.

Fox, William A. "Aboriginal Peoples, Archaeology and Parks Canada." *Plains Anthropologist* 44, 170 (1999): 35–42.

– "The Freelton/Misner Site Looting and Prosecution." *Arch Notes* (July/ Aug 1985): 31–9.

Francis, Daniel. *The Imaginary Indian: The Image of the Indian in Canadian Culture*. Vancouver: Arsenal Press, 1992.

Frank, Gloria Jean. "'That's My Dinner on Display': A First Nations Reflection on Museum Culture." *BC Studies* 125–6 (2000): 163–78.

Freedman, Jim, ed. *The History of Canadian Anthropology*. Canadian Ethnology Society Proceedings 3. Mercury Series. Ottawa: National Museums of Canada, 1976.

Friesen, Gerald. "The Manitoba Historical Society: A Centennial History." *Manitoba History* 4 (1982): 2–9.

Frost, Stanley Brice. "Science Education in the Nineteenth Century: The Natural History Society of Montreal, 1827–1925." *McGill Journal of Education* 17, 1 (1982): 31–43.

Gabriel, Mille and Jens Dahl, eds. *Utimut: Past Heritage – Future Partnerships: Discussions on Repatriation in the 21st Century*. Copenhagen: Eks-Skolens Trykkeri, 2008.

Gagnon, Hervé. "The Natural History Society of Montreal's Museum and the Socio-Economic Significance of Museums in Nineteenth Century Canada." *Scientia Canadensis* 18, 2 (1994): 103–35.

Galway, Elizabeth A. *From Nursery Rhymes to Nationhood: Children's Literature and the Construction of Canadian Identity*. New York and London: Routledge, 2008.

Garrad, Charles. *Commemorating the 350th Anniversary of the Dispersal of the Wyandots from Ontario, and Celebrating Their Return*. Petun Research Institute Bulletin 36 (2003): 1–17. www.wyandot.org/petun/ RB%2031%20to%2036/PRI36.pdf (31 July 2009) .

– *The Huron Institute and the Petun*. Petun Research Institute Bulletin 27 (1999): 1–16. www.wyandot.org/petun/RB%2021%20to%2030/ PRI27.pdf (31 July 2009).

– *Andrew F. Hunter and the Petun.* Petun Research Institute Bulletin 25 (1999): 1–17. www.wyandot.org/petun/RB%2021%20to%2030/PRI25. pdf (31 July 2009).

Gerson, Carole. *A Purer Taste: The Writing and Reading of Fiction in English in Nineteenth-Century Canada.* Toronto: University of Toronto Press, 1989.

– and Veronica Strong-Boag, eds. *E. Pauline Johnson Tekahionwake: Collected Poems and Selected Prose.* Toronto: University of Toronto Press, 2002.

Gidney, R.D. and W.P.J. Millar. *Professional Gentlemen: The Professions in Nineteenth-Century Ontario.* Toronto: University of Toronto Press, 1994.

– "'Beyond the Measure of the Golden Rule': The Contribution of the Poor to Medical Science in Nineteenth-Century Ontario." *Ontario History* 86, 3 (1994): 219–35.

Gillam, Robyn. *Hall of Mirrors: Museums and the Canadian Public.* Banff: Banff Centre Press, 2001.

Glassie, Henry. *Material Culture.* Bloomington: Indiana University Press, 1999.

*Glenbow* 8, 1 (1988). Special Issue. The Spirit Sings: Artistic Traditions of Canada's First Peoples.

Goldie, Terry. *Fear and Temptation: The Image of the Indigene in Canadian, Australian and New Zealand Literatures.* Montreal and Kingston: McGill-Queen's Press, 1989.

Grand Council of the Haudenosaunee. *Haudenosaunee Confederacy Policy on False Face Masks.* www.peace4turtleisland.org/pages/maskpolicy.htm (31 July 2009).

Grand General Indian Council. *Minutes of the Eighth Grand General Indian Council, Held upon the Cape Croker Indian Reserve, County of Bruce, from September 10th to September 15th, 1884.* Hagersville: The Indian Publishing Company, nd.

Grand Trunk Railway Company of Canada. *Annotated Time Table of the Tour Through Canada of Their Royal Highnesses the Duke and Duchess of Cornwall and York.* Montreal: Grand Trunk Railway of Canada, 1901.

– *The Tourist Route of America. Pen and Sunlight Sketches of Scenery Reached by the Grand Trunk Railway and Connections, With Summer Routes and Fares to Principal Points Including Niagara Falls, Thousand Islands, Rapids of the St Lawrence, Montreal, Quebec, Parry Sound, Georgian Bay, Muskoka Lakes, Adirondacks, Lake St John, Mackinac Island, Midland District Lakes, The White Mountains, The Saguenay River, Rangeley Lakes and the Sea-Shore.* Grand Trunk Railway of Canada, 1895.

– *A Few of the Many Points of Interest Noted in a Tour of Canada Over the System of the Grand Trunk Railway Co.* Toronto: A.H. Dixon, 1889.

Grant, George Monro, ed. *Picturesque Canada; The Country As it Was and Is.* Vols 1–2. Toronto: Belden Bros, 1882.

Gray, Charlotte. *Flint and Feather: The Life and Times of E. Pauline Johnson, Tekahionwake.* Toronto: HarperFlamingo Canada, 2002.

Great Lakes Research Alliance for the Study of Aboriginal Arts and Cultures. www.grasac.org/gks/gks_about.php (2 August 2009).

Gruber, Jacob W. "Ethnographic Salvage and the Shaping of Anthropology." *American Anthropologist* 72, 6 (1970): 1289–99.

– "Horatio Hale and the Development of American Anthropology." *Proceedings of the American Philosophical Society* 111, 1 (1967): 5–37.

Guest, W.E. "Ancient Indian Remains Near Prescott, C.W." *Annual Report of the Board of Regents of the Smithsonian Institution* (1856): 271–6.

Gulliford, Andrew. *Sacred Objects and Sacred Places: Preserving Tribal Traditions.* Boulder: University Press of Colorado, 2000.

– "Curation and Repatriation of Sacred and Tribal Objects." *The Public Historian* 14, 3 (1992): 23–38.

Haig-Brown, Celia and David A. Nock, eds. *With Good Intentions: Euro-Canadian and Aboriginal Relations in Colonial Canada.* Vancouver: University of British Columbia Press, 2006.

Hale, Horatio. "Indian Wampum Records." *Popular Science Monthly* 50 (1896–7): 481–6.

– "Four Huron Wampum Records: A Study of Aboriginal American History and Mnemonic Symbols." *Journal of the Anthropological Institute of Great Britain and Ireland* 26 (1897): 221–47.

– *An Iroquois Condoling Council: A Study of Aboriginal American Society and Government.* Ottawa, 1895.

– *Chief George H.M. Johnson, Onwanonsyshon: His Life and Work among the Six Nations.* New York, 1885.

– *The Iroquois Book of Rites.* Philadelphia: D.G. Brinton, 1883.

Halpin, Marjorie M. "Museum Review: 'The Spirit Sings: Artistic Traditions of Canada's First Peoples.'" *Culture* 8, 1 (1988): 89–93.

Hamil, Fred C. *The Valley of the Lower Thames, 1640 to 1850.* Toronto: University of Toronto Press, 1951.

Hamilton Association for the Advancement of Literature, Science and Art. *100th Anniversary, 1857–1957.* Hamilton: Davis-Lisson, 1958.

– *Proceedings of the Jubilee Celebration of the Hamilton Scientific Association, held at the Hamilton Conservatory of Music, November 8th, 1907: 1857–1907.* Hamilton: Heath and Hignelel, 1907.

– *Journal and Proceedings of the Hamilton Association.* Vols 1–30. 1882–1922.

– *Constitution and By-Laws of the Hamilton Association, Instituted 1857.* Hamilton: Gillespy and Robertson, 1857.

Hamilton, James Cleland. *The Georgian Bay: An Account of Its Position, Inhabitants, Mineral Interests, Fish, Timber and Other Resources.* Toronto: Carswell Company, Limited, 1893.

Hamilton, Michelle A. "'Anyone not on the list might as well be dead': Aboriginal Peoples and the Censuses of Canada, 1851–1916." *Journal of the Canadian Historical Association* 18, 1 (2007): 57–79.

Hanna, Margaret G. "Old Bones, New Reality: A Review of Issues and Guidelines Pertaining to Repatriation." *Canadian Journal of Archaeology* 27, 2 (2003): 234–57.

– "A Time to Choose: 'Us' versus 'Them,' or 'All of Us Together.'" *Plains Anthropologist* 44, 170 (1999): 43–53.

Harper, Russell. *The Early History of Haldimand County.* Caledonia: Grand River Sachem, 1950.

Harrington, M.R. "Vestiges of Material Culture among the Canadian Delawares." *American Anthropologist* 10, 3 (1908): 408–18.

Harris, Marvin. *The Rise of Anthropological Theory: A History of Theories of Culture.* Walnut Creek: AltaMira Press, 2001.

Harris, William Richard. *The Catholic Church in the Niagara Peninsula, 1626–1895.* Toronto: William Briggs, 1895.

Harrison, Julia and Regna Darnell, eds. *Historicizing Canadian Anthropology.* Vancouver: University of British Columbia Press, 2006.

Harrison, Julia. "Shaping Collaboration: Considering Institutional Culture." *Museum Management and Curatorship* 20, 3 (2005): 195–212.

– "Listening for the Conversation: The First People's Hall at the Canadian Museum of Civilization." *Anthropologica* 45, 2 (2003): 293–9.

– "'The Spirit Sings' and the Future of Anthropology." *Anthropology Today* 4, 6 (1988): 6–9.

– "The Great White Coverup." *Native Studies Review* 3, 2 (1987): 47–59.

Harvey, Kathryn. "Location, Location, Location: David Ross McCord and the Makings of Canadian History." *Journal of the Canadian Historical Association* 19 (2008): 57–81.

Haudenosaunee Standing Committee on Burial Rules and Regulations. *Haudenosaunee Policy on Wampum.* 2000.

Haycock, Ronald. *The Image of the Indian: The Canadian Indian as a Subject and a Concept in a Sampling of the Popular National Magazines Read in Canada, 1900–1970.* Waterloo: Waterloo Lutheran University, 1971.

Heidenreich, Conrad E. *Huronia: A History and Geography of the Huron Indians, 1600–1650.* Toronto: McClelland and Stewart, 1971.

Henry, Alexander. *Travels and Adventures in Canada and the Indian Territories Between the Years 1760 and 1776.* James Bain, ed. Boston: Little, Brown and Company, 1901.

Herrington, Walter S. *History of the County of Lennox and Addington.* Toronto: Macmillan, 1913.

Highet, Megan J. "Body Snatching and Grave Robbing: Bodies for Science." *History and Anthropology* 16, 4 (2005): 415–40.

Historical Committee, Nottawasaga Centennial Celebration. *Introduction to Nottawasaga "The Outburst of the Iroquois": Some Gleanings of the*

*Historical Committee in Connection with the Centennial Celebration of the First Settlements in the Township*. Duntroon, 1967.

*History of the County of Middlesex, Canada. From the Earliest Time to the Present; Containing an Authentic Account of Many Important Matters relating to the Settlement, Progress and General History of the County; and Including a Department Devoted to the Preservation of Personal and Private Records, etc*. London: Free Press Printing Company, 1889.

Hodgins, J. George. *A History of Canada and of the Other British Provinces of North America*. Montreal: John Lovell, 1866.

– *A School History of Canada and of the other British North American Provinces*. Montreal: John Lovell, 1865.

Holden, Mrs John Rose. *Burlington Bay, Beach, and Heights, in History*. Hamilton: W.J. Lancefield, 1898.

Holm, Margaret and David Pokotylo. "From Policy to Practice: A Case Study in Collaborative Exhibits with First Nations." *Canadian Journal of Archaeology* 21, 1 (1997): 33–43.

Hooper-Greenhill, Eilean. *Museums and the Shaping of Knowledge*. London and New York: Routledge, 1992.

Hulse, Elizabeth, ed. *Thinking With Both Hands: Sir Daniel Wilson in the Old World and the New*. Toronto: University of Toronto Press, 1999.

Hunter, Andrew F. *Historic Sites of Tay*. Bulletin of the Simcoe County Pioneer and Historical Society, November 1911. Barrie: Simcoe County Pioneer and Historical Society, 1911.

– *A History of Simcoe County*. Vols 1–2. Barrie: County Council, 1909.

– *Huron Village Sites Being an Appendix to the Report of the Minister of Education for the Year 1906*. Toronto: L.K. Cameron, 1907.

– *Notes on Sites of Indian Villages, Townships of North and South Orillia (Simcoe Co.)*. Toronto: Warwick Bros and Rutter, 1904.

– *Notes on Sites of Huron Villages in the Township of Oro (Simcoe County)*. Toronto: Warwick Bros and Rutter, 1903.

– *Notes on Sites of Huron Villages in the Township of Medonte (Simcoe Co.)*. Toronto: Warwick Bros and Rutter, 1902.

– *Notes on Sites of Huron Villages in the Township of Tay (Simcoe County)*. Toronto: Warwick Bros and Rutter, 1900.

– *Notes of Sites of Huron Village in the Township of Tiny (Simcoe County) and Adjacent Parts. Prepared with a View to the Identification of those Villages Visited and Described by Champlain and the Early Missionaries*. Toronto: Warwick Bros and Rutter, 1899.

– "New Aspects of the Old Huron Missions." *Massey's Magazine* (May 1897): 350–4.

– *National Characteristics and Migrations of the Hurons as Indicated by Their Remains in North Simcoe*. Toronto, 1892.

Huron Institute. *Papers and Records*. Vols 1–3. 1909–39.

Hutchison, Helen. "Introduction." *Lennox and Addington Historical Society Papers and Records* 14 (1972): 5–10.

Hyder, William D. and Lawrence L. Loendorf. "The Role of Avocational Archaeologists in Rock Art Research." *Discovering North American Rock Art*. Lawrence L. Loendorf, Christopher Chippindale, and David S. Whitley, eds, 228–39. Tucson: University of Arizona Press, 2005.

*Illustrated Atlas of the County of Simcoe*. Toronto: H. Beldon and Co., 1881.

*Illustrated Historical Atlas of the County of Elgin Ontario*. Toronto: H.R. Page and Co., 1877.

Jacknis, Ira. "A New Thing? The NMAI in Historical and Institutional Perspective." *American Indian Quarterly* 30, 3–4 (2006): 511–42.

– *The Storage Box of Tradition: Kwakiutl Art, Anthropologists, and Museums, 1881–1981*. Washington, DC: Smithsonian Institution Press, 2002.

– "George Hunt, Kwakiutl Photographer." *Anthropology and Photography, 1860–1920*. Elizabeth Edwards, ed., 143–51. New Haven and London: Yale University Press, 1992.

– "George Hunt, Collector of Indian Specimens." *Chiefly Feasts: The Enduring Kwakiutl Potlatch*. Aldona Jonaitis, ed., 177–224. Seattle and New York: University of Washington Press and American Museum of Natural History, 1991.

Jacobson, Lisa, ed. "Review Roundtable: The National Museum of the American Indian." *The Public Historian* 28, 2 (2006): 47–90.

Jalland, Patricia. *Death in the Victorian Family*. Oxford: Oxford University Press, 1996.

Jameson, Anna Brownell. *Winter Studies and Summer Rambles in Canada*. Vols 1–3. London: Saunders and Otley, 1838.

Janes, Robert R. and Gerald T. Conaty, eds. *Looking Reality in the Eye: Museums and Social Responsibility*. Calgary: University of Calgary Press and the Museums Association of Saskatchewan, 2005.

Janes, Robert R. "Personal, Academic and Institutional Perspectives on Museums and First Nations." *Canadian Journal of Native Studies* 14, 1 (1994): 147–56.

Jarrell, Richard A. "The Rise and Decline of Science at Quebec, 1824–1844." *Social History/Histoire Sociale* 10, 19 (1977): 77–91.

Jeffers, J. Frith. *History of Canada for the Use of Schools*. Toronto: James Campbell and Son, 1875.

Jenness, Diamond. *The Ojibwa Indians of Parry Island, Their Social and Religious Life*. National Museum of Canada Bulletin 78, Anthropological Series 17. Ottawa: J.O. Patenaude, 1935.

Johansen, Bruce E. "Kennewick Man: The Facts, the Fantasies, and the Stakes." *Enduring Legacies: Native American Treaties and Contemporary Controversies*. Bruce E. Johansen, ed., 283–303. Westport: Praeger Publishers, 2004.

Johnson, E. Pauline. *The Shagganappi*. Toronto: William Briggs, 1913.

Johnson, Elias. *Legends, Traditions and Laws, of the Iroquois, or Six Nations, and History of the Tuscarora Indians.* Lockport: Union Print. and Pub. Co., 1881.

Johnson, Evelyn H.C. "Chief John Smoke Johnson." *Ontario Historical Society Papers and Records* 12 (1914): 102–13.

Johnson, William Frederick. *Arkona Through the Years, 1821–1976.* Forest: J.B. Pole, 1976.

Johnston, Basil. *Ojibway Ceremonies.* Toronto: McClelland and Stewart, 1982.

Johnston, James. *Aurora: Its Early Beginnings.* Aurora: Aurora and District Historical Society, 1972.

Johnston, Richard B. *Archaeology of Rice Lake, Ontario.* Anthropology Papers 19. Ottawa: National Museum of Canada, 1968.

Jonaitis, Aldona. *The Yuquot Whalers' Shrine.* Seattle: University of Washington Press, 1999.

Jones, Edwin Bassett. *The Recollections of Edwin Bassett Jones.* With an Introduction by Grace Jones Morgan. 1974.

Jones, P.E. *Prospectus of "The Indian" A Paper Devoted to the Indians of North America.* Hagersville: Times Printing Company, 1885.

Jones, Peter. *History of the Ojebway Indians; with Especial Reference to their Conversion to Christianity.* London: A.W. Bennett, 1861.

– *Life and Journals of Kah-ke-wa-quo-na-by: (Rev. Peter Jones), Wesleyan Missionary.* Toronto: A. Green, 1860.

Judd, W.W. *Early Naturalists and Natural History Societies in London, Ontario.* London: Phelps Publishing Company, 1979.

Jury, Wilfrid. *Preliminary Report on the Train Farm Site, Simcoe County.* London: University of Western Ontario, 1947.

– and Elsie McLeod Jury. *Sainte-Marie among the Hurons.* Toronto: Oxford University Press, 1954.

Kan, Sergei, ed. *Strangers to Relatives: The Adoption and Naming of Anthropologists in Native North America.* Lincoln: University of Nebraska, 2001.

Kane, Paul. *Wanderings of an Artist among the Indians of North America from Canada to Vancouver's Island and Oregon Through the Hudson's Bay Company's Territory and Back Again.* London: Longman, Brown, Green, Longmans, and Roberts, 1859.

Kapches, Mima. "Henry Montgomery, PhD (1848–1919): Professor of Archaeologic Geology." *Ontario Archaeology* 75 (2003): 29–37.

– "Antiquarians to Archaeologists in Nineteenth-Century Toronto." *Northeast Anthropology* 47 (1994): 87–97.

– "What the People Said: An Archaeological Exchange Revisited (98 Years Later)." Royal Ontario Museum. *Archaeological Newsletter* 213 (1983): 1–4.

Karp, Ivan. "Introduction: Museums and Communities: The Politics of Public Culture." *Museums and Communities: The Politics of Public*

*Culture*. Ivan Karp, Christine Mullen Kreamer, and Steven D. Lavine, eds, 1–17. Washington, DC, and London: Smithsonian Institution Press, 1992.

– and Steven D. Lavine, eds. *Exhibiting Cultures: The Poetics and Politics of Museum Display*. Washington, DC, and London: Smithsonian Institution Press, 1991.

Karttunen, Frances E. *Between Worlds: Interpreters, Guides, and Survivors*. New Brunswick: Rutgers University Press, 1994.

Kaye, Frances W. *Hiding the Audience: Viewing Arts and Arts Institutions on the Prairies*. Edmonton: University of Alberta Press, 2003.

Ke-Che-Ah-Gah-Me-Qua. *The Life of Capt. Joseph Brant (Thayendanegea), an Account of his Re-interment at Mohawk, 1850, and of the Corner Stone Ceremony in the Erection of the Brant Memorial, 1886*. Brantford: B.H. Rothwell, 1886.

Keller, Betty. *Pauline Johnson: First Aboriginal Voice of Canada*. Montreal: XYZ Publishing, 1999.

– *Pauline: A Biography of Pauline Johnson*. Vancouver: Douglas and McIntyre, 1981.

Kenyon, Walter A. *Mounds of Sacred Earth: Burial Mounds of Ontario*. ROM Archaeology Monograph 9. Toronto: University of Toronto Press, 1986.

Kerber, Jordan E., ed. *Cross-Cultural Collaboration: Native Peoples and Archaeology in the Northeastern United States*. Lincoln and London: University of Nebraska Press, 2006.

Key, Archie F. *Beyond Four Walls: The Origins and Development of Canadian Museums*. Toronto: McClelland and Stewart, 1973.

Kidd, K.E. "Sixty Years of Ontario Archeology." *Archeology of Eastern United States*. James B. Griffin, ed., 71–82. Chicago and London: University of Chicago Press, 1952.

Killan, Gerald. *David Boyle: From Artisan to Archaeologist*. Toronto: University of Toronto Press, 1983.

– "The Canadian Institute and the Origins of the Ontario Archaeological Tradition, 1851–1884." *Ontario Archaeology* 34 (1980): 3–16.

– *Preserving Ontario's Heritage: A History of the Ontario Historical Society*. Ottawa: Love Printing Service, 1976.

Killion, Thomas W., ed. *Opening Archaeology: Repatriation's Impact on Contemporary Research and Practice*. Santa Fe: School for Advanced Research Press, 2007.

King, Thomas, Cheryl Calver and Helen Hoy, eds. *The Native in Literature*. Oakville: ECW Press, 1987.

Kirkconnell, Watson. *Victoria County: Centennial History*. Lindsay: Watchman-Warder Press, 1921.

Klesert, Anthony L. and Alan S. Downer, eds. *Preservation on the Reservation: Native Americans, Native American Lands, and Archaeology*. Navajo Nation Papers in Anthropology 26. Window Rock: Navajo National Archaeology Department, 1990.

Knowles, Norman J. *Inventing the Loyalists: The Ontario Loyalist Tradition and the Creation of Usable Pasts*. Toronto: University of Toronto Press, 1997.

Knudson, Ruthann and Bennie C. Keel, eds. *The Public Trust and the First Americans*. Oregon: Oregon State University Press, 1995.

Kreis, Karl Markus. "John O. Brant-Sero's Adventures in Europe." *European Review of Native American Studies* 15, 2 (2001): 27–30.

Krupat, Arnold. *Ethnocriticism: Ethnography, History, Literature*. Berkeley: University of California Press, 1992.

Krupnik, Igor. "'When our words are put to paper': Heritage Documentation and Reversing Knowledge Shift in the Bering Strait Region." *Etudes Inuit/Inuit Studies* 29, 1–2 (2005): 67–90.

– and William W. Fitzhugh, eds. *Gateways: Exploring the Legacy of the Jesup North Pacific Expedition, 1897–1902*. Washington, DC: Arctic Studies Center, National Museum of Natural History, Smithsonian Institution, 2001.

Laidlaw, George E. *Ontario Effigy Pipes in Stone*. Ontario, 1913.

– "Teeth Tools in Canada." *The American Antiquarian and Oriental Journal* 21, 4 (1899): 236–8.

– "Some Copper Implements from the Midland District, Ontario." *The American Antiquarian and Oriental Journal* 21, 2 (1899): 83–90.

– "Horn Relics – Ontario." *The American Antiquarian and Oriental Journal* 20, 2 (1898): 65–71.

– "Miniatures, or Dimunitive Relics." *The American Antiquarian and Oriental Journal* 20, 1 (1898): 37–44.

– "Remains in Ash Beds at Balsam Lake." *The American Antiquarian and Oriental Journal* 19, 5 (1897): 271–5.

– "Aboriginal Remains of Balsam Lake, Ontario." *The American Antiquarian and Oriental Journal* 19, 3 (1897): 138–45.

– "The Aboriginal Remains of Balsam Lake, Ontario." *The American Antiquarian and Oriental Journal* 19, 2 (1897): 68–72.

Langton, H.H. *Sir Daniel Wilson: A Memoir*. Toronto: Thomas Nelson and Sons, 1929.

Lauriston, Victor. *Romantic Kent: The Story of a County, 1626–1952*. Chatham: Shepherd Print Co., 1952.

La Vere, David. *Looting Spiro Mounds: An American King Tut's Tomb*. Norman: University of Oklahoma Press, 2007.

Lawlor, Mary. *Public Native America: Tribal Self-Representations in Casinos, Museums, and Powwows*. New Brunswick: Rutgers University Press, 2006.

Lawson, Barbara. "Exhibiting Agendas: Anthropology at the Redpath Museum (1882–99)." *Anthropologica* 41, 1 (1999): 53–65.

Layton, Robert, ed. *Conflict in the Archaeology of Living Traditions*. London and New York: Rutledge, 1994.

– *Who Needs the Past? Indigenous Values and Archaeology.* London and Boston: Unwin Hyman, 1989.

Leacock, Stephen. *Sunshine Sketches of a Little Town.* London: J. Lane, 1912.

Leighton, Douglas. "Assikinack, Francis." *Dictionary of Canadian Biography.* Vol. 9 (1861–70): 10–11.

Lennox and Addington Historical Society. *Papers and Records.* Vols 1–6. 1909–15.

Lepper, Bradley T. and Robson Bonnichsen, eds. *New Perspectives on the First Americans.* College Station, Texas: Center for the Study of the First Americans, 2004.

Liberty, Margot, ed. *American Indian Intellectuals of the Nineteenth and Early Twentieth Centuries.* Norman: University of Oklahoma Press, 2002.

Lighthall, W.D. *The Master of Life: A Romance of the Five Nations and of Prehistoric Montreal.* Toronto: Musson Book Co. Limited, 1908.

Literary and Historical Society of Quebec. *Centenary Volume of the Literary and Historical Society of Quebec, 1824–1924.* Quebec: L'Evenement Press, 1924.

Littlehales, Edward Baker. *Journal Written by Edward Baker Littlehales (Major of Brigade, etc.) of an Exploratory Tour Partly in Sleighs but Chiefly on Foot, from Navy Hall, Niagara, to Detroit made in the Months of February and March,* A.D. *1793, by His Excellency Lieut.-Gov. Simcoe.* Toronto: Copp, Clark and Company, 1889.

London and Middlesex Historical Society. *Transactions.* Vols 1–9. 1902–18.

Lovis, William A. et al. "Archaeological Perspectives on the NAGPRA: Underlying Principles, Legislative History, and Current Issues." *Legal Perspectives on Cultural Resources.* Jennifer R. Richman and Marion P. Forsyth, eds, 165–84. Walnut Creek: AltaMira Press, 2004.

Macdonald, Joanne. "From Ceremonial Object to Curio: Object Transformation at Port Simpson and Metlakatla, British Columbia in the Nineteenth Century." *Canadian Journal of Native Studies* 10, 2 (1990): 193–217.

Macdonald, Sharon. "Accessing Audiences: Visiting Visitor Books." *Museum and Society* 3, 3 (2005): 119–36.

Mackenzie, William Lyon. *Sketches of Canada and the United States.* London: E. Wilson, 1833.

Mallouf, Robert J. "An Unraveling Rope: The Looting of America's Past." *American Indian Quarterly* 20, 2 (1996): 197–208.

Mann, Barbara Alice. *Native Americans, Archaeologists, and the Mounds.* New York: Peter Lang Publishing, 2003.

Mark, Joan T. *A Stranger in Her Native Land: Alice Fletcher and the American Indians.* Lincoln: University of Nebraska Press, 1988.

– "Francis La Flesche: The American Indian as Anthropologist." *Isis* 73, 269 (1982): 497–510.

Marsh, Edith L. *A History of the County of Grey.* Owen Sound: Fleming
    Publishing Company, 1931.
Maud, Ralph, ed. *The Salish People: The Local Contribution of Charles
    Hill-Tout.* Vols 1–4. Vancouver: Talonbooks, 1978.
Mason, Ronald J. "Archaeology and Native North American Oral
    Traditions." *American Antiquity* 65, 2 (2000): 239–66.
"Massanoga, or Picture Lake." *Rod and Gun in Canada* (September 1901):
    1–3.
McCaffrey, Moira T. "Rononshonni-The Builder: David Ross McCord's
    Ethnographic Collection." *Collecting Native America, 1870–1960.*
    Shepard Krech III and Barbara A. Hail, eds, 43–73. Washington, DC,
    and London: Smithsonian Institution Press, 1999.
– et al. *Wrapped in the Colours of the Earth: Cultural Heritage of the First
    Nations.* Montreal: McCord Museum of Canadian History, 1992.
McIntosh, John. *The Discovery of America by Christopher Columbus and
    the Origins of the North American Indians.* Toronto: W.J. Coates, 1836.
McIntyre, James. *Poems of James McIntyre.* Ingersoll: Chronicle, 1889.
McKeough, George T. "The Early Indian Occupation of Kent." Kent
    Historical Society *Papers and Addresses* 4 (1919): 13–27.
McLachlan, Alexander. *Poems and Songs.* Toronto: Hunter, Rose, 1874.
McLoughlin, Moira. *Museums and the Representation of Native Canadians:
    Negotiating the Borders of Culture.* New York: Garland Publishing,
    1999.
McMillan, Alan D. and Eldon Yellowhorn. *First Peoples in Canada.*
    Vancouver: Douglas and McIntyre, 2004.
McTavish, Lianne and Joshua Dickison. "William Macintosh, Natural
    History and the Professionalization of the New Brunswick Museum,
    1898–1940." *Acadiensis* 36, 2 (2007): 72–90.
McTavish, Lianne. "Learning to See in New Brunswick, 1862–1929."
    *Canadian Historical Review* 87, 4 (2006): 553–81.
Medicine, Beatrice. "Ella C. Deloria: The Emic Voice." *Learning to Be an
    Anthropologist and Remaining "Native": Selected Writings.* Beatrice
    Medicine and Sue-Ellen Jacobs, eds, 269–88. Urbana: University of
    Illinois Press, 2001.
– "The Anthropologist as the Indian's Image-Maker." *Indian Historian* 4, 3
    (1971): 27–9.
Meighan, Clement W. "Another View on Repatriation: Lost to the Public,
    Lost to History." *The Public Historian* 14, 3 (1992): 39–45.
Merrill, William L. et al. "The Return of the Ahayu: da: Lessons for
    Repatriation from Zuni Pueblo and the Smithsonian Institution."
    *Current Anthropology* 34, 5 (1993): 523–67.
Messenger, Phyllis Mauch, ed. *The Ethics of Collecting Cultural Property:
    Whose Culture? Whose Property?* Albuquerque: University of New
    Mexico Press, 1989.

Meyer, Melissa L. and Kerwin Lee Klein. "Native American Studies and the End of Ethnohistory." *Studying Native America: Problems and Prospects*. Russell Thornton, ed., 182–216. Madison: University of Wisconsin Press, 1998.

Michaelsen, Scott. *The Limits of Multiculturism: Interrogating the Origins of American Anthropology*. Minneapolis and London: University of Minnesota Press, 1999.

Mihesuah, Devon A. *Repatriation Reader: Who Owns American Indian Remains?* Lincoln: University of Nebraska Press, 2000.

Miller, Daniel, ed. *Material Cultures: Why Some Things Matter*. London: UCL Press, 1997.

Miller, Pamela et al. *The McCord Family: A Passionate Vision*. Montreal: McCord Museum of Canadian History, 1992.

– *The McCord Museum Archives*. Montreal: McCord Museum of Canadian History, 1992.

Miller, Virginia P. "Silas T. Rand: Nineteenth Century Anthropologist among the Micmac." *Anthropologica* 22, 2 (1980): 235–50.

Mills, Barbara J. and T.J. Ferguson. "Preservation and Research of Sacred Sites by the Zuni Indian Tribe of New Mexico." *Human Organization* 57, 1 (1998): 30–43.

Mills, Stanley. *Lake Medad and Waterdown*. Hamilton, 1937.

Monkman, Leslie. *A Native Heritage: Image of the Indian in English-Canadian Literature*. Toronto: University of Toronto Press, 1981.

Morden, James C. *Historic Niagara Falls*. Niagara Falls: Lindsay Press, Limited, 1932.

Morgan, Cecilia. "'A Wigwam to Westminster': Performing Mohawk Identity in Imperial Britain, 1890s-1990s." *Gender and History* 15, 2 (2003): 319–41.

– "History, Nation and Empire: Gender and Southern Ontario Historical Societies, 1890–1920s." *Canadian Historical Review* 82, 3 (2001): 491–528.

Morgan, Henry James, ed. *The Canadian Men and Women of the Time. A Hand-Book of Canadian Biography*. Toronto: William Briggs, 1898.

Morrison, David A. *Arctic Hunters: The Inuit and Diamond Jenness*. Hull: Canadian Museum of Civilization, 1992.

Moyer, Bill. *This Unique Heritage: The Story of Waterloo County*. Kitchener, 1971.

Muller, Kathryn V. "The Two 'Mystery' Belts of Grand River: A Biography of the Two Row Wampum and the Friendship Belt." *American Indian Quarterly* 31, 1 (2007): 129–64.

Mulvaney, Charles Pelham. *History of the County of Peterborough, Ontario; Containing a History of the County; History of Haliburton County; their Townships, Towns, Schools, Churches, etc.; General and Local Statistics; Biographical Sketches; and an Outline History of the Dominion of Canada*. Toronto: C. Blackett Robinson, 1884.

– *The History of the County of Brant, Ontario, Containing a History of the County: Its Townships, Cities, Schools, Churches, etc., General and Local Statistics, Portraits of Early Settlers and Prominent Men, History of the Six Nation Indians and Captain Joseph Brant (Thayendanegea), History of the Dominion of Canada, Miscellaneous Matters, etc., etc., etc.* Toronto: Warner, Beers and Co., 1883.

*Muse* 6, 3 (1988). Special Issue. First Nations and Museums.

Museum of Anthropology. Reciprocal Research Network. www.moa.ubc/RRN/ (5 September 2009).

Nabokov, Peter. *A Forest of Time: American Indian Ways of History.* Cambridge: Cambridge University Press, 2002.

National Museum of the American Indian. *Facts and Figures from the Grand Opening of the Smithsonian's National Museum of the American Indian.* Press release. October 2004.

– "About the National Museum of the American Indian." www.nmai.si.edu/subpage.cfm?subpage=about (2 August 2009).

Need, Thomas. *Six Years in the Bush; or Extracts from the Journal of a Settler in Upper Canada, 1832–1838.* London: Simpkin, Marshall, 1838.

Niagara Historical Society. *Catalogue of Articles in Historical Room of Niagara Historical Society Collected Since May, 1896.* January 1899.

– *Annual Report.* 1897–1914.

– *Papers.* Vols 1–26. 1897–1914.

– *Niagara Historical Society: Motto, Ducit Amor Patriae, Constitution.* Niagara: 1896?

Nicholas, George P. and Thomas D. Andrews, eds. *At a Crossroads: Archaeology and First Peoples in Canada.* Simon Fraser University Publication 24. Burnaby: Archaeology Press, 1997.

Nicks, Trudy. "Partnerships in Developing Cultural Resources: Lessons from the Task Force on Museums and First Peoples." *Culture* 12, 1 (1992): 87–94.

Noble, Brian. "Niitooii: 'the same that is real': Parallel Practice, Museums, and the Repatriation of Piikani Customary Authority." *Anthropologica* 44, 1 (2002): 113–30.

Noble, William C. "George Edward Laidlaw." *Ontario Archaeology* 81/82 (2006): 73–5.

– "One Hundred and Twenty-Five Years of Archaeology in the Canadian Provinces." *Bulletin of the Canadian Archaeological Association* 4 (1972): 1–78.

Nock, David A. "A Chapter in the Amateur Period of Canadian Anthropology: A Missionary Case Study." *Canadian Journal of Native Studies* 2, 2 (1982): 249–67.

Nowry, Laurence. *Man of Mana, Marius Barbeau: A Biography.* Toronto: NC Press, 1995.

Nurse, Andrew. "'But Now Things Have Changed': Marius Barbeau and the Politics of Amerindian Identity." *Ethnohistory* 48, 3 (2001): 433–72.

Ontario Heritage Foundation. *Avocational Archaeologists: Roles, Needs, and Responsibilities, Proceedings of the Conference and Workshop Held at Trinity College, University of Toronto, 19 January 1991*. Toronto: University of Toronto Press, 1992.

Ontario Historical Society. *Catalogue, Canadian Historical Exhibition Victoria College, Queen's Park, Toronto Under the Patronage of His Excellency the Governor-General and the Countess of Minto*. Toronto: William Briggs, 1899.

– *Annual Report*. 1898–1914.

– *Constitution and By-Laws of the Ontario Historical Society*. Toronto, 1898.

Ottawa Field-Naturalists' Club. *The Ottawa Naturalist*. Vols 1–28. 1887–1915.

– *Transactions of the Ottawa Field-Naturalists' Club*. Vols 1–7. 1879–86.

Ottawa Literary and Scientific Society. *Transactions of the Ottawa Literary and Scientific Society*. Vols 1–4. 1897–1907.

– *Act of Incorporation and By-Laws of the Ottawa Literary and Scientific Society*. Ottawa: Hunter, Rose and Company, 1870.

*Ontario Public School History of England and Canada*. Toronto: Macmillan Company of Canada, 1917.

*Our Holiday Annual and Kent County Almanac for 1883*. Chatham: James Soutar, 1882?

Owsley, Douglas W. and Richard L. Jantz. "Archaeological Politics and Public Interest in Paleoamerican Studies: Lessons from Gordon Creek Woman and Kennewick Man." *American Antiquity* 66, 4 (2001): 565–75.

Parkman, Francis. *The Jesuits in North America in the Seventeenth Century*. Boston: Little, Brown and Company, 1867.

Parvin, Viola Elizabeth. *Authorization of Textbooks for the Schools of Ontario, 1846–1950*. Toronto: University of Toronto Press and Canadian Textbook Publishers' Institute, 1965.

Pass, Forrest D. "'The Wondrous Story and Traditions of the Country': The Native Sons of British Columbia and the Role of Myth in the Formation of an Urban Middle Class." *BC Studies* 151 (2006): 3–38.

Paudash, Robert and Johnson Paudash. Prepared by J. Hampden Burnham. "The Coming of the Mississagas." *Ontario Historical Society Papers and Records* 6 (1905): 7–11.

Pavlik, Steve, ed. *A Good Cherokee, a Good Anthropologist: Papers in Honour of Robert K. Thomas*. Los Angeles: UCLA American Indian Studies Center, 1998.

Pearce, Robert J. "Prehistory and Native Settlement." *London Township: A Rich Heritage 1796–1997*. Alice Gibb, ed., vol. 1, 1–10. Aylmer: Aylmer Express, 2001.

Pearce, Susan, ed. *Museums and the Appropriation of Culture*. London: Athlone Press, 1994.

– *Objects of Knowledge*. London: Athlone Press, 1990.

Peers, Laura and Alison K. Brown, eds. *Museums and Source Communities:
A Routledge Reader*. London and New York: Routledge, 2003.

Pensley, D.S. "The Native American Graves Protection and Repatriation
Act (1990): Where the Native Voice Is Missing." *Wicazo Sa Review* 20, 2
(2005): 37–64.

Petrone, Penny, ed. *First People, First Voices*. Toronto: University of
Toronto Press, 1983.

Petrone, S. Penny. "John Ojijatekha Brant-Sero." *Dictionary of Canadian
Biography*. Vol. 14 (1911–20): 137–9.

Phillips, Ruth B. "Jasper Grant and Edward Walsh: The Gentleman-Soldier
as Early Collector of Great Lakes Indian Art." *Journal of Canadian
Studies* 21, 4 (1986–87): 56–71.

– and Mark Salber Phillips. "Double Take: Contesting Time, Place,
and Nation in the First Peoples Hall of the Canadian Museum of
Civilization." *American Anthropologist* 107, 4 (2005): 694–704.

Pilon, Jean-Luc. "On the Nature of Archaeology in the Ottawa Area and
Archaeological Mysteries." *Ontario Archaeology* 75 (2003): 17–28.

Pioneer and Historical Association of Ontario. *Annual Report*. 1890–97.

Pocius, Gerald L., ed. *Living in a Material World: Canadian and American
Approaches to Material Culture*. St John's: Institute of Social and
Economic Research, Memorial University of Newfoundland, 1991.

Pokotylo, David and Neil Guppy. "Public Opinion and Archaeological
Heritage: Views from Outside the Profession." *American Antiquity* 64, 3
(1999): 400–16.

Porter, Joy. *To be Indian: The Life of Iroquois-Seneca Arthur Caswell
Parker*. Norman: University of Oklahoma Press, 2001.

Powell, Joseph F. *The First Americans: Race, Evolution, and the Origin of
Native Americans*. Cambridge: Cambridge University Press, 2005.

Powell, Shirley, C.E. Garza, and A. Hendricks, "Ethics and Ownership of
the Past: The Reburial and Repatriation Controversy." *Archaeological
Method and Theory* 5, 2 (1993): 1–42.

Pratt, Mary Louise. *Imperial Eyes: Travel Writing and Transculturation*.
London and New York: Routledge, 1992.

Price III, H. Marcus. *Disputing the Dead: US Law on Aboriginal Remains
and Grave Goods*. Columbia and London: University of Missouri Press,
1991.

Prucha, Francis Paul. *Indian Peace Medals in American History*. Lincoln
and London: University of Nebraska Press, 1971.

Radforth, Ian. *Royal Spectacle: The 1860 Visit of the Prince of Wales to
Canada and the United States*. Toronto: University of Toronto Press,
2004.

– "Performance, Politics, and Representation: Aboriginal People and the
1860 Royal Tour of Canada." *Canadian Historical Review* 84, 1 (2003):
1–32.

Raibmon, Paige. *Authentic Indians: Episodes of Encounter from the Late-Nineteenth-Century Northwest Coast.* Durham and London: Duke University Press, 2005.

Reed, T.A. "The Scaddings, a Pioneer Family in York." *Ontario History* 36 (1944): 7–20.

Reed-Danahay, Deborah E., ed. *Auto/Ethnography: Rewriting the Self and the Social.* Oxford and New York: Berg, 1997.

Rempel, Gwen. "The Manitoba Mound Builders: The Making of an Archaeological Myth, 1857–1900." *Manitoba History* 28 (1994): 12–18.

Richling, Barnett. "Diamond Jenness and the National Museum of Canada, 1930–1947." *Curator* 33, 4 (1990): 245–60.

Rider, Peter E., ed. *Studies in History and Museums.* History Division Paper 47. Mercury Series. Hull: Canadian Museum of Civilization, 1994.

Riding In, James, Cal Seciwa, Suzan Shown Harjo, and Walter Echo-Hawk. "Protecting Native American Human Remains, Burial Grounds, and Sacred Places: Panel Discussion." *Wicazo Sa Review* 19, 2 (2004): 169–83.

Riding In, James. "Without Ethics and Morality: A Historical Overview of Imperial Archaeology and American Indians." *Arizona State Law Journal* 24, 1 (1992): 11–34.

Ridington, Robin and Dennis Hastings. *Blessing for a Long Time: The Sacred Pole of the Omaha Tribe.* Lincoln and London: University of Nebraska Press, 1997.

Ridley, Frank. *Archaeology of the Neutral Indian.* Port Credit: The Weekly, 1961.

Riegel, Henrietta. "Into the Heart of Irony: Ethnographic Exhibitions and the Politics of Difference." *Theorizing Museums: Representing Identity and Diversity in a Changing World.* Sharon Macdonald and Gordon Fyfe, eds, 83–104. Oxford: Blackwell Publishers, 1996.

Rogers, Edward S. and Donald B. Smith, eds. *Aboriginal Ontario: Historical Perspectives on the First Nations.* Toronto: Dundurn Press, 1994.

Roness, Lori Ann and Kent McNeil. "Legalizing Oral History: Proving Aboriginal Claims in Canadian Courts." *Journal of the West* 39, 3 (2000): 66–74.

Rosenwig, Robert M. "Ethics in Canadian Archaeology: An International, Comparative Analysis." *Canadian Journal of Archaeology* 21, 2 (1997): 99–114.

Roy, Susan. "'Who Were these Mysterious People?' Cesna:m, the Marpole Midden, and the Dispossession of Aboriginal Lands in British Columbia." *BC Studies* 152 (2006–7): 67–95.

Royal Society of Canada. *Proceedings and Transactions of the Royal Society of Canada.* Series 2. Vols 1–12. 1895–1906.

Ruffins, Fath Davis. "Culture Wars Won and Lost: Ethnic Museums of
the Mall, Part I: The National Holocaust Museum and the National
Museum of the American Indian." *Radical History Review* 68 (1997):
79–100.

Russell, Loris S. *The National Museum of Canada, 1910 to 1960.* Ottawa:
Department of Northern Affairs and National Resources, 1961.

Russell, Steve. "Law and Bones: Religion, Science, and the Discourse of
Empire." *Radical History Review* 99 (2007): 214–26.

Ryerson, Egerton. "Canadian Archology [*sic*]." *Journal of Education for
Upper Canada* 18, 1 (1865): 3–4.

Sagard, Gabriel. *The Long Journey to the Country of the Hurons.* Ed.
George M. Wrong. Trans. H.H. Langton. Toronto: Champlain Society,
1939.

Scadding, Henry. *Toronto of Old: Collections and Recollections Illustrative
of the Early Settlement and Social Life of the Capital of Ontario.*
Toronto: Adam, Stevenson and Co., 1873.

– *On Museums and Other Classified Collections, Temporary or Permanent,
as Instruments of Education in Natural Science.* Toronto, 1871.

Schlereth, Thomas J., ed. *Material Culture Studies in America.* Nashville:
American Association for State and Local History, 1982.

Schmaltz, Peter S. *The Ojibwa of Southern Ontario.* Toronto: University of
Toronto Press, 1991.

Schoolcraft, Henry R. *Historical and Statistical Information, Respecting
the History, Condition and Prospects of the Indian Tribes of the United
States.* Vol. 1. Philadelphia: Lippincott, Grambo, 1851.

– *The Indian in His Wigwam or Characteristics of the Red Race of America
from Original Notes and Manuscripts.* Buffalo: Derby and Hewson,
1848.

Seton, Ernest Thompson. *Two Little Savages, Being the Adventures of Two
Boys Who Lived as Indians, and What They Learned.* New York: Dover
Publications, 1962.

Sheets-Pyenson, Susan. *John William Dawson: Faith, Hope and Science.*
Montreal and Kingston: McGill-Queen's University Press, 1996.

– "'Stones and Bones and Skeletons': The Origins and Development of the
Peter Redpath Museum (1882–1912)." *McGill Journal of Education* 17, 1
(1982): 45–64.

– "Better than a Travelling Circus: Museums and Meetings in Montreal
during the Early 1880s." *Transactions of the Royal Society of Canada* 20.
Series 5 (1982): 499–518.

Shimony, Annemarie Anrod. *Conservatism among the Iroquois at the Six
Nations Reserve.* Syracuse: Syracuse University Press, 1994.

Silverstein-Willmott, Cory. "Object Lessons: An Ojibway Artifact
Unraveled. The Case of the Bag with the Snake Skin Strap." *Textile
History* 34, 1 (2003): 74–81.

Simpson, Moira G. *Making Representations: Museums in the Post-Colonial World*. London and New York: Routledge, 1996.

Sioui, Georges E. *For an Amerindian Autohistory: An Essay on the Foundations of a Social Ethic*. Montreal and Kingston: McGill-Queen's University Press, 1992.

Slight, Benjamin. *Indian Researches; or, Facts Concerning the North American Indians; Including Notices of their Present State of Improvement, in their Social, Civil, and Religious Condition; with Hints for their Future Advancement*. Montreal: J.E.L. Miller, 1844.

Small, H. Beaumont. *The Canadian Handbook and Tourist's Guide Giving a Description of Canadian Lake and River Scenery and Places of Historical Interest with the Best Spots for Fishing and Shooting*. Montreal: M. Longmoore and Co., 1867.

Smily, Frederick, ed. *Canadian Summer Resort Guide: Illustrated Souvenir and Guide Book of some of the Principal Fishing, Hunting, Health and Pleasure Resorts and Tourist and Excursion Routes of Canada, with Tables of Railway and Steamboat Fares and Connections, Hotel Rates, etc.* Toronto: R.G. McLean, 1900.

Smith, Arthur M. "Missionary as Collector: The Role of the Reverend Joseph Annand." *Acadiensis* 26, 2 (1997): 96–111.

Smith, Claire and H. Martin Wobst. *Indigenous Archaeologies: Decolonizing Theory and Practice*. London and New York: Routledge, 2005.

Smith, Donald B. "Jones, Peter Edmund." *Dictionary of Canadian Biography*. Vol. 13 (1901–10): 530–1.

– *Sacred Feathers: The Reverend Peter Jones (Kahkewaquonaby) and the Mississauga Indians*. Lincoln: University of Nebraska, 1987.

– "The Life of George Copway or Kah-ge-ga-gah-bowh (1818–1869) and a Review of His Writings." *Journal of Canadian Studies* 23, 3 (1988): 5–38.

– "The Dispossession of the Mississauga Indians: A Missing Chapter in the Early History of Upper Canada." *Ontario History* 73, 2 (1981): 67–87.

Smith, Joseph Henry. *Historical Sketch of the County of Wentworth and the Head of the Lake*. Hamilton, 1897.

Smith, Pamela Jane and Donald Mitchell, eds. *Bringing Back the Past: Historical Perspectives on Canadian Archaeology*. Archaeological Survey of Canada, Paper 158. Mercury Series. Hull: Canadian Museum of Civilization, 1998.

Smith, Sherry L. "Francis LaFlesche and the World of Letters." *American Indian Quarterly* 25, 4 (2001): 579–603.

Smith, Thaddeus. *Point Au Pelee Island: A Historical Sketch of and an Account of the McCormick Family, Who Were the First White Owners of the Island*. Amherstburg: Echo Printing Company, Limited, 1899.

Society of American Archaeology. Repatriation Policy. www.saa.org/AbouttheSociety/GovernmentAffairs/RepatriationIssues/SAARepatriationPolicy/tabid/242/Default.aspx (2 August 2009).

Spicer, Elizabeth. *A History of the London Public Library, 1899–1905*.
    Occasional Publication 5, London Public Library and Art Museum.
    London: London Public Library and Art Museum, 1967.
*The Spirit Sings: Artistic Traditions of Canada's First Peoples*. Toronto:
    McClelland and Stewart, 1987.
Squier, E. George and E.H. Davis. *Ancient Monuments of the Mississippi
    Valley Comprising the Results of Extensive Original Surveys and
    Explorations*. New York: AMS Press, 1973.
Squires, W. Austin. *The History and Development of the New Brunswick
    Museum (1842–1945)*. Publications of the New Brunswick Museum.
    Administrative Series 2. Saint John: New Brunswick Museum, 1945.
Stanley, Nick, ed. *The Future of Indigenous Museums: Perspectives from the
    Southwest Pacific*. New York: Berghahn Books, 2007.
Stapp, Darby C. and Michael S. Burney. *Tribal Cultural Resource
    Management: The Full Circle to Stewardship*. Walnut Creek: AltaMira
    Press, 2002.
St Denis, Guy. *Tecumseh's Bones*. Montreal and Kingston: McGill-Queen's
    University Press, 2005.
Stevenson, Hugh A. "James H. Coyne: An Early Contributor to Canadian
    Historical Scholarship." *Ontario History* 54, 1 (1962): 25–42.
Strathern, Marilyn. "The Limits of Auto-Anthropology." *Anthropology at
    Home*. Anthony Jackson, ed., 16–37. London and New York: Tavistock
    Publications, 1987.
Strickland, Samuel. *Twenty Seven Years in Canada West, or, the Experience of
    an Early Settler*. Agnes Strickland, ed. Vols 1–2. London: R. Bentley, 1853.
Strong-Boag, Veronica and Carole Gerson. *Paddling Her Own Canoe:
    The Times and Texts of E. Pauline Johnson (Tekahionwake)*. Toronto:
    University of Toronto Press, 2000.
Sullivan, Martin. "Return of the Sacred Wampum Belts of the Iroquois."
    *History Teacher* 26, 1 (1992): 7–14.
Swayze, Nansi. *The Man-Hunters: Jenness, Barbeau, Wintemberg*. Toronto
    and Vancouver: Clarke, Irwin and Co., 1960.
Swidler, Nina et al. *Native Americans and Archaeologists: Stepping Stones to
    Common Ground*. Walnut Creek: AltaMira Press, 1997.
Szasz, Margaret Connell, ed. *Between Indian and White Worlds: The
    Cultural Broker*. Norman: University of Oklahoma Press, 1994.
Talman, James J. "Some Precursors of the Ontario Historical Society."
    *Papers and Records of the Ontario Historical Society* 40 (1948): 13–21.
Taylor, C.J. *Negotiating the Past: The Making of Canada's National
    Historic Parks and Sites*. Montreal and Kingston: McGill-Queen's
    University Press, 1990.
Teather, J. Lynne. "Universities, Museums, and Civic Formation: A Case
    Study of the University of Toronto Museum of Natural Science, 1840–
    1890." *Museum History Journal* 2, 2 (2009): 181–209.

– *The Royal Ontario Museum: A Prehistory, 1830–1914.* Toronto and London: Canada University Press, 2005.
– "'Delighting the Eye and Mending the Heart': Canadian Proprietary Museums of the Early Nineteenth Century." *Ontario History* 94, 1 (2002): 49–77.
Thomas, David Hurst. *Skull Wars: Kennewick Man, Archaeology, and the Battle for Native American Identity.* New York: Basic Books, 2000.
Thompson, Samuel. *Reminiscences of a Canadian Pioneer for the Last Fifty Years: An Autobiography.* Toronto: Hunter, Rose & Company, 1884.
Thorold and Beaverdams Historical Society. *Jubilee History of Thorold Township and Town from the Time of the Red Man to the Present.* Thorold: Thorold Post Printing and Publishing Company, 1897–8.
Thwaites, Reuben G., ed. *The Jesuit Relations and Allied Documents.* Vols 1–73. Cleveland: Burrows, 1896–1901.
Tivy, Mary. "The Local History Museum in Ontario: An Intellectual History, 1851–1985." PhD. dissertation, University of Waterloo, 2006.
– "Museums, Visitors and the Reconstruction of the Past in Ontario." *Material History Review* 37 (1993): 35–51.
– "The Quality of Research Is Definitely Strained: Collections Research in Ontario Community Museums." *Material History Bulletin* 27 (1988): 61–8.
Todd, Henry Cook. *Notes upon Canada and the United States of America. In the Year MDCCCXXXV by A Traveller.* Toronto: W.J. Coates, 1835.
Tooker, Elisabeth. "A Note on the Return of Eleven Wampum Belts to the Six Nations Iroquois Confederacy on Grand River, Canada." *Ethnohistory* 45, 2 (1998): 219–36.
– *An Ethnography of the Huron Indians, 1615–1649.* Midland: Huronia Historical Development Council, 1967.
– "Isaac N. Hurd's Ethnographic Studies of the Iroquois: Their Significance and Ethnographic Value." *Ethnohistory* 27, 4 (1980): 363–9.
Traill, Catharine Parr. *Canadian Crusoes: A Tale of the Rice Lake Plains.* Ed. Agnes Strickland. Toronto: McClelland and Stewart, 1923.
– *Pearls and Pebbles; or Notes of an Old Naturalist.* Toronto: William Briggs, 1895.
– "The Indian Maiden's Grave." *Canadian Magazine of Politics, Science, Art and Literature* 4 (1894–95): 280–2.
Trigger, Bruce G. *The Huron Farmers of the North.* Chicago: Holt, Rinehart and Winston, 1990.
– "A Present of Their Past? Anthropologists, Native People, and Their Heritage." *Culture* 8, 1 (1988): 71–9.
– *Natives and Newcomers: Canada's "Heroic Age" Reconsidered.* Montreal and Kingston: McGill-Queen's University Press, 1985.
– "Indians and Ontario History." *Ontario History* 74, 4 (1982): 246–57.
– "Giants and Pygmies: The Professionalization of Canadian Archaeology." *Towards a History of Archaeology Being the Papers Read at the First*

*Conference on the History for Archaeology in Aarhus, 29 August–2 September 1978.* Glyn Daniel, ed., 69–84. London: Thames and Hudson, 1981.
– "Archaeology and the Image of the Indian." *American Antiquity* 45, 4 (1980): 662–76.
– "William J. Wintemberg: Iroquoian Archaeologist." *Essays in Northeastern Anthropology in Memory of Marian E. White.* William E. Engelbrecht and Donald K. Grayson, eds, 5–21. Occasional Publications in Northeastern Anthropology 5. Rindge: Franklin Pierce College, 1978.
– *The Children of Aataentsic: A History of the Huron People to 1660.* Montreal and Kingston: McGill-Queen's University Press, 1976.
– "Sir Daniel Wilson: Canada's First Anthropologist." *Anthropologica* 8, 1 (1966): 3–28.
– "Sir John William Dawson: A Faithful Anthropologist." *Anthropologica* 8, 1 (1966): 351–9.
United Empire Loyalists Association of Ontario. *Annual Transactions.* Vols 1–7. 1897–1916.
Vaccarelli, Vito. "Nineteenth Century Archaeological Thought in Ontario: David Boyle and the Mound Builder Myth." *Origins of the People of the Longhouse: Proceedings of the 21st Annual Symposium of the Ontario Archaeological Society.* André Bekerman and Gary Warrick, eds, 129–39. North York: OAS, 1995.
Van Dusen, Conrad. *The Indian Chief: An Account of the Labours, Losses, Sufferings and Oppression of Ke-zig-ko-e-ne-ne (David Sawyer), a Chief of the Ojibbeway Indians in Canada West.* London: W. Nichols, 1867.
Van West, John J. "George Mercer Dawson: An Early Canadian Anthropologist." *Anthropological Journal of Canada* 14, 4 (1976): 8–12.
"Views of a Mohawk Indian." *Journal of American Folklore* 18, 69 (1905): 160–2.
Vitelli, Karen D., ed. *Archaeological Ethics.* Walnut Creek: AltaMira Press, 1996.
– and Chip Colwell-Chanthaphonh, eds. *Archaeological Ethics.* Lanham: AltaMira Press, 2006.
Vogel, M.L. Vanessa. "The Glenbow Controversy and the Exhibition of North American Art." *Museum Anthropology* 14, 4 (1990): 7–11.
Volkert, James, Linda R. Martin, and Amy Pickworth. *National Museum of the American Indian: Map and Guide.* London: Scala Publishers Ltd, 2004.
Wall, Sharon. "Totem Poles, Teepees, and Token Traditions: 'Playing Indian' at Ontario Summer Camps, 1920–1955." *Canadian Historical Review* 86, 3 (2005): 513–44.
Wallace, W. Stewart, ed. *The Royal Canadian Institute Centennial Volume, 1849–1949.* Toronto: Royal Canadian Institute, 1949.

Wakeham, Pauline. *Taxidermic Signs: Reconstructing Aboriginality*. Minneapolis: University of Minnesota Press, 2008.

Warrick, Gary. *A Population History of the Huron-Petun*, A.D. *500–1650*. Cambridge: Cambridge University Press, 2008.

Watkins, Joe. *Indigenous Archaeology: American Indian Values and Scientific Practice*. Walnut Creek: AltaMira Press, 2000.

Waugh, Frederick W. "Indian Art in Pottery." *Popular Science News* (October 1901): 230–1.

Weaver, Emily P. *A Canadian History for Boys and Girls*. Toronto: Copp, Clark Company, 1900.

Weaver, Jace. "Indian Presence with No Indians Present: NAGPRA and Its Discontents." *Wicazo Sa Review* 12, 2 (1997): 13–30.

Weaver, Sally. "Seth Newhouse and the Grand River Confederacy at Mid-Nineteenth Century." *Extending the Rafters: Interdisciplinary Approaches to Iroquoian Studies*. Michael K. Foster, Jack Campisi, and Marianne Mithun, eds, 165–82. Albany: State University of New York Press, 1984.

Weir, Reverend F.G. *Scugog and Its Environs*. Port Perry: Star Print, 1927.

Wentworth Historical Society. *Journal and Transactions of the Wentworth Historical Society*. Vols 1–10. 1892–1922.

West, W. Richard, ed. *The Changing Presentation of the American Indian: Museums and Native Cultures*. Seattle and London: University of Washington Press, 2000.

Whiteley, Peter M. "Archaeology and Oral Tradition: The Scientific Importance of Dialogue." *American Antiquity* 67, 3 (2002): 405–15.

Willey, Gordon R. and Jeremy A. Sabloff. *A History of American Archaeology*. New York: W.H. Freeman and Company, 1980.

Williams, Stephen. *Fantastic Archaeology: The Wild Side of North American Prehistory*. Philadelphia: University of Pennsylvania Press, 1991.

Williamson, Ronald F. et al. "Ruthven and the Collection of Andrew Thompson: A Case Study of a Nineteenth Century Antiquarian." *Arch Notes* 7, 2 (2002): 7–34.

Wilson, Daniel. *Prehistoric Man: Researches into the Origin of Civilisation in the Old and New World*. Vols 1–2. London: Macmillan and Co., 1862.

Wintemberg, W.J. *Lawson Prehistoric Village Site, Middlesex County, Ontario*. Anthropological Series 25. National Museum of Canada Bulletin 94. Ottawa: J.O. Patenaude, 1939.

– *Roebuck Prehistoric Village Site, Grenville County, Ontario*. Anthropological Series Number 19. National Museum of Canada Bulletin 83. Ottawa: J.O Patenaude, 1936.

Winter, Barbara J. "William Beynon and the Anthropologists." *Canadian Journal of Native Studies* 4, 2 (1984): 279–92.

Withrow, W.H. *Our Own Country: Canada, Scenic and Descriptive: Being an Account of the Extent, Resources, Physical Aspect, Industries, Cities and Chief Towns of the Provinces of Nova Scotia, Prince Edward Island,*

*Newfoundland, New Brunswick, Quebec, Ontario, Manitoba, the North-West Territory and British Columbia, with Sketches of Travel and Adventure*. Toronto: W. Briggs, 1889.

Women's Canadian Historical Society of Toronto. *First Canadian Historical Exhibition Held at Victoria College, Queen's Park, Toronto, June, 1899 Report of the Secretary and Treasurer*. Toronto: The Society, 1900.

– *Annual Report and Transaction*. Vols 1–10. 1897–1910.

Wright, Donald A. *The Professionalization of History in English Canada*. Toronto: University of Toronto Press, 2005.

– "W.D. Lighthall and David Ross McCord: Antimodernism and English-Canadian Imperialism, 1880s-1918." *Journal of Canadian Studies* 32, 2 (1997): 134–53.

Wright, James V. and Jean-Luc Pilon, eds. *A Passion for the Past: Papers in Honour of James F. Pendergast*. Archaeology Paper 164. Mercury Series. Gatineau: Canadian Museum of Civilization, 2003.

Wright, James V. *A History of the Native People of Canada*. Vols 1–3. Archaeology Paper 152. Mercury Series. Hull: Canadian Museum of Civilization, 1995.

York Pioneer and Historical Society. *Annual Report*. 1906–10.

York Pioneers' Association. *Constitution and By-Laws of the York Pioneers' Association with a List of Members*. Toronto: Copp, Clark and Co., 1883.

Young, Brian J. *The Making and Unmaking of a University Museum: The McCord, 1921–1996*. Montreal and Kingston: McGill-Queen's University Press, 2000.

Zaslow, Morris. *Reading the Rocks: The Story of the Geological Survey of Canada, 1842–1972*. Toronto: Macmillan Company, the Department of Energy, Mines and Resources, and Information Canada, 1975.

Zeller, Suzanne. *Inventing Canada: Early Victorian Science and the Idea of a Transcontinental Nation*. Toronto: University of Toronto Press, 1987.

Zimmerman, Larry, Karen D. Vitelli, and Julie Hollowell-Zimmer, eds. *Ethical Issues in Archaeology*. Walnut Creek: AltaMira, 2003.

## INTERVIEWS AND COMMUNICATIONS

Hunter, Jamie. Director, Huronia Museum, Midland, ON. Interview with author. December 2009.

Kapches, Mima. Senior curator of Archaeology, Royal Ontario Museum, Toronto, ON. Email communication with author. January 2004.

Lazenby, Richard. President of the Canadian Association of Physical Anthropologists. Email communication with author. September 2002.

O'Neal, Paul. Chief archaeologist, Mayer Heritage Consultants, London, ON. Interview with author. September 2002.

Six Nations Ethics Committee, Six Nations Council. Ohsweken, ON.
 Correspondence with author. 2002–04.
Williams, Paul. Haudenosaunee Standing Committee on Burial Rules and
 Regulations. Interview with author. March 2004.

## MUSEUM COLLECTIONS AND EXHIBITS

Canadian Institute/Ontario Provincial Museum Collection. Royal Ontario
 Museum, Toronto, ON.
Dundurn Museum Collection. Department of Anthropology, McMaster
 University, Hamilton, ON.
Andrew F. Hunter Collection. Simcoe County Museum, Minesing, ON.
Huron Institute Collection. Museum at the Station, Collingwood, ON.
Lundy's Lane Historical Society Collection. Lundy's Lane Museum,
 Niagara Falls, ON.
*Mohawk Ideals, Victorian Values: Oronhyatekha M.D.* Exhibit produced
 by the Woodland Cultural Centre, Brantford, ON, 2002.
Niagara Historical Society Collection. Niagara Historical Museum,
 Niagara-on-the-Lake, ON.
Ottawa Literary and Scientific Society Collection. Canadian Museum of
 Civilization, Gatineau, QC.
Oxford Historical Society Collection. Woodstock Museum, Woodstock,
 ON.
Stratford-Perth Historical Society Collection. Stratford-Perth Museum,
 Stratford, ON.

# INDEX